Corporate Social Responsibility in India

About the Author

Dr. Sanjay Kumar Panda, born in 1955 in Odisha, had a brilliant academic career with two University **Gold Medals**, as the **Best Graduate** and in the **Post Graduation,** a **Silver Medal** in **Diploma in Public Administration**. He holds a **Diploma in Forestry** and a **Ph.D. in Economics**.

As a distinguished civil servant, he served in the **Indian Administrative Service** (1980 batch) for 35 years in the states of Tripura, Odisha, and in the Government of India. As the **Chief Secretary, Tripura** (2010-14) and **Secretary, Ministry of Textiles, Government of India** (2014-15), he headed the bureaucratic set up. The author combined within himself a brilliant academician and an able administrator, with professional competence and concern for the poor and disadvantaged.

His **dealing with the welfare** of the Scheduled Castes/Minorities and Backward Classes as the **Joint Secretary**; followed by a **stint in the Steel Authority of India Limited** and a **study** for diploma in Public Administration formed the backdrop of his interest and publication **"Corporate Social Responsibility (CSR) in India – Past, Present and Future"** in 2008, one of the **first publications** on the subject.

Work for **Empowerment of Tribal Women through Mulberry Sericulture** brought him international applause with the conferment of **Louis Pasteur Award** in 2016 for outstanding contribution to **sericulture and silk industry** by the International Sericultural Commission. His Ph. D. in economics, publication **"Mulberry Sericulture – Empowering Tribal Women"** and film **"Soil to Silk"**, based on this work are valuable contribution to promotion of sericulture.

While working as **Chief Secretary**, Tripura, he took up mobilising the team with positive mindset and use of appropriate technology on various welfare schemes, which yielded transformative results. These have been documented in his publication **"Making One Plus One Eleven"** in 2014.

His areas of interest relate to **Empowerment of the Poor and Disadvantaged Segments** of the society in the field of promotion of **handloom, handicraft, sericulture** and **skill development** in general and development of the **North Eastern Region**, the tribal areas in particular.

After his superannuation from service, Dr. Panda dealt with **Skill Development** as the **Chairman**, Executive Committee in the Tripura Skill Development Mission.

Corporate Social Responsibility in India

Sanjay Kumar Panda

CONCEPT PUBLISHING COMPANY PVT. LTD.
NEW DELHI-110059

ISBN-13: 978-93-86682-46-8

First Published 2018

Published and Printed by

Concept
Since 1974

Concept Publishing Company Pvt. Ltd.
A/15-16, Commercial Block, Mohan Garden,
New Delhi-110059 (INDIA)
T: +91 11 25351460, +91 11 25351794
E-publishing@conceptpub.com; *W*: www.conceptpub.com

Cataloging in Publication Data--Courtesy: D.K. Agencies (P) Ltd. <docinfo@dkagencies.com>

Panda, Sanjay Kumar, 1955- **author.**
Corporate social responsibility in India / Sanjay Kumar Panda.
pages cm
Includes bibliographical references and index.
ISBN 9789386682468

1. Social responsibility of business--India. 2. Social responsibility of business. I. Title.

LCC HD60.5.I5P36 2018 DDC 658.4080954 23

Dedication

This work is offered
as a floral tribute on the feet of
Bharat Mata,
our esteemed motherland.

धर्मेन्द्र प्रधान
ଧର୍ମେନ୍ଦ୍ର ପ୍ରଧାନ
Dharmendra Pradhan

मंत्री
पेट्रोलियम एवं प्राकृतिक गैस;
कौशल विकास एवं उद्यमशीलता मंत्रालय
भारत सरकार, नई दिल्ली
Minister
Petroleum & Natural Gas ;
Skill Development & Entrepreneurship
Government of India
New Delhi

Message

Under the visionary leadership of Shri Narendra Modi, Hon'ble Prime Minister, the present government at the centre has taken up several bold steps for developing India as *"Shrestha Bharat"*. Empowerment of the youth, the women and the disadvantaged segments have been assigned high priority under *Make in India, Skill India, Digital India, Start-up India, Stand-up India, MUDRA Yojana, Jan Dhan - Aadhaar- Mobile (JAM)* platform and other initiatives launched in the past three years. The corporate and business houses are required to support these Government initiatives under their **Corporate Social Responsibility (CSR)** for making the development inclusive.

The Ministry of Petroleum & Natural Gas has been guiding the Central Public Sector Enterprises as well as the private sectors working with the Ministry in implementation of CSR, which became mandatory in 2014. **Swachh Bharat** initiatives including construction of toilets separately for boys and girls in all government schools of the country within a specified time under CSR has marked a beginning in CSR dealing with national issues. It is hoped that many such projects will come up in the coming years with CSR making meaningful difference in the lives of the common man.

In this background, **"Corporate Social Responsibility in India",** authored by Dr. Sanjay Kumar Panda, a former bureaucrat with wide experience of working in the Central and State Governments, has come as a timely input. It provides a comprehensive and cogent account of theoretical and practical aspects of CSR. Based on the study of a number of corporates in the public and private sectors, the author has suggested best practices, which can be replicated for optimising benefits from CSR interventions. Among other things, the author has laid stress on corporate voluntarism and using CSR as last mile connectivity for filling the gaps in the ongoing government schemes, which have the potential to bring about transformative results.

While complementing the author for his painstaking, sincere work in bringing out a useful publication, I also hope that this will help and guide the corporate and other stakeholders in empowering the disadvantaged segments, in general, and in making the development participative and inclusive, in particular.

New Delhi
September, 2017

(Dharmendra Pradhan)

Ministry of Petroleum & Natural Gas : 201-A, Shastri Bhawan, New Delhi-110001 Tel : +91-11-23386622 FAX : +91-11-23386118
Ministry of Skill Development & Entrepreneurship : 2nd Floor, Annexe Building Shivaji Stadium, Shaheed Bhagat Singh Marg, Connaught Place, New Delhi-110001, Tel. : +91 -11 -23450811, FAX : +91 -11 -23450864

संतोष कुमार गंगवार
SANTOSH KUMAR GANGWAR

वित्त राज्य मंत्री
भारत सरकार
नई दिल्ली–110 001
Minister of State for Finance
Government of India
New Delhi- 110 001

Message

Under the visionary leadership of **Hon'ble Prime Minister, Shri Narendra Modi**, the new government at the centre has started its journey for expediting socio-economic development with specific stress on making the Growth Socially Inclusive and Participative **"Sabka Saath Sabka Vikas"**. Active cooperation of all stakeholders of the society is being sought for empowering the people with skill, technology and assets, giving particular attention to the disadvantaged segments of the society. As corporate operate in the society, they have a responsibility towards the society in general, and in supplementing the Government initiatives for making the development sustainable, in particular.

India has been a pioneer in making **Corporate Social Responsibility (CSR)** mandatory under the Companies Act, 2013, which requires all corporate with turnover/net worth/net profit exceeding the limit, to spend two percent of profit on social activities listed in the Schedule every year. There are several reports of corporate taking up CSR interventions with innovation and commitment, making a difference in the lives of the target group.

In this context, the publication **"Corporate Social Responsibility in India"**, by Dr. Sanjay Kumar Panda has come as a timely step. Coming from a retired officer of the Indian Administrative Service with three and a half decades of service at the Centre and State in different capacities including heading the State Administration as Chief Secretary and as Secretary in the Ministry of Textiles, this book provides a lucid account of theory and practice of CSR in India. Dr. Panda has been studying the subject over last decade and had one of the first publications titled **"Corporate Social Responsibility in India—Past, Present and Future"** on the subject in 2008.

The present book provides salient features of the concept, global practices, and CSR practices in India before and after Independence, under the liberalised economic policy (post 1991), in the new millennium and under the mandatory provision. Action taken by selected corporate in the private and public sectors have been discussed as case studies in the book along with best practices. The author has advocated for looking beyond money, mobilising corporate voluntarism and using CSR fund as last mile connectivity for getting transformative results. Evolving synergy in functioning of the corporate, the government and civil society of repute for addressing national issues has been stressed for CSR achieving the social and economic objectives in the true sense. We owe a deep sense of gratitude to Dr. Panda for his labour of love and suggesting a pattern of development for achieving the national goal of food, health, education and work for all.

India, with its large youth population is destined to play a leading role in the global economy in the coming decades. Empowering the youth with education, health and skill for livelihood is critical for ensuring this. The environment aspects of development are also required to be given due attention for checking global warming and making the development sustainable. In this context, this publication will be useful to all the stakeholders in mobilising corporate action for making CSR initiative an effective tool for welfare of the society along with enhancing the corporate brand image and socio-economic development.

(Santosh Kumar Gangwar)

138, नॉर्थ ब्लाक, नई दिल्ली–110001 दूरभाष : 23093783, 23092377, 23094108 फैक्स : 23092680
138, North Block, New Delhi-110001 Phone : 23093783, 23092377, 23094108 Fax : 23092680

M.S. SWAMINATHAN RESEARCH FOUNDATION

M.S. Swaminathan
Founder Chairman
Ex-Member of Parliament (Rajya Sabha)

Foreword

Corporate plays an important role in the society by creation of wealth and employment on the one hand and providing quality goods and services to the consumer at reasonable rate on the other hand. Responsibility of the corporate beyond the shareholders towards the society has been under debate for decades. However, a general consensus has been emerging that as the corporate functions in the society and owes their existence to the society; it is but natural that they have a responsibility towards the society. Accordingly, the yardstick for measuring corporate performance has been broadened covering Planet (for environment) and People along with Profit, under the three Ps—*Triple Bottom Line* approach.

Dr. Sanjay Kumar Panda, a former bureaucrat with concern for the society, has been studying corporate initiatives for social causes for over a decade and had one of the first publications titled **"Corporate Social Responsibility in India—Past, Present and Future"** on the subject in 2008. In the present publication **"Corporate Social Responsibility in India"**, Dr. Panda has dealt with the concept, global scenario, CSR practices in India from the pre-and post-independence days till the two years' of becoming mandatory under the Companies Act, 2013 in a comprehensive manner. Action taken by selected corporate in the public and private sectors have been documented as case study along with best practices, which can be replicated. Based on the analysis of the CSR initiatives and its impact, the author has advocated for evolving synergy in functioning of the corporate, the government and civil society of repute, mobilising corporate voluntarism for addressing national issues, which will make the CSR achieving its objective in the true sense. We owe a deep sense of gratitude to Dr. Panda for his labour of love and suggesting a pattern of development, which will help in achieving the national goal of food, health, education and work for all.

Adoption of Sustainable Development Goals (SDGs): 2030 by the UN General Assembly Summit with effect from 2016 has come up as a major challenge for the humanity in general and the developing countries in particular. The seventeen SDGs and 169 targets of SDGs envisage "Transforming our world: the 2030 agenda for sustainable development". As a major stakeholder of the civilised society, the corporate has a responsibility towards the society in dealing with people, planet, prosperity, partnership and profit in a holistic manner. Along with adherence to ethical values, taking up CSR in a comprehensive manner with due concern for the environment will play an important role in making the development sustainable and achieving the SDG 2030.

M.S. Swaminathan

3rd Cross Road, Taramani Institutional Area, Chennai (Madras)—600 113, India
Phone: +91-44-2254 2790, 2254 1698 Fax: +91-44-2254 1319
E-mail: founder@mssrf.res.in, swami@mssrf.res.in

Preface

My association with Corporate Social Responsibility (CSR) has its origin in my personal life as a student, remaining sensitive to social needs. After completing my education, I joined the Indian Forest Service in 1978, which gave me a good understanding of the technical aspects of forest and environment and its importance in the life of a common man at the micro-level and on sustainable development related issues at the macro-level. Subsequently, I joined the Indian Administrative Service in 1980 and was allotted Tripura part of the Manipur –Tripura cadre in the North-Eastern Region. The state was then passing through turbulent times in the post-ethnic riot (June 1980) period, with lakhs of displaced families living in camps, in the midst of distrust among tribal and non-tribal communities and large scale poverty. In course of my field postings as the Block Development Officer, Khowai; Sub-Divisional Officer, Dharmanagar; Additional District Magistrate & Collector, South Tripura District and District Magistrate & Collector, North Tripura District; I had the opportunity of closely interacting with the common people, while dealing with the implementation of various plans and programmes. I am deeply indebted to the legendary late Shri S.R. Sankaran (an IAS officer of Andhra Pradesh on deputation to Tripura), the then Chief Secretary, for the valuable insight and guidance in the formative period of my service career. This, in fact, had shaped my understanding and remaining sensitive to the needs of the poor and under-privileged. Later, as Director of Textiles, Odisha, I had the opportunity of working with women belonging to Scheduled Tribes, who were introduced to mulberry plantation, silk worm rearing, production of silk yarn as well as assisting the skilled handloom weavers in earning a decent livelihood. My interest in social issues was further reinforced while dealing with implementation of Social Welfare & Social Education Programmes in Tripura; followed by working at the national level as the Joint Secretary, Ministry of Social Justice & Empowerment for welfare of the Scheduled Castes, Minorities and Other Backward Classes during 2000-02. As the Director (Sports), Ministry of Youth Affairs and Sports, I was instrumental in working out details of the

National Sports Development Fund (NSDF) for mobilising corporate support for promotion of sports, in general, and assisting talented sports persons, in particular, during 1997-1999.

My close interaction with the corporate world started in 2002, while working as the Chief Vigilance Officer, Steel Authority of India Limited (SAIL). Along with system based approach for ethical practices, probity and transparency; I took interest in implementation of welfare activities under Peripheral Developmental Programmes (PDP). Immediately thereafter, I attended the 30th Advance Professional Programme on Public Administration in the Indian Institute of Public Administration (IIPA). As a requirement of this course, I worked on CSR in India for a dissertation and collected facts on CSR for a number of private and public companies along with views of corporate executives, government officers, peoples' representatives and a cross-section of people for understanding the way corporate have been discharging their responsibility towards the society. The dissertation, submitted to the Panjab University for my Diploma in Public Administration, was later developed and published under the title "**Corporate Social Responsibility in India – Past, Present and Future**". I am grateful to Prof. M.S. Swaminathan, the distinguished Agricultural Scientist, for writing a foreword for the book. The book was released in 2008 by Shri Montek Singh Ahluwalia, Deputy Chairman of the erstwhile Planning Commission of India. Evolving synergy in activities of the Corporate, the Government and the Non-Governmental Organisation (NGO) was advocated in this book for making the best out of CSR. The book had appreciation from the students as well as practitioners. I have continued my study and practice of CSR as a passion; by sharing experience with corporate executives, government officials, academicians and civil society, more as a way of giving back to the society what one has been privileged to get in all these years.

The 1st April, 2014, with CSR becoming mandatory under the Companies Act, 2013, marked a defining moment for **CSR in India**. Under the Act, not only the corporate having net worth, or turnover, or profit above the prescribed limit are required to adopt a policy and spend at least two-percent of the average profit on the listed activities, but also are required to disclose relevant details of their CSR activities during the year. This has led to increase in the interest in CSR by manifold within the corporate as well as in government, academic institutions, civil society, NGOs, the press and media.

In this background, the present publication has been attempted by updating the study and publication made in 2008, along with subsequent developments particularly under the mandatory provisions. The mandatory provisions requiring the corporate to publicise details on the website has made the recent study relatively easier, more authentic and analytical. The best practices, observed during the study, have been updated and incorporated as boxes for facilitating reading. This publication has two parts. The **first part** deals with **theoretical aspects** of CSR, covering the concept, the way it evolved and is being practiced in different countries of the world. Strength of the book lies in the **practical aspects** of CSR, dealt in the **second part** covering salient features of the initiatives taken, its impact on the society in general and the disadvantaged segments in particular in the **case studies and best practices**. It is hoped that this book will serve as a handbook for the corporate executives in learning about CSR, others' experience and designing their own interventions suitably, for **getting a better value for the money spent**.

In the 21st Century, we are all living in a fast changing world. Fuelled by awareness, education, digital print, electronic and social media; expectations of an average Indian youth have increased at a phenomenal rate, as reflected in the statement "*Today, an young Indian has five dreams, starting with a five digit monthly salary, a four wheeler, a three bed room flat, two children and one wife*". Due to obvious reasons, the national governments have been finding it difficult to fulfil such expectations. The unfulfilled expectations in turn have been leading to frustration, anger and violence. Future of CSR in India has to be carved out in this background for meeting these emerging challenges in the Indian way. Instead of looking at statutory CSR as a mere few thousand crores of rupees, it has to be evolved as active partnership between the Corporate and the Government for bringing about **transformative change** (rather than a mere change) like ***"a caterpillar's metamorphic change to a butterfly".*** This has brought an opportunity for the corporate to **play a meaningful role in the National development** in discharging their responsibility towards the society (CSR) in the real sense. In this context, I feel it is worth quoting a hypothesis, advocated in my book ***Making One plus One Eleven***, based on the experiences while working as the Chief Secretary, Tripura. The hypothesis proposes that "W***orking with positive mind-set and attitude, in a team and use of appropriate technology increases the end result by manifold",*** which, I feel, applies to CSR as well, in bringing about transformative changes for meeting the expectations of the youth.

The observation ***"Business cannot succeed in a society that is failing"*** has been substantiated by number of incidents in the recent past;

where the corporate have failed to exploit existing business opportunity due to unrest in the society. The challenge ahead lies in evolving synergy in implementation of CSR projects with ongoing government interventions and help of NGOs; which will make the mandatory CSR truly relevant for the society. It is hoped that the present book will be of help in guiding the corporate in the troubled (waters) society, like the "*Polestar* guiding ships in the troubled high seas" to reach the much cherished destination of sustainable development along with environmental conservation, peace and prosperity.

In course of my four decades long career in the civil service, I have noticed that while there is a general consensus for upliftment of the poor and disadvantaged segments and on other social issues; often there is communication gaps, lack of understanding and cohesion among various agencies dealing with development, which led to protracted correspondence, delays and underachievement. This applies to the implementation of CSR projects as well. This book is a *humble attempt to bridge* the trust deficit and make the stakeholders—the corporate, the Government and the civil society—join hands in working for the society.

ॐ सह नाववतु। सह नौ भुनक्तु । सह वीर्यं करवावहै।
तेजस्वि नावधीतमस्तु मा विद्विषावहै।
ॐ शान्तिः शान्तिः शान्तिः।।

Om Saha Naav[au]-Avatu |Saha Nau Bhunaktu |Saha Viryam Karavaavahai |Tejasvi Naav[au]-Adhiitam-Astu Maa Vidvishaavahai | Om Shaantih Shaantih Shaantih ||

Meaning:

Om, May God Protect us Both (the Teacher and the Student) (during the journey of awakening our Knowledge),

May God Nourish us Both (with that spring of Knowledge which nourishes life when awakened),

May we Work Together with Energy and Vigour (cleansing ourselves with that flow of energy for the Knowledge to manifest),

May our Study be Enlightening (taking us towards the true Essence underlying everything), and not giving rise to Hostility (by constricting the understanding of the Essence in a particular manifestation only),

Om, Peace, Peace, Peace.

April 15, 2018

Sanjay Kumar Panda
sanjaypandaias@gmail.com

Acknowledgements

I thankfully acknowledge the views and supports received from a wide range of persons including people's representatives, corporate leaders and executives, bureaucrats, colleagues for the present publication. I have referred to write up and views published in various newspapers, magazines and other media sources in course of the study, for which I convey my sincere thanks to concerned authors / publishers.

I am grateful to Shri Narendra Modi, Hon'ble Prime Minister of India, for his visionary leadership for developing India as the *Eka Bharat - Shrestha Bharat*. It inspired me to explore scope of **CSR** in its new version as a tool for making the development inclusive and participative "*Sabka Saath Sabka Vikas*". I am thankful to the Government and people of Tripura for giving me the opportunity to study the changing needs of the society in general and the expectations of the youth in particular; which in turn, helped me in suggesting appropriate CSR interventions."

I am grateful to Shri Dharmendra Pradhan, Hon'ble Union Minister for Petroleum & Natural Gas and Skill Development & Entrepreneurship, and Shri Santosh Kumar Gangwar, Hon'ble Minister of State for Finance for their encouraging words for the book. I am highly grateful to Professor M.S. Swaminathan for sparing his valuable time and writing the foreword for the book.

I would like to thank Shri Praveen Agarwal, Director of Industries and Commerce, Tripura; Shri V. Ramachandran, Ministry of Textiles; Shri Tarun Joshi, Cotton Corporation of India; Shri Pradeep Mahato, Tripura Natural Gas Company Limited and Shri Tapan Bhattacharya, my Private Secretary, for their active help in preparing the manuscript.

I acknowledge the cooperation extended by Shri Nitin Mittal and all other concerned persons of the Concept Publishing Company Private Limited, New Delhi in bringing out this publication.

On the eve of completion of this work, I fondly remember my late mother, Smt Janaki Devi for her divine blessings, which has been the guiding spirit in undertaking this work. I would sincerely and thankfully acknowledge the love and support of Aruna, my wife; our daughter, Saswati; son-in-law, Sourabh and son, Aditya for their affection, which helped me a lot in undertaking this work.

Preface for the Earlier Edition

In course of rendering public service in different capacities over the last three decades, I got the rare opportunity of looking at issues concerning the poor and the disadvantaged from close quarters. Notwithstanding the cynicism, doubts and apprehensions expressed by a section of the intelligentsia, it was fascinating to come across the enthusiasms, hopes, and aspirations at the grassroots level. Resilience of the common men and women living under difficult situations – be it the handloom weavers or the first generation Scheduled Tribes practicing sericulture in Orissa, or the cane and bamboo handicraft artisans in Tripura – with whom I had occasions to interact, have been striking. It was interesting to come across instances, where favourable conditions created by motivation, co-operation and understanding along with committed action have yielded significant results, which have proved the critics wrong.

My interest in the present subject dates back to early 2000, while working in the Ministry of Social Justice and Empowerment, I had the opportunity of looking at the way intensions for welfare of the disadvantaged are translated into action – the achievements, the constraints and the limitations. Later, while working in the Steel Authority of India Limited, a *Nava Ratna* Public Sector Company, I got the benefit of understanding the way the corporate functions. These provided the background for undertaking a study on **"Corporate Social Responsibility (CSR) in India"** as a part of the training, I attended at the Indian Institute of Public Administration, Delhi in 2004-05. The study, done initially with reference to the steel industry, was later on expanded to cover corporates dealing with other sectors. In addition to the study of selected corporate, in the public and private sector, action taken by the associations of industries, NGOs dealing with welfare activities and initiatives taken by the Government for mobilizing corporate support were also studied. Articles published on the subject in various newspapers, magazines and websites were also referred. Some economists and academicians, starting with Milton Friedman, have expressed reservations about CSR. As CSR relates to the society, it is but natural that there are diverse views either supporting or opposing it. The present study seeks to provide a broad overview of various initiatives taken and which can be taken by the Corporate in the Indian context, keeping in view their relevance for the society on a pragmatic basis. As CSR activities of Tata Steel and SAIL were studied in greater detail, there are many references to the steps taken by them. It is a fact that other corporates have also taken excellent initiatives, which could not be covered due to limitations, inherent in a work of this nature and magnitude. I look forward to all such suggestions in this regard.

This book has two parts. Major issues relating to CSR have been dealt in the first part, based on case studies, which have been dealt in the second part in chapters seven to seventeen. After a brief introduction to the subject in the first chapter, theoretical concept and evolution of CSR have been dealt in the second chapter. Developments relating to CSR in various countries have been covered in the third chapter. Developments in India in the pre- and post-independence period, after adoption of the new economic policy in 1991 have been covered in the fourth chapter on past of CSR in India.

Based on the study, present status of CSR in India has been discussed in the fifth chapter. From the study, it appears that the awareness about CSR has been increasing among the Indian Corporate, both in the public and private sectors in the recent years. Several Public Sector Enterprises (PSEs) have adopted CSR policy and some PSEs have earmarked a part of the profit for CSR activities. Among the private sectors, some have adopted CSR policy. Even though private sectors have not earmarked part of profit for CSR, the expenditure on CSR activities has been increasing. Some corporate surplus have taken up mobilizing voluntarism of the employees and deploying surplus machineries, and buildings for solving social problems and providing quality services to the poor. A wide range of activities are being undertaken under CSR out of which provision of health, education, and income generating skill facilities, appeared to be the major ones. The CSR initiatives were found to have helped the target group both in quantitative and qualitative terms. Quality of education and health services provided under CSR in some cases was found to be superior to similar services provided by the Government. CSR interventions, taken up with imagination, commitment and dedication, were found to have made a difference in the lives of the poor and facilitated social inclusion.

The first and foremost responsibility of the corporate towards the society relates to being a good corporate citizen by following the laws of the land, taking care of the investors, the consumers, and adhering to ethical business practices. There are instances of corporate interventions for empowering the poor and making them potential consumers. Such measures have helped both the corporate in expansion of business and the poor, leading to a "win-win" situation. Besides, some corporates have taken up strategic interventions for diversification keeping in view the long-term requirements of business. Such measures have helped the corporate in promoting their commercial interest no doubt, but have also enabled the common man in acquiring skill and accessing the market. In the Indian context, such measures were found to have facilitated social inclusion and are required to be promoted. So far as social welfare activities meant for the common man are concerned, it was found that synergy of action taken by the corporate, with involvement of the NGOs and support of the Government agencies, have empowered the target groups on a sustainable basis and paid dividends to the concerned corporate as well.

Based on the analysis of best practices taken up under CSR interventions, a roadmap for the future of CSR in India has been suggested in the sixth chapter. Role of the corporate, the government, the media, the NGOs and the civil society have been briefly outlined for making the CSR interventions sustainable and effective.

Dr. Prasant Mahapatra, Dr. Veena Chotray, Shri Raj Kishore Mishra, and Shri Chabirendra Roul had gone through the draft and made valuable suggestions. These have added value to the work, for which I am highly thankful to them. I have consulted available literatures on the subject, for which I thankfully acknowledge the concerned authors and publishers. My sincere thanks are due to Mr. N.J. Yasaswy and the team at the ICFAI University Press, Hyderabad for taking up the publication of this book. I am immensely grateful to Dr. M.S. Swaminathan for the encouragement and writing a foreword for this book.

I have done this publication in my personal capacity and the views expressed are my personal.

Socio-economic development of a developing economy like India is a complex task. As one of the major stakeholders of the National development, the corporate has to take appropriate action for sharing the benefit of growth with the less privileged. This book seeks to generate awareness and sensitize all corporates, irrespective of the nature and size of business, for undertaking appropriate CSR interventions as per ability.

In this context, replication of successful interventions will be useful by getting the benefit of others experiences. It is beyond doubt that undertaking CSR will provide considerable mileage to the corporate in expansion of business while remaining at peace with the society. The Civil society, including the NGOs, needs to support and supplement this process. The Government will of course have a major role in promoting CSR as it will facilitate achieving the national goal of growth with distributive justice. It is hoped that the major stakeholders of national development – the Government, the Corporate, the NGOs and the Media – will come forward for using CSR as an effective tool in making the economic growth socially inclusive and sustainable. This calls for each of the stakeholder to work in unison with trust, understanding and cooperation rather than raising finger at one another, as has been aptly reflected in the *Oriya* couplet.

"Andhar Boli Kara Nahi Gola, Dipa Tiye Diya Jali,
Jaliba Tahinru Sahasra Deepali, Andhakar Jiba Chali."

"Let us not shout that there is darkness all round, rather let us light a *Dipa* (earthen lamp) each, from which thousands of lamps will glow and the darkness will go for ever".

February 11, 2008

Sanjay Kumar Panda

Contents

Abbreviations

AA 1000	Account Ability 1000
AGM	Annual General Meeting
APRDDC	Air Pollution Research and Disease Diagnostic Centre
ART	Anti Retroviral Therapy
ASSOCHAM	The Associated Chambers of Commerce and Industry of India
BAIF	Bharatiya Agro Industries Foundation
BHEL	Bharat Heavy Electricals Limited
BPCL	Bharat Petroleum Corporation Limited
BPL	Below Poverty Line
BRGF	Backward Region Grant Fund
BSP	Bhilai Steel Plant
BSR	Business for Social Responsibility
CAPART	Council for Advancement of People's Action and Rural Technology
CCR	Centre for Corporate Responsibility
CII	Confederation of Indian Industries
CINI	Child In Need in India
COPU	Committee on Public Undertakings
CPSE	Central Public Sector Enterprises
CRY	Child Relief and You
CSC	Common Service Centres
CSO	Civil Society Organisation
CSR	Corporate Social Responsibility
CSTI	Construction Skills Training Institute
DTI	Department of Trade and Industry
EGS	Education Guarantee Scheme
ESG	Environmental Social Governance
EVA	Economic Value Addition
FDI	Foreign Direct Investment
FICCI	Federation of Indian Chambers of Commerce and Industries

FMCGs	Fast Moving Consumer Goods
FNN	Forum for Nurturing Nature
FSNL	Ferro Scrap Nigam Limited
GAIL	Gas Authority of India Limited
GDP	Gross Domestic Product
GGA	Grameen Gyan Abhiyan
GNP	Gross Natioanal Product
GNRC	Guwahati Neurological Research Centre
GRI	Global Reporting Initiative
HDFC	Housing Development Finance Coproration
HDI	Human Development Index
HPCL	Hindustan Petroleum Corporation Limited
HSBC	Hong Kong and Shanghai Banking Corporation
HSCE	High School Certificate Examination
ICC	Indian Chemical Council
ICDS	Integrated Child Development Services
ICFAI	Institute of Chartered Financial Analysts of India
ICICI	ICICI Bank
ICT	Information and Communication Technology
IFC	International Finance Corporation
IIFT	Indian Institute of Foreign Trade
IIIT	Indian Institute of Information Technology
IIPA	Indian Institute of Public Administration
IISCO	Indian Iron and Steel Company
IIS	Indian Institute of Science
IMR	Infant Mortality Rate
IOCL	Indian Oil Corporation Limited
IPF	India Partnership Forum
IRS	ICFAI Republic School
ISKCON	International Society for Krishna Consciousness
ISPs	Integrated Steel Plants
IT	Information Technology
ITES	Information Technology Enabled Services
JFMC	Joint Forest Management Committee
JNURM	Jawaharlal Nehru Urban Renewal Mission
KIOCL	Kudremukh Iron Ore Company Limited
KISS	Kalinga Institute of Social Sciences
LABS	Livelihood Advancement Business School
LCA	Life Cycle Approach
LSE	London Stock Exchange

MDGs	Millennium Development Goals
MEL	Maharashtra Elektrosmelt Limited
MKCIS	Mahila Karmodyaga Co-operative Industrial Society
MNCs	Multi National Corporates
MOIL	Manganese Ore India Limited
MoU	Memorandum of Understanding
MRP	Mixed Recall Period
MSSRF	M S Swaminathan Research Foundation
MTNL	Mahanagar Telephone Nigam Limited
NABARD	National Bank for Agriculture and Rural Development
NACO	National AIDS Control Organisation
NALCO	National Aluminium Company Limited
NEGP	National E-Governance Plan
NFHS	National Family Health Survey
NGOs	Non-Governmental Organizations
NIF	National Innovation Foundation of India
NMDC	National Mineral Development Corporation Limited
NREGP	National Rural Employment Guarantee Programme
NRHM	National Rural Health Mission
NSKFDC	National Safai Karmacharis Finance and Development Corporation
NSLRS	National Scheme for Liberation and Rehabilitation of Scavengers
NTPC	National Thermal Power Corporation Limited
NTTF	Nettur Technical Training Foundation
OBCs	Other Backward Classes
ODA	Official Development Assistance
ONGC	Oil and Natural Gas Corporation Limited
ORSE	Observatoire sur la Responsabilite Societale des Enterprises
PAF	Project Affected Families
PAP	Project Affected Persons
PCPNDT	Pre-Conception and Pre-Natal Diagnostic Techniques
PDI	Peripheral Development Institute
PDP	Peripheral Development Programme
PFI	Population Foundation of India
PPSC	Planned Parenthood of Stark Country
PR	Public Relation
PSEs	Public Sector Enterprises
PURA	Provision of Urban facilities in Rural Areas

PwC	PricewaterhouseCoopers
RBH	Rural Business Hub
RBI	Reserve Bank of India
RCH	Reproductive Child Health
REDA	Renewable Energy Development Agency
RIL	Reliance Industries Limited
RPDAC	Rehabilitation and Periphery Development Advisory Committee
RSP	Rourkela Steel Plant
RSVY	Rashtriya Sama Vikas Yojana
SA	Social Auditing
SAIL	Steel Authority of India Limited
SC	Scheduled Caste
SEBI	Securities and Exchanges Board of India
SEDF	South Asia Enterprise Development Facility
SEDP	Socio-Economic Development Policy
SELCO	Solar Electric Light Company
SEZ	Special Economic Zone
SGSY	Swarna Jayanti Gram Swarojgar Yojana
SHGs	Self Help Groups
SIGMA	Sustainability Integrated Guidelines for Management
SOP	Standard Operating Procedure
SRI	Socially Responsible Investment
ST	Scheduled Tribe
TELCO	Tata Engineering and Locomotive Company
TERI	The Energy and Resources Institute
TIFR	Tata Institute of Fundamental Research
TISCO	Tata Iron and Steel Company Limited
TMH	Tata Memorial Hospital
TSCP	Tata Steel Centenary Project
TSFIF	Tata Steel Family Initiatives Foundation
TSRDS	Tata Steel Rural Development Society
UNDP	United Nations Development Programme
USP	Unique Service Propositions
VISL	Visvesvaraya Iron & Steel Plant Limited
VKC	Village Knowledge Centres
VRC	Village Resource Centres
WATSAN	Water and Sanitation Programme
WBCSD	World Business Council for Sustainable Development
WHO	World Health Organization
XLRI	Xavier Labour Relation Institute

List of Case Studies

List of Boxes

List of Tables

1

Introduction

Evolution of Society

The term 'society' has its origin in the Latin word '*societas*', meaning a bond or interaction between individuals/parties that are friendly. The concept of society basically relates to bondage and the advantages derived by individuals being members of a group. It is related to the perception that an individual has limited means as an autonomous unit and being in the group or in the society enables the individual to transact business with ease as well as in getting safety and security. Living in a group or society or social behaviour is common to the animal kingdom from the small one like the ants living in colony to sheep, monkey and the big and powerful elephants and lions living in herd. Living in a group or herd requires each member of the group to obey certain basic norms or rules, which is often enforced by the leader of the group.

Aborigine human beings started living in groups for getting protection from wild animals as well as for facilitating hunting and gathering food. Settling down at one place for agriculture marked the beginning of formal society, which gradually evolved as the "Feudal society", where ownership of land decided the status of individuals. Farmers were made to cultivate the landowner's land and get a share of the crop. In due course, this extended to seeking protection against invaders and the landowners exploited the peasants in lieu of providing food, crops, crafts and other services.

Industrial revolution brought the next phase of "Industrial society", which relied on machines powered by fuels like coal and oil for production and transportation of goods. Formation of capital with means of production being privately owned gave rise to capitalism. Competition for production and marketing of produced goods led to exploring new markets and setting up colony outside the country. The agriculture based feudal societies gradually broke down with people migrating from agriculture to industrial sectors for employment. Improvement in productivity and healthcare increased the longevity and birth rate, and reduced death rate. These developments led to rapid increase in population. Use of machines in place of men and animals created surplus of labour and reduced the wage for hiring of labour. Increase in population on the one hand and machines replacing labour on the other increased the incidence of unemployment. Social inequality arising out of the skewed ownership of land in the feudal society got somewhat intensified in the industrial society based on ownership of capital and productive assets.

The second part of the 20th century saw rapid growth in technology with information and services dominating the production. There was a shift from manufacturing to services sector covering education, health, law, banking, marketing, research and governance.

Notwithstanding the technological advancement, staying together in the society continued to be an integral and inseparable part of human life. The concept of responsibility towards the society accordingly evolved as an essential requirement and a part of individuals paying back for the support derived from the society. Since individuals constitute society, they form the units of society. As a member of the society, all individuals were required to behave in a manner, which is good for all and is helpful in promoting the welfare of society. Society called upon the individuals to follow certain norms as the obligations or duties. Rights and duties are related to each other like the two sides of the same coin. The rights of one are the duties of the other and *vice versa*. In the absence of duties, rights become insignificant and duties are fruitless in the absence of rights. With the evolution of the concept of state, which guaranteed the enjoyment of certain rights to individuals, citizens are required to perform certain duties in the society. These are broadly of two types, *viz*. legal and moral. Legal duties, enforceable by law, cover respecting the constitution, paying taxes regularly and honestly etc. Moral duties, on the other hand, cover obligations such as showing respect to parents, elders, and teachers, behaving well with the brothers, sisters and the relatives, which one is expected to observe of one's own and are not legally enforceable.[1]

Evolution of Business

Business is defined as the regular production or purchase and sale of goods undertaken with the objective of earning profit and acquiring wealth through the satisfaction of human wants. The business evolved progressively through five broad stages. The first and initial stage related to local business starting with a barter economy, followed by the village economy and the town economy. The second stage related to the regional business, which grew as a result of cooperation between states. The third stage related to the national business, which covered the business presence in the entire country. The next stage related to the international business covering more than one country. The final stage of business covered the entire world as one huge market as the global business.

The concept of responsibility towards the society applies to organizations, which operate in the society on similar lines as individuals. Being Socially Responsible[2] requires the individual citizens and organizations operating in the society to conduct themselves in an ethical manner with sensitivity on all social, cultural, economic and environmental issues. Remaining responsible towards the society helps individuals and organizations and has a positive impact on development, business and society as a whole. It makes a positive contribution to the bottom line of the business as well, by creating a "win-win" situation for all the stakeholders. Relationship between the individuals and the society has been summed up in the words of George Bernard Shaw, "I am of the opinion that my life belongs to the whole community and as long as I live, it is my privilege to do for it whatever I can. I want to be thoroughly used up when I die, for the harder I work the more I live."

Impact of Industrial Revolution

The industrial revolution started in Europe in the 18th century and gradually spread over to other continents. It had impact on almost all aspects of human life. It transformed the agrarian society to industrial society along with significant changes in the means of production, ownership and other socio-economic spheres. It laid the foundation of the organized industry, trade and commerce. In the agrarian society, the skills were traditional being inherited from the father and forefathers. It was not necessary to go out of the family to acquire knowledge and skill except for the members of the royal family. However, in the industrial society, formal training in institutions became a necessity and basic prerequisite for acquiring skills as per the need of market in undertaking production as well as trade and commerce. Individuals, who had access to such facility, were able to enter the market and derive the benefits. On the other hand, those, who didn't have such facility, got deprived and continue in the low productivity jobs with limited earning. Such deprivation led to genesis of socio-economic exclusion.

Development of science and technology gave a boost to production on a commercial scale and to formation of organized industries and commerce, popularly known as Corporate. The corporate took advantage of the new technology and diversified their activities fast. They took up mobilization of human and financial resources and moved from place to place for marketing their products. In due course, business entities dealing with production and marketing of goods and services emerged as a powerful force all-over the world.

Corporate played an important role in the development of the society by creation of wealth and employment opportunity. Expansion of business intensified competition and compelled them to look for new markets for selling their products. Competing commercial interest often led to conflicts. In due course, trading activities extended beyond national boundaries and led to political mobilization and colonization. Adoption of unfair trade practices gave rise to exploitation and affected the economy of the host countries. Such trade related factors were also partly responsible for the World Wars.

Development of business and trade got a new lease of life after the Second World War on account of the reconstruction and development related activities. This gave a boost and maintained the growth of the corporate in the second part of the twentieth century. Adoption of latest technology often led to replacing labour by machines and to jobless growth. Overemphasis on the bottom line and maximization of profit resulted in laying-off of labour. Even though training and capacity building of the surplus labour and deploying them in alternate occupation was promised, it seldom happened. As a result, the retrenched labours became unemployed and were exposed to poverty, hunger and misery, which led to frustration and social unrest.

Development of science and technology acquired new dimensions in the last part of the twentieth century, which continued over to the new millennium. Development of faster means of transportation on land, water and air facilitated movement of raw material and finished goods. Information Technology based interventions like Internet and World Wide Web (WWW) redefined the concept of space and time and made globalization a reality. These have evolved as an unavoidable part of human life all-over the world. Armed with such powerful technology, the corporate expanded their activities both within and across countries and acquired enormous economic clout. Control over wealth, vast production and distribution base enabled the business entities to expand its control of over the polity and society, affecting almost all aspects of human life.

Sustainable Development—Areas of Concern

Social "Rich-Poor" Divide

Fruits of development of science and technology did not spread equally to all segments of the society. A smaller segment, which had the requisite skill, ability and resources, derived the benefits whereas a larger segment, which lacked such ability, was left behind. The gap between the 'Haves' and 'Have-nots' arising out of material based prosperity on the one hand and illiteracy, disease, hunger, malnutrition, and poverty based deprivation on the other posed one of the major global challenges in the twenty-first century. The world has got divided into two parts[3]. On the one hand, billions of people lack the opportunity to meet their basic needs. On the other hand, a relatively smaller segment is consuming resources in ways, which are environmentally unsustainable and often inimical to its own well-being. The distortion is evident from the fact that about 1.2 billion of the global population is estimated to be poor, while the richest one per cent of the world's population enjoys income equal to that of the bottom fifty-seven per cent[4]. This has necessitated a comprehensive, multifaceted and integrated approach to harness forces of global integration and technological advancement to reduce human deprivation. While the economic deprivation is a matter of concern for all nations, it has become more conspicuous in case of the developing ones.

Environmental Degradation

Another adverse consequence of rapid industrialization related to the exploitation of natural and physical resources at a rate faster than the rate at which nature can replenish itself. Growth in the industrial activities, trade and commerce led to pollution of air, water and environment, with adverse consequences for the common man both in the short and long terms.

Degradation of environment and widening of the rich-poor divide are interrelated. Those with less capital resources are more dependent on nature and hence are more vulnerable to degradation of environment. Study[5] on impact of Climate Change on Women in Agriculture in an increasingly feminizing agriculture sector indicated that the women farmer and farm labourer bear the brunt of climate change. Women at the farm level are doubly disadvantaged as their overall workload increases with men migrating out of the village when agriculture production gets affected due to climate change on the one hand and their access to resources like land, credit and information gets reduced on the other. Prevailing social customs restricts women's access to food and nutrition due to intra-household inequities. During the periods of scarcity, women have to travel longer distances to fetch fuel, water, fodder, which exposes them to greater risk of violence. The findings indicate that the perceptions of climate change adaptation differ between men and women. While men play a dominant role in the short term in crisis, decisions are more equally shared. For climate change adaptation, preference of men and women differ for long-term coping strategies, as men migrate out whereas women tend to find wage labour locally.

Human deprivation and suffering of sizeable population on the one hand and overexploitation of natural resources on the other have raised serious concern about sustainability of the contemporary model for economic development.

The corporate operate in the society and owe their existence to the society. Its existence is based on meeting the demand for goods and services in the society by taking up production and supply of goods and services. Corporate continue to be in business so long as it fulfils the commercial purpose of meeting the demand of the consumers. In case any corporate fails to deliver as per the expectations of the consumers and the investors, who represent the society, it is but natural that the said corporate loses its relevance and has to wind up its business. A closer look at the business process indicates that profit made by a corporate in any commercial endeavour comes partly from internal factors like the mobilization of capital, entrepreneurship etc. Other part of the profit is due to external factors like imperfect market conditions; aberrations like information asymmetry due to provision of incomplete or inadequate information to the investors/consumers; and monopolies leading to inadequate competitions. Further, in addition to making monetary profit, the corporate draws non-monetary benefits like reputation and social capital from the society for carrying on its business. It is difficult to quantify such benefits in monetary terms. These features of business clearly indicate the relevance of the society for the business. Accordingly, it is said that *the business needs the society to remain in business*. As a natural corollary, it is obligatory on the part of the business to take care of the society. In this background, observations of Milton Friedman that "the Business (Corporate) has only one responsibility to make profit for the owner-share holders" needs reconsideration in the contemporary society in general and the context of the developing countries in particular.

As corporate operate in the society, they need to take care of the stakeholders other than the shareholders, namely the customers, employees, suppliers and the society at large. However, often financial interest of the shareholders becomes not only the prime but also the only concern in determining the policy and functioning of the corporate. While interest of the customers and employees are considered to some extent, interest of the common man in the society is either ignored or at best paid lip service. The socio-economic impact of deprivation in general and frustration of the youth in particular has made it imperative for the corporate to redefine their responsibility towards the society for continuing business in the society. The concept of "Profit" alone deciding the success of a commercial enterprise was accordingly broadened with the inclusion of "Planet" (environment) and "People" (society) along with "Profit", making "three Ps" instead of "one P" as the essential parameters for sustainable business. This led to emergence of Triple Bottom Line (TBL) as the principles guiding the responsibility of the corporate towards the society. Further, issues relating to ethics, transparency and fair business practices gathered momentum all-over the world, both in the developed and the developing countries. Concerns for the society and environment along with ethical behaviour led to rise of Corporate Social Responsibility (CSR) as central feature of corporate governance all-over the world.

In the Indian context, the responsibility of business towards the society is best reflected in the theory of trusteeship, advocated by Gandhi[6] "*As corporations are created by the society, they should remain in the public domain and their vast economic power should be exercised in the interest of not only the shareholders but also of the customers, employees and the society at large*". This approach appears to be pragmatic and appropriate for meeting the emerging challenges of a developing country like India.

After Independence, India adopted the socialistic pattern of development and promoted state owned public sector enterprises for undertaking production and service sector activities. This policy was radically modified with adoption of the new economic policy based on Liberalization, Privatization and Globalization in 1991. The new policy gave a boost to growth of private corporate in India. Economic liberalization for facilitating growth of the private sector was pursued subsequently in the technology led globalised world. This led to significant growth of the private sector by exploiting the market potential both within and outside the country. Favourable government policy enabled the Indian entrepreneurs to capture the market all-over the world, which is most visible in the success of Information Technology (IT) based enterprises. Large number of startup new enterprises came up both within the country and abroad in a record time, with leading corporate like Infosys, Wipro scaling great heights.

However, in the new millennium, India has been witness to number of violent incidents affecting law and order as well as loss of human life and property such as at Kalinganagar[7] in Orissa, Singur[8] and Nandigram[9] in West Bengal, Khammam[10] in Andhra Pradesh, activities of the left-wing extremists (LWEs)[11] in Bihar, Jharkhand and disruptive elements in the North-eastern region.[12] These incidents have raised questions about the sustainability of the development process. Subsequently, in 2014 before the last general elections to the 16th Lok Sabha, there was a gruesome attack[13] by the LWEs, in which seven members of a polling party, including five CRPF personnel moving in an ambulance and a bus, were killed by landmine blast in Bijapur and Bastar districts of Chhattisgarh. In another such bizarre incident, an ambulance (108 *Sanjeevani*) carrying CRPF personnel was attacked, in which four persons got killed in Darbha police station area in Kamanar. Such happenings at periodic intervals are attributed to a number of factors including human deprivations and have raised doubts about the so-called economic development. Along with socio-economic and political aspects, such incidents have frustrated corporate efforts for launching new initiatives for exploiting existing market potential at considerable cost to the corporate and the society as well.

Corporate growth related issues affecting the society are not unique to India. Such incidents have happened in other parts of the world as well. Even in one of the most developed nations like the United States of America, there were protests by the unemployed and the poor against the rich and the resourceful. The "*Occupy Wall Street (OWS)*"[14] protest in New York, USA on the 17th September, 2011 had its origin in the social and economic inequality, greed, corruption and the perceived undue influence of corporations on government, particularly in the financial services sector. This is evident from the slogan coined by the protesters, "*We are the 99 per cent*". This arose out of the inequality in income and wealth distribution in the developed economy between the wealthiest one per cent and the rest of the population. To achieve their goals, protesters have evolved consensus, which emphasized on "*direct action over petitioning authorities for redress*". This trend indicates the restlessness of the youth and the urgency required in addressing the issues.

In the Indian context, corporate related issues, which had impact on the society in the recent decades broadly fall under two heads, namely (i) in acquisition of private land for industrial uses; and (ii) in handling labour. The corporate require land for setting up units for production and sale of goods and services. The overall land resource is limited; further land available for corporate use has been shrinking due to rapid urbanization, use of land for housing and physical infrastructure like rail, road, airport, port. Consequently, acquisition of private land and/or diversion of forestland for non-forestry use are the only way for getting land for corporate use. Acquisition of private land falls in the State List of the Constitution and is dealt by the State Government as per provisions of the Land Acquisition Act of 1894. This Act was enacted before independence. During the initial years, more land was available and such requirements were few and far between. The compensation amount for the land acquired used to be relatively low and the private landowners were contended with the amount received. However, this position has changed with urbanization, development of housing projects and rapid expansion of the service sector. The educated youth from the landowners' family became aware of the importance and value of a limited commodity like land. Unlike his father and forefathers, the modern youth is no longer satisfied with the paltry compensation received for handing over his private land. Further, in some cases, the land requirement for the project was bloated up and private land was acquired in excess of the actual requirement. At a later stage, after the main project came up, part of the land acquired for the project was diverted for development of housing, market complex and real estate purposes. As a result of development, value of the acquired land became much higher than the price paid to the original landowner. In this process, the corporate made huge profit and the original landowner felt cheated. This in turn led to distrust and heartburning among the landowners.

Diversion of forestland for non-forestry use is another case of similar nature, where interest of the forest dwellers is required to be appreciated and protected for making the land diversion process smooth and acceptable to the forest dwellers. The forest dwellers, usually belonging to the Scheduled Tribe, depend on forest for livelihood. Following diversion of forest land, they not only lost their homestead, assets but also livelihood opportunity. Meager financial compensation received often was not adequate for the person to look after self and family.

Analysis of land acquisition for the *Nano* small car plant at Singur in West Bengal, Steel plant at Kalingnagar in Odisha and mega POSCO Steel plant[15] in Odisha indicated that all recent cases of acquisition of private land for corporate use has to be dealt with sensitivity, after due consultation with the stakeholders about rehabilitation of the displaced persons and making them partners in development rather than giving some money as compensation. Providing part of the developed land to the original landowners for alternate use would help in making them owning the project and the operation smooth.

Labour related issues is another area, on which corporate need to give due attention particularly to the social implication. At times, extraneous factors like change in technology, improvement in quality require induction of new technology, which reduces the labour size for remaining competitive. As such measures often led to loss of livelihood, it need to be dealt with care and compassion. The Jet Airways laying off about 1900 staff in October 2008 was a case, which was dealt in a hurry without due sensitivity. This led to agitation and considerable commotion, which had to be finally reversed.

Induction of new technology and rightsizing the employee often become inevitable for survival in the market. As this related to livelihood of the workers and affect the society, the challenge lies in the corporate remaining sensitive to the need of the labour, looking beyond profit and empowering the surplus labour with new skill sets for alternate jobs or starting their own enterprise. There are instances, where the corporate anticipate it, take the labour into confidence, invest in skilling so that the surplus labour became employable and get redeployed in alternate jobs either in the same or other project/corporate. In such cases, labour reduction does not cause much hardship and is accepted by the labour. On the other hand, when such important matter is dealt in a casual manner by the corporate without giving due attention and taking due care, the surplus labour is left to look after itself with hardship and suffering. This led to agitation and social unrest. In the modern society, the corporate need to be careful in dealing with employees in general and in separation scheme in particular with provision of due consultation and taking the employees into confidence.

In both the cases discussed above, it needs to be appreciated that in the earlier times the poor used to get reconciled to economic deprivation as a matter of fate and accepted things. This has however changed with spread of literacy, education, generation of awareness created by television and other mass media. In the past, the poor did not know how wealthy the riches were, nor did they care too much because so few were rich. However, things have changed over the last decade. Advertisements for generating demand for consumer and luxury goods have fuelled the expectations for such goods among the people in general and the youth in particular. Unfulfilled expectation arising out of the gap between expectation and opportunity is leading to frustration, frustration leading to anger and anger leading to violence.

Such developments at individual level had its impact on the society, at regional, state and national levels. In the globalized world, this has been extending beyond national boundaries affecting development and peace all-over the world. Reflecting on this aspect of human deprivation and changing mindset. Nobel laureate Wangari Maathai had observed "it was important to manage our resources in a responsible way and to share them equitably in order to pre-empt the root cause of conflict and war. Looking at wars, be it regional or international, indicates that they are over access and control to resources. Those who are denied, discriminated against and marginalized are trying to seek justice through whatever means available. Call them terrorists, thieves or militants, if we want to live in a peaceful world, we must add issues of resource management, governance and equity, which are important ingredients for peace".[16]

Rapid industrialization related socio-economic deprivations are making it increasingly evident that economic development shall have to be considered beyond immediate, short-term gain. Any meaningful development has to be sustainable on long-term basis taking care of the interest of the future generations. Relevance of sustainable development for continuation of life in the planet is best reflected in the words of George Bernard Shaw, "*Life is no brief candle to me. It's a sort of splendid torch, which I've got to hold up for the moment and I want to make it burn as brightly as possible before handing it on to future generations.*" Experiences of development all-over the world indicate that industrialization and economic development is essential and can be made sustainable by making it socially and economically inclusive. This calls for capacity building for facilitating social inclusion along with taking care of the environment.

Impacts of the industrialization and economic development on the society have special dimensions for developing countries like India. India has to face severe constraints of natural resources for meeting needs of nearly one-sixth of the population with one-sixteenth of global natural resource. Meeting the growing aspirations of the world's largest youth population make the development process extremely challenging. This necessitates mobilization of the physical, human and financial resources in an innovative and effective manner for boosting up the pace of economic development in general and overcoming the human deprivation in particular. Human deprivation is a complex issue and requires an integrated approach. While the government is responsible for the welfare of the disadvantaged segment, the corporate sector needs to come forward and join this effort which will not only help the disadvantaged but also in restoring peace. This is essential for development and enabling the corporate to exploit available potential. The corporate have to remain sensitive to the emerging social needs and carry the society along with a human touch. It has to ensure providing required support for empowering the poor and the disadvantaged in the real sense rather than dealing it as a mere financial matter to be settled with some money as compensation. This is essential for the corporate's own sustenance and doing business in the society. While requirement of land for the project is required to be kept at the bare minimum level, the landowner/forest dweller (in case of forestland) are required to be taken into confidence and explained the advantages of the diversion and alternate use of land. This is the only way to overcome the resistance, get land and set up the project.

Charity and philanthropy has been a part of the Indian culture and tradition for centuries. Over years, this has got focused and refined with some corporate taking up social causes like providing health care and education, as a part of their internal policy. After decade long deliberations, India has set an innovative example by making CSR mandatory with effect from the 1st April, 2014. Since then, more than three years have been passed with the mandatory CSR. Under the new provision, the corporate with net worth/turnover/profit above the prescribed amount, have been mandated to spend two per cent of their profit on notified social activities. The corporate have been given full liberty to formulate and implement projects as per the broad guidelines laid down. The only requirement is to disclose details of the CSR projects taken up with the earmarked amount every year and indicate the reason, in case of inability to spend the amount. It would be in the interest of the corporate to ensure that the mandated CSR provision is implemented with sincerity and commitment so that it solves the social issues concerning the common man in general and the displaced families and persons affected by activities of the corporate in particular. Such step will not only help the society and make the growth inclusive but also give the best value for the money spent to the corporate. The challenge ahead lies in corporate taking it up seriously and stakeholders of the civilized society to appreciate various aspects of CSR in general and in mobilizing corporate support for addressing the major social issues relating to health, education, skill for livelihood to each and every citizen in particular for achieving the desired objectives of the Constitution. There are several examples of Indian corporate contributing significantly to the social cause along with doing good business and making profit. One of such examples relates to Infosys, one of the leading IT companies. In addition to emerging as a giant IT corporate, maintaining high ethical standards, it has taken up CSR activities in innovative manner through Infosys Foundation for improving the quality of education, nourishing young talents, provision of nutritious meals in collaboration with the Akshaya Patra Foundation. Such focused activities taken up under active support and guidance of its mentor provide valuable lessons for other corporate in using CSR as an effective tool responsible towards the society.

Responsibility of the corporate towards the society in India has come a long way from traditional charity to structured interventions under Triple Bottom Line, to earmarking a part of the profit for social purpose. This has culminated with CSR becoming mandatory, which is in an evolving stage. As CSR relates to the society, like other social issues, there are doubts and apprehensions about CSR as well, with apprehensions like "CSR interventions of the corporate are too small to make any meaningful difference", "Can CSR make a difference?", "CSR is a mere publicity stunt and an eye wash". It is necessary to approach the case with open mind and make an impartial and unbiased assessment of various aspects on a holistic and pragmatic basis.

Peace is essential for development. No business can grow unless there is peace. It hardly needs any emphasis that the future of business is linked up with peace in the society. The corporate need the society to carry on business. Further, peace and order in the society are prerequisites for doing business on a sustainable basis on a long term. The growth process has to be socially inclusive to be sustainable over time. The role and responsibility of the business towards the society in the changing socio-economic scenario has necessitated a paradigm shift from a "charity based" approach to an "empowerment based" approach based on empowering and enabling the disadvantaged to access market as active partners. CSR has the potential to create a "win-win" situation for all the stakeholders of the business instead of confining it to only the shareholders and management. Relevance of CSR in the Indian context is required to be appreciated and pursued keeping in view relevant issues for bringing about synergy between business and the society for sharing the benefits of economic development in a fair, equitable and just manner in the globalized world. These are essential for checking social unrest and having peace, which is a must for the society and the business to grow. This has to be appreciated as a basic need of good business and not as mere morality.

References

1. http://www.politicalsciencenotes.com/essay/moral-and-legal-duties-of-individuals-towards-society/268
2. http://www.imasocialentrepreneur.com/social-responsibility/
3. *Human Development Report*, 1998, UNDP.
4. Milanovic, B., 2002, "True World Income Distribution 1988 and 1993, First calculations based on household survey alone", *The European Journal*, Vol. 112, No. 476.
5. http://www.tandfonline.com/doi/abs/10.1080/13552070215904
6. Gidwani, Sushila, 1986, "Gandhian Trusteeship, A Corporate Management Strategy for Economic Justice", *Trusteeship – The Gandhian Alternative*, Gandhi Peace Foundation, p. 189.
7. On the 2nd January, 2006, police opened fire on a group of tribals protesting against the acquisition of land for setting up of steel plant at Kalinganagar in the Jajpur district of Orissa. Death of 13 tribals in this incident led to violent protest and closure of traffic on the Daitari-Paradip express highway, connecting the mineral-rich backyard of Orissa to the port, used for transportation of minerals for export. The project has to *be abandoned*.
8. There were oppositions to acquisition of land for setting up of a small car plant project at Singur in West Bengal during 2006-07. This matter could not be settled, project has to *be abandoned* after considerable time and efforts.
9. There were oppositions to acquisition of land for setting up of a Special Economic Zone (SEZ) at Nandigram in West Bengal during 2006-07. SEZ aimed at boosting up industrial production, generating higher exports, Foreign Direct Investment (FDI) and employment by promotion of export oriented industrial units. Following violent clashes, this project has to *be abandoned*.
10. There were oppositions to land acquisition for industrial projects in Khammam district in Andhra Pradesh during 2007, which led to loss of lives and property and delay in undertaking the project.
11. Activities of the Left Wing Extremists (LWEs) in the central plateau in Bihar, Jharkhand, Andhra Pradesh, Odisha, mainly inhabited by Tribals, continue to be a major concern. Apart from loss of life and property, such

incidents severely affected development of the area in general and setting up of projects for exploiting the rich minerals resources in particular.

12. The North-eastern region of the country is marked by geographical isolation, inadequate infrastructure and incidence of poverty and unemployment. Activities of some misguided youth at periodic intervals have been affecting law and order situation of this region in general and economic development in particular.
13. On the 12th April, 2014 there was an attack on election party deployed for conduct of general elections to the 16th Lok Sabha in Bijapur and Bastar districts of Chhattisgarh.
14. "Occupy Wall Street (OWS)" began on September 17, 2011, in Zuccotti Park, Wall Street financial district, New York, USA.
15. Acquisition of private land in Jagatsinghpur District of Odisha was initiated for setting up a mega steel plant by the South Korean steel maker, POSCO involving one of the largest Foreign Direct Investment (FDI) was objected by the landowners for more than a decade. In spite of the decision to reduce the size of the plant and quantum of land required, required land could not be provided and the plant could not come up.
16. Rajiv Gandhi Foundation Lecture, Delhi, March 21, 2007, "The marginalized have right to be listened", *The Hindu*, March 22, 2007, p.11.

2

The Concept

A corporation or corporate is defined[1] as a legal entity that has been incorporated either directly through legislation or through a registration process established by law. Incorporated entities have legal rights and liabilities that are distinct from their employees and shareholders, and may conduct business as either a profit-seeking business or not-for-profit business. Early incorporated entities were established by charter. Registered corporations have legal personality and are owned by shareholders, whose liability is limited to their investment. Shareholders, do not typically, actively manage a corporation; shareholders instead elect or appoint a board of directors to control the corporation in a fiduciary capacity.

Origin of Corporate

The origin of corporate as organized business started with the Industrial revolution in England and other European countries in the second half of the eighteenth century. Commencing with the invention of steam engine, industrialization and related developments over the next century, this revolution altered England and the whole of Europe in a manner, which was unprecedented in the history of mankind. The revolution transformed the common man from a farmer/shepherd to a manipulator of machines, run by inanimate energy. The revolution was spearheaded by a wide range of energy such as coal, oil, electricity and later nuclear energy. Fossil fuel and electricity empowered human in a manner, which was inconceivable in the earlier times, when animals were the source of energy.

The social power structure also shifted[2] accordingly. In the agrarian society, land was the main economic resource and the social power structure was monopolized by groups, who had control over land and land based activities. As a result of industrialization, agriculture got gradually replaced by manufacturing, trade and commerce, inspired by profit motive, expediency and to some extent, reason and logic. Social position of the warlords and the monks were replaced by the merchants and the professionals. Growth in manufacturing, trade and commerce led to emergence of a merchant class with managerial ability, economic power, social and political influence. This change required efficient manpower, and professionals with special skill for managing the machines, production activities, trade and commerce.

Impact of Industrial Revolution on Individuals

The industrial revolution had significant impact on man, as the industrial society required a new type of man. In the pre-industrial society, a farmer was able to pursue his occupation with the traditional skill, acquired from his father and forefathers. It was not necessary to have formal education for pursuing the production activities. But in an *industrialized society, there was no place for the so-called uneducated and the unskilled.* In order to survive in an industrial society, each and every individual needed several years of instructions. It was necessary to develop a *new mindset in which intuition got replaced by rationality, approximation by precision, and emotion by calculation.* Further, in an industrial society, it was necessary to cope up with the technological changes, which were both rapid and continuous. In the new society, with advancement in science and technology, established systems as well as men were required to change and adapt to evolving changes fast, failing which they became obsolete. The agricultural worker could live his whole life on a few ideas learnt in his adolescence. But the industrial worker had to survive in a system, which almost continuously forced him to be advanced. In the agricultural society, *the old man was the wise one but there was no such virtue in an industrialized society.* Division of labour and need for teamwork in an industrial venture required impersonal relation with the workers and subordinates in a precise and continuous basis.

Impact on Families

The agrarian society was characterized by joint family with many members, which comprised of all age groups, living together under one roof. Along with its basic function of procreating, raising and grooming the new generations, the family accepted the responsibility of providing '*social security*' to the young and the old. In the industrial society, the joint family broke down as people had to move out for education, acquisition of skill and in search of employment and job. The joint family was replaced by nuclear units, with relatively fewer functions. As a result, it became necessary for the State to look after the functions, which were traditionally extended by the joint family. Nature of family changed from being a large nucleus in a numerically small society in the agricultural set up, to a small nucleus in an ever-increasing large society in the industrialized set up.

Impact on State

The role of State also changed for meeting the changing social and economic needs of an industrialized society. Scope and nature of taxation was expanded for generating revenue for the State and regulating consumption of scarce commodities. Taxes imposed by the government along with extractions by landlords and the church kept the peasants at subsistence level in many parts of Europe. Public expenditure increased by manifold for meeting the requirements of social services of the industrial society. Along with this, conflict among countries leading to war became increasingly common and complex. This further stepped up the need for taxation, and direct tax in the form of income tax was introduced in England. Growing industrialization and urbanization demanded improvement in standards of literacy and education for meeting the emerging needs, which led to expansion of the formal educational facilities managed by the government. Local self-government bodies also took up managing schools, hospitals and levy taxes for meeting the expenditure thereon.

Industrial revolution had profound impact on the economic and social structure. It transformed the agrarian society with more than fifty per cent of the population primarily dependent on agriculture living in the countryside, to a stage where dependence on agriculture reduced considerably. Sizeable population migrated from rural to urban areas in search of employment with better remuneration. The agriculture-based rural villages were replaced by industrialized towns and cities for accommodating greater number of people. Changes in demographic and economic activities had impact on socio-cultural spheres like customs, ideas and beliefs as well.

Success of the industrial revolution in England and neighbouring countries is attributed to a number of factors such as political structure, mental attitude and social values, which were favourable to industrialization. Industrial revolution spread to other countries in Europe and North America with relative ease, as prevalent conditions were similar to those of the English society. However, its expansion to other countries faced limitations as prevailing socio-cultural milieu was different and not so favourable for industrialization. Conversion of an agrarian economy to an industrialized economy happened to be a *fairly complex process* involving political, social and cultural factors rather than mere economic and technological factors.

Impact at Global Level

Improvement in communication and transport facilities gave a boost to industrialization. Countries, where conditions were favourable, saw economic growth at a much faster pace than others. However, the demand for industrialized products grew all-over the world. This led to export of manufactured goods from the more industrialized nations to less industrialized nations. Export of manufactured goods was much higher than the agricultural produce, in terms of value, which resulted in tilting of the international trade in favour of the industrialized nations and gave rise to trade deficits. As a result of uneven industrialization over the next century, the trade deficit continued to grow and divided the world into two unequal parts—the developed and the underdeveloped countries. Countries, which were able to reap benefits of industrialization, saw economic development at a fast rate, while others, which could not, continued in the pre-industrial stage. Limitations in physical infrastructure, facilities for education and skill formation, mindset of dependence and helplessness were some of the factors, which hindered the growth of the underdeveloped countries.

State and Industrialization

The initial phase of industrialization and economic growth in Britain was a market-based phenomenon in which the State played a minimal role. As the impact of industrial revolution spread, role of State changed for meeting the emerging social and economic challenges. By the second half of the twentieth century, the role of the State was strengthened for facilitating industrialization and regulating it for checking any adverse impact. Suitable mechanisms were put in place for attainment of the national objectives and meeting the emerging challenges from changeover of a traditional, agricultural society to a modern, industrialized society. Control of individual over land, the major asset in an agrarian society, was regulated by the State and land tenure system was introduced for effective use of natural resources and labour. The industrial revolution had impact on almost all aspects of human lives along with transformation of an agrarian society to an industrialized society. Acquisition of new skills and ability to change became increasingly important in deciding the position of individuals in the society.

Pace of Industrialization

The impact of the industrial revolution remained somewhat uneven both within a country and across countries. Geographical areas, economic sectors and social groups within the same country moved with different dynamics and speed. Traditional activities and old institutions, which could change and adapt to new situations managed to survive, while others, which could not, perished. Impact of the industrial revolution spread to other European countries and the United States by the middle of nineteenth century. In due course, it extended to Sweden, Italy, Russia, Japan and Argentina and later to India, China and Africa by the mid-twentieth century.

The industrial revolution was a continuous process, which passed from one stage to another. The more advanced industrial societies faced problems of social restructuring, cultural and political renewal. Technological progress and demographical changes led to the subsequent stage of industrialization. Rapid industrialization had its impact on social and personal life. With machines determining the pace of development, the process, which solved the problems in the past, posed new problems.[3] Such developments continued to be areas of concern in an industrialized society.

Evolution of Corporate

The industrialized society was characterized by production of goods on a mass scale with the use of machines. Such production process required mobilization of men, money, materials and machines. These are required to be managed with appropriate technology with expertise and managerial ability. This gave birth to corporate as business entities for undertaking production and marketing activities. Importance of the corporate grew in magnitude and diversity continuously with improvement in trade and commerce. Gradually, the corporate acquired sizeable economic and political clout as well.

Evolution of CSR

Making profit was the major concern of industries and business since the evolution of the organized industries. The State evolved mechanisms for regulating conduct of the business, which was resisted by the corporate initially. There were instances of corporate houses adopting the strategy of obeying the law in a minimal extent and lobbying to defeat the regulatory mechanisms. They often got into litigations by retaining good corporate lawyers. Thus, in its initial years, the business evolved merely as an 'economic institution' with hardly any concern for the society.

Concern of the business houses towards the society was first reported[4] around 1930s. In the subsequent period, this developed in an organized manner with the realization that corporate need the consumers and the market for selling their products. This got intensified at the time of the Great Depression. The business houses felt that it would be in their interest to look after the consumers particularly for generating purchasing power, which would increase the demand for their products. It seems that initial response of the business towards the welfare of the society arose *more out of a selfish motive* for its own survival rather than as a genuine, altruistic, selfless, philanthropic concern.

Gradually, the responsibility of the corporate towards the society gained importance in theory and practice as well as in law, economics and politics. Merrick Dodd of Harvard University had advocated that corporations served a social purpose along with profit-making. However, this view was challenged by others, who held that the corporate primarily and exclusively pursued the financial goals of making profit and providing a decent return to the investors on the capital deployed. This debate continued over the subsequent decades.

The Great Depression of the 1930s pushed the business houses through a churning process and forced them to evolve appropriate business strategy for survival. Reaction of the business to this crisis covered measures like introducing advanced technology, improving quality, reducing costs for earning the goodwill of the consumers. Simultaneously, ethical issues also came up for adhering to principles that distinguished "*the good from the bad*" and "*the right from the wrong*". Business ethics became a topic of interest with the realization that ethical misconduct could cost dearly to a company. This made several companies to lay down *corporate code of ethics* for their managers seeking action in conformity with values, beliefs of the company as well as ethical behaviour in general. Over the next decade, ethical behaviour was enlarged to include economic, social and environmental issues. Gradually, concern for the consumer, the workers and later for the environment acquired importance, which formed the basis of responsibility of the corporate towards the society.

These concepts evolved over the next decades. It was felt that the business was answerable to the shareholder public, whose money was used for conducting the business. It was recognized that business and social responsibility were not mutually exclusive but inclusive. The definition of a stakeholder, who impacted organization activities, was enlarged beyond shareholder.[5] Social responsibility of corporate gathered momentum amid growing concern about large corporations and their power after the fall of the Berlin wall. Subsequent developments in the Enron, WorldCom and dubious accounting practices raised doubts about conduct of corporate houses and pressed the need for adoption of ethical practices.

Over years, it was realized that although performance of corporate is judged by economic parameters, they are inalienable organs of the society and must fulfil certain basic responsibilities towards the society.

Corporate Social Responsibility (CSR): The Concept

Corporate Social Responsibility (CSR) comprised of three words meaning the responsibility of the corporate towards the society. As per legal provisions, a company is a registered body owned by the shareholders and carry on its activities as per its bye-laws, regulated as per the provisions of the Companies Act. The company is primarily responsible to its shareholders. The board of management deals with the day-to-day managerial functions. The company also owes responsibility towards other stakeholders, namely the customers, workers, employees, and suppliers. The concept of CSR originated from the need for making the development process sustainable. This is based on taking a macro view and looking beyond the shareholders, earning profit, declaring of dividends and return on investment. From time to time, the corporate houses took up charity and philanthropic activities. CSR as a management function evolved towards the later half of the twentieth century.

CSR: Definitions

Although the concept of CSR has been developing since the early 1970s, there is no single, commonly accepted definition of CSR.

One of the early references to CSR was made by Friedman who was of the view that the one and only social responsibility of business is "to use its resources and engage in activities designed to increase its profits so long as it stays within the rule of the game."[6]

The World Business Council for Sustainable Development (WBCSD) has defined CSR as "the continuing commitment of business to behave ethically and contribute to economic development while improving the quality of life of the workforce and their families as well as of the local community and society at large."[7]

Business for Social Responsibility (BSR) defined CSR as "Operating a business in a manner that meets or exceeds the ethical, legal, commercial and public expectations that society has of business. CSR is seen by leadership companies as more than a collection of discrete practices or occasional gestures, or initiatives motivated by marketing, public relations or other business benefits. Rather, it is viewed as a comprehensive set of policies, practices and programmes that are integrated throughout business operations, and decision-making processes that are supported and rewarded by top management."

The European Union defined CSR as "the concept that requires an enterprise to remain accountable for its impact on all relevant stakeholders. It is the continuing commitment by business to behave fairly and responsibly and contribute to economic development while improving the quality of life of the workforce and their families as well as of the local community and society at large."

Michael Hopkins defined CSR as treating the stakeholders of the firm ethically or in a responsible manner.[8] "Ethically responsible" means treating stakeholders in a manner deemed acceptable in civilized societies. "Social" includes economic responsibility as well. Stakeholders exist both within a firm and outside—for example the natural environment is a stakeholder. The wider aim of social responsibility is to create higher and higher standards of living, while preserving the profitability of the corporation, for people both within and outside the corporation.

Kotler and Lee have defined CSR as "a commitment to improve community well-being through discretionary business practices and contribution of business resources."[9]

A more comprehensive definition of Corporate Social Responsibility (CSR) describes it as "a concept whereby organizations consider the interests of society by taking responsibility for the impact of their activities on customers, employees, shareholders, communities and the environment in all aspects of their operations. This obligation is seen to extend beyond the statutory obligation to comply with legislation and sees organizations voluntarily taking further steps to improve the quality of life for employees and their families as well as for the local community and society at large."[10]

Social Responsiveness *vs.* Responsibility

Ackerman and Bauer have argued that Corporate Social "Responsiveness" will be a preferred provision,.as "Responsibility" represents the process of merely assuming an obligation and places emphasis on motivation rather than on performance. They have argued that motivation is not enough as responding to social demands requires more than deciding what to do. Social Responsiveness relates to management of doing, what one has decided to do, to become Socially Responsible.

Mallen Baker had advocated that CSR related[11] to the way companies manage the business processes to produce an overall positive impact on the society (**Box 2.1: Impact of the Business on Society**). Activities of the companies can be visualized as two concentric circles, the *inner circle* covering the quality of *their own management*, both in terms of people and processes, surrounded by an *outer circle* comprising its impact on *society*. In the traditional management, the company used to be concerned only with the inner circle relating to the workers and the consumers. However, things have been changing with the outside stakeholders taking an increasing interest in the activity of the company in terms of its products and services, as well as its impact on the environment and on local communities.

CSR: Negotiating between Wealth and Welfare

Generation of wealth has been the basic and major concern of the corporate. As any charity or philanthropic activity has a cost, often there is a conflict between making profit and spending money on the society beyond the direct shareholders. The interrelationship between private goods in terms of return to the shareholders and public goods in terms of welfare of the society at large needs elaboration. Under real life situations, there are variations and profit for the organization and welfare of the

Box 2.1: Impact of the Business on Society

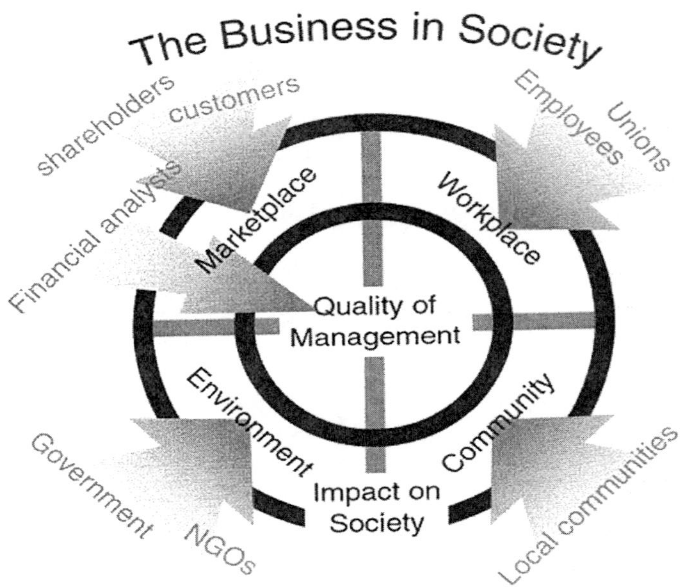

Diagram by Mallen Barker.

society does not necessarily go together. There are four types of situations, which can be depicted in the form of a matrix.[12] **(Box 2.2: Negotiating between Wealth and Welfare)**

Good Management

Under ideal conditions, ethically sound business practices generally enhance both profitability and public goods. Any steps for adopting sound management practices like dealing honestly with employees, suppliers, and customers, lead to a "W*in-Win*" situation. Such measures improve profitability on a long-term basis due to good market image, branding and advance public good at the same time. These measures are popularly known as "*Good Management*" practices.

Burrowed Virtue

There are cases where social welfare activities are taken up at the

Box 2.2: Negotiating between Wealth and Welfare

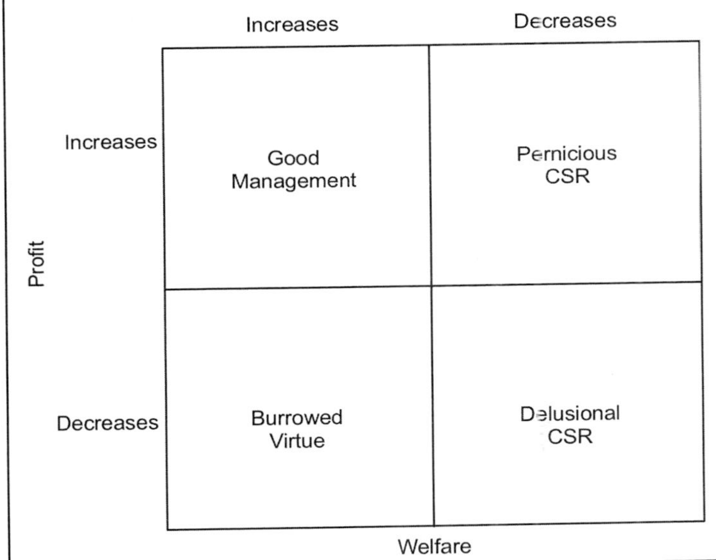

organization's expense for the benefit of a few individuals, without bringing in tangible benefits to the organization and society. Such activities lead to outgo of resources of the organization without much gain. For example, at times the corporate houses give awards and sponsor events for promoting individuals, which do not have the approval of the owner-shareholders. It amounts to a few persons doing charity with the shareholders' money and does not constitute CSR in the real sense. Any such case of charity or philanthropy with corporate fund, without explicit knowledge of the shareholders, essentially amounts to an unethical practice, notwithstanding the purpose. Such cases are indeed more unfortunate as these are cases of spending money taken not from strangers, but from persons, who have placed the management in a position of trust to safeguard their interest. It amounts to not only misuse of fund but breach of trust as well. Such instances of corporate philanthropy represent cases of "*Burrowed Virtue*".

However, there are exceptions where the charitable trusts were set up by individual philanthropists heading corporate. In such cases, the money is spent out of the amount due to them as individual shareholder and not part of the fund of the company, which belongs to the shareholders.

Such activities of a number of trusts have been laudable in promoting institutions of excellence in the field of education and research.

Pernicious CSR

The third category relates to measures, which lead to increase in profit at the cost of society. For example, recycling of waste has a financial cost to the company. In case "Profit" is taken in the limited sense of private benefit minus private cost, recycling may not be desirable. In some cases, the organizations take a myopic view and do not undertake such practices. This leads to compromising with the larger interest of the society. However, in case the social costs and benefits are considered taking into account depletion of natural resources, impact on environment, public health etc., this position changes. Such cases of avoiding the environmental compliance or social responsibility merely for limiting expenditure and increasing profit are examples of "*Pernicious CSR*".

Delusional CSR

The fourth category relates to interventions, which reduce both profit and social welfare. This includes activities taken up merely for achieving target without any commitment. Supporting activities without looking into relevant factors leads to reduction of profit without commensurate social welfare. For example, supporting NGOs of doubtful integrity and without proper monitoring do not bring social welfare to the desired extent even though valuable resources of the company are doled out. Similarly, funding welfare activities, which increases dependency syndrome of the target group, are harmful to the beneficiaries, as such measures are not sustainable in the long run. Such activities ultimately become a delusion for the beneficiaries and are regarded as "*Delusional CSR*".

CSR Dimensions

Social responsibility of business has three different dimensions[13], namely social obligation, social reaction and social responsiveness. The first and most important dimension "*Social Obligation*" relates to the obligation of the corporate to use the resources, undertake activities and operate in the market in a free and fair manner for making profit without indulging in any fraudulent practice. The second dimension, "*Social Reaction*" means the response of the business houses to the prevailing social norms, values and expectations. This relates to a firm's contribution in solving problems prevailing in the society. In more specific terms, this implies the firm's acceptance of social obligation voluntarily without the requirements of law and not in reaction to the pressure groups, consumer boycotts or with fear of adverse publicity. The third dimension, "*Social Responsiveness*", is somewhat broader and relates to taking stand on public issues. It involves accounting for actions of any group, anticipating the future needs of society and moving towards satisfying them. At times, it requires interventions including making a continuous dialogue with the government regarding existing and anticipated socially desirable legislation. It places the organization and its managers in a broader position of social responsibility instead of being concerned only with its own affairs.

CSR as Partnership

CSR can also be visualized as a partnership, which stands for a relationship between two or more parties which transact business for mutual benefits. It provides a forum to bring together strengths, capacities, approaches, skills and methodologies of different actors, thereby creating powerful synergies and ability to overcome barriers. From the corporate perspective, partnership can be seen as a platform to manage expectations, deliver messages and reduce dependencies—which led to financial and social gains in due course. For the society, it provides avenues for capacity building and gain in physical and financial terms to individuals. Partnership provides valuable source of insights, expertise and innovations on issues of concern. Study of successful corporate indicates that the real strength of a corporate comes not from the assets that it owns or the employees that it supervises, but from the domain of trust[14], it has established among the stakeholders. For any corporate house, 'trust' relates to the image the company has among its consumers, shareholders, employees, government and the communities at large. In case the corporate fails to 'take care' of the environment and the society, the trust level reduces and eventually breaks down. Partnership offers an effective tool for achieving and improving level of trust. There are several innovative examples of interface and engagement of the corporate with the society, which have proved to be useful to the society and the corporate as well in building up their brand image.

CSR and Trusteeship

Any discussion on the role and responsibility of the corporate towards the society will remain incomplete without reference to the theory of trusteeship advocated by Mahatma Gandhi. Based on study and understanding of the Indian society, Gandhi had evolved the principle of *trusteeship*, which is derived from the ideal of non-possession (*aparigraha*) given in the *Ishopanishad.* This principle proposes that private property should be under the control of individual, who should regard himself as its protector (trustee) and not as its master (owner). It is different from the western concepts of capitalism or socialism.

The theory of trusteeship[15] envisages economic equality in the true sense and is derived from the understanding "*The world has enough for meeting everybody's need but not greed*" and desiring more than the basic needs amount to misuse and theft, deserving punishment. Accordingly, any surplus wealth belongs to the society and should be held in trust. Gandhi was not in favour of restricting growth of intellectual attainments of the people and wanted them to make full use of their talents in the interest of the community. Trusteeship requires a change of heart or mindset of the rich property-owners for considering themselves not as the absolute owners of what they possess, but as the custodians or trustees utilizing the property for the good of the whole community. Expressing his reservation on the capitalist system and concept of inheritance, Gandhi had advocated that the choice of a trustee or successor should be subject to the final approval of the community. He had suggested that the State should make a law for checking any misuse of trust property, regulating private property system, and confiscating illegally held wealth with minimum use of force.

Gandhi's theory of trusteeship is often criticized as being utopian and not pragmatic in the contemporary society, where Man's love for wealth is so ingrained that he may forget as to who had killed his father but not as to who usurped his property. Even Jawaharlal Nehru had questioned, "Is it reasonable to believe in the theory of trusteeship to give unchecked power and wealth to an individual and to expect him to use it entirely for the public good? Are the best of us so perfect as to be entrusted in this way?" Notwithstanding this debate, the theory of trusteeship propounded by Gandhi continues to be an important milestone and like a light house guiding the path for CSR.

Stages of Corporate Responsibility

Mirvis and Googins (2006) advocated that there is no single developmental pathway but there is a natural progression. They developed a model built on ideas of behavioural psychology and like individuals, exhibit distinct patterns of behaviour at different stages of development, activities of companies becoming more complex and sophisticated as they mature. This was based on five identified stages of corporate citizenship – elementary, engaged, innovative, integrated and transforming – representing "distinct patterns of activity at different points of development." The stages are measured along seven dimensions covering definition, purpose, leadership support, structure, issues management, stakeholder relationships and transparency.

The seven areas of management, which determines the level of maturity of the company, cover (i) Citizenship concept—covering the way corporate responsibility is defined and its comprehensiveness; (ii) Strategic Intent – reflecting the purpose of the company's corporate responsibility; (iii) Leadership – indicating the support given by company managers; (iv) Structure – indicating the day-to-day management of corporate responsibility team within the company; (v) Management covering Responses to social, environmental; and other relevant issues; (vi) Stakeholder relationships— covering Managing the relationship with key constituencies within and outside the company; and (vii) Transparency— covering Openness, transparency, and disclosure about different aspects of corporate responsibility performance. A matrix, covering the seven areas in the five stages of companies discharging the CSR functions, given in Table 2.1 explains the position.

Socially Responsible Investment (SRI)[16]

Mobilization of financial resources is one of the essential prerequisites for any business. Investment of resources is normally guided by factors like financial return and security. But it has social implication as well. The concept of Socially Responsible Investment (SRI) emerged in the 1920s, when churches divested the so-called '*sin stocks*'—alcohol, tobacco and gambling from their portfolio in view of its undesirable social impact. Later, environment-conservation-related movements of the 1970s and the 1980s strengthened this concept. The 'negative' or 'avoidance' screening approach is being replaced by 'positive' or 'inclusionary' screening approach for guiding the investors in choosing companies with better policies and practices.

Table 2.1: Stages of Corporate Responsibility

Dimensions	Stages				
	Stage 1	*Stage 2*	*Stage 3*	*Stage 4*	*Stage 5*
Citizenship concept	Jobs, profits, taxes	Philanthropy, environmental protection	Stakeholder management	Sustainability/triple bottom line	Change the game
Strategic intent	Legal compliance	Maintain license to operate	Make Business case	Integration of value and values	Create new markets/social change
Leadership	Minimal	Supportive	On top of the issues	Ahead of the curve	Visionary
Structure	Marginal	Functional ownership	Cross-functional coordination	Organizational alignment	Integrated into mainstream
Management issues	Defensive	Reactive	Responsive	Proactive	Defines the issues
Stakeholder relationships	Unilateral	Interactive	Mutual influence	Alliances and partnerships	Multi organizational
Transparency	Enough to protect flanks	Public relations	Public reporting	Assurance	Full disclosure

Source: Adopted from Mirvis and Googins (2006).

Kofi Annan, former UN Secretary-General, formally launched the principle of SRI in April 2006. It aims at integrating consideration of Environmental Social Governance (ESG) issues by institutional investors into investment decision-making and ownership practices and thereby improving long-term returns. SRI basically favours corporate practices, which are environmentally responsible, community-friendly, support workplace diversity and increase product safety and quality. It advocates that investment should be made in a manner that builds a better tomorrow while earning competitive returns. Interpretations of SRI however vary in practice from (i) identification of 'sin-stocks' like tobacco, pornography, alcohol, weapons, nuclear power to; (ii) positive choices dealing with good business practices relating to the workplace or the environment; and (iii) community investment like welfare of the disadvantaged, low income communities.

Several organizations are working on this concept by undertaking study on the policies and practices of SRI. Their findings are yielding valuable information to the ordinary investors in making decisions. The corporate have also started realizing its importance and are extending cooperation for making quantifiable assessments of corporate behaviour and suitability. This has helped in the development of more inclusive company rankings and SRI indices. A number of SRI indices such as Dow Jones Sustainability World Index, FTSE4 Good Global Index, Domini 400 Social Index, Humanix, and JSE SRI Index have come up based on this concept.

SRI technique has grown up in the developed markets. However, it is yet to take a definite shape in the emerging markets. As a result of globalization, issues relating to racial discrimination, human rights violation, child labour, climate change are getting attention in the market. With the developing countries emerging as attractive investment destinations, SRI technique will become useful to the investors in making their investment decisions. As SRI technique aims at guiding the investment for making the business socially responsible, it complements CSR to a considerable extent.

Advantages of CSR

CSR has been evolving as a concept associated with a genuine culture of "doing the right thing". It has been helping the corporate in building up brand name based on distinctive ethical values[17] and getting loyalty of the customers at the marketplace. There are instances of reputations, which took decades to build up, getting ruined in hours due to corruption, scandals, environmental accidents etc. Such unfortunate incidents draw adverse attention from the regulators, courts, governments and media and become a major source of embarrassment for the corporate at the marketplace. CSR interventions, which are holistic in nature, help the corporation in management of risk[18] by offsetting such risks at the market place. Besides, CSR activities also contribute positively in personnel matters[19] involving recruitment and retention of staff, which are of critical importance for survival in the highly competitive markets. Firms with a comprehensive CSR policy attract committed persons, which give them a distinct advantage over others. It also helps in improving the perception about the company among its existing staff, particularly when the staff get involved in CSR through payroll giving, fund raising activities or community volunteering, contributing directly to a sense of fellow-feeling. Reputation at the marketplace along with committed workforce enables the CSR committed corporate to retain their supremacy in the competitive markets. Attempts have been made to develop mechanism for measuring the impact of CSR interventions.

Criticism on CSR

The primary objective of any corporate relates to make profit and maximize value for its shareholders. As undertaking any CSR activity leads to outgo of resources and reduction of profit, CSR activities appear to contradict the corporate objective of making money in the short-run. Based on this logic, Milton Friedman had expressed reservation[20] on CSR with the observation "there is one and only one social responsibility of business—to use its resources and energies in activities designed to increase profits so long as it stays within the rules of the game, which is to say, engages in open and free competition without deception or fraud."

This approach was based[21] on the consideration that it is difficult and rather impossible to distinguish a profit motive from a charitable motive in any particular corporate action. As such, it becomes difficult to judge the propriety of any managerial decision in pursuing CSR. Factors like natural monopoly, market failure and public corporations set up by government affect operations of an ideal market. Based on the facts that issues like environmental protection, employees' welfare, sale of goods at below market price, community development and support of cultural, educational and medical facility etc. are taken up under CSR, it has been argued that such purposes are effectively private concerns. The corporations, who hire the employees, owe a responsibility towards them as well as towards the community by following the laws of land. There cannot be any public interest in undertaking such activity. Based on this, it is argued that CSR amounts to a distortion, which is often used by the vested interests for controlling private wealth at the cost of capitalist venture.

Social Capital—Concept

Relevance of CSR in the larger social context can be better appreciated with an understanding of the concept of "*Social capital*". Social capital[22] has its origin on the benefits or capital, which is accrued as a result of personal relationship formed when people interact with each other in families, workplaces, neighbourhoods, local associations and a range of informal and formal meeting places. Social capital, a multidimensional concept, has been defined[23] as "a set of social norms, social networks, solidarity, and civic associations that affect relations among people and are assets as a means for the individual collective production of well-being". Based on his study, Robert Putnam[24] had observed that social capital includes all forms of association and relationship aimed to benefit all those in association and is sustained due to the presence of trust between people and groups facilitating cooperation and co-ordination for mutual benefit. It refers to the networks either formal or informal, which enable collective action. It describes the pattern and intensity of networks among people and the shared values, which arise from those networks. The term '*social capital*' emphasizes not just warm and cuddly feelings, but a wide variety of quite specific benefits that flow from trust, reciprocity, information and cooperation associated with social networks. It has been found that such network creates value in the form of social capital not only for the people who are directly connected but for others as well.

Social Capital—Types

Depending upon the types of networks, social capital can be broadly divided into three types—

- Bonding social capital
- Bridging social capital
- Linking social capital

Bonding social capital is generated as a result of close connection between people. It is characterized by strong bonds as in the case of members of a family or of the same ethnic group and is considered useful for 'getting by' in life.

Bridging social capital arises by networking between people at more distant connections. It is characterized by relatively weaker bonds as in the case with business associates, acquaintances, friends from different ethnic groups, friends of friends, etc., and is considered useful for 'getting ahead' in life.

Linking social capital arises as a result of interrelationship between people in positions of power. It is characterized by relations between persons within a hierarchy at different levels of power and is considered useful for accessing support from formal institutions.

Social capital works through multiple channels such as (i) through *information flows* e.g., learning about jobs, learning about candidates running for office, exchanging ideas at college, etc.; (ii) through *mutual aid or reciprocity*, which is either *bonding networks* that connect persons, who share similar particularized (in-group) reciprocity or *bridging networks* that connect individuals, who are diverse and sustain generalized reciprocity; and (iii) through *collective action* e.g., consumers of a particular good or service getting together for fighting for their legally admissible dues. Such social networks lead to greater solidarity, ultimately translating an "I" mentality into "we" and facilitate individuals and organizations in transacting business in the society.

In this context, it is worth mentioning that Social Responsibility initiatives and concern for the disadvantaged enhances the market reputation, i.e. *Brand building of the corporate*. In several parts of the world, corporate leaders like Warren Buffet, Bill Gates have pursued social activities very keenly. This has earned them tremendous goodwill in the contemporary society, where projects funded by them have benefitted the common men. Such goodwill in turn has tilted consumer preference in favour of their products directly and also enhanced their public image.

Civil Society—Concept

Civil Society[25] is a conception of society as a set of interlocking institutions and practices that cannot be philosophically simplified. By nature, human beings form groups and associations. Further, already associated human beings change their mode of association and form new associations.

Broadly speaking, civil society consists of the whole society except the military and the government. It has been found that associational power based on the social relations of any particular association within its members affect the outcome of any action. Participation in the civil society enables an ordinary member to derive benefits from other members in position of power and influence. It leads to a '*Win-Win*' situation for all members of the group as a whole.

The concept of civil society has its origin in Aristotle's work "*Polis*" in which a city is described as the political community or partnership. '*Polis*' is conceived as an association of persons, who cannot exist without one another. Civil society was brought into focus by the Central European dissidents as a name for the complex non-governmental 'social capital' required for liberal society.[26]

The definition of civil society by the *London School of Economics Centre for Civil Society* appears to be most illustrative. "Civil Society[27] refers to the arena of un-coerced collective action around shared interests, purposes and values. In theory, its institutional forms are distinct from those of the State, family, and market, though in practice, the boundaries between State, civil society, family, and market are often complex, blurred, and negotiated. Civil society commonly embraces a diversity of spaces, actors and institutional forms, varying in their degree of formality, autonomy and power. Civil societies are often populated by organizations such as registered charities, non-governmental organizations, community groups, women's organizations, faith based organizations, professional associations, trade unions, self-help groups, social movements, business associations, coalitions and advocacy groups".

Civil Society—Types

Several types of institutions are formed in a modern society sharing commercial, political, familial, recreational, associational and religious interest, which often criss-cross one another. As an individual can join one or many of such institutions, there is a wide range of choice of such institutions. Even though these institutions don't have direct control over one another, there are informal interactions. Participation in one or several such institutions enables an individual to derive strength from a number of institutions, which help in generation of social capital.

So far as the interrelationship between civil society and market is concerned, markets are a necessary but not sufficient condition for the modern civil society. The basic difference[28] between civil society and market lies in the fact that civil society is a dimension of public social existence and experience, which is relatively uninterested and uncoordinated. On the other hand, market is an organized and coordinated entity. The dimension, in which social members act and experience themselves as living together according to civil rules, is different from the way they carry on business in market.

Studies[29] indicate that social cohesion or social capital plays a critical role in the success of developmental programmes in the short run and particularly in making the development sustainable. There are positive correlations[30] between higher levels of social capital and better health, education, employment status and even lower crime rate. In other words, people having extensive social networks are more likely to be housed, healthy, hired (employed) and happy. Such situation also provides the green house environment conducive for promotion and growth of market and the corporate as well.

The quality of public life and the performance of social institutions are powerfully influenced by the norms and networks of civic engagements, which are commonly known as the civil society. The presence of associations is a forecaster of successful outcomes in many areas, including education, poverty alleviation, and unemployment, control of crime and drug abuse, and health. It has been generally experienced that in societies, where there is greater interaction between individuals there is greater goodwill. This in turn leads to organizations outside the government playing a positive role in furthering the common cause and public good. This gives rise to a '*Win-Win*' situation and improves the quality of governance. Social capital produces good governance in so far as it produces trust in others, including trust in government by facilitating coordination and cooperation for mutual benefit. On the other hand, societies where there is mistrust, it becomes difficult for the civil society to grow and contribute to the social cause. In such societies, there is a '*Lose-Lose*' situation, which retards the growth and development.

Democracy—Emerging Challenges

Democracy is defined as a form of Government which is by the people, for the people and of the people. Keeping in view the definition of development[31] as the process of enlarging people's choices, democracy represents the most developed form of government. Limitation and shortcomings noticed in some of the democratic set up in different parts of the globe have been attributed to factors which arise out of operation rather than the basic structure of democracy. The earlier concept that governance mainly concerns the State and the society is just an appendage, has been challenged and a consensus has been emerging that for a democracy to succeed[32], it has to be "*Society and people-centric*" rather than "State-centric". The State-centric approach is concerned with assessing the political and institutional capacity of the State to steer society towards certain goals associated with the public good. The Society-centric approach, on the other hand, is concerned with involvement of the civil society in the governing process and its relation with the State through a variety of governance forms or institutional arrangements. It includes the government as the dominant player, but transcends it by taking in the private sector and the civil society. Active participation of these three stakeholders is critical for sustaining human, economic and social development. Under ideal situation, the government creates conducive political, legal and living environment, the private sector promotes enterprises and generates jobs and income and the civil society facilitates mobilizing groups to participate in economic, social and political activities.

Success of democracy therefore depends, to a great extent on the synergy between the civil society, the private sector and the government. It is determined by a number of interrelated factors such as involvement of the minorities and other disadvantaged segments of the society in the decision-making process, transparency and accountability at all governmental and societal levels, citizens' participation in the process of social and public welfare, economic growth and development, a balanced relationship between all bodies of government and civil society. It also requires probity in public dealings on the part of the government, social auditing of government policies and programmes, mandatory establishment of ombudsman institutions and non-discriminatory judicial system etc. Further, decentralization plays an important role in strengthening democracy by taking the administration closer to the people and ensuring active participation of the people. Erosion of civil society robs the democracy of its base in the society. Active participation of the civil society is therefore of critical importance for success of any democracy.

Democracy, Civil Society and Social Capital

Effective participation of people, transparency, responsiveness, consensus, equity and inclusiveness, rule of law, effectiveness and efficiency, accountability, and strategic vision form the basic ingredients of good governance. These are crucially value-laden and constitute the bedrock of any democracy. In a parliamentary democracy, the decision-making is with a small group of elected people's representatives. There are instances of democracy, which should be "of the people" becoming "off the people". This necessitates systemic solutions to the problems. In a democracy, the civil society influences policy and project formulation through membership of committees, submission of memoranda directly or through elected representatives, and interactive rule-making in the implementation of policies, projects and schemes affecting common citizens. Civil society acts through social capital and enhances the capacity of people to act together in pursuing their common long-term interest.

In a homogeneous, egalitarian society, formation of civil society and social capital is relatively easier. However, in a pluralistic heterogeneous society like India, there are constraints in formation of social capital and operation of civil society in realizing its full potential in general and contributing to good governance in particular. In a heterogeneous society, civil society becomes active under extraordinary situations like natural calamities or under the leadership of a charismatic leader like Mahatma Gandhi, who could mobilize people overcoming narrow loyalties. Mobilization of people and civil society in a similar manner and magnitude however does not happen in ordinary, day-to-day situations. Making the civil society effective in a heterogeneous society therefore offers a real challenge. It is not possible for individuals to take on the huge political-bureaucratic machine that the government is, nor can the entire civil society act on behalf of every citizen. However, improvements in education and awareness lead to formation of social capital and civil society coming up through compact, focused organizations, which play a critical role in strengthening democracy[33] in a heterogeneous society.

Notwithstanding its limitations, democratic form has emerged as the best form of governance for ensuring protection of basic human rights and sustainable development. However, a crisis was experienced in the democracy with public confidence in the government declining around the middle period of the twentieth century. Confidence or trust in an institution arises out of its competence and motivation to perform. It is required to be appreciated that Democracy is much more than just election. It also endorses transparent public conduct, an impartial judicial system and an empowered citizenry.[34] It is this that enabled western democracies to deliver tangible benefits to its people, from universal healthcare to minority rights, at unimaginable speed. This also explains why, in spite of the American Dream, corruption in the West is not quite as bad as it is elsewhere. Sadly, the pressure is gathering there as well; how else can one explain the 2008 banking crisis led by Lehmann Brothers? Collapse of Enron and WorldCom have brought to surface the deterioration in the performance of the public institutions affecting trust and competence. These have been attributed to the decline in the capacity and fidelity, with which the political agents are supposed to act in citizen's interest. There has been a growth in the activities of the voluntary sector in the last decade. While presence of the voluntary sector is important, it shall have to be kept under watch for avoiding a similar crisis. It is felt that the traditional checks and balances operating through formal legal mechanism in a democracy are required to be buttressed. Keeping in view its nature, potential of the civil society and social capital is required to be availed for putting democracy on the right track and to ensure that interest of the common man is protected and any exploitation by the vested interests is thwarted.

Conclusion

CSR is often considered as an obligation on the part of a corporate and business house to take such actions, which protect and improve the welfare of the society as a whole and also safeguard their own interest of creating surplus. Attitude of corporate towards the community, within which they are operating, has undergone considerable changes. However, the scope of CSR is required to be reoriented by covering all stakeholders as a long-term commitment towards the shareholders and the society. It needs to cover preservation of depleting environmental resources, emergence of effective workplace practices as well as narrowing the gulf between the rich and poor. It is beyond doubt that the corporate with the active support of the civil society can make the CSR interventions effective and meaningful in solving important social issues on a sustainable basis, which would generate social capital, thereby create a 'Win-Win' situation for the corporate and the society at large. Civil society, social capital and CSR interventions of the corporate are closely interrelated issues. By evolving proper synergy, the civil society can provide the base on which CSR interventions can operate generating social capital for the corporate on the one hand and social welfare on the other, which will strengthen the democracy in the long run.

References

1. http://en.wikipedia.org/wiki/Corporation
2. Carto M. Cipolla (editor), *The Economic History of Europe – The Industrial Revolution*, Fontana/Collins Volume 3, p.12.
3. The new generation is often anguished because the problems are many, formidable and pressing. There is no area of human activity, no corner of society which does not need new solutions. We seem to lack the necessary time and imagination to solve these problems, encumbered as we are with institutions inherited from a world now dead, impeded by tradition, out-of-date scales of values, customs and points of view, unable to distinguish between fact and fantasy. The young people protest when they realize the inadequacy of the old institutions and the older generation, but they have no better diagnosis and no better cures. The young often give vent to their frustration in surges of violent anarchy and curious hatred against their inheritance, or try to escape reality either by destroying their consciousness or by a desperate search for new religions. *The Economic History of Europe – The Industrial Revolution*, Editor Carlo M. Cipolla, Fontana/Collins.
4. James W. Mekie, 1974, "Social Responsibility and the business predicament", Brooking institutions, Washington DC.
5. Van Buren, 2006, University of New Mexico Management Presentation.
6. M. Friedman, 1962, *Capitalism and Freedom*, University of Chicago Press, p. 133.
7. *www.wbcsd.org*
8. Michael Hopkins, 2003, *The Planetary Bargain, Corporate Social Responsibility Matters*, Earthscan Publications, p.10.
9. P. Kotler and Lee, N., 2005, *Corporate Social Responsibility: Doing the Most Good for Your Company and Your Cause,* John Wiley & Sons, NJ, USA.
10. Wikipedia.
11. Mallen Baker, *www.mallenbaker.net/csr/files/definition.html*
12. The Future of the Company, *The Economist*, December 22, 2001.
13. *Ibid.*
14. *Ibid.*
15. J.C. Johari, *Principles of Modern Political Science*, Sterling Publishers Private Limited, pp. 823-825.
16. Sunil Sinha, 2007, "Socially Responsible Investment (SRI)", *Rating Scan*, April, p. 19.
17. Ethics and Brand Value: Strategic Differentiation (*http://www.scu.edu*).
18. Risk: A Model for Multinationals (*http://www.ksg.harvard.edu*)
19. *The Economist's* CSR Survey (*http://www.economist.com*)
20. Milton Friedman, "The Social Responsibility of Business is to increase its profits", *The New York Times Magazine*, September 13, 1970.
21. Henry G. Manne, Dean Emeritus of the George Mason University School of Law "Corporate Social Responsibility is Bunk", November 24, 2006.

22. Australian Bureau of Statistics, 2000. "Measuring Social Capital: Current Collections and Future Directions".
23. *http://www.uniromal.it/soccap.eng-index.html*
24. R.D. Putnam, 1995, "Bowling Alone: America's Declining Social Capital", *Journal of Democracy,* 6(1): 65-78.
25. Cahoone Lawrence, 2002, *Civil Society, the Conservative Meaning of Liberal Politics*, Blackwell Publishers, p. 205.
26. *Ibid.*, p. 217.
27. *http://www.lse.ac.uk/collections/CCS/what_is_Civil_society.html*
28. *Ibid.*, p. 229.
29. *http://www1.worldbank.org/prem/poverty/capital/index.html*
30. Woolcock, "The Place of Social Capital in Understanding Social and Economic Outcomes", *Canadian Journal of Policy Research*, 2 (10): 11-17.
31. http://www.unhistory.org/briefing/8HumDev.pdf
32. M.G. Devasahayam, "Governance key to equitable growth", *The Hindu*, August 14, 2005, p.14.
33. P.K. Doraiswamy, "The role of civil society in good governance", *The Hindu*, August 26, 2007, p. 16.
34. Dipankar Gupta, "Corruption of the American Dream", *The Times of India*, 25th May, 2013.

3

The Global Scenario

Growth of Corporate, Global Trade and Commerce

Starting with the industrial revolution, Corporate grew rapidly in the subsequent decades. Technology-led developments gave a big boost to corporate activities for production and marketing of goods and services as well as trade and commerce in the Twentieth century. Invention of computer, internet and Information Technology Enabled Services (ITES) had a major impact on bridging geographical distance and time. On the other hand, biotechnology based research had profound impact on productivity and quality of plant and animal produces as well as on provision of healthcare facilities. These changes continued unabated with new technology replacing the old at regular intervals. Digital technology based interventions, mobile telephone, television, music, and other entertainments changed the life of human being as never before.

Rapid development in science and technology opened vast opportunity for the corporate in form of new demand for production and marketing of goods and services. Arrival of new technology at a fast rate made the earlier version obsolete, which boosted the demand for new products leading to diversification and expansion of the market. Faster mode of transportation by land, air and sea for movement of raw material and finished products supplemented by Information Technology based faster means of communication; further facilitated growth of business, which were exploited by the corporate. These changes, over the past decades, have transformed the world into a virtual *Global village*. Activities of the corporate expanded beyond national boundaries and assumed Multi-National character. Over years, the Multi National Corporations (MNCs) acquired financial assets, clout and power, which even exceeded those of several sovereign countries. MNCs made all out efforts for exploiting the opportunities and often exerted pressure on countries to open up their boundaries to them for business. International bodies like the World Trade Organization (WTO) were set up and the General Agreement on Trade and Tariff (GATT) were laid down to regulate the barriers in international trade and facilitate free movement of goods from the producing countries to the consuming countries.

The impact of technology on industrial growth and economic development varied widely from country to country based on available resources, both natural and human, as well as on prevailing culture, mindset, customs, levels of education and skill of the people; nature and quality of governance, status of business and corporate. The pace of development even varied from region to region within a country; depending upon relevant parameters. This led to uneven growth and economic development among and within the countries across the world. As a result, the world gradually got divided into two broad groups *viz.*, the developed countries with huge financial assets on the one side and the developing and underdeveloped countries with limited assets on the other. Further, environment related issues came up as an important area of concern for making the development sustainable. The development in science and technology brought about significant changes in almost all aspects of human life. Its impact has been visible in agricultural and industrial activities, where introduction of appropriate technology led to significant increase in production and productivity, as evident in the case of the Green Revolution in India during the 60s and 70s. Discovery of new high yielding variety of wheat along with suitable economic and administrative support turned India from a food deficit country to a food surplus country, producing enough for feeding its domestic population and for export.

On the health front, discovery of new medicines along with improved healthcare facility led to eradication of communicable diseases like small-pox and controlling incidence of cholera, tuberculosis, leprosy, and blindness. Improvement in the economic condition, availability of food, drinking water etc. led to increase in the human longevity in almost all countries.

In the new millennium, expansion of Information Technology and particularly Internet redefined the concept of geographical distance and time. Mobile Phone based applications came up as a major tool in empowering the poor in providing access to market for gainful employment with a decent earning.

On the impact of technology, way back in 1970, Vinton Cerf, who played an important role in developing Internet in the 1970s, had predicted that the television industry would change rapidly as it approached its "iPod movement". He had mentioned[1] that television was rapidly approaching the same kind of redundancy that the music industry faced with the arrival of the MP_3 and analogue photography faced with the advent of digital technology. That about eighty-five per cent of all video programmes are being watched now are pre-recorded. A time will come soon when such items would be downloaded for viewing as per convenience, like the iPod. This will restrict viewing television live to only a few areas like—news, sporting events, and emergencies. It was also predicted that the influence of Internet, which had been radically altering the television businesses, would continue and that people would soon be watching the majority of television programmes through the Internet. This development would *herald the death of the traditional broadcast television channels* in favour of new interactive services. These predictions have come true today showing the powerful impact, new technology has on the society and human life **[Box 3.1: Impact of Technology on Human Life].**

Sustainability of Development

In this rapidly changing technology-led development, sustainability of the development process is being questioned on two fronts, namely (i) Environmental aspects relating to conservation of nature and checking adverse impact on account of climate change; and (ii) Social aspects relating to the rich-poor gaps, which has been widening. Latter issue has been getting intensified due to the impact of media and internet on the mindset and expectations of the youth.

Environment Aspects of Sustainable Development

Out of various challenges thrown up by the technology-led development, impact on environment has been significant. Industrialization and urbanization at a rapid rate have led to sharp rise in the consumption of fossil fuels like coal and petroleum products. This stepped up carbon emission, adversely affected the environment, led to global warming along with several other undesirable consequences like increase in earth's temperature, melting of the glaciers, drying of rivers and depletion of the natural flora and fauna. These developments have been leading to environmental disasters like tsunami, hurricanes and fires in South-east Asia.

Box 3.1: Impact of Technology on Human Life

Industrial revolution, which started in the 18th century with invention of steam engine-based mechanical production, led to the second stage of production in the moving assembly lines (in 1923). The next, third stage of industrial revolution involved programmable logic controller (in 1969) which has led to the latest, fourth stage, *Industry 4.0* with production on real time/ self-optimising connected systems (started in 2014).

The latest *Industry 4.0* stage represents a paradigm shift from the previous era of rigid, efficiency-focussed and manual manufacturing to a more dynamic, agile, and automated manufacturing. It marks a shift of focus from *mass production to mass customisation, enabled by flexible production and shorter lead times.* For production, there will be a transition *from large-scale factories specialised for product to smart factories* with high-technological equipment that can produce multiple products at competitive cost.

Evolution of *Industry 4.0* will lead to increased use of automation and robots in the shop floor. As robots will be capable of performing tasks, multiple times with high levels of accuracy and within shorter time duration than humans, *robots will act as an efficient replacement for labour.* For example, an employee whose job is to fix a specific part while assembling an engine will be *replaced by a robot, which will carry out the same job accurately and in lesser time.* The quantum of job loss, however, is expected to vary with country, industry and employed levels of automation.

In the *Industry 4.0,* use of robots in production process would be a necessity for multiple advantages like faster and uniform production, less defect, better quality, lower cost and time; which are essential for remaining competitive. However, it will have adverse social implications due to displacement of workers by machines. It will worsen unemployment and create tension; leading to anger and violence in the society.

Bill Gates[1], founder of Microsoft has expressed scepticism about society's ability to manage rapid automation. His worries are based on the threat from activities like driving or managing warehouses, where automated machine will displace manual labour causing misery in an economy already awash with abundant, cheap labour. This will worsen the employment situation leading to social tension and violence. To forestall a social crisis, Mr. Gates proposed[2] to tax robots to compensate for the job they take from human. The money so generated could be used to retrain workers, and perhaps to finance an expansion of healthcare and education, which provide lots of hard-to-automate jobs in teaching or caring for the old and sick.

Adoption of new and appropriate technology is a must and cannot be avoided for economic development. However, the corporate needs to remain sensitive to the social aspects and the delicate balance between the commercial interest and social interest while undertaking the change, for making the development process sustainable.

References

1. The Economist News, Bill Gates's proposal revealing about challanges automation poses why taxing.
2. River Sutra: Being Human in Legal parlance, *The Economic Times*, the 25th March, 2017, p. 1.

Adverse impacts of environmental degradation were brought to the general public view in the United States of America and Europe around the 1980s. However, the business took the matter rather casually. This was possibly due to the fact that such admission would have given the business additional responsibility and provision of resources, which would have affected their bottom line. As a matter of fact, shortly after an intergovernmental panel was set up by the United Nations to establish a consensus on climate change, some of the big carbon emitters took[2] measures for diverting the attention from this important area of concern.

The impact of global warming has been discussed at various international forums in the last decades. Initially, the developed countries remained rather indifferent to this cause and argued that the proposed measures would be unfair to them as these sought to restrict emissions in the rich countries and allowed the poor countries to grow unfettered.

Adoption of the ***Kyoto protocol***[3] on the 11 December, 1997 in Kyoto, Japan, marked a major milestone in the endeavour to tackle the problem of climate change. This was ratified by one hundred seventy five countries endorsing their commitment to reduce greenhouse gas emissions below a specified level. Rules for the implementation of the protocol were adopted at Conference of Parties (CoP7) in Marrakesh, Morocco, in 2001, popularly known as the "*Marrakesh Accords.*" The protocol came into force on 16 February, 2005 with a commitment period from 2008 to 2012 and a target for reducing the total greenhouse gas emissions by at least 5 per cent from 1990 levels by 2012.

In response to the effects of carbon emission and global warming, various countries adopted regulatory measures like imposition of additional taxes/duty on the industry emitting carbon as well as promotional measures like subsidizing interventions for promoting use of alternate sources of clean energy like solar, wind and biomass. Further, carbon trading system was evolved for keeping the overall global carbon emission under control. Introduction of regulatory measures for checking emission led to promotion of cleaner technologies based on solar, biological, electric and fuel-cell energy. These measures also generated new business opportunities.

General awareness and concern about climate change, global warming and environment related issues, grew in subsequent years. The developed countries started investing in better technology and restricting the use of fossil fuel. The industry[4] found it useful to talk about global warming as it enhanced their brand worth in the public. Besides, it is also helping them in attracting clever, idealistic, young people with higher commitment to work for them. Steps taken for checking carbon emission are being reported in the Annual Report by several forward looking companies.

There are several positive developments on the commitment to check global warming. Japan planned to reduce carbon emissions to half by 2050, whereas Britain planned to reduce it by 60 per cent. The European Union agreed to reduce its emissions by 20 per cent by 2020. The best commitment appeared to be from Norway, which had planned to become the world's first "carbon neutral" country, by reducing its emissions to zero by 2050.

Notwithstanding so-called commitments, the overall global emissions were found to be on the rise. According to a study[5], worldwide emissions which were growing by 1.1 per cent per year in the 1990s increased by threefold to more than 3 per cent per year, between 2000 and 2004. Further, the fact that the *rate of emission during this period remained higher than the rate of economic growth* implies that *the world is not just consuming more energy, but also doing it even more dirtily*. This increasing trend of global emissions has become a matter of serious concern for the entire humanity.

The next major event on Environmental sustainability, the United Nations Conference on Sustainable Development (UNCSD), also known as ***Rio 2012 or Earth Summit 2012***[6], *was* held in Rio de Janeiro, Brazil from 13 to 22 June, 2012. It marked completion of two decades of the Earth Summit/United Nations Conference on Environment and Development (UNCED) held in the same city in 1992 and one decade after the World Summit on Sustainable Development (WSSD) held in Johannesburg. However, the developed and the developing countries, participating in this consultation, were at loggerheads particularly in reaching any understanding for restricting the emissions levels. The conference marked a push on major policy shifts to meet the proposed goals, with some *financial assistance from the rich nations to the poor*. Some of the major *recommendations adopted* in this conference on sustainable development and poverty eradication related to:

- contribute to eradicate poverty as well as sustained economic growth, enhancing social inclusion, improving human welfare and creating opportunities for employment and decent work for all, while maintaining the healthy functioning of the Earth's ecosystems;
- strengthen international cooperation, including the provision of

financial resources, capacity-building and technology transfer to developing countries;
- contribute to closing technology gaps between developed and developing countries and reduce the technological dependence of developing countries by using appropriate measures;
- enhance the welfare of indigenous peoples and their communities, other local and traditional communities and ethnic minorities, recognizing and supporting their identity, culture and interests, and avoid endangering their cultural heritage, practices and traditional knowledge, preserving and respecting non-market approaches that contribute to the eradication of poverty;
- enhance the welfare of women, children, youth, persons with disabilities, small holder and subsistence farmers and those working in small and medium-sized enterprises, and improve the livelihoods and empowerment of the poor and vulnerable groups in particular in developing countries; and
- mobilize the potential and ensure the equal contribution of both women and men.

United Nations Framework Consultation on Climate Change (UNFCCC), Paris, 2015

The next major event, United Nations Climate Change Conference, was held in Paris, France, from 30 November to 12 December, 2015. It is also known as **COP 21** marking the 21st yearly session of the Conference of the Parties (COP) to the 1992 United Nations Framework Convention on Climate Change (UNFCCC) and **CMP 11** as the 11th session of the Meeting of the Parties to the 1997 Kyoto Protocol.

A global agreement on the reduction of climate change, popularly known as "**Paris Agreement**" was negotiated and finalized in this conference by consensus of 196 participating countries. In order to be legally binding, the agreement required to be endorsed by at least 55 countries, which together represent at least 55 per cent of the total global greenhouse gas emissions. The participating countries were required to adopt it within their own legal system and sign the agreement in New York between 22 April, 2016 (Earth Day) and 21 April, 2017.

In the adopted version of the Paris Agreement, the parties seek to "pursue efforts to" limit the temperature increase to 1.5 °C, which will require zero emissions between 2030 and 2050. This was in place of limiting global warming to less than two degrees compared to pre-industrial levels.

Prior to the conference, 146 national climate panels publicly presented draft national climate contributions, called "**Intended Nationally Determined Contributions**" (INDCs). These suggested commitments were estimated to limit global warming to 2.7 degrees Celsius by 2100. For example, the EU suggested INDC is a commitment to a 40 per cent reduction in emissions by 2030 compared to 1990. The agreement establishes a "global stock take", which revisits the national goals to "update and enhance" them every five years beginning with 2023.

The Paris accord, aiming to phase out net greenhouse gas emissions by this century, was a breakthrough after more than two decades of negotiations, driven by increased scientific certainty that man-made emissions drive heat waves, floods and rising sea levels. The threshold for entry into force of the Paris Agreement was achieved on the 5th October, 2016 and the Paris Agreement entered into force[7] on 4 November, 2016.

COP 22, Morocco, November, 2016

The Conference of the Parties, serving as the Meeting of the Parties to the Paris Agreement, (CMA-1) has its first session in Marrakech in November, 2016, in conjunction with COP 22 and CMP 12 with participation of about 200 nations.

In his address on the 15th November, 2016, Ban Ki-moon, the UN Secretary-General, said that action on climate change has become "unstoppable" and hoped that US president-elect, Donald Trump, would drop his view that man-made climate change is a hoax and review his pledge to withdraw from the Paris agreement and to quit a global accord aimed at weaning the world off fossil fuels.

The Kyoto Protocol was adopted in 1997 and the 1st commitment period was from 2008-2012. At Doha in 2012, the amendments to Kyoto Protocol for the 2nd commitment period (the Doha Amendment) were successfully adopted for the period 2013-2020. Developed countries started implementing their commitments under the 'opt-in' provisions of the Doha Amendment. India had emphasized the importance of climate actions by developed country Parties in the pre-2020 period. Besides, India had advocated climate actions based on the principles and provisions of the Convention, such as the principles of *Equity and Common But Differentiated Responsibilities and Respective Capabilities* (CBDR & RC). After intense negotiations in Kigali, Rwanda, 197 nations struck a legally-binding deal to phase down Hydro-Fluoro-Carbons (HFC-23), a potent greenhouse gas with high global warming potential, to mitigate climate change in October 2016.

India occupies[8] an intriguing dual position in global climate politics, as a developing economy with low levels of historical per capita emissions, and a large and rapidly growing economy with rising emissions. Indian climate politics has substantially been shaped around the first perspective, and increasingly, under international pressure, is being forced to grapple with the second.

On the 1st June, 2017, America, under President Donald Trump, announcing[9] to withdraw from the historic Paris Agreement has come as a concern for the global effort for checking carbon emission and climate change, which was adopted by 195 nations at Paris in December 2015 and came into force on the 4th November, 2016.

As per a recent study[10] by the Climate Action Tracker shows that the vacuum created by the rollback of US climate policies can be filled up to a great extent by China and India, who are at number one and three producers of green house gases. China has reduced coal use for successive three years and recently scrapped plans to build over one hundred coal power plants. Sale of electric vehicle has gone up by seventy per cent in China last year. Similarly, in India about forty per cent of the total electricity is expected to be generated from non-fossil fuel sources by 2020, much ahead of schedule 2030. The cost of solar power has gone down significantly in India as a result of favourable policy initiatives.

It appears that USA had also backed out from international pact on climate change earlier in 2001, when newly elect President George W. Bush had decided not to abide by the Kyoto Protocol. However unlike Paris accord, Kyoto Protocol was shorter and less detailed involving only the developed countries meant to tackle global warming by implementing a cap-and-trade deal. It had not included China and India, which have emerged as major carbon emitters. The Paris accord is different, endorsed by 195 countries—both developed and developing, is more detailed and has come into force after endorsement by over 55 per cent countries emitting over 55 per cent of the total carbon emission.

US President, Donald Trump's decision is based on the feeling that this agreement would undermine US economy, hamstring workers and weaken US sovereignty and would give undue advantage to India and China, the world's leading polluters at the cost of US' interest. In this context, as per the World Bank, the largest producers of carbon-dioxide emissions worldwide, in 2016 based on their share of global CO_2 emissions, include China (28.2%), US (15.99%), India (6.24%), Russia

(4.53%) and Japan (3.67%).[11] It is noteworthy that both India and China as well as number of European countries have indicated their firm commitment to the accord, irrespective of the stand taken by others. The challenge ahead lies in persuading US administration by mobilizing the world opinion with help of media and the civil society, to reconsider its decision and continue its commitment for a cause, which is linked with the very existence and continuation of human race on the planet and achieving the Sustainable Development Goals (SDG 2030) in the larger interest of the entire humanity including the US.

Economic Disparity—"*Rich-Poor divide*" Increasing

The second aspect of sustainable development, which caused considerable concern, relates to the economic aspect arising out of the *Rich-Poor divide*. Adoptions of technology, industrial development and promotion of trade and commerce at differential rates in different parts of the world intensified economic disparities. Provisions of basic facilities covering nutrition, education, health and livelihood have been a matter of concern in several parts of the world. Prevalence of disease, poverty, unemployment and lack of basic amenities of life has raised doubts about the nature of development. These have questioned the basic approach to development as to "*Is this development sustainable*?" While the national governments are primarily responsible for provision of basic health, education and skill upgradation facilities and removal of poverty; conduct of corporate sector, which is a major beneficiary of the present development, has also come under the scanner.

As per an estimate[12] India-born Hinduja brothers Gopichand and Srichand, with interests across automotive, real estate and oil, with an asset of £11.9 billion have emerged as the richest in Britain. Russian tycoon, Alisher Usmamov Arsenal shareholder came second with £10.65 billion, followed by Laskshmi Mittal with £10.25 billion. Increasing wealth of individuals at global level is evident from the fact that the number of billionaires in the world, as estimated by *Forbes*, have gone up by 19 per cent from 793 in 2006 to 946 in 2007 and their combined net worth by $900 million to $ 3.5 trillion. Bill Gates was estimated to be the richest person for the 13th consecutive year, with a net worth of $56 billion, followed by Warren Buffett with $52 billion. Carlos Slim of Mexico had overtaken Bill Gates as the richest man in the world. As per the *Forbes* list 2017, Bill Gates, founder of Microsoft again topped the list with an estimated net worth of US$ 76.6 billion followed by Amancio Ortega with a net worth of US$ 73.5 billion.

Such enormous amount of wealth held by a small segment of the society offers a sad contrast with the incidence of high level of poverty and human deprivation at the other end. A study[13] conducted by using household poverty data from 1990 to 2004 indicated that there were about 162 million poorest people, who survived on less than 50 cents a day and about one billion people, who live on less than a dollar a day in the world. *Inability of poor families to invest in the education of their children, limited access to credit for those with few assets, and reduced productivity due to malnutrition have been identified as the common causes of poverty.*

The poor have been further categorized as (i) *Subjacent poor*, who live on 0.75 to one dollar a day; (ii) *Medial poor*, who live on 0.5 to 0.75 dollar a day; and (iii) *Poorest (ultra) poor*, who live on less than 0.5 dollar a day. The ultra-poor appeared to be in poverty trap from which they cannot get out without external assistance. It has been assessed that the ultra-poor have *benefited the least from the poverty reduction* interventions during the last decade. Further, if the decline had been equal in all three categories of poverty, the number of ultra-poor people would have fallen by nearly 4 per cent, but actually it declined only by less than 2 per cent, which was less than half the expected rate. *This calls for innovative and more focused action to improve the livelihood opportunity along with provision of social protection to the poorest segments.*

Initiatives for Sustainable Development

Efforts of Nations

In response to the challenges in growth and development in the post-Second World War period, the United Nations set up a Commission in 1983 for suggesting ways to improve human well-being in the short-term without threatening the local and global environment on a long-term basis. Report of the Commission, popularly known as ***Brundtland Report,*** published in 1987, stressed on increased cooperation among nations and the participatory role of the business community among other things.

Issues relating to sustainable development were subsequently deliberated in the United Nations Conference on Environment and Development, commonly known as the *Rio Summit*, held in Rio de Janeiro, Brazil in 1992.

Efforts of Corporate Sector

The corporate world responded to sustainable development in January 1995, with the setting up of the *World Business Council for Sustainable Development* (WBCSD), as a coalition of 160 international companies, sharing their commitment covering three vital issues relating to *economic growth, ecological balance and social progress*. The council sought to promote the business as a catalyst for change towards sustainable development and to support the business to operate, innovate and grow in a world increasingly shaped by sustainable development issues. It provided a platform for companies to explore sustainable development, share knowledge, experiences and best practices, and to advocate business positions on these issues in a variety of forums, working with governments, non-governmental and intergovernmental organizations.

Evolution of concept of CSR and Sustainable Development

In 1998, WBCSD deliberated on sustainable development. Responsibility of the corporate towards the society was discussed and importance of CSR interventions were reiterated as the *continuing commitment of business*[14] *to behave ethically and contribute to economic development, while improving the quality of life of the workforce and their families as well as of the local community and society at large.*

Triple Bottom Line (TBL)

The Triple Bottom Line (TBL) concept was first mooted by John Elkington, the founder of a British consultancy called *SustainAbility*, in 1994. It is based on the logic that in order to make the development sustainable, the traditional way of measuring success of a corporate in terms of profit as the "*Bottom line*" of the profit and loss account needs to be widened with the inclusion of two more parameters. The second bottom line relates to the company's "people account" as a measure of how socially responsible the organization has been throughout its operations. The third bottom line relates to the company's "planet" account as a measure of how environmentally responsible the company has been. The TBL thus consists of three "P"s—Profit, People and Planet aiming at measuring the financial, social and environmental performance of the company. The concept is based on using the stakeholder theory to measure and mange the impact of CSR that reflects economic, social and environmental performance.

However, measuring the Triple Bottom Line is difficult as impact/ contribution of "Planet" and "People" cannot be quantified and measured, as is the case with "Profit" being measured in monetary. For example, impact of an oil-tanker spillage on the environment, displacing the primitive communities to clear forests for setting up industrial unit(s), or engaging child labour, which deprive them to learn; on the society are too big and complex to be measured in the conventional way.

Millennium Development Goals (MDGs) 2015

At the beginning of the new millennium, the United Nations initiated a consultation on major issues relating to human welfare in the new century. Following this consultation, the millennium declarations[15] were adopted in September 2000 with a view to express global solidarity and concern for improving the lot of the poor and disadvantaged, particularly in the developing countries. The Millennium Development Goals (MDGs) and targets were evolved as a set of interrelated parameters for achieving the broad objectives of the declaration [**Box 3.2: Millennium Development Goals (MDGs) 2015**]. This initiative called for active partnership between the developed and developing countries "to create an environment—at the national and global levels alike—which is conducive to development and the elimination of poverty". One hundred and eighty nine countries including India endorsed this declaration and pledged to achieve these goals by 2015.

Provision of certain basic services to billions of people around the world, who have been deprived of basic amenities and services such as clean drinking water and sanitation etc. was deliberated in the next World Summit on sustainable development was held in Johannesburg, South Africa, in 2002. Strategy for meeting the challenges of removing poverty globally and creating conditions for sustainable development involving various stakeholders namely, the private sector, government, civil society and academic and research institutions were discussed in this summit. Among other things, this summit deliberated upon the role and responsibility of the corporate sector in solving some of the most daunting and intractable problems facing the human society.

Mid-term Review of MDG (2007)

A mid-term review[16] done in 2007, indicated several positive developments as well as areas of concern in respect of the MDGs.

Box 3.2: Millennium Development Goal (MDG)s 2015

Goals (8 no.) and Targets (17 no.)

Goal 1: Eradicate extreme poverty and hunger

Target 1: Halve, between 1990 and 2015, the proportion of people whose income is less than one dollar a day.

Target 2: Halve, between 1990 and 2015, the proportion of people who suffer from hunger.

Goal 2: Achieve universal primary education

Target 3: Ensure that, by 2015, children everywhere, boys and girls alike, will be able to complete a full course of primary schooling.

Goal 3: Promote gender equality and empower women

Target 4: Eliminate gender disparity in primary and secondary education, preferably by 2005, and in all levels of education no later than 2015.

Goal 4: Reduce child mortality

Target 5: Reduce by two-thirds, between 1990 and 2015, the under-five mortality rate.

Goal 5: Improve maternal health

Target 6: Reduce by three-quarters, between 1990 and 2015, the maternal mortality ratio.

Goal 6: Combat HIV/AIDS, malaria and other diseases

Target 7: Have halted by 2015 and begun to reverse the spread of HIV/AIDS

Target 8: Have halted by 2015 and begun to reverse the incidence of malaria and other major diseases.

Goal 7: Ensure environmental sustainability

Target 9: Integrate the principles of sustainable development into country policies and programmes and reverse the loss of environmental resources.

Target 10: Halve, by 2015, the proportion of people without sustainable access to safe drinking water and basic sanitation.

Target 11: By 2020, to have achieved a significant improvement in the lives of at least 100 million slum dwellers.

Goal 8: Develop a global partnership for development

Target 12: Develop further an open, rule-based, predictable, non-discriminatory trading and financial system. Includes a commitment to good governance, development and poverty reduction—both nationally and internationally.

Target 13: Address the special needs of the least developed countries, includes tariff and quota free access for the least developed countries' exports; enhanced programme of debt relief for Heavily Indebted Poor Countries (HIPCs) and cancellation of official bilateral debt; and more generous ODA for countries committed to poverty reduction.

Target 14: Address the special needs of landlocked developing countries and Small Island Developing States (through the Programme of Action for the Sustainable Development of Small Island Developing States and the

outcome of the twenty-second special session of the General Assembly).
Target 15: Deal comprehensively with the debt problems of developing countries through national and international measures in order to make debt sustainable in the long-term.
Target 16: In cooperation with developing countries, develop and implement strategies for decent and productive work for youth.
Target 17: In cooperation with pharmaceutical companies, provide access to affordable essential drugs in developing countries.
Target 18: In cooperation with the private sector, make available the benefits of new technologies, especially information and communications.

Reference: www.undp.org/mdggoallist.s.html

On eradication of poverty and hunger, the trend has been positive about meeting the target as the number of people in developing countries living on less than $1 a day fell from 1.25 billion in 1990 to 980 million in 2004 and the proportion of people living in extreme poverty fell from nearly one-third to 19 per cent during this period. However, there are concerns that the benefit of economic growth in the developing world has not been equally shared, both within and amongst countries. This has been of particular concern in eastern Asia where the share of consumption among the poorest people appeared to have declined during the period.

On universal primary education, the positions in terms of late enrolment ratio and out of school children improved. However, improvement in respect of the poorer household and gender aspects relating to girl students, particularly in the rural areas, continued to be a matter of concern. Empowerment of women in terms of participation in paid and non-agricultural employment as well as in the political process increased slowly.

Incidence of infant and child mortality declined. However, there was considerable scope for its improvement particularly in the vulnerable first month of birth. Interrelated factors like regular education of the mother and provision of basic health services particularly in rural areas continued to be areas of concern with regard to achieving the targeted goals in child and maternal health. It was deemed necessary to intensify the interventions for achieving the target by 2015.

Threats of HIV and AIDS continued to persist, with women being more prone. Increase in the magnitude of the problem necessitated intensifying preventive measures on urgent basis. Conversion of forest to agricultural land and for non-agricultural uses increased in the developing countries, along with greater threat to the ecosystem and sustainability of the environment.

On the promise for partnership for development, the development aid provided by the donor countries remained uneven, with a decline in 2006. There was little progress in extending benefits of globalization available to all countries. Further, there was no agreement on overall programmes in the World Trade Organization meet held at Doha in 2001, which put the developing countries at a disadvantage.

So far as making benefits of new technology available with the participation of private sector is concerned, while the growth in access to mobile cellular phone was found to be spectacular, the progress in use of Internet remained slow with only 9 per cent and 1 per cent of the people accessing the facility in the developing countries and the least developing countries respectively, as against 50 per cent in the developed countries.

Revision of the strategy and preparing a concerted plan of action covering interrelated issues like health, education, gender sensitivity concerning welfare of the common man was deemed necessary for achieving the MDG by 2015. Provision of effective healthcare services, for example, reduced child mortality encouraged the poor households to adopt small family norms due to increased confidence about survival of their children to adulthood. Investments in child healthcare therefore have a positive impact on checking population growth in poor countries. In this context, availability of *financial resources was one of the major constraints in achieving the goals* within the time schedule, particularly in case of the poorer nations. It was estimated that about 3 billion US dollars per year would be required for controlling malaria, only in Africa. Similar is the magnitude of funds required for achieving the other MDGs within the time schedule, which posed a major challenge to all developing nations.

Sustainable Development Goals (SDGs) 2030

Achievements in respect of the various goals under MDG 2015 were assessed for deciding the next course of action with specific thrust on making the development sustainable. Sustainable development has been defined *as the development that meets the needs of the present without compromising the ability of future generations to meet their own needs.* It calls for concerted efforts towards building an inclusive, sustainable and resilient future for people and planet and to harmonize three core elements namely economic growth, social inclusion and environmental protection. These elements are interconnected and are crucial for the well-being of individuals and societies. Eradicating poverty in all its forms and dimensions is an indispensable requirement for sustainable development. This calls for promotion of sustainable, inclusive and equitable economic growth, creating greater opportunities for all, reducing inequalities, raising basic standards of living, fostering equitable social development; and management of natural resources and ecosystems in an integrated manner.

The Sustainable Development Goals (SDGs)[17] with 17 goals and 169 targets of the 2030 Agenda were adopted in September 2015 at an historic UN Summit and came into force on 1st January, 2016 [**Box 3.3: Sustainable Development Goals (SDGs) 2030**]. These new Goals, which apply universally to all countries, require the member countries to mobilize efforts to end all forms of poverty, fight inequalities and tackle climate change, and ensuring that no one is left behind.

The SDGs were built on the success of the Millennium Development Goals (MDGs) and aim to go further to end all forms of poverty. The new Goals are unique in the sense that they call for action by all countries, rich, poor, and middle-income; to promote prosperity while protecting the planet. They recognize that ending poverty must go hand-in-hand with strategies that build economic growth and address a range of social needs including education, health, social protection, and job opportunities,

Box 3.3: Sustainable Development Goal (SDG)s 2030

1. **End poverty** in all its forms everywhere.
2. **End hunger**, achieve food security and improved nutrition and promote sustainable agriculture.
3. **Ensure healthy lives** and promote well-being for all at all ages.
4. **Ensure inclusive equitable quality education** and promote lifelong learning opportunities for all.
5. **Achieve gender equality and empower all women and girls**.
6. Ensure availability and sustainable **management of water and sanitation for all**.
7. Ensure access to **affordable, reliable, sustainable and modern energy for all**.
8. Promote sustained, inclusive and sustainable economic growth, **full and productive employment** and decent work for all.
9. Build resilient infrastructure, promote **inclusive and sustainable industrialization and foster innovation**.
10. **Reduce inequality within and among countries**.
11. Make **cities and human settlements inclusive, safe, resilient and sustainable**.
12. **Ensure sustainable consumption and production patterns**.
13. Take urgent action to **combat climate change** and its impacts.
14. Conserve and **sustainably use the oceans, seas and marine resources** for sustainable development
15. Protect, restore and promote **sustainable use of terrestrial ecosystems**, sustainably manage forests, combat desertification, and halt and reverse land degradation and halt biodiversity loss.
16. **Promote peaceful and inclusive societies for sustainable development,** provide access to justice for all and build effective, accountable and inclusive institutions at all levels.
17. Strengthen the means of implementation and revitalize the **Global Partnership** for Sustainable Development.

Reference: www.un.org/sustainable–development–goals.html

while tackling climate change and environmental protection. Even though the SDGs are not legally binding, governments are expected to take ownership and establish national frameworks for the achievement of the 17 Goals. Countries are primarily responsible for follow-up and review of the progress made in implementing the Goals, based on collection of quality, accessible and timely data. Regional follow-up and review will be based on national-level analyses and contribute to follow-up and review at the global level.

SDGs differ from the earlier version MDGs in three major ways, namely (i) The SDGs are *universal and apply to all countries*, whereas the MDGs were intended for action in developing countries only, (ii) The SDGs have strong *focus on means of implementation, mobilization of financial resources, capacity-building and technology*, as well as data and institutions, and (iii) SDGs recognize that *tackling climate change is essential* for sustainable development and poverty eradication, with SDG 2030 aiming to promote urgent action to combat climate change and its impacts.

The means of implementation, including mobilization of financial resources to achieve the sustainable development agenda, from a core feature of the new agenda. In order to achieve the Sustainable Development Goals (SDGs), substantial investment will be required, in both developed and developing countries.

As achievement of SDGs requires mobilization of support of all the stakeholders at the national level, *CSR interventions of the corporate* will play an important and meaningful role in this regard. Apart from financial resources, corporate are required to lend their managerial expertise and corporate voluntarism which will make the corporate support to be of critical importance in optimizing use of the resources, the country governments have at their command in achieving the goals by 2030. It is a fact that Official Development Assistance (ODA) will be necessary to help the least developed countries in particular, to achieve sustainable development. CSR intervention and support of corporate are expected to help in building on the success of the MDGs in pursuing goals to address inequalities, economic growth, provision of decent jobs, cities and human settlements, industrialization, oceans, ecosystems, energy, climate change, sustainable consumption and production, peace and justice as envisaged in SDG, 2030.

Aid for Development

One of the basic prerequisites of sustainable development relates to mobilization of financial resources for undertaking the economic intervention. While internal resources of the country/nation, both natural and human, are of critical importance, it is often necessary to supplement it with assistance from outside; either in form of outright grant or as loan with low rate of interest or both. Similar is the case with individual families in the disadvantaged groups. Keeping this in view, provision of external aid for development is pursued on bilateral and multilateral basis.

Aid from Nations and Institutions

With a view to make the development process more equitable and sustainable, the developed countries have periodically come up for assisting the developing countries. In 1961, the United Nations General Assembly had deliberated on this issue and resolved to double foreign assistance from the developed to the developing countries from an existing level of 0.5 per cent to 1 per cent of the combined national incomes of the economically advanced countries as soon as possible. However, in practice, provision of international aid to the developing countries declined. By early 1990s, Official Development Assistance (ODA) fell to about 0.33 per cent of the GNP[18] of donor countries, which further declined to about 0.22 per cent of GNP by the 2000s. Adoption of MDGs in the new millennium brought this back to discussion with renewed stress on the developed countries for increasing international aid to the developing and underdeveloped countries substantially; for achieving the MDG targets by 2015. However, the actual flow of aid varied widely from country to country. As per an estimate, in case of the US, Official Development Assistance (ODA) was about 0.15 per cent of the GNP, as against military expenditure of about 4 per cent of the GNP ($500 billion a year). This indicated that the US spends around 30 times more on its military than on developmental aid to the poor countries. It appears that only five countries—Denmark, Luxembourg, Netherlands, Norway, and Sweden are contributing 0.7 per cent of GNP for international aid and another six countries—Belgium, Finland, France, Ireland, Spain and the United Kingdom are planning to increase aid to 0.7 per cent of GNP by 2015.

Besides the developed countries, international agencies like the World

Bank, Asian Development Bank, DFID etc. have been providing financial and technological assistance to the developing countries. World Health Organization (WHO)[19] has been supporting initiatives to check the menace of diseases by provision of drugs and other measures. It has been stated that provision of available drug in right time and quantity can cure tuberculosis and many other diseases. On the requirement of resources for human development in poor countries, it is estimated that for checking tuberculosis only, about US$56 billion would be required in the next 10 years, including US$47 billion for medicine and treatment and balance US$9 billion for research. This resource will provide treatment to about 50 million people and prevent about 14 million deaths due to this disease alone.

As per available information in 2015, USA overseas development assistance was US$30.765 billion, either as bilateral aid or through international organizations such as the World Bank or UN; followed by Germany with $20.855 billion and UK with $19.920 billion, as the major donors. As a percentage of gross national income, Sweden topped the list of donors with a net ODA amounting to 1.41 per cent of gross national income, followed by UAE (1.09%), Norway (1.05%); with UK (0.71%) and Germany (0.52%). Sweden had committed to keep the figure above 1 per cent notwithstanding need of resources for multifarious activities. The UN called for economically advanced countries to spend at least 0.7 per cent of gross national income on ODA.

Aid from Individuals

Provision of financial aid by the rich developed nations to developing nations is guided by factors like the national policies, international relation, philosophy of the political party in power etc. Barring a few exceptions, provision of international aid by the rich nations generally remained lukewarm.

However, corporate and High Net Worth individuals have taken up supporting philanthropic causes generously. **Stanford University**[20] was set up with the generous grant from Mr. Leland Stanford, Governor of California, in memory of his son, Leland Jr., who died at the age of 15 years. Similarly, **Harvard University** received a generous grant from John Harvard in 1638. As a matter of fact, numbers of US universities were set up with private philanthropy, which with independent governance and support from distinguished alumni have emerged as leading institutions in higher education and research in the world.

Institution of the Nobel Prize by Swedish scientist, **Alfred Nobel**, inventor of dynamite, provided an interesting and remarkable instance of philanthropy. Moved by an obituary published on the death of his brother, Ludvig, mistaking it as his death, "*The merchant of death, Dr. Alfred Nobel", who became rich by finding ways to kill more people faster than ever before, died yesterday*"; Mr. Nobel made a will in 1895, setting aside bulk of his personal wealth around USD 472 million, to establish Nobel Prizes; awarded for outstanding contribution to physical science, chemistry, medical science, literature and peace every year.

Increase in Wall Street's profit brought a new wave of wealthy people donating generously for preschool education to park benches with naming rights, which became attractive to individual donors. Naomi Levine, Chairperson of the George H. Heyman Jr. Center for Philanthropy and Fund-raising, New York University attributed such development to the feeling "*Every one of us wants to be remembered*". The responses varied from naming the children's health centre at Presbyterian hospital, New York, after Phyllis and David H. Komansky, the former CEO of Merrill Lynch & Co. to the Medical College, Cornell University after Chairman of Citigroup Inc. The Weill Medical College attracted more than $1 billion by offering naming opportunities ranging from buildings to hallways. The school was named in honour of the Stanford Weill, an alumnus of Cornell, after donation of $200 millions in 1998 and 2002. The New York Central Park initiated an innovative scheme for encouraging people, who want to make smaller contribution in 1986 and was able to get 1,200 out of 9,000 benches of the park adopted by individuals with a silver plaque bearing a message of donor's choosing by donating $7,500 per bench.

Bill Gates, founder of **Microsoft Corp**[21], pledging US$900 million to fight tuberculosis, with an initial contribution of US$31 million, represent one of the major contributions in the recent decades. Another such initiative related to the support for development of an inexpensive vaccine to fight pneumonia[22], taking lives of about a million children every year; as many lives as by AIDS, malaria and tuberculosis. The Bill and Melinda Gates Foundation awarded $75 million to *"Path"*, a Seattle based non-profit group to create a new, inexpensive vaccine for preventing pneumonia.

The general economic development has been leading promotion of **charity and philanthropy**.[23] Many wealthier individuals **will come forward**[24] to contribute a portion of their huge wealth to make a difference in the lives of millions of less fortunate people, living in other parts of the planet. A two pronged strategy, based on *encouraging the rich to donate along with a transparent method of utilizing the donated amount* for the specified purpose with *active support of the civil society and the media* will help in mobilizing this and in turn making the development inclusive and sustainable.

Rays of Hope

In the last decade, the pace of development of the developing countries remained a mixed one. While some countries have seen significant economic and social progress leading to achievements of standards comparable with the developed countries, other countries continue to lag behind with overall progress varying from poor to dismal. In recent years, **two developments**[25], namely invention of **powerful technologies** and **ability to raise resources** in adverse conditions have come as pleasant surprises. These have generated hope for making a big difference in the lives of the world poor in the coming years.

Impact of appropriate technology is evident from the multi-pronged strategy adopted for tackling malaria covering the use of treated bed net to protect especially children from mosquito bite, insecticides to stop breeding of malaria-transmitting mosquitoes and making medicines available at a reasonable price. This has paid rich dividends[26] in checking malaria, a major killer in the developing countries. This indicates the scope for using appropriate technology in tackling major issues relating to human development in the developing countries.

The other development in mobilization of resources relates to the response of people from across the world providing aid for relief and rehabilitation of families affected by the *Tsunami,* which hit several Asian countries in December 2004. The magnitude of assistance, in terms of money and material, mobilized within a short time for this humane cause has been phenomenal, which led Bill Clinton, the then US President, calling it a process of "*democratization of development assistance*".

The challenges ahead therefore lie in converting and institutionalizing such enthusiastic response usually received at the time of a crisis; for dealing with social issues on a routine and long term basis for welfare of the society. It has been estimated that a meager contribution of *just three dollars in a year* by individuals living in the developed countries will generate enough resources to solve the problem of child healthcare in all the developing and underdeveloped countries. While for an individual, extending such financial assistance is affordable, the challenge lies in mobilizing and sustaining it at a macro level over a long term. Evolving suitable institutional policy mechanism. Commitment of the national governments and promoting community participation are critical in this regard. Change in the mindset, sound management practices, introduction of appropriate technology, reducing wastage, ensuring people's participation would be essential for ensuring this. CSR intervention of the corporate, as one of the major stakeholders of the society, is required to be viewed in this perspective.

Mobilizing Resources for SDGs 2030

The resources needed to achieve the 2030 agenda for sustainable development is extremely large, on the order of trillions of dollars annually. It is necessary to mobilize public and private investment globally to meet the financial resources and align it with sustainable development. This would involve public finance, policies and regulatory frameworks, unlocking the transformative potential of people and the private sector and incentivizing changes in consumption, production and investment patterns to support sustainable development.

On the 16th July, 2015, 193 UN Member States attending the Third International Conference on Financing for Development held in Addis Ababa, Ethiopia, agreed on a series of bold measures, known as the *Addis Ababa Action Agenda*, to overhaul global finance practices and generate investments for tackling a range of economic, social and environmental challenges. It provided a policy framework to realign financial flows with public goals. While Official Development Assistance (ODA) remains crucial, particularly for the developing countries, aid alone will not be sufficient. The Agenda seeks to mobilise all sources of finance: public and private, domestic and international on a holistic manner.

The ambitious 2030 agenda for sustainable development will put significant demands on public budgets and capacities, which would require scaling-up and more effective international support, including both concessional and non-concessional financing. In that regard, developed countries recommit to their ODA targets, including 0.70 per cent of Gross National Income (GNI) provided as ODA, with 0.15 to 0.20 per cent to least developed countries. Developed countries further commit to reversing the declining trend of ODA to the least developed countries, and are encouraged to set a target of providing at least 0.20 per cent of

ODA/GNI to least developed countries, with the European Union promising to do so by 2030.

The Action Agenda invites businesses to apply their creativity and innovation for solving sustainable development challenges and to engage as partners in the development process. It encourages businesses to embrace a core business model that takes into account the environmental, social and governance impacts of their activities, including integrated reporting, and also encourages impact investing. In particular, private foundations are encouraged to use their endowments actively, through impact investment, to better support sustainable development. Success will rely on countries' own sustainable development policies, plans and programmes, which will be led by the countries concerned. SDGs seek to act as a compass for aligning countries' plans with their global commitments. The 2030 agenda will be (i) *Nationally owned and country-led sustainable* development strategies and require resource mobilization and financing strategies; (ii) All *stakeholders*: governments, civil society, the private sector, and others, are required to contribute to the realization of the new agenda; (iii) *A revitalized global partnership* at the global level is needed to support national efforts; and (iv) *Multi-stakeholder partnerships* have been recognized as an important component of strategies that seek to mobilize all stakeholders around the new agenda.

Monitoring SDGs

For monitoring the 17 SDGs and 169 targets of the new agenda, the Inter-Agency and Expert Group on SDG Indicators (IAEG-SDGs) developed global indicator framework. There were 232 indicators, on which general agreement has been reached. These were agreed upon at the 48th session of the United Nations Statistical Commission in March 2017. Achieving Sustainable Development Goals is closely linked with controlling the Climate Change, which has been impacting public health, availability of food and water security, migration, peace and security. Climate change, left unchecked, will worsen economic condition of the poor and disadvantaged and roll back the development gains made over the last decades and will make further gains impossible. Accordingly, investments in sustainable development shall have to address climate change by reducing greenhouse gas emissions and building climate resilience. Tackling climate change and fostering sustainable development are mutually reinforcing and represent two sides of the same coin, which need to be pursued together.

Reporting Corporate Social Responsibility

With a view to measure the CSR initiatives, efforts have been made for measuring and reporting action taken by corporate. Such reporting should be reliable for building trust among stakeholders and enhancing reputation of the corporate by demonstrating the purpose, vision, mission and responsible business operations clearly. It helps in leading the change; stimulate dialogues for creation of awareness on sustainable practices.

Any CSR reporting is required to be based on five parameters of reporting namely: (i) Defining reporting goals and CSR programme; (ii) Assigning specific target and measurements; (iii) Deciding reporting standards; (iv) Understanding the stakeholders; and (v) Assigning roles and responsibilities. Accordingly, numbers of reporting mechanism have been developed for reporting of CSR by different organizations, including the following:

Social Auditing

Social Auditing (SA) technique was introduced for dealing with defining, observing and reporting measures of ethical behaviour and social impact of an organization in relation to its aims and those of its stakeholders.

Ethical Accounting Statement (EAS)

Ethical Accounting Statement (EAS) was developed at the Copenhagen Business School basing on the stakeholders' approach. However, this approach does not believe in benchmarking with reference to external sources on the ground that such measures are meaningless.

Global Reporting Initiative (GRI)

The Global Reporting Initiative (GRI)'s reporting guidelines were initially launched in March 1999. Subsequently in 2002, GRI was set up as a permanent, independent, international body with a multi-stakeholder governance structure with headquarters in Amsterdam. Based on sustainability concept, GRI provides a framework to assess and measure CSR. It has been attempting to devise a set of indicators so that companies can report progress in meeting the Triple Bottom Line (TBL) covering (i) Principles of social responsibility, (ii) Process of social responsibility and (iii) Products (or outcomes), as they relate to the firm's societal relationships.

Accountability 1000 (AA 1000)

Another technique, Accountability 1000 (AA 1000) was launched in November 1999 by the ISEA. AccountAbility deals with linking various CSR management tools, such as the Global Reporting Initiative (GRI), the Sustainability Integrated Guidelines for Management (SIGMA), the Balanced Scorecard and other initiatives.

International Standards (SA 8000)

In 2002, Social Accountability International (SAI) developed new International standards (SA 8000) indicating the auditable requirements on a broad range of issues such as child labour, health and safety, freedom of association, right to collective bargaining, discrimination, disciplinary practices, working hours and remuneration.

Accounting for Sustainability

Accounting for Sustainability was set up by HRH the Prince of Wales in 2004 "To help ensure that sustainability—considering what we do not only in terms of ourselves and today, but also of others and tomorrow—is not just talked and worried about, but becomes embedded in organizations' "DNA". The integration of environmental and social factors into management decision-making and reporting will allow the connection between strategic direction, financial performance and sustainability impacts to be made and thereby drive a better and more sustainable return into the future.

AA1000

Accountability's AA1000 series were further refined and evolved in 2008 as principles-based standards to help organizations in becoming more accountable, responsible and sustainable. It covers issues relating to governance, business models and organizational strategy, as well as providing operational guidance on sustainability assurance and stakeholder engagement. The AA1000 standards are designed for the integrated thinking required by the low carbon, green economy and support integrated reporting and assurance. The standards are developed through a multi-stakeholder consultation process, which ensures they are written for those they impact, not just those who may gain from them. They are used by a wide range of organizations, covering multinational businesses, small and medium enterprises, governments and civil societies. Account Ability publishes guidance and research materials to enhance the understanding and application of the AA1000 Series. Guidance materials for the AA1000 Assurance Standard 2008 include Guidance for Assurance Providers, Guidance for Reporting Organizations and Guidance for Stakeholders

ISO 26000:2010

ISO 26000:2010 was launched in 2010, after five years long negotiations between different stakeholders across the world. It provides guidance rather than requirements and helps in clarifying as to what is social responsibility, how it helps businesses and organizations, translate principles into effective actions and shares best practices relating to social responsibility. It applies to all types of organizations regardless of their activity, size or location. CSR primarily relates to management practices, which promote sustainable development and generate higher social capital for the corporate. CSR practices are to be viewed as business practices to be evolved by mutual consensus for meeting the greater needs of the society and promoting the interest of the corporate as well.

Carbon Disclosure Project (CDP)

The Carbon Disclosure Project (CDP) is an independent not-for-profit organization, working to drive greenhouse gas emissions reduction and sustainable water use by business and cities. It provides a transformative global system for thousands of companies and cities to measure, disclose, manage and share environmental information. When provided with the necessary information, market forces can be a major cause of change. Working with the world's largest investors, businesses and governments, CDP is uniquely positioned to catalyze action towards a more sustainable economy.

UN Global Compact

The Global Compact asks companies to embrace universal principles and to partner with the United Nations It has grown to become a critical platform for the UN to engage effectively with enlightened global business. [**Box: 3.4. Global Compact**].

Box 3.4: Global Compact

Global Compact was developed by United Nations in 1999 as an important measure for guiding the voluntary initiatives and code of conduct of the corporate. It has ten basic principles covering human rights, environmental sustainability, labour rights and ethical conduct as indicated below:

Human Rights

1. Business should support and respect the protection of internationally proclaimed human rights; and
2. Make sure that they are not complicit in human rights abuses.

Labour Standards

3. Businesses should uphold the freedom of association and the effective recognition of the right to collective bargaining;
4. The elimination of all forms of forced and compulsory labour;
5. The effective abolition of child labour; and
6. The elimination of discrimination in respect of employment and occupation.

Environment

7. Businesses should support a precautionary approach to environmental challenges;
8. Undertake initiatives to promote greater environmental responsibility; and
9. Encourage the development and diffusion of environmentally friendly technologies.

Anti-Corruption

10. Businesses should work against all forms of corruption, including extortion and bribery.

UN Secretary General, Kofi Annan had called upon the global corporate leadership to join in a "*Global Compact*" in order to marshal the creative forces of private entrepreneurship to address the needs of the *disadvantages* and requirements of future generations. Launching of the *Global Compact* helped in sensitizing the corporate managements across the world to these principles and to some extent marked the beginning of Corporate Social Responsibility. However, as there was no mechanism for enforcing these principles, it had attracted criticism that corporate by referring to this utilized the name of UN without complying with the requirements.

Reference: http://www.unglobalcompact.org.

Ceres

The Exxon-Valdez oil spill, a major environmental disaster, shook public confidence in corporate America in 1989. Nearly 11 million gallons of oil poured into Alaska's Prince William Sound, devastating one of the world's most pristine habitats. Suddenly, the environmental cost of doing business became painfully clear and it was apparent that companies weren't doing enough to account for the environmental and social impacts of their operations. Six months after the spill, a group of investors launched a non-profit organization called "*Ceres*" to tackle this problem. Ceres, a 501(c) (3) non-profit organization, introduced a bold new vision to the business community—a vision of a world in which business and the capital markets promote the well-being of human society and the protection of the Earth's environment. It seeks to mobilize a powerful network of investors, companies and public interest groups to accelerate and expand the adoption of sustainable business practices and solutions to build a healthy global economy with a mission to "Mobilizing investor and business leadership to build a thriving, sustainable global economy."

CSR: Country-wise Experiences

Based on the level of economic development, socio-cultural and environmental settings, CSR practices of the countries have developed over the last decade. Salient features of which are discussed below for facititating appreciation of the status of CSR at global level.

The United Kingdom

Following a number of financial scandals, a committee was set up under Lord Adrian Cadbury to draw up a code of best practices and suggest specific procedures on corporate governance. The Committee made a number of recommendations on how large companies should conduct their business in its report, submitted in December 1992. This is popularly known as the "***Cadbury Code***", which constituted a landmark in corporate governance. Cadbury Code relates partly to financial control and partly to ethical practices followed by the company.

Provisions of this code were not legally binding. However, the London Stock Exchange (LSE) had advised all the listed and unlisted companies to include a statement indicating compliance in respect of the Cadbury Code in their Annual Report. As per survey[27] conducted by the Confederation of British Industry, 81 per cent of the respondents indicated that the code had caused them to review the structure and the operation of their Board.

Subsequently, the matter was looked into by another study group headed by Greenbury in July 1995, with particular reference to the remuneration of the company Directors. This group recommended that companies should publish a statement regarding compliance with the best practices including provision of remunerations. Adherence to the Cadbury and Greenbury codes does not necessarily imply that the company is an ethical organization. However, it was felt[28] that following practices as indicated in the Cadbury Report would lead to a corporate governance regime, which is open and has lesser chance of domination by few people and would put a check on the remuneration package of senior executives. The LSE introduced "Principles of good governance and code of best practices" in 1998, which is popularly known as Hampel Report. These guidelines provided that the Board of Directors should review the effectiveness of all controls, including operational, financial, compliance control and business risk management with the objective of protecting and increasing shareholders' value. To that extent, it helps the corporate in fulfilling their responsibility towards the stakeholders.

The Reports of Cadbury, Greenbury and Hampel were combined by the LSE as the "***Combined Code***", which laid down guidelines to be followed by the listed and unlisted companies in UK. Subsequently, Turnbull looked at the interpretation of the provisions of the Combined Code in 1999. The extent of compliance with the guidelines varies widely from company to company. Nonetheless, it is felt that ethics in business plays a crucial role for any organization as it relies on the ability of individuals to apply the ideal of the social contract in day-to-day decisions and actions. The real test of ethics lies in the manner that ethics must be applied[29] in a way that leaves no doubt in the mind of observers outside the enterprise.

Importance of the code of ethics spread in UK with more and more companies adopting a code. As per a survey[30] held in 1998, about 55 per cent of the respondents were found to have a code for business ethics. These developments appeared to have *formed the core of CSR extending beyond the premises of the company and the national barrier*. This has been reflected in the case of "*Burton*", a British firm dealing with clothes and having business set up in Myanmar. Following adverse criticism about unethical practices relating to child labour and violations of human rights in Myanmar, the firm initially tried to change the approach of the military rulers in power but finally closed down[31] its business and withdrew from Myanmar in 1992.

In UK[32], CSR issues are dealt by the Department of Trade and Industry (DTI). In implementation of CSR, based on the approach—"*there is no one size fits all";* companies are encouraged to develop their own practices keeping in view the nature of their business and its impacts. The government activities mainly relate to raising awareness about good practices and encouraging businesses to improve their CSR performance. DTI has sponsored *Annual Awards for Excellence* for recognizing leading examples of good practice among businesses, small and large. The awards recognize achievements of the companies and their partners, while stimulating innovative CSR practices. DTI also sponsored the Business in the Community *Corporate Responsibility Index* since its establishment in 2002. The Index helps businesses to improve their impact on society and the environment by assessing how well their CSR policies are embedded in their business operations, while allowing them to benchmark their performance among their peers.

The UK passed a number of regulations designed to complement voluntary initiatives to encourage CSR. The Companies Act, 2006 compelled directors to act in the interests of the company's shareholders, but taking into account the wider interests of stakeholders. It also required companies to provide information in their annual report on their strategies, performance and risks (the so-called Business Review). Quoted companies additionally should disclose, to the extent necessary for an understanding of the business, information on environmental, workplace, social and community matters in their annual reviews, as well as information about any policies in relation to these matters and about the effectiveness of those policies.

The United States of America

After the Second World War, the reconstruction related activities gave a boost to the US economy, which continued over the next decades. Necessity for regulating the corporate and business got attention in the US after the market crashed in September 1987. The National Commission on Fraudulent Financial Reporting (NCFFR), popularly known as the "*Tread way Commission*" was set up for suggesting corrective measures. This commission laid emphasis on functioning of Boards and recommended formation of Audit Committees with independent directors. However, the US Security Exchange Commission (SEC) did not support these recommendations. Issues relating to Corporate Governance got acceptability in 1989, with the National Association of Securities Dealers (NASD) making it mandatory for all the companies listed on the National Market System. Code of ethics was developed as a part of Corporate Governance for ensuring ethical conduct of the corporate.

A survey[33] held in 1992 indicated that about 83 per cent of the US companies had a code of ethics, which was higher than that of Europe with a compliance rate of about 50 per cent. Ninety three per cent of the *Fortune 1000* companies were found to have a code of ethics. There are instances of extending these commitments beyond the company's premises. For example, "Gap", dealing with retail clothing, had put pressure[34] on its suppliers in the developing countries to improve the working conditions of labour and reinstate the leaders of the trade union before renewal of contract. Organizations like the Interfaith Centre on Corporate Responsibility, Business for Social Responsibility (BSR) have been dealing with code of ethics and social responsibility of the corporate. Social issues such as prevention of child labour, prison or forced labour, discrimination on ground of sex, age and race, extension of basic social benefits, working hours etc., are being looked into as a part of ethical behaviour in accordance with local standards.

However, corporate scandals leading to bankruptcies of Enron and WorldCom had an impact on the conscience of the American business. These led to enactment[35] of the *Sarbanes-Oxley Act*, widely known as SOX, in July 2002 leading to the setting up of the Public Company Accounting Oversight Board, for regulating conduct of auditors, giving protection to the whistle-blowers etc.

U.S. businesses freely acknowledge their ethical and social obligations. They accepted the idea that businesses have economic, legal, ethical, and discretionary responsibilities. Discretionary responsibility relates to the presumption that a company will voluntarily serve society. Such service reaches beyond economic, legal, and even ethical responsibilities. Most businesses support the fight against hunger. The U.S. Sentencing Commission's Guidelines for Organizations seek to facilitate such goals, which cover almost all businesses including labour unions, partnerships, unincorporated organizations and associations.

Japan

Japanese tradition of corporate being responsible towards the society is different from that of other countries, which keep on changing as per emerging needs of the society. In the 1960s, this basically related to resolving conflicts between the labour and the management, which changed by the 1970s to cover compliance with pollution and environment-related issues. Canon Inc. emerged as a leader in CSR activities in Japan by adopting a code of conduct, which envisages a corporate culture dedicated to contributing to society through business operations. The company sought to excel in the areas of advanced technologies, global business deployment, and diverse specialized human resources through diversification for meeting the changing needs of globalization. Capitalizing on these strengths with the aim of contributing to the betterment of society as a good corporate citizen, the Canon Group established its CSR Activity Policy[36] in January 2012. As a part of this policy, five key activities have been defined for the Canon Group to address. This approach ensures that the entire Group shares a core set of values, while pursuing CSR activities specifically tailored to individual countries and regions to create a corporate group that grows together with society.

With quality and cost competitiveness integral parts of the Japanese business culture, corporations have been pursuing the goal of supplying quality products at reasonable rates for winning satisfaction of the consumer Japanese citizens. Further, the corporate give attention to issues like reducing excessive work hours for enriching family life of the workers/ executives while safeguarding the interest of other stakeholders as the core of CSR in Japan.

In Japan, Management awareness about social responsibility changed from social contribution through philanthropy and mercenary activities to solving social issues through business activities. The Report by the Study Group on "*Social Responsibility for a Safe and Comfortable, Sustainable Future*" in Japan was compiled in May 2008. The Ministry of the Environment (environment), Ministry of Health, Labour and Welfare (labour), and Ministry of Economy, Trade and Industry (internal control, intellectual property) established their own guidelines on optional disclosure. In March 2011, a "*Collaborative strategy*" was established to realize a safe, comfortable and sustainable society, under which each organization assumed their social responsibilities.

Germany

Germany had a history of the corporate getting involved in social issues since the nineteenth century. In addition to the church and the scientific community, the business also took interest in social matters. After the Second World War, social market economy (*Soziale Marktwirtschaft)* was adopted, which comprised capitalist economy, along with market regulations for safeguarding interest of labour and providing social security. Relatively sound social and educational services were provided through the public sector for decades in Germany; which made involvement of the corporate in social issues somewhat secondary.

This position changed subsequently. The educational and social services organization started looking to corporate support for upgrading equipment, facilities and meeting establishment and salary related expenditure. There are instances of social responsibility of corporate extending beyond national boundaries; as was the case with putting pressure on developing countries like Nepal for checking child labour engaged in carpet weaving. The National Strategy for Corporate Social Responsibility in the form of an "*Action Plan for CSR*" was adopted in October 2010, which seeks to bring about a change in attitude and generate awareness that practicing corporate social responsibility is good for the business and the society. CSR was seen as an opportunity not only to boost the international competitiveness of enterprises but also to provide solutions to social challenges.

France

The corporations were either wholly or partially owned by the State in France. As public funded institutions, these corporations remained sensitive to social issues. Among the private firms, there was a feeling that they have been paying enough as taxes and social charges to the State, which should deal with the social issues. Consequently, social responsibility was not a priority for the French companies. However, "*Observatoiresur la Responsabilite Societale des Enterprises (ORSE)*" was set up by the French trade unions and some companies as an institution to promote socially responsible investment and activities relating to labour and environment issues. Further, legislative measures were initiated to encourage Corporate Social Responsibility and Socially Responsible Investment practices in business. *NRE Act on New Economic Regulation* requires the listed companies to disclose information on the measures taken into account regarding the environmental and social impacts of their activities in their annual report. Companies were found to have taken steps for some effort in terms of reporting. It was becoming apparent that incorporating sustainable development was their core.

South Africa

In South Africa, Social responsibility of corporate was brought to the forefront in 1994 based on the recommendations of the *King Committee*, which examined various aspects of the corporate governance from a wider perspective. In addition to the issues dealt by the Cadbury Committee, it recommended effective worker participation in decision making, adoption of affirmative action as a part of business plans as well as respecting interests of constituencies, which do not have any contractual links with the company. South Africa's Code and Report on Governance Principles was revised for the third time, as *King III Report* in March 2010. The new report focused on sustainability and risk issues, while continuing to highlight the importance for companies to respond to all stakeholders. In a survey conducted by Globe Scan Incorporated in 2011, about half of the interviewees reported having considered rewarding social responsible companies, while 20 per cent actually did so. This position is expected to improve in due course.

India

Modern approach to social responsibility of the corporate in the Indian context has its origin in the concept of "*Trusteeship*", advocated by Mahatma Gandhi. Numbers of industrial houses like the Tata, Birla took the charity based approach ahead as institutionalized philanthropy.

Setting up of Security Exchange Board of India (SEBI) in 1992 marked the beginning of streamlining corporate governance in India. Later, a National Task Force on Corporate Governance was set up under the chairmanship of Rahul Bajaj, which gave its recommendations in 1996. Subsequently, these issues were examined by other committees, which were incorporated in the Clause 49 of the listing agreement of companies with the stock exchanges.

As per a survey, environmental, social, and governance programmes were seen as an opportunity to create new revenue streams. Given investors' demand for financial data, it was deemed necessary to develop metrics that focus on integrating the financial effects of environmental, social, and governance programmes with the rest of the company's finances. CSR professionals took measures for making their investors aware about the company's environmental, social, and governance programmes.

India achieved the rare distinction by making CSR mandatory under the Companies Act in 2013 with effect from 1st April, 2014. As per the mandated provision, companies having a net worth of rupees 500 crore or more, or a turnover of rupees 1,000 crore or more, or a net profit of rupees 5 crore or more became liable to spend two per cent of the average net profits of last 3 years on CSR activities, specified in Schedule VII of the Act. Developments of CSR in India, both in theory and practice, have been dealt at length in the next chapter.

Conclusion

Experiences of different counties indicate that science and technology-led developments increased production, trade, commerce and profits of the corporate substantially in the second half of the twentieth century. This got a further boost in the new millennium. The rate and impact of growth however varied widely from country to country, depending on several factors. The corporate were benefited by the technology-led growth. However, these developments had its adverse effect in terms of environmental degradation and increasing economic inequality. The gap between the rich and the poor and the have and the have-nots widened, which in turn led to frustration, anger and violence.

Studies of developing economies have indicated that the trickle-down economics theory failed to deliver as envisaged, due to limitations in the way markets operate and other related factors. The logic that economic growth is the panacea and would be automatically socially inclusive was found to be not correct. There are several cases where there was economic growth, but conditions of the poor worsened instead of improving. In a globalized economy, the national economy is affected by external pulls and pressures. In certain cases, the national governments are succumbing to external influence. The so-called "Safety nets for the poor" had limitations in taking of the poor and yielding desired result. As a result, the poor farmer, weaver, trader etc., got further marginalized. Many times pressures from the vocal urban consumers led to import for giving a better deal to the consumers, which put the domestic producers at considerable disadvantage. Besides, while the educated and skilled have been able to derive benefits from the globalization; those form the disadvantaged segments without requisite skill and knowledge, including women, got further marginalized. This has been posing challenges to the developing countries in facing the competition from the developed countries. Often the developed countries force political and economic agenda on the developing countries either to give in or face sanctions. This is aggravating human deprivation in the developing countries further and affecting the global peace and prosperity, notwithstanding the technological miracles, man has at his command.

While the national governments are primarily responsible for taking care of the poor by suitable policy interventions and providing good governance; the corporate, which are major beneficiaries of the economic growth cannot afford to remain as silent spectators. The market forces would continue to play an important role in the globalized world. In order to make this growth sustainable, issues relating to distributive justice by empowerment of the poor with provision of education, skill, health and resources for accessing the market, have to be given due attention. In this context, the corporate can facilitate this, in view of their control over vast financial and human resources and managerial skill. The pressure on business to play a role in social issues has been growing in the last decade, which is likely to intensify further. There are instances of corporate and the NGOs working together on several social issues, which have provided success stories on business taking a lead in addressing social and economic issues, in which the corporate have an interest. Such instances have provided valuable lessons in areas, where government agencies have been struggling to come up with a viable solution. One such example relates to tackling the depleting fish stocks, where *Unilever* supported sustainable fisheries development based on effective use of their supply chain and made a difference in the lives of many fishermen with limited assets.

While this does not necessarily mean that the *corporate can or should solve all problems of the society*, it only indicates that the corporate are in a position to make a difference in selected areas, where they have interest and the circumstances are conducive for enabling them to take up identified social activities, while pursuing their commercial interest.

It has been observed that synergy of action between the national governments, the corporate and the civil society can empower the poor and the unskilled by creating a 'Win-Win' situation for the corporate and the society. These would facilitate sustainable development on a long-term basis, which form the core of CSR interventions as a distinct improvement over the short-term, charity-based approach adopted earlier. This approach will help in distributing the benefits of growth evenly, reducing the skewed concentration of wealth in the hands of a few and would have positive impact in reducing human deprivation, leading to greater social inclusion and making the development sustainable on a long-term basis.

References

1. Bobbie Johnson, "Coming television's iPod moment", *The Hindu*, August 28, 2007, p. 9.
2. Setting up Global climate coalition.
3. http://unfccc.int/kyoto_protocol/items/2830.php
4. Emma Duncan, "*Cleaning up*", *The Economist*, June 02, 2007, A special report on business and climate change, p.3.
5. American Academy of Sciences, *The Economist*, June, 2007, pp. 57-58.
6. https://en.wikipedia.org/wiki/United_Nations_Conference_on_Sustainable_Development
7. http://unfccc.int/paris_agreement/items/9485.php
8. *WIREs Clim Change* 2013, 4:191–201. doi: 10.1002/wcc.210 http://onlinelibrary.wiley.com/doi/10.1002/wcc.210/full
9. http://www.livemint.com/Politics/D7bKh6aZsXLBNCIpMM57fP/Donald-Trump-withdraws-US-from-Paris-climate-deal.html?utm_source=newsletter&utm_medium=email&utm_campaign=newsletter
10. Nidhi Sharma, "Climate Change US Frozen, Chindia warms up", *The Economic Times*, May 31, 2017, p. 12.
11. *ENERDATA*, World Bank.
12. Annual list of the superrich made by *Sunday Times*, London; *The Hindu*, May 12, 2014.
13. Gargi Parsai, "World's poorest people being left behind", International Food Policy Research Institute (IFPRI), *The Hindu*, November 10, 2007, p. 8.
14. Holme, R. and Watts, P., 2000, "*Corporate Social Responsibilities: Making Good Business Sense*", London, Rio Tinto and Royal Dutch/shell.
15. http://www.un.org/millennium/declaration/ares552e.html
16. The Millennium Development Goals Report 2007, United Nations, New York, 2007.
17. http://www.un.org/sustainabledevelopment/development-agenda/
18. Sachs Jeffrey, D., "Giving till it heals", *The Economic Times*, April 06, 2005.
19. Marcos Espinal, WHO, *The Hindu*, January 28, 2006.
20. Vineet Gupta, "Role of private sector in creating Centres of excellence", *The Times of India*, April 30, 2014, p. 9.
21. "Microsoft Corp's founder Bill Gates pledges US $900 million for TB eradication", on Friday, 27 January, 2006 at Davos, Switzerland, *The Hindu*, January 28, 2006.
22. "Gates Foundation gives $75 million for pneumonia vaccine research", *The Financial Express*, April 09, 2006.
23. "Wall Street Profits Fuel Philanthropy", *The Financial Express*, April 09, 2006.
24. J.D. Sachs, "The healthier poor", *The Economic Times*, September 03, 2007, p. 14.

25. "*Investing in Development*", A Practical Plan to Achieve the Millennium Development Goals.
26. *Ibid.*
27. Confederation of British Industry 1996, CBI at work, CBI News.
28. Kittson and Robert Campbell, 1996, "*The Ethical Organisation: Ethical Theory and the Behavior*", Alan, p. 115.
29. Sajhau Jean-Paul, 1997, "*Business Ethics in the Textiles, Clothing and Footwear (TCF) Industries: Code of Conduct*", Working paper 110, ILO, Geneva.
30. Simon Webley, 1992, "*Business ethics and company codes: Current best practices in UK*", Institute of Business Ethics.
31. "*The Principles People Pull out of Burma*", Andrew Marshall (1977), www.jubileecampaign.co.uk/
32. "*Business in the Community*", CSR research review, London, United Kingdom website.
33. G.R. Weaver, 1993, "Corporate Code of Ethics: Purpose, Process and Content Issues", *Business and Society*, Vol. 33(1): 46.
34. Jean-Paul Sajhau, 1997, "*Business Ethics in the Textile, Clothing and Footwear (TCF) Industries: Code of Conduct*", Working paper, ILO, Geneva.
35. "Five years under the thumb", *The Financial Express*, July 30, 2007, p. 7.
36. http://www.canon.com/csr/vision/policy.html

4

The Indian Scenario

Responsibility Towards the Society— A Part of Indian Culture and Tradition

Universal happiness and prosperity as reflected in the Sanskrit *sloka,* "*Sarve Bhavantu Sukhinah, Sarve Santu Niramayah . ..*" forms the core of the Indian culture and tradition. The spirit of sacrifice and philanthropy is an integral part of this tradition. There are several instances of the kings, nobles, and businessmen contributing generously for social causes. "*Daan*" or donating food, cloth, money to the poor and needy is considered as an essential prerequisite for getting salvation (*Moksha*) and forms main component of all Hindu rituals. There are similar reference in Islam as well. *Wakf,* constituted by donation of land and property by the rich in the name of *Allah,* aims at helping the poor, destitute, orphans and the travellers, thereby serving social purpose. In Sikhism, provision of "*Langar*", food and shelter free of cost in the *Gurudwaras* out of donations made by the devotees, is yet another illustration of institutionalized philanthropy. There are similar examples in all religions forming a part of the pluralistic society, typical to India. Along with helping the disadvantaged, these have led to active involvement of the civil society and promoted social cohesion, peace and goodwill.

Concern of the rich for the poor and disadvantaged has been documented in Kautilya's *Arthashastra*. There are references to taking care of the family of deceased soldiers, helpless, weak, aged, and workers as one of the major responsibilities of the king (State). This was supplemented by the rich and wealthy segment of the society out of their own means. History of CSR in India has been shaped based on this tradition, modified by subsequent social and economic development.

CSR before Independence (Pre-1947)

In its early phase, concern of the business towards the society was limited to charity and philanthropy. The response of trade and business was based on the prevailing social values, religion and culture. Wealthy merchants were sparing a part of their wealth for social purposes like assisting the poor and the needy and for public institutions like temples.

History of modern corporate in India started with the trading activities of the British East India Company in the eighteenth century. The company was primarily concerned with safeguarding the interest of the British owners, with little concern for the Indian society, even in difficult times like drought, famine, outbreak of epidemics. In the pre-Independence period, Indian business scene was dominated by British firms with a handful of firms of Indian origin. Notwithstanding small number and prevailing insecurity, some Indian firms actively supported the struggle for Independence at considerable risk to their business interest. Documentation of such cases will be a source of inspiration for the corporate of modern India.

During this period, Mahatma Gandhi had advocated the concept of "*trusteeship*" on the role and responsibility of the commercial enterprises towards the society. His vision for free India was based on the ideology of "*Simple living and high thinking*" and the presumption that the "*World has enough for meeting everyone's need but not greed*". He had held that the customers, employees and the society at large are as important for the business/corporation as the shareholders and evolved the philosophy of trusteeship[1] based on "*As the corporations are created by the society, they should remain in the public domain and their vast economic power should be exercised in the interest of not only the shareholders but the customers, employees and the society at large.*" Inspired by this ideal, Indian corporate had established trusts, set up and ran schools, colleges, hospital and institutions to pursue education, science and technology. Further, Empowerment of weaker sections of the society and women, abolition of untouchability, development of rural areas were pursued by these trusts in line with Gandhiji's philosophy. Hailing from a family dealing with business, Mahatma Gandhi had appreciated the role of business and its importance in generating wealth for national development. He had reiterated the need for promotion of *Business with ethics and concern for the common man,* as evident from his address[2] in FICCI in April 1931, *"I cannot forget the services rendered by the commercial clans, but I want you to make Congress your own and we would willingly surrender the reins to you. The work can be better done by you. But if you decide to assume the reins, you can do so only on the condition that you should regard yourselves as trustees and servants of the poor, your commerce must be regularized for the benefit of the toiling millions."*

Swami Vivekananda, the great Indian philosopher and thinker, had also stressed on the role of business remaining sensitive to the needs of the society in his observation, *"By doing the duty which is nearest to us, the duty which is in our hands now, we make ourselves stronger; and improving ourselves in this manner, step by step, we may even reach a State in which it will be our privilege to do the most coveted and honoured duties in life and society. Every duty is holy and devotion to duty is the highest form of worship of God."*

Before Independence, the Indian business was controlled by the foreign rulers. After Independence, most of the businessmen of foreign origin left India within a period of one year. Jute, tea and textiles constituted the main businesses, which were controlled by about 25 firms. Overall business ambiance before and immediately after Independence was not very exciting[3] as several industrialists lost parts of their business and production in the partition. Independence brought lots of enthusiasm to all including the corporate; however this feeling took time to sink in. There was not much improvement in business in the initial years and industrial expansion took place gradually.

There was a gradual shift in the approach of business in responsibility towards the society from ethical conduct to supporting welfare measures for the poor living in the peripheral areas of the plant and units. G.D. Birla, the founder of the Birla Group of Industries, had supported the poor through charitable works, which were taken forward by his successor, Aditya Birla with a paradigm shift for helping the people in a way so that they are able to stand on their own feet and earn money continuously instead of depending on charity. The group espoused the trusteeship concept of management, which entails ploughing back part of its profit into community. Kumaramangalam Birla's commitment to CSR lies in "Triple Bottom Line" approach to management, where accountability involves factoring holistically the interest of the stakeholders, namely the shareholders, customers, employees and community at large. Other private sectors also took up social activities for helping the poor and disadvantaged. One example of private sector pursuing issues of national importance is reflected in the letter of JRD Tata expressing his concern and seeking interventions of Pandit Jawaharlal Nehru, the then Prime Minister for checking the rapidly increasing population.

Social activities of the Tata Group, one of the major Indian corporate were guided by the approach of its founder, Jamshetji N. Tata to business of putting "*People before Profit*". This formed a part of the organization's philosophy "*The wealth, which comes from people must, as far as possible, go back to the people*". Observations of Jamshetji *"In a free enterprise, the community is not just another stakeholder in business, but in fact the very purpose of its existence"* reflected the concern of the group towards the society. Importance attached and the range of activities taken up by the group for the welfare of the society in general and people living in the periphery of the industrial units in particular is evident from the letter[4] Jamshetji Tata, wrote to his successor Dorabji Tata in 1902 "*Be sure* to lay wide streets planted with shady trees, every other of a quick growing variety. *Be sure* that there is plenty of space for lawns and gardens. *Reserve large areas* for football, hockey and parks. *Earmark areas* for Hindu temples, Mohamedan mosques and Christian churches." On success of an enterprise, he had further observed *"We think we started on sound and straightforward business principles, considering the interests of the shareholder our own, and the health and welfare of the employees the sure foundation of our prosperity."* The group set up several endowments for philanthropy and took steps for promotion of education, science and technology. Tata Institute of Fundamental Research (TIFR) at Mumbai, the Indian Institute of Science (IIS) at Bangalore and Tata Energy Research Institute (TERI), Delhi are some of such bodies, which evolved as major Centre of Excellence and earned worldwide acclaim.

Among the instances of philanthropic activities[5] of corporate before independence, one noteworthy case related to the spontaneous donation of Rs. 26 lakh by Ardeshir Godrej to the Tilak Fund for the upliftment of Harijans in 1926. This initiative was applauded by Mahatma Gandhi as contribution for a right cause. Pirojsha Godrej, brother of Ardeshir, pursued this and set up the Pirojsha Godrej Foundation in 1972. One-third share of the holding company, Godrej & Boyce Manufacturing Company Ltd., was donated to this foundation and the income from the dividend is being utilized for providing free medical care to the poor and critically ill, for education to poor students and relief in case of natural disasters. Shri G.D. Birla, founder of Birla Group had espoused the trusteeship concept of management. Birla Institute of Technology in 1964 has over years evolved as one of the top Engineering and Business School of India. The Bajaj Group under leadership of Jamnalal Bajaj had taken steps for promoting social welfare. This tradition continued and got expanded after Independence with more corporate taking up such measures.

CSR after Independence (1947-1991)

After Independence, the Constitution was adopted in 1949, which envisaged securing "Justice—Social, Economic and Political, Liberty and Equality for all the citizens" as enshrined in the Preamble. Welfare State formed the cornerstone of State policy, details of which are outlined in the Directive Principles of State Policy, in Article 38 *"(1) The State shall strive to promote the welfare of the people by securing and protecting as effectively as it may be a social order in which justice, social, economic and political, shall inform all the institutions of the national life. (2) the State shall, in particular, strive to minimize the inequalities in income, and Endeavour to eliminate inequalities in status, facilities and opportunities not only amongst individuals but also amongst groups of people residing in different areas or engaged in different vocations."*

This has been elaborated further in Article 39 that *"the State shall in particular direct its policy towards securing that the ownership and control of the material resources of the community are so distributed as best to subserve the common good and that the operation of the economic system does not result in the concentration of wealth and means of production to the common detriment"* and Article 41 that *"the State shall, within the limits of its economic capacity and development, make effective provision for securing the right to work, to education and to public assistance in cases of unemployment, old age, sickness and disablement, and in other cases of undeserved want."* These principles guided the course of formulation and implementation of the Five Year Plans for socio-economic development aiming at growth with distributive justice.

Development of the Corporate and its responsibility towards the society after independence fall *under two broad heads*.

Firstly, in accordance with the objective of the Constitution for establishing a socialistic society, distributing benefits of developments over all segments of the society, as envisaged under the Directive Principles of the State Policy, became the guiding principles for the Government. Number of plans and programmes were launched by Government from time to time with provision of sizable financial resources for provision of basic services and welfare of the disadvantaged segments of the society. As a result, corporate intervention for social activities became somewhat secondary.

The *second aspect* related to promotion of Public Sector Enterprises (PSEs), substantially owned and controlled by the Government both at the national and state levels, for production and sale of goods and services.

Under the Soviet model of planned development, PSEs were set up and vigorously pursued in different sectors as engines of growth. Even though the PSEs were set up primarily as commercial units, there was a social purpose as well, which is evident in the Industrial Policy Resolution, 1956, which *inter alia* envisaged, *"The adoption of the socialist pattern of society as the national objective as well as the need for planned and rapid development, require that all industries of basic and strategic importance, or in the nature of public utility services should be in the public sector."* Simultaneously, the private sector was regulated with stringent rules and regulations for safeguarding interest of the labour, protection of environment. The policy of industrial licensing, taxation and restrictions stifled private initiatives to some extent, led to unhealthy competition, and malpractices in the corporate sector. These factors affected the growth and competiveness of the Indian corporate and are often described as an "Era of command and control".

Social responsibility of the *PSEs covered three broad areas*, namely (i) provision of direct employment, (ii) development of ancillaries, and (iii) development of peripheral area with health, education and livelihood opportunity to the displaced families.

Along with commercial activities, PSEs were looked forward for creating employment opportunity. The affirmative action for reservation for the Scheduled Caste (SC) and Scheduled Tribe (ST) in employment was made mandatory for the PSEs as well. Besides, PSEs implemented Peripheral Development Programmes (PDPs) for provision of health, education and skill generation facilities to the families living near the plant/units. For the purpose, school and hospitals were set up in the peripheral areas in addition to extension of education and healthcare facilities from the infrastructure developed for the employees and workers. PSEs also promoted ancillaries for meeting the captive demand of the plant, which in turn generated employment opportunities in the peripheral areas.

Social Responsibilities and Public Accountability of State-Run Public Sector Undertakings were looked into by the Parliamentary Committee on Public Undertakings (CoPU) in 1991-92 with reference to the benefits accruing to region/area and the Project Affected Persons (PAPs). In its report, the Committee had observed[6] that *"being part of the State, every Public Undertaking has the moral responsibility to play an active role in discharging the social obligations endowed on a Welfare State, subject to the financial health of the enterprise; that although massive investments have been made for expansion of public enterprises, the macro and micro objectives and obligations in the sphere of social responsibilities have not been defined. As a result, social responsibilities to be discharged by Public Undertakings have remained ambiguous"*. The committee had recommended that *"projects for fulfilment of social responsibilities should be selected by individual undertakings keeping in view specific requirements of the areas where the units are located in consultation preferably with the peoples' representatives, renowned social workers of the district and non-governmental organizations. However, fulfilment of social responsibilities by the public enterprises should be linked to their profitability"*.

Acting on these recommendations in November 1994, the Central Public Sector Enterprises were advised to take appropriate action by availing help of State Government, the district administration and people's representatives, whenever necessary. Boards of the PSEs were advised to take appropriate action for identification and implementation of Social Responsibilities based on the power vested under the articles of Associations.

State-run enterprises continued commercial activities on similar lines, with support and protection from concerned State Governments in getting raw-materials and marketing products.

Importance of the PSEs in the economy is evident from the fact that the *number of Central Public Sector Enterprises (CPSEs) grew*[7] from 5 with an investment of Rs. 29 crores in 1951 to 248 (excluding 7 insurance companies) with a total investment of Rs. 6,66,848 crores as on 31st March, 2011.[8] Out of 277 CPSEs, 229 were operating on 31st March, 2013. Gross revenue/turnover of the operating CPSEs recorded growth rate varying from 6.79 per cent in 2012-13 to 21.63 per cent in 2011-12. Net profit of the profit making CPSEs increased from Rs. 1,25,929 crores in 2011-12 to Rs.1,43,559 crores in 2012-13. At the aggregate level, the net profit of all CPSEs (aggregate net profit – aggregate net loss) increased from Rs. 98,246 crores during 2011-12 to Rs. 1,15,298 crores in 2012-13.

So far as *generation of employment is concerned*, 38,500 persons belonging to SC (18.8%) and 16,100 to ST (7.9%) were engaged in the CPSEs as on 01.01.1995, as part of the affirmative action. The representation for the weaker section grew further to 19 per cent for SC and 8.4 per cent for ST respectively by 01.01.2003. Even though the percentage of representation increased, *absolute number of SC and ST persons employed in the CPSEs fell* to 31,300 and 13,900 respectively during this period, which was attributed to overall downsizing of the

CPSEs. Representation of SC excluding the safai *karmacharis* in the CPSEs improved from 17.44 per cent in 1980 to 17.99 per cent in 2012 and 18.19 per cent in 2013. Similarly, representation of ST increased from 7.6 per cent in 1980 to 9.58 per cent in 2012 to 10.24 per cent in 2013. The overall representation, being higher than the percentage of population 15 per cent in case of SC and 7.5 per cent in case of ST, indicate the importance attached by the PSEs to this important and sensitive social aspect.

Private Sector after Independence

Notwithstanding the importance and support extended to public sector under the socialistic model of economic development adopted after Independence, the private sector continued to play an important role. Along with their commercial interest, private sector corporate took interest in social issues. Social responsibility of the private sectors was referred[9] to by the Parliamentary Committee as the obligations of companies, like TISCO, showed beyond the shareholders to the community and society at large, in which the company operates. The committee had observed that *"It would not be an exaggeration to say about the private sector that it is the public money, which is being managed by private individuals. Suitable ways and means may be devised for the private enterprises also to discharge certain social responsibilities, which could be linked to profitability."* The committee referred to these obligations arising from the company's own understanding of what it owes to society and that such an understanding is based on values and norms that have been traditionally nurtured in India.

CSR under the New Economic Policy (1991-2000)

Economic and political developments like advent of Information and Communication Technology (ICT), disintegration of the Soviet Russia, rapid growth in global trade and commerce brought about significant changes in the Indian business scenario. With a view to meet the emerging challenges, the new economic policy based on Liberalization and Privatization for meeting the challenges of Globalization (LPG) was adopted in 1991. Promotion of private sector was stressed by relaxation of controls and regulations for facilitating growth in general and unleashing the power of the private sector in particular. However, no specific reference to the social responsibility of the corporate could be located in this economic policy.

Regulation of the Corporate

Under the new economic policy, accountability and transparency of the corporate towards shareholders and the society at large are stressed, which were regulated by the Securities and Exchange Board of India (SEBI). With a view to safeguarding the interest of the shareholders, SEBI issued a set of guidelines titled "Listing Agreement", to be executed by each company wishing to list its securities on the stock exchange [**Box 4.1: SEBI Guidelines on Listing**].

Box 4.1: SEBI Guidelines on Listing

Following acceptance of the Cadbury committee report in UK in 1991, accountability and transparency of the corporate towards the shareholders and the society at large assumed importance in corporate governance all over the world.

The Securities and Exchange Board of India (SEBI) was established on April 12, 1992 as per the provisions of the Securities and Exchange Board of India Act, 1992. SEBI has laid down *Listing Agreement*, which is required to be signed by every company wishing to list its securities on a stock exchange. The agreement has 51 clauses covering guidelines on listing and responsibilities of the company management. Clause 49 of the agreement, dealing with corporate governance, covers mandatory and non-mandatory norms for companies to comply with.

Clause 49 is applicable to companies seeking listing for the first time as well as to already listed companies with a paid-up share capital of more than Rs.3 crore or a recorded net worth of Rs.25 crore anytime. Thus, virtually all listed companies are required to comply with clause 49, which requires the company to make certain critical disclosures regarding party transactions, accounting statement, risk management practices, proceeds from public issues, remuneration of directors and management discussion and analysis.

Provisions of clause 49 were amended in February 2000 based on the recommendations of a committee set up under Kumaramangalam Birla and later in October 2004 based on recommendations of another panel set up under N.R. Narayana Murthy.

Reference: Clause 49 of the Listing Agreement, *The Financial Express*, January 02, 2006.

While pursuing commercial objectives, PSUs had taken up social welfare initiatives for the benefit of the families, who were displaced for getting land for setting up the plants. The private sector had also taken up other social initiatives. However, such initiatives were limited to a few firms and were on a limited scale. Under the new economic policy, private sector got a big boost and spread their wings beyond India. With economic development, social activities got redefined for meeting changing needs of the society. Several corporate took up replacing the traditional charity-based approach by a participative, empowerment-based approach. With changing needs of the market and shareholders, the corporate started exploring new ways of doing business taking into account all the stakeholders, valuing the differences and adopting inclusive policies so that the growth process is sustainable. Successful Information Technology corporate like Wipro, Infosys took up social issues with focus and substantial resources for provision of quality education which marked a new chapter in the history of CSR in India, in addition to the traditional corporate like Tata.

CSR in the New Millennium (2000-2014)

At the beginning of the new Millennium, there were *two major global developments* relating to CSR. *Firstly,* serious financial irregularities were noticed in functioning of Multinational Companies, like Enron and WorldCom in the US, which reiterated the importance of values and ethics in business. Adhering to values and principles became a matter of concern all-over the world in the context of responsibility of the Corporate towards the society. *Secondly*, adoption of the Millennium Development Goals (MDGs) 2015 became an important global issue, which had impact on the approach of the corporate towards the society in general and the disadvantaged segments in particular. These had impact on the Indian corporate scenario as well.

In the post liberalization period, CSR initiatives of about 1000 companies were surveyed by the Confederation of Indian Industries (CII) in collaboration with United Nations Development Programme, the British Council and Price Waterhouse Coopers (PwC) in 2002. Some of the major findings of the survey indicated the following:

- Definitions of Corporate Social Responsibility vary as per the perceptions of the promoters. Notwithstanding the differences, there was a near unanimity that CSR is very much included in the domain of corporate action and passive philanthropy is no longer sufficient to meet the emerging needs.

- There is a shift in the approach to CSR from 'Trusteeship-Ethical Model' to 'Statist Model' i.e., where companies perceive CSR as contribution to nation building, holding social wealth in trust, strategic investments in employees and as the means to enhance long-term stakeholder value.
- Promotion of brand, "Reputation of being a good corporate citizen" has been the main factor for undertaking CSR activities. "Intention to improve relationship with local communities" and "stated philosophy of the founder fathers" were the other important factors. Companies, that see themselves as leaders or early movers, are taking keen interest in CSR.
- Provision of tax duty and custom benefits and inclusion of CSR performance as a parameter for assessment and clearing new projects were suggested for boosting up CSR activities.
- There was no direct relationship between profit and CSR expenditure.
- Lack of comprehension and capacity to implement projects appeared to be the major concern of the Corporate Sector in taking up CSR on a wider scale. Increasing demands from benefited community, increase in operating cost, political interference in implementation and non-availablity of tools and mechanisms to measure, evaluate and report CSR performance appeared to be the other barriers.

Social Charter for the Corporate

The ten point *Social Charter*, [**Box 4.2: Social Charter for the Corporate**], announced by Dr. Manmohan Singh, the then Prime Minister, in May 2007 marked one of the major interventions in directing the strength of the Indian corporate to social issues in the new Millennium. It sought to provide a platform for fostering a "Government-Industry Partnership" for making the growth socially inclusive. The role of Indian corporate in meeting the emerging challenges faced by the country and taking care of the social needs were reiterated for carrying on business on a sustainable basis in the society. Referring to the Gandhi's concept of trusteeship, importance of CSR was stressed to be taken up within the framework of corporate philosophy, keeping in view the needs of the community and the region, in which a corporate functions.

Box 4.2: Social Charter for the Corporate

In the context of the responsibility of business in a modern, democratic society, Prime Minister, Manmohan Singh referred to ten basic issues, as indicated below, for ensuring growth with distributive justice:

1. *"Have healthy respect for workers and invest in their welfare:* Unless workers feel they are cared for at work, we can never evolve a national consensus in favour of much-needed more flexible Labour laws aimed at ensuring that our firms remain globally competitive.
2. *Corporate social responsibility* should be defined within the framework of a corporate philosophy which factors the needs of the community and the regions in which a corporate entity functions.
3. *Industry must be proactive in offering employment to the less privileged*, at all levels of the job ladder. The representation companies give to SC/STs, OBCs, minorities and women in their workforce must increase.
4. *Resist excessive remuneration to promoters and senior executives* and discourage conspicuous consumption.
5. *Invest in people and in their skills* to make youth employable.
6. *Desist from non-competitive behaviour:* The operation of cartels by groups of companies to keep prices high must end. Even profit maximization should be within the bounds of decency and greed.
7. *Invest environment friendly technologies:* As a country of a billion plus people, with a scarcity of natural resources on a per capita basis, we cannot afford the wasteful lifestyles of the Western world. Conspicuous consumption must be reduced not just because it is socially undesirable at our level of development, but also because it is environmentally unsustainable.
8. *Promote enterprise and innovation* within your firms and outside. If our industry has to make the leap to the next stage of development, it must be far more innovative and enterprising.
9. *Fight corruption at all levels:* Corruption need not be the grease that oils the wheels of progress. There are many successful companies today that have refused to yield to this temptation. I commend them, and I urge others to follow.
10. *Promote socially responsible media and finance socially responsible advertising*: Through your advertisement budgets and your investments in media, you can encourage socially responsible media to grow and flourish. You can promote socially relevant messages and causes."

Reference: Annual Summit of CII, May 24, 2007.

National Voluntary Guidelines on Social, Environmental and Economical Responsibilities of Business

Potential of mobilizing corporate support for nation building in general and making the development inclusive in particular has been an ongoing process in India. The Ministry of Corporate Affairs issued guidelines for promoting social interventions by the relatively bigger corporate in 2009. These were modified and issued in July 2011 for all corporate irrespective of size, sector, or location as "National Voluntary Guidelines on Social, Environmental and Economical Responsibilities of Business". These guidelines laid down comprehensive principles to be adopted by companies as part of their business practices and a structured business responsibility reporting format requiring certain specified disclosures, demonstrating the steps taken by companies to implement the said principles. It was mandatory to prepare Business Responsibility Report ("BR reports") covering salient features of the work done during the year in the Annual Reports. Business Responsibility Reporting (BRR) for top 100 listed entities mandated by The Securities and Exchange Board of India (SEBI) in 2012 was extended[10] to top 500 listed entities in 2015.

Department of Public Enterprises issued "Guidelines on Corporate Social Responsibility for Central Public Sector Enterprises" in March 2010. [**Box 4.3: CSR Guidelines for the CPSEs**].

Study Done in 2004-05

A study of selected corporate in public and private sectors, was done by the author in 2004-05. Analysis of the compiled information indicated that CSR expenditure by Tata Steel in relation to the turnover remained consistent during these years. The fact that CSR activities not only continued but also increased during the period, when national and international steel market was going through a slow down, reflects the sincerity and importance attached by the Tata Steel to CSR. On the other hand, CSR expenditure of SAIL (a CPSE) fluctuated from year to year and plant to plant. However, continuation of CSR activities during the period, when the company was incurring loss, remained a noticeable feature.

Analysis of expenditure incurred by SAIL on Public Relation (PR) activities indicated that expenditure on PR during 2001-02 to 2003-04 remained around 0.04 per cent of the turnover irrespective of the profit or loss of the company in a particular year. However, during this period, expenditure on CSR remained erratic. For any corporate, PR is not only required to be continued but also stepped up suitably and sharpened to make it more effective in facing the competitors. In this context, it needs to be appreciated that with proper planning and implementation, CSR interventions can augment social capital for the corporate considerably and generate goodwill in the market, which will be in fact sustainable on a long term, yielding better results than PR exercise, which is essentially a short term measure.

Box 4.3: Guidelines on CSR activities of the Central PSUs

Thrust should be given wherever possible to areas related to the business of the CPSEs as a natural corollary to the business.

Investment in CSR should be project-based. Mere donations to philanthropic/charity or other organizations would not come under the category of CSR.

CSR activities should generate community goodwill, create social impact and visibility.

For every project, the time-frame and periodic milestones should be finalized at the outset.

CSR activities should also involve the suppliers in order to ensure that the supply-chain also follows the CSR principles.

CSR activities should help in building a positive image of the company in the public perception.

CSR activities may be related to United Nations Global Compact Programme on Environment.?

CSR projects may be closely linked with the principles of Sustainable Development, based on the immediate and long-term social and environmental consequences of their activities.

Every CPSE should shoulder responsibility for restoring/compensating for any ecological damage that is taking place as a result of its operations. Care may be taken to ensure that CPSEs work towards fulfilment of the National Plan goals and objectives, as well as the Millennium Development Goals adopted by our country, ensure gender sensitivity, skill enhancement, entrepreneurship development and employment generation by co-creating value with local institutions/people.

Central Public Sector Enterprises should redefine their business continuity plan to factor in hazards, risks and vulnerabilities. They should also create value in innovative social investments in the community and may focus on the areas of "Preparedness and Capacity Building" in Disaster Management (DM).

Public-Private Partnership between the Government and the Central Public Sector could also be encouraged to leverage the strengths of the latter in Disaster Management. CPSEs need to network with the Ministries in Government of India/NOMA at the National level and State Governments/ SOMAs at the State level to strengthen and formalize their role in the DM process for ensuring preparedness of the communities towards disaster resilience.

Reference: Guidelines issued by Department of Public Enterprises in March 2010.

In the first decade of the new millennium (2000-2010), number of CPSEs institutionalized CSR, adopted CSR policy and earmarked part of the profit made in the previous year for CSR activities. NALCO appeared to be the first CPSE to commit spending around one per cent of its net annual profit for peripheral development in 2001-02. ONGC took a similar decision in 2003 to allocate 0.75 per cent of the net profit on Socio-Economic Development Programmes (SEDP). However, the expenditure actually incurred by these CPSEs during 2000-01, 2001-02 and 2002-03 remained below the targeted level.

Ministry of Steel had directed all the profit making CPSEs in the steel sector to spend at least two per cent of distributable profits on CSR every year, which had an impact on improving the CSR interventions of the CPSEs under the Ministry.

Among the private sector, number of corporate like Tata Steel, Wipro, and Infosys took up CSR intervention in a planned manner with allocation of sizeable resource and focus on the result. Active involvement of the head of the corporate led CSR interventions in making an impact on the society. While a number of middle size corporate started taking interest in CSR, relatively smaller ones were yet to join. However, unlike the public sector, the private sector was usually shy of disclosing the amount spent on CSR.

Allocation and actual expenditure on CSR by selected CPSEs for the years 2011-12, 2012-13 and 2013-14 are given in Table 4.1. Analysis of these figures indicated that allocation of resource for CSR as a percentage of profit of the previous year(s) varies from 0.5 per cent in case of NTPC, BHEL up to 2 per cent in case of ONGC [**Table 4.1: Fund allocated and spent on CSR activities by the CPSEs during 2011-14**]. During these years, expenditure in case of NTPC increased from 0.5 per cent to 1 per cent; whereas in case of BHEL, it increased from 0.5 per cent to 1.2 per cent. However, the amount earmarked for CSR could not be spent in full by several of the corporations.

It appeared that out of the 16 *Navratna* PSUs, four viz. BHEL, GAIL, Hindustan Petroleum and RINL could not utilize the amount allocated for CSR fully. Five other *Navratna* PSUs, *viz*. Bharat Petroleum, National Aluminium Company, Oil India, PFC and Rural Electrification Corporation reported to have utilized the funds fully. Remaining six *Navratnas*—Bharat Electronics Ltd., Hindustan Aeronautics, NMDC, Neyveli Lignite Corp., Power Grid and Shipping Corporation exceeded the limit of allocated amount, except MTNL which was making loss and hence not mandated to earmark funds for CSR activities.

Table 4.1: Fund Allocated and Spent on CSR Activities by the CPSEs during 2011-14

Name of CPSE	*2011-12*		*2012-13*		*2013-14*	
	CSR Fund Allocated	*CSR Spent*	*CSR Fund Allocated*	*CSR Spent*	*CSR Fund Allocated*	*CSR Spent$*
ONGC (in Crore Rs)	378.48	121.08	502.46	262.13	418.52	143.50*
As %age of PAT (in %)	2	1.31	2.00	0.64	2.00	
SAIL Rs/Crore	64.00	61.25	42.00	53.29	40.00	23.15#
As %age of PAT	1.3	1.25	1.19	1.5	1.84	
IOCL Rs/Crore	95.60	82.73	100.89	78.97	64.88	25.61*
As %age of PAT	1.28	1.11	2.55	2	1.3	
NTPC Rs/Crore	45.51	49.44	56.37	79.42	98.94	67.10*
As %age of PAT	0.5	0.54	0.61	0.86	1.00	
CIL Rs/Crore	43.14	2.59	22.47	31.15	66.17	108.26*
As %age of PAT	1.92%	0.12	1.33	1.85	1.45	
GAIL Rs/Crore	71.22	61.98	73.08	61.63	80.44	40.00*
As %age of PAT	2	1.74	2	1.69	2	
BHEL Rs/Crore	30.05	4.87	35.20	63.11	79.38	70.26*
As %age of PAT	0.5	0.08	0.5	0.89	1.2	

Source: Department of Public Enterprises, $ Up to Sept'13#/Dec'13*.

Department of Public Enterprises included CSR as one of the parameters in the MoU, executed by PSUs with the government, for assessing performance during a year. This marked a positive development in institutionalizing CSR of the PSEs. Further, some of the administrative ministries, like the Ministry of Steel, had issued specific directives reiterating commitment to social issues.

Prior to 2014, several private corporate took up CSR and some adopted CSR policy. However, unlike the public sector, private sector was generally shy of divulging financial details on expenditure incurred on CSR. The nature and extent of welfare activities undertaken by the private corporate generally increased in good times, when the company was making profit. According to a study[11] the donation made by the Indian corporate for philanthropic purposes increased by about 30 per cent from Rs. 314 crores in 2006 to Rs. 411 crores in 2007.

In course of interview[12] conducted in 2004-05 before CSR became mandatory, persons holding responsible positions in the CPSEs had expressed concern that in case CSR provision get quantified and linked up with profit, there would be unwanted pressure on the management for spending the money earmarked. There were apprehensions that such measures would get manipulated and misused by rent seeking persons, which would bring bad name to the corporate as well as CSR. It will amount to putting good money for bad use. As CSR primarily related to social issues, there was a feeling that it should remain voluntary and not be linked with profits of the previous year. They expressed the need for evolving Standard Operating Procedure (SOP) for ensuring that the fund earmarked for CSR is spent in a meaningful manner and avoiding any sort of wastage or misuse, covering proper coordination with ongoing government programmes with the same objective, avoiding duplication, bridging gaps on last mile connectivity basis, proper delegation and involvement of the local community and the beneficiaries.

CSR under Statutory Provision (1st April, 2014 onwards)

Discharging responsibility towards the society and other stakeholders is integral to functioning and success of any business enterprise. The extent and nature of discharging this responsibility keep on changing based on various economic, social and political developments. As it relates to the society, there cannot be any standard prescription, which will apply to all across countries. It is necessary to keep the approach flexible for meeting the changing needs of the society.

Background of making CSR Mandatory

The Constitution of India seeks to secure to all its citizens; Justice, social, economic, political; Liberty of thought, expression, belief, faith and worship; Equality of status and opportunity; and to promote among them all; Fraternity, assuring the dignity of the individual and the unity and integrity of the nation.

With a view to address the wide gap in social and economic status, special provisions have been made for the disadvantaged segments through affirmative action (positive discrimination) by way of reservation for Scheduled Castes (SCs) and Scheduled Tribes (STs) in employment under government in the Constitution of India. This was later extended to admission in educational institutions managed by government. Subsequently, these measures were extended to include the Other Backward Classes (OBCs) as well. These measures have come under judicial scrutiny and Hon'ble Supreme Court has issued reasoned directions with qualitative exclusion—relating to creamy layer, and quantitative restrictions—that overall reservation should not exceed fifty per cent.

Reservation in government employment was guided by provision under Article 16(4) of the Constitution of India. In due course, this extended to the Public Sector Enterprises, which have been raised with public money and managed by the government. The private corporate was also pursued for providing reservation. However, private corporate did not agree to this on the ground that said provisions do not apply to private organization. Inclusive development and taking care of the disadvantaged segments have been an important issue and area of concern. CSR was considered as a medium for mobilising corporate support for welfare of the disadvantaged segment, like a safety valve for easing out the public pressure, which is of critical importance in a Democracy.

In the Indian context, number of old corporate like Tata, Birla as well as new corporate like Infosys, Wipro, etc. have taken up CSR with all seriousness with active involvement of the founder/top management. However, there was a debate as to if CSR should be kept voluntary or made mandatory.

The New Legislation

After considerable debate, CSR was made mandatory with effect from the 1st April, 2014 by an amendment to the Companies Act, 2013 and insertion of a specific **legal provision under Section 135** for the first time making CSR mandatory for the relatively bigger profit making companies.

Criteria for the companies, which come under purview of this legal provision, has been laid down under Sub-Section (1) of Section 135 as those which have:

- Net worth of Rs. 500 crore or more, or
- Turnover of Rs. 1,000 crore or more, or
- Net Profit of Rs. 5 crore or more during any financial year.

The statutory liabilities of the companies, which become liable under the above, fall under four broad heads, *viz.*

(i) Constitution of a **board level CSR committee** consisting of three or more directors, out of which at least one director shall be an independent director [under Sub-Section (1) of Section 135].

(ii) **Obligation of the CSR committee**—To formulate and recommend a **CSR policy** indicating the activities to be undertaken by the company.

Activities, which can be **undertaken under these provisions,** are specified in the **Schedule-VII** of the Act. The Schedule-VII was first notified on the 27th February, 2014 and amended subsequently from time to time. The updated Schedule is given at the Appendix 4.2.

(iii) **Expenditure of at least two per cent** of the average net profit of the company during the three immediately preceding financial years, on these activities in pursuance of the CSR policy. [Under Sub-Section (5) of Section 135]

The committee shall recommend the amount of expenditure to be incurred on activities and monitor implementation of the CSR policy. [under Sub-Section (3), Clause (b) and (c) of Section 135]

(iv) **Disclosure and reporting on CSR activities**—Disclosing constitution and composition of the CSR committee, activities undertaken during a year in the annual report, **along with reasons** in case the stipulated amount of **two per cent of the average net profit could not be spent** in a particular year. [under the second proviso of Sub-Section (5) of Section 135].

The Companies' (CSR) Policy Rules, 2014 were notified on the 27th February, 2014, which gives details of the modalities for implementation of the above provision.

Penalty for Failure in Compliance

Each and every company, coming under purview of the aforesaid legal provision, is liable for failure to set up CSR committee and/or formulation of CSR policy etc. as per the general provisions guiding violation of any provisions of the Companies Act.

So far as failure to spend the prescribed amount, i.e. two per cent of the average profit of the preceding three years, is concerned, the legal requirement relates to reporting the expenditure incurred along with reasons in the event of failure to spend the prescribed amount. There is no penalty for not spending the prescribed amount. However, **failures for reporting the reasons, make the company liable to penalty** under Section 134(8) of the Act. The company, which fails to give the reason in its Annual Report, shall be *"punishable with a fine which shall not be less than fifty thousand rupees but which may extend up to twenty five lakh rupees. Further, every officer of the company, who is in default, shall be punishable with imprisonment for a term which may extend up to three years or with fine which shall not be less than fifty thousand rupees but which may extend up to five lakh rupees or with both"*.

Omissions, which are not clearly specified, will come under the Section 450, read with Section 451, which provides for residual provision. Under Section 450, this fine may extend up to ten thousand rupees, and where the contravention is a continuing one, a further fine to one thousand rupees for every day after the first during which contravention continues is imposed.

A high level committee (HLC) was constituted in February 2015 for looking into implementation of the legal provision. Some of the recommendations made by the HLC have been taken into account for modifying the Schedule and provisions the Rules for implementation of the legal provision.

The government has clarified various issues relating to implementation of the legal provision in the Circular dated the 18th June, 2014.

Provisions of Section 135 of the Companies Act; the Schedule-VII indicating the list of activities, which are permissible under CSR; the

Rules giving the procedural aspects of implementation; and clarification issued by the Ministry of Corporate Affairs on this legal provision are given as **Appendix 4.1, 4.2, 4.3 and 4.4** respectively.

The intention behind the aforesaid legal provision appears to have been guided by the consideration to *persuade and encourage the corporate rather than forcing them to support social issues*. The legal provision on expenditure on CSR has been linked with the average profit made in the last three years; thereby *exempting the loss making companies*. Earmarking two-per cent of the profit for CSR activities similarly appeared to have been made based on the existing practices in a number of Governments managed Central Public Sector Enterprises.

In implementation of CSR, the concerned **company has been given the full freedom for choosing and designing the projects and implementing it**. For ensuring optimum utilization, it has made mandatory for such companies to have an exclusive arrangement with a *board level CSR committee*, with at least one independent director. Further, for long term impact, it has been made mandatory for such companies to formulate a *policy on CSR*. The company has been given the option either to take up projects in the peripheral areas of its units establishment, where the people are affected by activities of the company or in other areas within the country. The companies are required to prepare projects indicating the linkages for making the interventions sustainable and meaningful.

The **control on implementation of CSR has been kept indirect** by making it mandatory for each company to disclose details of the CSR activities during the year in the annual report indicating the list of projects taken up and the amount spent. On the expenditure of two per cent of the profit, the *requirement has been kept mainly for disclosing the actual amount spent* and in case it is *less than the prescribed limit of two per cent to indicate the reason* for which the amount could not be spent. This legal provision and approach is aligned with the spirit of democracy and the Constitution for disclosing details so that the stakeholders comprising of the investors, workers, consumers and the society at large are aware of the importance given by the company to CSR and the activities undertaken. The **underlying, principle envisages that it is for the consumer and the market to appreciate the CSR interventions of a particular company**. This will in turn guide consumer behaviour and determine the brand value and image of the company at the market place.

Accordingly, the penalty has been kept only for failure to disclose details. As a result, in case a company fails to spend the two per cent earmarked amount, it is not taken to have violated the provision, provided it makes details available to the public about its CSR activities and the reasons for which it has not been able to spend the prescribed amount of two per cent of profit. The punishment arises only in case of failure to disclose in time, which would make the defaulting company as well as the individual officer dealing with the subject liable for the omission.

The legal provision guiding CSR has been innovative in the sense that it seeks to encourage the companies to spend on CSR projects and disclose. Availability of this information in the annual report of the company has started coming with effect from October 2015. These details are being analysed by Government, Academic institutions and Non-governmental Organizations.

Amount Spent on CSR

While processing the amendment to the Companies Act for making CSR mandatory, IICA had assessed that out of about 11,00,000 registered Corporate in the country, about 16,000 will come under purview of the CSR provision. As 2 per cent of the net profit, about Rs. 20,000 crores will be available for CSR activities annually.

Analysis of the information on CSR disclosed by the companies by the Ministry of Corporate Affairs[13], administrative Ministry dealing with the subject, indicates that during the year 2014-15, the first year after CSR was made mandatory, Rs. 6,337 crores was spent on CSR by 460 companies including 51 Public Sector Undertakings (PSUs) (Rs. 2,386.6 crores) and 409 Private sector corporate (Rs. 3,950.76 crores). As per a subsequent compilation[14], covering 142 PSUs and 2,997 Private Sector Companies, expenditure on CSR was found to be Rs. 8,803 crores, details of which is given in Table 4.2.

As per another compilation[15] for the Central Public Sector Enterprises (CPSEs), 120 CPSEs spent Rs. 2,450.31 crores on CSR during the year 2014-15. ONGC topped the list with an expenditure of Rs. 495.24 crores, followed by NTPC (Rs. 205.5 crores) and NMDC (Rs. 188.6 crores).

During the year 2015-16, CSR expenditure of CPSEs increased substantially to Rs. 4,100.93 crores for 106 companies, including the highest by ONGC (Rs. 421 crore), followed by South-Eastern Coal Field (Rs. 270.85 crore) and Rural Electrical Corporation (Rs. 256 crore).

Table 4.2: CSR Expenditure during 2014-15

Sl. No.	Company Type	Total Companies	No. of Companies with CSR Expenditure	No. of Companies with no CSR Expenditure	Actual CSR Expenditure (in Rs. Crore) (2014-15)
1.	PSUs	226	142	84	2,497
2.	Private Sector Companies	7,108	2,997	4,111	6,306
	Total	**7,334**	**3,139**	**4,195**	**8,803**

Source: Reply in Lok Sabha on the 9th December, 2016.

As per an elaborate recent compilation*, 5,097 companies spent Rs. 9,822 crore on their CSR intervention during 2015-16. Analysis of the State/Union Territory-wise projects undertaken depicted a skewed pattern, with majority of these projects implemented in the economically and industrially advanced states, *viz.* Maharashtra (1,138), Karnataka (408), Gujarat (338) and Andhra Pradesh (379). Uttar Pradesh had only 322 projects and no project taken up in the North-Eastern States and Union Territories.

The Companies Act was amended in 2013 making CSR mandatory for the corporate with a view to mobilise corporate support, to the extent of two per cent of the average profit of the last three years. Using available infrastructure, corporate voluntarism of the executives for supplementing the government efforts for undertaking various social sector activities in health, education, skill development livelihood activities will make the interventions more effective. With a view to make the development inclusive, it is necessary that the relatively backward region/states of the country get higher attention and more resources to bridge the gap and expedite the development at par with the advanced region. However, from the expenditure pattern of CSR, indicated above, the position appears to be otherwise.

Under the Companies Act, the corporate have full discretion in selection of projects, in terms of activities and geographical area; only requirement being to follow the list of activities indicated in Schedule-VII. Under normal circumstances, the corporate will like to undertake projects near their area of activities, where they are more comfortable, as has happened in the case indicated above with CSR projects getting concentrated in the industrialised states of the country. The possible way

* "State-specific CSR", *The Hindu*, June 09, 2017.

to overcome **this would require the State Government of the less developed states becoming proactive, for supporting and encouraging the corporate to implement projects in their states** as well for supplementing the ongoing developmental activities with deployment of financial and managerial resources of the corporate under CSR.

This would help in overcoming the distortion indicated above and removal of regional disparities.

With a view to recognise and encourage the Corporate to put in their best for CSR, achievements are being discussed and awards conferred for exemplary CSR interventions from time to time. Association of corporate and civil society organisations have joined the Government in this effort. Such events were organised by *NGO Box* in 2014 and subsequently on the 7th and 8th October, 2015 in Bangalore. All the stakeholders *viz.* business, government and civil society organizations were brought together for sharing experience and best practices in CSR.

Study on CSR

CII-ITC Centre of Excellence

Analysis[16] of disclosures made by 1,181 BSE-listed companies shows that Rs. 6,400 crore was spent for CSR activities during 2014-15. Out of the total amount, about 55 per cent was spent on projects for promotion of education, skills, livelihoods, health and sanitation and only two per cent contributed to Prime Minister's relief fund. Maharashtra and Gujarat had got the largest chunk of the CSR fund. 97 per cent of the companies analyzed had board-level CSR committee and 94 per cent had a CSR policy. 87 per cent of the companies have spent on CSR activities, however 52 per cent shelled out less than the two per cent requirement. Being the first year, time taken in understanding *a fairly complex piece of legislation*, projects spreading over multiple years, not finding the right projects or implementing agencies were stated as some of the reasons for under-spending.

NGO Box[17]

Analysis of disclosure made by 100 Companies listed in the Bombay Stock Exchange (BSE) indicated that 27 per cent companies spent more than the prescribed 2 per cent of their profit on CSR, 9 per cent spent amount as required, 64 per cent less than the prescribed amount and

2 per cent did not spend any amount on CSR. VIP Industries emerged as the best performer by spending more than the double of prescribed CSR spend (210%), followed by Tech Mahindra Ltd. (172%) and UPL Ltd. (153%).

So far as the bank and financial companies are concerned, commitment to CSR was somewhat lukewarm, as only one company managed to spend the prescribed CSR spend among 17 banking and Finance sector companies and about 50 per cent of the companies could not spend even half of the prescribed CSR spend.

KPMG (2015)

A survey[18] of Corporate Responsibility (CR) Reporting by 4500 companies across 45 countries done by KPMG in 2015 placed India as the leading country in terms of reporting Corporate Responsibility. The key findings of the survey indicated that, *inter alia*, India has the highest CR reporting rates with a 27 percentage point increase between 2013 and 2015. This rise in reporting appears to be primarily driven by the reporting requirements under the law from April 2014.

Techno Park (2015)

CSR Policy

Having a policy on CSR is a mandatory requirement under the Companies Act w.e.f. the 1st April, 2014. A study[19] of 238 companies indicated that only 32 per cent companies had CSR Policy in 2010-11, which increased to 46 per cent in 2012-13, to 72 per cent in 2013-14 and 93 per cent in 2014-15 leaving only 16 companies to frame a CSR policy.

CSR Committee

In respect of having a board level CSR committee, it appeared that only 5 per cent companies had constituted a CSR Committee in 2010-11, which improved marginally to 14 per cent in 2012-13 to 64 per cent companies in 2013-14. Making it mandatory increased compliance level to 89 per cent of the companies having CSR committee in 2014-15. The comparative position is given in the Table 4.3.

Table 4.3: Adoption of CSR Policy and CSR Committee during 2010-11 to 2014-15

YEAR	*2010-11*	*2011-12*	*2012-13*	*2013-14*	*2014-15*
Number of companies	238	238	238	238	238
CSR Policy framed	78 (32%)	82 (34%)	110 (46%)	172 (72%)	222 (93%)
CSR Committee formed	12 (5%)	14 (6%)	35 (14%)	153 (64%)	214 (89%)

Table 4.4: CSR Spending of Companies, with Profit After Tax Higher than Rs. 5 Crore Per Annum, during 2010-11 to 2014-15

(Amount in Crores Rs.)

	2010-11	*2011-12*	*2012-13*	*2013-14*	*2014-15*
Number of companies	10	15	74	85	208
Combined Profit after tax (PAT)	25,364	50,670	2,20,140	2,50,933	3,20,601
CSR Expenditure on CSR	277	530	2,451	3,661	5,029
Exp. on CSR as part of PAT (in %age)	1.10%	1.05%	1.11%	1.46%	1.68%

Trend of CSR expenditure, given in Table 4.4, showed that companies having profit after tax higher than 5 Crores during 2010-11 to 2014-15, average expenditure on CSR during 2010-11 was 1.10 per cent of profit after tax, which improved to 1.68 per cent in 2014-15.

IICA (2015)

Another survey of 1000 Companies was done by the Indian Institute of Corporate Affairs (IICA). Out of these, details of CSR activities were not disclosed on the website by 569 companies. However, some companies took up CSR activities, notwithstanding incurring loss during the preceding year.

During 2014-15, Rs. 6107 Crores (75%) was spent on CSR against Rs. 8,130 crores to be spent, as two per cent of the profit. This was estimated to increase by 8.14 per cent to about Rs. 8,792 crores during 2015-16.

Out of the 431 Corporate studied, 23 per cent (101 Cos.) spent more than 2 per cent of net profit, 18 per cent (78 Cos.) equal to 2 per cent on CSR. Out of the remaining 7 per cent (30 Cos.) did not incur any expenditure, 21 per cent (91 Cos.) up to 33 per cent of the prescribed amount, 16 per cent (68 Cos.) 33 per cent to 66 per cent of the prescribed amount and 15 per cent (63 Cos.) 66 per cent to 99 per cent of the prescribed amount.

Reliance Industries Limited topped the list with a reported expenditure of Rs. 763 Crore on CSR, which was higher than Rs. 533 crore as two per cent of profit. ONGC figured second with an expenditure of Rs. 495 crore, which was less than the mandated amount of Rs. 660 crore. Infosys Limited ranked third with an expenditure of Rs. 240 crore against marginally less than the mandated Rs. 243 crore followed by Tata Consultancy Services Limited spending Rs. 219 crore (against mandated Rs. 285 crore). Remaining included ITC Limited spending Rs. 214 crore (against mandated Rs. 213 crore), NTPS Rs. 205 crore (against mandated Rs. 283 crore), NMDC spending Rs. 189 Crore (prescribed Rs. 210 Crore), Tata Steel Rs. 171 Crore (prescribed Rs. 168 crore), Oil India Rs. 133 crore (prescribed Rs. 98 crore) and Wipro Rs. 133 Crore (prescribed Rs. 128 crore).

CSRY (2015)

Study of 50 PSUs and 381 private Corporate, indicated that expenditure of private companies remained 78 per cent (Rs. 3,784 crores against Rs. 4,850 crore prescribed), higher than the public sector companies 70.85 per cent (Rs. 2,324 crores against Rs. 3,280 crore prescribed).

Analysis of modalities for execution of CSR projects indicated that 28 per cent projects were implemented directly by the Company, 5 per cent by foundation, trusts managed by the Company, and 6 per cent by other NGOs, 29 per cent was done jointly by the Company and NGOs, 25 per cent by Company, its own foundation and NGOs and 7 per cent by own foundation and NGOs.

Analysis of the activities selected for utilization of CSR amount indicated that majority of 357 (82.8%) companies implemented projects on health, poverty, malnutrition, etc., 385 (89.3%) on education, differently abled, livelihood related, 209 (48.4%) environment, animal welfare related, and 123 (28.5%) Rural development projects.

Expenditure on health took the largest share (24%) of available CSR fund, followed by education (21%), environment (20%), rural development (12%), and skill development (4%).

Analysis of the geographical area in which CSR projects were implemented indicated that CSR projects were implemented in the industrially prosperous western states, namely Maharashtra, Gujarat,

Tamil Nadu, Karnataka and Rajasthan. Share of CSR projects in the North Eastern region was few and far between.

Analysis of the reasons for inability to spend the prescribed amount indicated that majority (28%) attributed failure due to first year of implementation, followed by non-availability of suitable NGO.

NextGen

Analysis of reported data for top 100 companies, listed on the National Stock Exchange by NextGen, a Bengaluru-based CSR management company indicated[20] the following:

- CSR spending of 33 firms rose by 22 per cent over the previous year to Rs. 2,167 crore in fiscal year 2016.
- Companies partnered with more than 150 non-governmental organizations (NGOs) across 450 projects during the year for implementation of CSR projects.
- Tata Consultancy Services Ltd. (TCS) topped the list with an expenditure of Rs. 294 crore, followed by ITC Ltd. and Infosys Ltd.

FICCI (March 2016)

A survey[21] of CSR activities of selected companies by FICCI gave the following findings:

- 79 per cent of the companies have constituted board level CSR committee with independent director.
- Ethical consideration is the prime motivation for CSR activities. There is an increasing trend for integrating business with the community to create shared value; with 49 per cent companies stating shared value as the motivation factor followed by social compliance.
- Promoting education, special education and vocational skill is the major activity under CSR (21%) followed by reduction of hunger, poverty, malnutrition, promoting healthcare, sanitation and safe drinking water, ensuring environmental sustainability and rural development projects.
- Majority of the companies (95%) have aligned their CSR activities with major flagship government initiatives namely

Swachchh Bharat Mission, *Skill India* and *National Health Mission*.

- Majority of the companies (40%) implement the projects through company owned foundation with focus on involvement of the local community in implementation of the project.
- Project for welfare of children was the most preferred activity (31%), followed by women (22%), disabled (10%), senior citizens (8%), sportsmen (6%), war veterans (4%) and transgender (3%).
- Budget provision for CSR during 2014-15 increased over the previous year by majority (77%), companies, of which 5 per cent made provision for the first time. There was no change for 6 per cent and decline for remaining 12 per cent.
- 83 per cent anticipated increase in CSR expenditure in the coming years, 9 per cent indicating no change and 6 per cent anticipating decline.
- 54 per cent of the companies got their CSR activities audited by the third party and majority of them intend to use the outcome in implementation of CSR projects in future.

The Economic Times (2016)[22]

CSR intervention of 217 companies was analyzed in an unbiased, quantitative and analytical manner by *The Economic Times* in partnership between IIM, Udaipur, *Futurescape*. Some of the major findings of the survey are as follows:

- Out of the 217 companies whose CSR activities in 2014-15 were studied, data was available only for 173 firms. Their CSR expenditure came to Rs. 5,752 crore i.e. on average Rs. 33.25 crore per company. This worked out to 1.4 per cent of average PAT, lower than 2 per cent required under the statute.
- Education and healthcare activities got largest share 21 per cent and 24 per cent respectively both making 45 per cent of the total CSR spends. However, Empowerment of women, support for senior citizens and armed forces veterans were not opted by any.
- Government emphasis on *Swachchh Bharat* gave a push to sanitation with 39 per cent of companies opting for it. Besides,

59 per cent of the companies surveyed took up promotion of solar energy.

- Only the top 33 per cent firms appeared to have taken a long-term view on responsible business and Sustainability is at the heart of high performing companies.
- Governance for business responsibility sees improvement with more than 54 per cent companies having scored more than half the marks as compared with 47 per cent in the previous year.
- Disclosure on sustainability reporting however remained inadequate. Further, Emissions disclosure needs more focus. Only 36 per cent of India's top 200 companies disclosed data on GHG emissions against 38 per cent in the previous year, while 54 per cent participated in carbon specific initiatives such as Carbon Disclosure Project (CDP).

KPMG

Survey[23] of top hundred companies by revenue in 49 countries indicated that the companies are under increasing pressure from the investors to disclose their CSR activities. Corporate action for linking United Nation's Sustainable Development Goals (SDGs) with CSR activities has been increasing in India, even though it has been lower than the global average of over a third of the corporate doing this. Indian companies have however shown higher commitment to human rights in their business as compared to the global average. Commitment to checking carbon emission has been increasing from 58 per cent in 2015 to 67 per cent in 2017.

Analysis of CSR Activities

CSR activities of selected Indian corporate, both in the public and private sectors, were studied[24] during 2004-05 with particular reference to the steel industry. This was done based on issues typical to steelmaking like requirement of vast stretch of land, related displacement and resettlement of persons etc. make CSR more relevant for such corporate. CSR interventions of mega steel corporate, namely Tata Steel (in the private sector) and Steel Authority of India Limited (SAIL), Rashtriya Ispat Nigam Limited (RINL) (in the public sector) were studied along with a few other corporate. Relevant information for the years 2001-02 to 2003-04 was collected in a framed questionnaire and analyzed along with study of available literature, views of persons living in the peripheral areas as well as executives dealing with CSR related issues in the corporate. Findings of the study were later updated based on the Annual Report, statement of the Chairman in the Annual General Meeting and other available information during 2014 to 2017, which saw transition of CSR from voluntary to mandatory with effect from the 1st April, 2014. **Salient features of CSR activities of the Corporate studied are given as Appendices**. Salient features of CSR activities of these corporate in the Indian scenario are given below.

Public Sector Enterprises

Oil

Bharat Petroleum Corporation Limited (BPCL) dealing with petroleum products initiated CSR interventions in 1984 in pursuance of its philosophy "to give back to the society/community our best", with a view to help the people enrich their lives, be it employees or their families or villagers living in peripheral areas. Starting with helping inhabitants of Mahul village near its Mumbai refinery in 1986, a range of activities covering education, health and other support were taken up through NGOs. Further, counselling in HIV and AIDS care, environmental conservation measures by setting up green fuel terminal and station, developing renewable energy sources, R&D on bio-fuel including ethanol and promoting better corporate governance were taken up. Under Livelihood component titled "Economic Empowerment and Income Generation", BPCL assisted 600 rural women in earning their livelihood with the skill of *Chikankari* art work near its LPG Bottling Plant in Lucknow, for which it got the *Aaj Tak CSR Award* June 2012.[25]

Hindustan Petroleum Corporation Limited (HPCL) started its CSR initiative in 1984, with emphasis on primary education, healthcare, drinking water, vocational training, development of infrastructure in rural areas, adoption of villages and assistance to the physically challenged. It adopted villages in the peripheral areas of its refinery and took up rehabilitation of shifting cultivators belonging to Scheduled Tribes with provision of education, health and irrigation facilities. Family members of martyrs of Kargil were provided LPG dealership. CSR projects of HPCL like *Bal Haq*, *Muskan*, *Unnati*, *Nanhi Kali*, *Akshaya Patra*, *Swavalamban*, *Jal Tarang*, *Rasoi Ghar* etc. have been appreciated.[26]

Oil and Natural Gas Corporation Limited (ONGC) adopted Socio-Economic Development Policy (SEDP) in 2001-02, which envisaged allocation of 0.75 per cent of net profit of the previous year for SEDP activities. Under this, the corporate supported education, healthcare, entrepreneurship development, water management and disaster relief. '*Project Saraswati*' and *ONGC Pura* are claimed to be its landmark CSR initiatives. Over the years, ONGC expanded its CSR activities with inclusion of Community development programme, Global Compact programme in collaboration with United Nations along with programmes for Environment Protection and Safety.

Indian Oil Corporation Limited (IOCL) took up CSR initiatives under "Looking beyond Profit" reiterating its commitment to conservation of energy, reduction of carbon emission, commercializing bio-fuels, adoption of other clean development mechanism as well as "to engage with community in the neighbourhood of its location in synergistic business activities that create livelihood for money and raise standard of living". Its first sustainability Report, published in 2005-06, gave an account of its economic, social and environmental initiatives based on the "*Triple Bottom Line*" approach. The earmarked fund was sub-allocated (5%) for donation/contribution. 30 per cent on scholarship earmarking 50 per cent for weaker section, 30 per cent on community development and 35 per cent for natural calamities or any other national cause.

Gas Authority of India Limited (GAIL) set high standards of discharging social responsibilities by earmarking one per cent of PAT of the previous year for CSR. Its CSR interventions covered a range of activities such as setting up of Air Pollution Research and Disease Diagnostic Centre (APRDDC), mobile health clinics in the deep interiors of rural areas, empowering village women with vocational training, construction of check and stop dams, adopting villages, distribution of insecticides to control diseases, installation of waste bins in prominent public places, promoting plastic waste modified bitumen for road carpeting, health camps, legal awareness, adult education and award of scholarships to underprivileged children. Fund for CSR was later stepped up to 2 per cent of PAT of previous year to be spent on Healthcare (15%), Environment protection (5%), Community Development (28%), Water/sanitation (4%), Education (10%), Skill development (9%) and Infrastructure (29%).[27]

Power

National Thermal Power Corporation Limited (NTPC) initiated CSR as an "article of faith" and set-up NTPC foundation for undertaking CSR initiatives with the vision "to serve and empower the physically challenged and economically weaker sections of the society". Under its CSR intervention, steps were taken to improve the socio-economic status of the project affected persons in the peripheral area. Besides, it took up provision of power to inaccessible and remote villages in backward areas and imparting IT skills to disabled in partnership with the Delhi University.

Steel

Steel Authority of India Limited (SAIL) decided to earmark one per cent of its profit of the previous year for CSR activities. SAIL had earmarked Rs.100 crores on CSR for discharging its responsibility towards the society in 2007-08. However, this amount decreased to Rs. 64 crores in 2011-12 on account of poor utilization of fund.[28] It took up provision of healthcare, education as well as management of solid wastes and conservation of environment on sustainable basis around its plants and units.

Private Sector

Steel

Among the private sector, Tata group of industries continued its tradition of taking care of the community along with business. Tata Steel adopted a CSR policy on the 1st February, 2003. "*Putting principles taught by him* (JRD Tata in 1969) *into practice*" was reiterated, as stated in its annual report for 2003-04. Achievements under the Corporate Sustainability Initiative are covered in the Annual Report before financial parameters like turnover, profit, return etc., which indicates the commitment of Tata Steel to CSR, continuing the legacy of philanthropic activities initiated by its founder, Jamshetji. On the eve of completing 100 years of steel production in the country, commitment to CSR is reflected in the observations of Ratan Tata *"the (Tata) Group held a view and a sense of purpose that our companies are not in existence just to run our business and to make profit and that we are responsible and as good corporate citizens over and above our normal operations... we shoulder community responsibility as part of social responsibility of our nation. And, these responsibilities are not to be confused with employee welfare, (because) they go beyond our own employees and in fact concentrate on contribution to the community and to the nation".*

Fast Moving Consumer Goods (FMCGs)

ITC Limited, dealing with FMCG adopted CSR as a strategic intervention and dealt it in its Annual Report at a greater length than its commercial activities. Its approach "*Redefining Corporate Contribution—ITC in pursuit of the triple bottom line*" reflected a paradigm shift in the importance attached by the company to CSR. This trend continued over years. CSR interventions of the company have been covered so extensively in the chairman's address in the Annual General Body meetings that *mention about turnover and profit looked somewhat mundane*. Its E-choupal intervention for empowering the villagers with Information Technology was referred to in the Budget Speech for 2006-07 by the Union Finance Minister, which appeared to be an interesting development of government recognizing activities of the corporate having social impact.

Software

Infosys Technologies Ltd. set up Infosys Foundation in December 1996 with the objective of fulfilling its social responsibility by supporting and encouraging the underprivileged sections of society. The Foundation undertook social activities such as providing medical facilities in remote rural areas, organizing novel pension schemes, aiding orphans and street children, reconstruction of old school buildings, setting up of rural science centres, supporting dying traditional art and culture forms. Under its rural education programme titled "*A library for every school*", 5,500 libraries were set up in government schools in rural areas.

Another software giant, Wipro, set up Azim Premji Foundation with a personal grant of Rs. 400 crores from the promoter, Aziz Premji. He contributed nearly Rs. 9,000 crore for promoting education, which made him the first Indian to dedicate a majority of his wealth for philanthropy.[29]

ICICI Bank set up ICICI Foundation in 2007 and decided to contribute one per cent of the bank's profits to the corpus every year.

Associations of Corporate

Associations of corporate like Confederation of Indian Industry (CII),

Federation of Indian Chambers of Commerce and Industry (FICCI) also took up promoting CSR with help of their member corporate. The interventions covered three broad areas: (i) sensitizing the member corporate to the social needs; (ii) implementing social welfare projects by pooling resources of the member corporate; and (iii) recognizing innovative initiatives/performers with awards.

CII set up the Social Development Council in 1995 with a view to ensure that the benefits and opportunities emerging out of the industrial growth are made available to all. It pursued its member corporate for undertaking social welfare activities relating to promotion of health, women empowerment, education and literacy, control of HIV/AIDS, community development, empowerment of disadvantaged youth, disabled etc. In collaboration with UNDP, CII launched India Partnership Forum (IPF) in February 2001 and provided a platform to facilitate dialogue on the role and responsibilities of business in development and to bring the business, civil society organizations and government together.

FICCI set up FICCI Socio-Economic Development Foundation (FICCI-SEDF), as a not-for-profit body in December, 1995. SEDF is providing an institutionalized arrangement and extends guidance and assistance to the member corporate for implementation of welfare projects under CSR. FICCI-SEDF along with *Business World* and *Compaq* instituted "Social Responsiveness Award" in 1999 to promote the concept of business with conscience.

ASSOCHAM set up a foundation and mobilized efforts of its member corporate for social activities.

An account of the steps taken by these associations for promotion of CSR is given in the Annexure.

Standing Conference of Public Enterprises (SCOPE), an apex organization representing the Central Government Public Enterprises, some State Enterprises, banks and other institutions also pursued promotion of CSR. It had instituted[30] "SCOPE Meritorious Award" and organized workshop, Seminar, Conference to create awareness in capacity building on CSR.

Government Initiatives for Promoting CSR

Government also took initiatives for institutionalising mobilization of corporate support for social purpose. The National Culture Fund set up by the Ministry of Culture in 1997, marked the beginning of such effort for mobilisation of corporate support for preservation of ancient monuments and promotion of culture. Later in 1998, the Ministry of Youth Affairs and Sports set up the National Sports Development Fund with similar objective of mobilizing corporate support for promotion of sports. Ministry of Health and Family Welfare set up Jana Sankhya Sthirata Kosh for mobilization of corporate support for socially relevant purposes like population stabilization.

Financial incentives in form of exemption or reimbursement of Income Tax/Central Excise Duties were also provided for encouraging corporate çontribution to these funds. The Ministry of Health and Family Welfare took steps for encouraging corporate support for control of HIV and AIDS. However, outcome of such efforts for mobilization of corporate sector support were barely visible and remained somewhat limited.

Civil Society/Non-Governmental Organizations (NGOs) Promoting CSR

The civil society organizations and NGOs came forward to utilize CSR fund. They networked with corporate for implementation of social welfare projects with financial support from the corporate. Further, NGOs organised seminars, discussions and given awards in recognition of good work for promoting CSR from time to time.

The Child In Need in India (CINI), Kolkata, an NGO dealing with child welfare, organized seminar on CSR in collaboration with the Indian Institute of Management, Kolkata. The Smile Foundation, a charitable trust, promoted by a group of young professionals from corporate and business sectors took up child centric welfare initiatives, with support from ASSOCHAM and Indian Institute of Foreign Trade (IIFT). Academic institutions dealing with Management studies like the India Institute of Management (IIM) included CSR as a topic in their curriculum for sensitizing the corporate leader of future, to the social issues.

Media Promoting CSR

The media houses also took upspreading of awareness on CSR. *The Financial Times* carried exclusive coverage of CSR under "Common Cause", "Corporate Citizen" giving details on innovative practices adopted by corporate having an impact on the society. *The Economic Times* covered such cases under Corporate Governance.

Analysis of CSR initiatives taken by various corporate indicates the following:

Awareness and Policy on CSR

CSR in structured form started sporadically in the eighties by a few corporate, peaked up in the nineties and got crystallized in the first decade of the new millennium.

Based on turnover, profit and other techno-economic parameters, the seven CPSUs were categorized as *Maharatnas* (Great Jewels), fourteen CPSUs as *Navratna* (Nine Jewels), and 72 CPSUs as *Mini Ratnas* (Small Jewels) in December 2013.[31] It was found that all these companies have adopted CSR policies for guiding various CSR activities.

As per available information, CSR expenditure of the *Maharatna* companies went up to Rs. 1,100 crores in the first six months of 2011 financial year.[32]

Compared with 2004-05, when the survey was last made, CSR interventions of both the public and private sectors have undergone a sea change, as is evident from the facts, that when several attempts for getting details on CSR interventions did not yield much response, to the corporate being keen for disclosing their CSR interventions in 2011-12. Coverage of CSR activities has been finding a central place in the Annual Report. Corporate, dealing with the production of steel, cement, mining etc., which requires vast stretch of land, leading to displacement and discontentment, have been keen for taking up CSR seriously for easing off the public resistance to land acquisition. On the other hand, corporate dealing with software, have been pursuing CSR vigorously as a tool for brand building and emerging as market leaders. However, while some followed the policy of watch and act, many are yet to get sensitized and look beyond their own interest to the society. On the whole, during the period 1990-2014 till it became mandatory, CSR grew which is a healthy sign, both for the business and the society.

Activities taken up under CSR

A wide range of activities varying from short term measures like giving awards in recognition of excellence to long term project for sustainable development were taken up under CSR depending on the nature, area of operation, and other issues of interest to the particular corporate. These fall under two broad categories. The first category includes corporate dealing with production of steel, cement, mining etc. require sizable land, which affect the local inhabitants adversely due to displacement, loss of occupation etc. Such corporate were under increasing pressure for taking up rehabilitation and welfare of the project-affected persons and those living in the periphery of the plants seriously. Consequently, major part of the resources available for CSR interventions of such corporate remain committed for development of the peripheral area of the plant/units and only a smaller part is spent for other purposes like relief and rehabilitation in case of natural calamity. For example, 80 per cent of the total resources earmarked for CSR activities by NALCO is spent for undertaking developmental works in areas where the company's major production facilities are located and only 20 per cent is used for undertaking developmental work in other areas as well as on provision of relief and rehabilitation to persons affected by natural calamities.

In respect of other corporate dealing with software, information technology and service sector, there is no such obligation, as their activities do not lead to any displacement and related impact on the population of its periphery. In such cases, CSR activities are decided as per its own policy and priorities assigned by the top management.

Short-Term *vs.* Long-Term

Short term measures relate to the event of any major calamity, like the super cyclone in Orissa (1999), earthquake in Gujarat (2001), Tsunami (2004), causing loss of human lives and property on a large scale. Almost all corporate came forward with help in cash and kind for provision of assistance for relief and rehabilitation the affected persons.

So far as CSR interventions on a long term basis is concerned, bulk of the initiatives relate to education, healthcare and livelihood covering the three major components of human resource development.

In course of the study, it was found that prior to 2005 CSR interventions were sporadic in nature. Project-based approach, covering all aspects and making the development inclusive and sustainable, was at initial stage. Similarly, there were no instance of corporate working with the government schemes in general and for bridging the gaps in particular.

Barring a few exceptions, general approach of the corporate in taking up CSR activities was found to be publicity oriented using it as a medium for promoting the image and brand name of the company. It was found that health and education related activities were supported on standalone basis without proper planning, required linkages and providing for maintenance of the created assets. Completion of the project taken up under CSR often took lot of time and benefits to the target group remained uncertain.

However, corporate like Infosys, Wipro, Tatas took up few CSR activities in a project based approach with clear objectives and focus on implementation for achieving the objectives.

Implementation of CSR Projects

CSR interventions were executed in either of three methods, namely (i) through society/foundation set up and managed by the corporate itself, (ii) NGOs, and (iii) as contribution to funds managed by government.

Foundation under the Management of the Corporate

Execution of CSR projects through Society or foundation set up by the corporate appeared to be the most common and most sought after route. Tata Steel set up Tata Steel Rural Development Society (TSRDS) in 1972 for implementing its CSR activities in the peripheral areas. The society was managed by a committee, with the Managing Director of the plant as the President, other officials, President of the Labour Union and academicians as members. Over years, this society acquired professionalism in implementing CSR activities, which helped in providing quality services.

In case of SAIL, the position remained a mixed one. Major works relating to construction were executed by the agency dealing with provision of civic amenities in the township area. *Mahila Samiti*, an NGO organized with women members and wife of the Managing Director as the chairperson for taking up social and cultural activities, was entrusted with running of CSR projects as well. Implementation of CSR activities through *Mahila Samiti* faced inherent constraints due to lack of required expertise/skilled manpower. In this context, setting up a Peripheral Development Institute (PDI) by the RSP unit of SAIL along with *Bharatiya Agro Industries Foundation* (BAIF), Pune, an NGO of repute, appeared to be an innovative step for institutionalising the mechanism for implementation of CSR projects.

Number of corporate in the private sector set up their own institutions like Azim Premji Foundation, Infosys Foundation for implementing CSR activities as per the policy and priorities of the corporate. These institutions worked under the direct supervision of the head of the corporate or his/her close family member. This appeared to be a preferred mechanism as it had the trust, support and active involvement of head/mentor of the corporate.

NGOs

Several NGOs came forward to utilise CSR fund in their area of activity. They found it to be attractive as the procedure followed was less cumbersome than that of the Government scheme. NGOs of credibility like Population Foundation of India, BAIF, and Children In Need in India (CINI) implemented projects with professionalism and skill. However, there are other NGOs, where the output was doubtful. Selection of the NGO, funding, monitoring etc. is done by the corporate itself based on their internal assessment and impressions, which made this relatively simple.

Government Managed Institution

The third mode of undertaking CSR activities relates to government supported mechanism like contribution to the National Culture Fund, National Sports Development Fund etc. From available information, it appeared that notwithstanding its noble intention, response of corporate for channelizing their CSR fund through government managed societies/ fund generally remained lukewarm and restricted to the Prime Minister Relief Fund particularly in the event of any natural calamity. Neither the corporate were aware of, nor the concerned Government Ministries were eager to mobilize corporate support. It appeared that the government sponsored mechanism have remained more on paper due to lack of visibility, complicated procedure; leading to lack of interest. Central Ministries have generally preferred to raising their demand for a larger share of public fund from the Ministry of Finance and Planning Commission rather than tapping CSR. The corporate, on the other hand, find the mechanism of selection, procedure for implementation too cumbersome and insensitive to the choice of the donor.

In some states, like Odisha, government guidelines require welfare activities in the peripheral area for rehabilitation of the displaced persons to be implemented through the government departments. These are decided by a committee set up with the Revenue Divisional Commissioner as the Chairman. In course of study, factors like complicated procedure, delay, apathetic and rent seeking behaviour of government officers appeared to limit implementation of CSR projects through this method.

Expenditure on CSR

There is a general impression that achievement under CSR is often exaggerated for benefit of the corporate. In this context, the amount spent gives an objective indication of the commitment of the corporate towards CSR. In course of survey in 2004, the corporate were approached to share the expenditure incurred on CSR activities during 2000-01, 2001-02 and 2002-03. Barring a few corporate like Tata Steel, SAIL, ONGC, NALCO, which sent available details, there was no response to sharing financial details. Certain corporate regretted indicating that "no information on budgets can be made public". However, this position changed from 2014-15, as disclosure of information on CSR, became mandatory under the Companies Act.

Impact

In course of field study (done in 2004-05), it was found that the CSR interventions improved access of the disadvantaged particularly those living in the interior rural and tribal areas to education and healthcare services. The gap in public health and education could be bridged to some extent with CSR. However, there was no such feeling in case of skill and livelihood and the impact remained sporadic and not visible. Further, intervention on environment related issues got limited attention except for a few corporate like ITC.

Creation of physical infrastructure for health and education services was the preferred activities under CSR. Utility of the physical infrastructure created by the Rourkela Steel Plant of SAIL under its CSR interventions was specifically looked into during the field study. It was found that community centre and additional rooms constructed in a primary school were useful to the local community. However, construction of a building in a privately managed girl's high school appeared to be of little use to the community, as evident from the quality of the education, *viz.* less than 10 per cent students of the school passing the final examination. The later project was taken up under CSR on a stand-alone basis, without looking into required linkages. Such project, being taken up under pressure from the local influential people, could not be ruled out. Such CSR project had limited utility for the community and appeared to be a case of "***Burrowed CSR***" **i.e., doing charity with others' money**. On the other hand, the school run by Bhilai Steel Plant of SAIL for imparting quality education to Scheduled Tribe students appeared to be serving a well-defined purpose. Along with use of idle infrastructure, active involvement and voluntary support of the employees, this CSR intervention sought to empower the disadvantaged segments in the real sense. It is hoped that with passage of time, students benefited under this innovative programme would pursue higher education and occupy higher positions as engineers and doctors, in the society, which would lead to social inclusion in the real sense and remove the sense of deprivation from among the local inhabitants.

For quality education, provision of soft infrastructure like trained teachers, commitment and supervision are more critical than hard infrastructure like brick and mortar buildings. During the study, it appeared that mobilization of volunteerism of employees of the corporate for CSR is a vast untapped potential, which can serve a more meaningful purpose in improving quality of education, than mere construction of buildings. It would be worthwhile to innovate and explore new projects involving employees and NGOs, while taking up CSR projects instead of continuing the routine approach of raising buildings in a mechanical manner with sizable financial implications.

Steps taken for capacity building and imparting income-generating skills vary widely from corporate to corporate. A wide range of activities were supported as per the local demand. Empowering the villagers with appropriate technology in the rural areas by ITC Ltd., appeared to be an innovative initiative in this regard. It appeared that participation of the target group and interest taken by the senior officers played an important role in success of the CSR interventions.

So far as social responsibility of bank and other financial institutions is concerned, social obligation was one of the major considerations behind nationalization[33] of Banks in India. The economic policy of 1991 brought in major changes and facilitated setting up of private Banks. The nationalized banks were associated with the implementation of poverty alleviation programmes and supporting livelihood generation activities by the unemployed youth and disadvantaged groups by provision of institutional finance. Provision of microfinance to the Self-Help Groups (SHGs), without insisting on adequate assets as collaterals/security, was another important development in the context of social responsibility of the banks. Some of the banks also supported provision of primary education and healthcare. According to MoU of ICICI Bank, *"there are layers of CSR activities, while primary education and health connect the poor and uneducated to the larger economy, activities in health and microfinance have a direct link with the bank's business."* In addition to individual efforts, there are attempts for pooling resources, as done by the Standard Chartered Bank under its "Mumbai Marathon" initiative. Though Standard Chartered Bank was the title sponsor, ICICI Group,

Citibank, HDFC and HSBC joined this cause for making the operation a success. So far as the financial commitments are concerned, though no one was willing to specify actual amounts, almost all participating banks in this event confirmed that allocation for social spending was on the rise.

From the study, it appeared that CSR interventions helped the weaker section considerably, in accessing primary health and education facilities in the rural areas. This is evident from the number of people (other than workers and employees) availing facilities from the hospitals as well as the mobile health facilities and health camps organized at different places. It is noteworthy that in terms of number of persons getting services, coverage under CSR remained higher than the services provided by the government system. Further, *quality of healthcare facilities provided under CSR interventions*, in terms of presence and availability of doctors and supply of medicine etc., were *felt to be superior than the facilities provided under the government managed public healthcare system.*

So far as education is concerned, literacy rate in the peripheral areas of the integrated steel plants of SAIL was higher than that of the national average and much higher than the average for the district and the State in which the plant is located.

Performance of students in the Board Examination in case of those studying in the schools *managed by SAIL was better than the government schools*. In the High School Certificate Examination conducted by the Board of Secondary Education, Orissa, success rate of students studying in the schools run by the RSP was 92.8 per cent as against 42 per cent for schools run by State Government located in the same area (2003-04).

These confirm the *superior quality of education provided* by the corporate under the *CSR interventions* in the peripheral area. The fact that such quality services are provided in interior areas of developing States like Orissa, Chattishgarh, Jharkhand, having concentration of families *belonging to Scheduled Tribes* and facing left-wing extremist activities provided *a special dimension to such initiatives* of the corporate in the context of social inclusion.

Social Audit

Audit basically relates to ascertaining if the resources have been spent and used in a judicious manner in achieving the desired objectives. It originated with examining the use of public fund by the government machineries by the audit wing within the government. The concept of

"Social audit" evolved for assessing the impact of social welfare programmes. In order to overcome the bias in favour of the implementing agency and hiding the truth which defeat the real purpose of auditing. "Social audit" is done by an outside body. In India, the concept of the social audit was started by *Mazdoor Kisan Shakti Sangathan* (MKSS), a civil society working in Rajasthan for checking corruption in the public works in the early 1990s. It was extended to other areas as a part of transparency and ethical behaviour. Some corporate adopted this method for getting their CSR activities examined by a third party outside the corporate and the Government for ascertaining the true position of work done under CSR.

Tata Steel conducted the first social audit in 1980 by a committee of independent persons of eminence namely Mr. Justice S.P. Kotval, Professor Rajni Kothari and Professor P.C. Mavalankar for assessing the impact of its CSR interventions. The social audit was done for the second time in 1990s by another committee with Justice D.N. Mehta (Retired), Professor P.G. Mavalankar and Professor Satchidananda, which had looked into the extent to which the company had fulfilled the objectives contained in the Articles of Association regarding its social and moral responsibilities to the consumers, employees, shareholders, society and the local community. The audit indicated that Tata Steel fulfilled its social obligation by distributing wealth in the area.

Making CSR Interventions Effective

In course of the study, interest taken by the person heading the corporate was found to be one of the main factors in making the CSR interventions effective, which was conspicuous in case of the private sector. Impact of the CSR interventions of corporate like Tatas, Infosys, Wipro and ITC has been visible due to the interest taken by the person heading these organizations. It is felt that arrangement for undertaking CSR activities needs to be institutionalized for providing continuity on a long-term basis in general and during change of guard in a corporate in particular.

The most striking part of CSR being mandatory has been the disclosure of CSR activities, as a part of statutory requirement under Section 135 of the Companies Act. All the corporate studied were found to have set up a board level committee with independent director for dealing with CSR activities and have a policy on CSR.

All the companies studied have disclosed the CSR activities as a separate annexure in the annual report, giving an account of the average profit made in the last three years, two per cent of profit which is to be spent on CSR, the amount spent, brief details of the activities undertaken and the reason for shortfall, if any. This information has made it easier for undertaking study of the CSR activities.

So far as spending of the two per cent of the profit of the last three years is concerned, the private corporate studied appeared to have complied with and in some cases, spend more than the earmarked amount barring few exceptions. However, in case of public sector, the actual expenditure was less than the prescribed amount during 2014-15 by a number of corporate and the reason for shortfall was attributed to 2014-15 being the first year after CSR was made mandatory and details on the procedure not being known. The same public sectors have however reported a higher expenditure during 2015-16, by taking care of the shortfall during the previous year, 2014-15.

The most critical aspect of CSR is the nature and quality of work done. The activities to be undertaken are listed in Schedule-VII of the Act, which broadly covers the three components of human resource development, i.e. education, healthcare and skill for livelihood. Besides, issues relating to environment, promotion of culture, promotion of games and sports, support to ex-servicemen and disadvantaged groups have been indicated. Projects for urban development and rural development cover an umbrella with bunch of activities. Following the emphasis given by the new government at the centre to sanitation and launching of "*Swachh Bharat Abhiyan*", number of public sector undertakings spent major part of their CSR fund during 2014-15 for construction of toilet in schools as a part of their "*Swachh Vidyalaya Abhiyan*." Provision of nutritious meal by setting up mechanized kitchen with help of "*Akshaya Patra Foundation*" has been another example of taking up CSR in a coordinated manner. The new guidelines envisaged taking up CSR activities on a project mode with proper planning, execution and monitoring. However, this appeared to be in a formative stage.

Among the initiatives taken for improving quality of education, relatively small corporate, like Thermax, adopted municipal schools and provided a package of services to the students which resulted in increasing the pass percentage and with distinction significantly.

These offer rich lessons to other corporate for making best use of their fund under CSR for providing better quality service required by the people in general and the disadvantaged segments in particular. This will pay a rich dividend to the company in improving their brand name. The point, which came up again and again in course of the study, is that involvement of the top management played a critical role in CSR getting embedded into the organizational culture, everybody owning it and contributing for making it a success. That has led to meaningful work and overcome the normal criticism that CSR activities have targeted for short term attention and publicity in the print and electronic media.

While there are number of success stories about CSR making a difference in education, experience in health, skill and livelihood and environment have been mixed one. Some corporate have attempted working with government departments and ongoing government programmes for filling the gaps. However, difficulties were expressed by the corporate about government officials not coming forward to avail CSR funding. Similar reservations also exist on the side of the government officials and the non-governmental organizations of repute. *The challenge*, therefore, *lies in bringing the corporate executive* dealing with CSR, the *government officer dealing with developmental* programmes and NGOs implementing the developmental schemes *to work together in a team for improving the quality of services and empowering the disadvantaged segments in the real sense.*

Task Ahead

From findings of the studies discussed above, it is evident that CSR being made mandatory under the Companies Act with effect from the 1st April, 2014 has improved CSR interventions of the corporate operating in India, both in quantity and quality for promotion of health, education, skill for livelihood, rural development as well as conservation of environment.

The challenges ahead lie in working out models for evolving synergy between CSR projects and ongoing Government sponsored plans and programmes for providing last mile connectivity, which will ensure provision of better quality service to the common man and in making the development socially inclusive on the one hand and giving the best value for the money spent on CSR to the corporate concerned on the other.

Future of CSR will primarily depend upon making the expenditure purposeful so that the Corporate get the best value out of its CSR activities and does not consider it as an additional tax. This would require the projects to be implemented in a manner to create desired impact by providing *better quality services than those available under the ongoing government programmes*. Satisfaction of the beneficiary belonging to the disadvantaged groups, who lacks the financial resources to avail quality services is the ultimate factor in deciding the efficacy of CSR interventions.

This would be possible by the corporate coming forward to implement CSR with seriousness, mobilization of corporate volunteerism and active involvement of the top management. Spirit of CSR is required to be embedded in the value system and culture of the organization. Several cases confirm that once CSR is taken up with commitment and voluntary zeal, it generates goodwill and provides distinct mileage to the Corporate in *getting trust of the society and enhance its brand name in the market.* This will ensure achieving the objective of CSR.

The *rationale behind making CSR mandatory* lies in the fact that social indicators of the country in terms of poverty, hunger, malnutrition, access to quality education and health services and level of skill has remained moderate in general and for the disadvantaged segments in particular; notwithstanding favourable macro-economic indicators like economic growth and foreign exchange reserves. Further, implementation of government plans and programmes have not yielded the desired result due to poor implementation and part of the resource being siphoned out by unscrupulous persons wielding power and authority, adversely affecting the interest of the common man. There are instances of the gap between the rich and the poor increasing. This *offers both a challenge and an opportunity to the corporate* India for making a meaningful difference. By extending their financial and managerial resources, the corporate can expedite the development process for welfare of the disadvantaged groups.

Corporate Social Responsibility (CSR) in India has been changing over the last decades, starting with charity based approach to the society. Corporate took it up in an organized manner, which took shape in post-1991 and in the new millennium. Private sectors like Tata, Birla set up educational institutions of eminence for development of human resource. Under Government directives, the public sector took up social work in its peripheral area for benefit of the people living nearby the plant/units in general and those displaced for getting land for industry in particular. The post-liberalization period saw significant growth of the private sector. Number of Information Technology companies like Infosys and Wipro spread their wings all-over the world and made sizeable profits. Persons mentoring these corporate took personal interest and made meaningful contribution for welfare of the society. This continued to the new millennium with significant growth in business opportunities led by Information Technology and globalization.

However, increase in literacy awareness fuelled expectation of the youth by manifold, which in turn led to frustration. Often, the agitating youth created roadblock to acquisition of private land for setting up industrial units. Several proposals for land acquisition for the Tata Plant in Singur, West Bengal, for Posco Plant in Odisha met with stiff resistance from the locals and could not see light of the day. This led to the realization that the corporate has to carry the society along for doing business in the society and opened a new dimension for CSR as a necessity for operating in the society peacefully.

After considerable debate, CSR was made mandatory by an amendment to the Companies Act with effect from the 1st April, 2014. The mandatory provision requires the corporate, with turnover/net worth/profit beyond a limit, to spend two per cent of their profit on CSR, have a board level CSR committee, a CSR policy and more importantly to disclose the action taken for CSR in compliance with the said provision. Against an initial estimate of about Rs. 15,000 crore being made available for CSR annually, over Rs. 6,000 crore was reported to have been spent on CSR activities during 2014-15, which increased to over Rs. 8000 crores in 2015-16. Number of corporate is yet to disclose details on CSR. Some corporate have indicated expenditure less than the prescribed amount due to some reason or other. This position would improve with time and more corporate will come forward to discharge their statutory responsibility, which will make more financial resources available for CSR in the coming years. In this background, it would be necessary to focus on the following aspects for making the best out of CSR:

- CSR related interventions are required to be taken up in a professional manner on project mode with clearly defined and measurable targets. This would require capacity building of corporate executives dealing with CSR.
- Database of NGOs of credibility needs to be evolved, who can be entrusted with the responsibility of implementation so that the Corporate can use their experties and give more time to business. This would require building up capacity of existing and new manpower both in the Corporate and NGO sector.
- The government agency dealing with development programmes need to remain sensitive and extend required support to the cooperate for achieving the aim and objectives of CSR.
- Trust deficit between Corporate, Civil Society and Government agencies dealing with CSR needs to be bridged.

Conclusion

CSR in India has come a long way starting from the charity based approach linked up with Indian tradition to several private sectors taking it up on a systematic and organized manner. The state owned Public Sector Enterprises joined with sizeable resources for social activities as per the government directions. CSR made mandatory, under the Companies Act with effect from the 1st April, 2014, has been a landmark initiative for mobilising corporate support for inclusive development.

Under mandatory provision, the companies are exploring as to what to do and how to implement CSR in a manner so as to get the best out of the money spent. Discussion on CSR in the boardrooms are getting focused on efficacy and there is a shift from charity and philanthropy approach to sustainable development, which will solve national issues and truly benefit India. Best practices adopted on CSR are being discussed for exploring ways to scale up the efforts, which broadly cover four areas.[34]

Firstly, generation of awareness about CSR in general and the best practices evolved in particular is of critical importance. The second issue would relate to building up capacity relating to CSR within the corporate and government for making the best out of CSR. On the modalities for implementation of CSR, the private corporate have opted for foundation managed by the corporate. However, the need for developing credible Non-Governmental Organizations of competence and expertise have been felt, with whom the corporate can partner for implementation of CSR. Thus, development of civil society/non-governmental organization with expertise in various social sectors is an area which need attention. Use of technology and innovation is another area for making best use of the money spent. Most of the corporate have been concentrating on education, healthcare and skill development for livelihood while planning activity for CSR intervention. As the government has been spending huge resources in these areas, partnering with government for providing last mile connectivity through civil society of expertise would be of significance in scaling up and creating a "Win-win" situation for all the stakeholders. In brief, the managerial ability of the corporate along with the financial resources to be spent on CSR mandatorily has the potential to forge alliance with government and NGOs, which along with use of innovation and technology would lead to CSR initiatives contributing to social change in the true sense.

Indian corporate has a legacy of philanthropic activities. Corporate houses have supported a wide range of benevolent activities like giving food to the poor, distribution of blankets in winter, construction of temples, excavation of ponds, construction of sheds for the pilgrims etc. However, the time has changed and CSR is being viewed as a medium for empowering the community rather than giving alms. While CSR has been important for the business at all times and in all countries, it is of special significance for the developing countries. This is due to the fact that in a developing country, the civil society and other institutions are in a formative stage. As a result, often initiatives taken by the government for welfare of the poor, the weak and the disadvantaged meet roadblocks and affect achieving the desired objectives affect. Improvement of governance, enforcing accountability, having proper reward and punishment system etc., in a developing democracy like India is a complex and would take time to evolve. As corporate are active members of the society, they cannot remain silent spectators in his interim period. A better alternative, which some corporate have already taken up, lies in using their resources in a positive manner for empowering the disadvantaged to join the national mainstream. This will make the growth process socially inclusive and sustainable. Visualizing this as an opportunity would enable the corporate to exploit the potential for growth and solve the problems of the society as well.

References

1. Gidwani, Sushila, 1986, "Corporate Management Strategy for Economic Justice, Trusteeship – the Gandhian Alternative", New Delhi: Gandhi Peace Foundation, p. 189.
2. Address in the 4th annual session of FICCI on 7th April, 1931, "Business and beyond—Leadership, through Quality and Excellence", FICCI Publication.
3. Anuradha Himatsingka, B.K., "Birla Reminisces about the Austere life in the Tumultuous Days before Independence", *The Economic Times*, August 14, 2007.
4. "A century that forged a company of steel", *The Financial Express*, August 25, 2007.
5. "Trusteeship of Wealth", Special Report on CSR, *The Economic Times*, November 8, 2004, p. 4.
6. *Ibid.*
7. 24th Report of the Parliamentary Committee on Public Undertakings (CoPU) 1993-94, on Social Responsibilities and Public Accounting of Public Undertakings, p. 54.
8. Public Enterprises Survey 2011-12, Ministry of Heavy Industries and Public Enterprises, Government of India.

9. *Ibid.*, 24th Report of CoPU, 1993-94, p. 65.
10. SEBI notification dated 22.12.2015.
11. Arup Gupta, The Economic Times Group, Mumbai, *The Economic Times*, October 18, 2007.
12. Field study (2004), *ibid*.
13. Reply to Rajya Sabha Unstarred question no. 1957 on the 15th March, 2016.
14. Reply in Lok Sabha on the 9th December, 2016.
15. Reply to Lok Sabha Unstarred Question no. 794 on the 7th February, 2017, *source*: PIB, Ministry of Corporate Affairs.
16. CII-ITC Centre of Excellence for Sustainable Development Report on CSR Expenditure for FY-2015.
17. Study done by NGOBOX in July 2015.
18. Reply to unstarred question in the Lok Sabha on 26th February, 2016 by Minister of Corporate Affairs. The KPMG report is available in public domain.
19. Technopark report "CSR relating to the Textile Sector for its Impact and scope for Future", November 2015.
20. Arundhati Ramanathan, August 03, 2016, http://www.livemint.com/Companies/3WSHLVqdonhIbh6bMRRvFO/CSR-gets-greater-acceptance-in-year-two.html
21. FICCI Survey of CSR, March 2016.
22. "Blending CSR with Responsible Growth", Utkarsh Majumder, Namrata Rana and Neeti Sanan, *The Economic Times*, 15th September, 2016, p. 14.
23. "Indian companies top global list on reporting CSR", *The Economic Times*, October 21, 2017, p. 11.
24. S.K. Panda, *Corporate Social Responsibility in India—Past, Present and Future*, ISBN-978-81-314-1965-6, 2008.
25. http://www.bharatpetroleum.in/EnergisingSociety/csr_accolades.aspx?id=2
26. http://www.hindustanpetroleum.com/En/UI/CSR2007n2008Activities.aspx
27. http://www.gail.nic.in/final_site/resourcesforCSR.html
28. http://post.jagran.com/cil-ongc-sail-did-not-fully-utilise-funds-on-csr-in-fy12-1355227223
29. *The Economics Times*, 20th February, 2013.
30. Compendium on CSR contribution by CPSEs, published in August 2014.
31. http://dpe.nic.in/publications/list_of_maharatna_navratna-and_miniratna
32. Dean Roy Nash, "CSR: Contributions of 'Maharatna' Companies of India", *Asian Journal of Resecrch in Business Economics and Management*, Vol. 2, Issue 4, April 2012, http://www.aijsh.org
33. 14 largest commercial banks with effect from the midnight of 19 July, 1969.
34. Deliberations in the seminar, organized by the *Times of India Group* on the 21st December, 2016 in Delhi.

5

The Road Ahead

Corporate Social Responsibility (CSR) relates to the responsibility of the corporate towards the society. As corporate operate in the society and owe their existence to the society, it is but natural that they have a responsibility towards the society. Further, in order to be meaningful, the approach and interventions in discharge of this responsibility shall have to remain dynamic, changing with time and the changing needs of the society.

A developing democracy like India, which has to meet the expectations of over 1.25 billion people, constituting 1/6th of the total global population, with hardly 1/16th of the global natural resources, faces several challenges. Multiple factors like increase in awareness, literacy, education, emerging leadership at the grass-root level following the Panchayat Raj movement, impact of the print and electronic media have led to expectations of the youth growing very fast; somewhat like in a geometric progression. As a result of various developmental activities, the opportunity has also been increasing, but at a much lesser rate; somewhat like in an arithmetic progression. This has led to the unfulfilled expectations increasing fast; which, in turn, is leading to frustration, frustration fuelling anger and anger surfacing as violence.

Peace is essential for development of any society on a sustainable basis. In today's context, peace can come only by creating more opportunities for fulfilling the unmet expectations of the youth, which will restore harmony in the society. This calls for empowering the youth with information, skill, assets and mentoring for accessing the market and earning livelihood. These features are typical to a developing democracy like in India, which corporate operating therein needs to appreciate and come forward to support the Government for creating a "win-win" situation for all the stakeholders of the society.

CSR—Dimensions in a Developing Country

Responsibility of the corporate towards the society in a developing democracy like India covers three broad areas namely, (i) Compliance with the laws of the land and ethical principles; (ii) Strategic interventions for a "Win-Win" situation; and (iii) Looking beyond immediate gains for meeting the social needs, as a responsible stakeholder.

Compliance with the Laws of the Land and Ethical Principles

The *first and foremost aspect* of Corporate Social Responsibility undoubtedly relates to compliance with the laws, rules and regulations in both letter and spirit. The corporate remaining responsible to the society *starts with* complying with the laws of the land. This covers the wide range of laws, rules and regulations, enacted with a view to safeguarding interest of the shareholders, the customers, the workers, the employees, the consumer and the common man as well. There are instances of corporate violating laws of the land and/or resorting to manipulation and frauds like fudging of accounts, engaging child labour, failing in payment of minimum wage as per statute, not complying with the pollution control norms, etc. Such conducts are prejudicial to the interest of a civilized society. Unless a corporate fulfils this, it cannot be considered as responsible to the society merely by giving some donation for charitable purpose or construction of a hospital or a school. Complying with the laws of the land, in letter and spirit, forms the basic and non-negotiable component of the CSR and precedes all other activities.

Following the basic principles of ethics, honesty and truthfulness, which may not necessarily be written and hence not be legally enforceable, is another equally important aspect of CSR. These are essential for doing business in the society and are expected of the corporate as an important stakeholder of the society. Complying with statutory provision for safeguarding interest of the customer, avoiding any exaggerated/ misleading publicity about the products, paying the due tax in time, complying with laid down norms for control of pollution of water, air and environment, avoiding adoption/abetment of corrupt practices/ emission of any pollutant etc. are essential prerequisites for doing good business in the society. Corporate dealing with harmful products needs to be extra careful for avoiding any accident like gas leak in the Union Carbide plant, in Bhopal [**Box 5.1: Lesson from Bhopal Gas Tragedy**]. Failure to comply with law not only make the corporate liable under law but also give the stigma of not being a responsible stakeholder of the

Box 5.1: Lesson from Bhopal Gas Tragedy

Methyl IsoCyanate (MIC) gas leak from the Union Carbide India Ltd. (UCIL)'s pesticide plant in Bhopal, Madhya Pradesh on December 2, 1984 night, causing large scale death and injury has been one of the major industrial disasters in India. Over 3,000 persons died in the incident and about ten times as many were injured, which increased to 5,73,588 people claiming compensation. Response of the US-based multinational company, Union Carbide Corporation (UCC), which owned the plant through its subsidiary UCIL, dealing with such a massive human tragedy however remained *too little and coming too late*.

Union Carbide used trade secrecy as a prerogative to withhold information on the exact composition of the leaked gases. Though it was known that MIC, on reacting with water at high temperatures, could release as many as 300 highly toxic chemicals, research was carried out only to check the toxicity of pure MIC—that also on animals. So, the treatment has been symptomatic. In 1989, UCC paid US $470 million as compensation for the disaster, which was one-seventh of the demand made from the Indian Government.

The Environment (Protection) Act (EPA) of 1986 was enacted in the post-Bhopal period. The pollution norms and management of hazardous waste were laid down under the Hazardous Waste (Management and Handling) Rules, other Central rules and regulations for management, storage and import of hazardous chemicals. The Public Liability Insurance Act was enacted (in 1991) to provide for immediate relief to persons affected by accidents while handling hazardous substances.

The Bhopal tragedy offers several major lessons in the context of Corporate remaining responsible towards the society (CSR). The first one relates to complying with the laid down procedures before commissioning of the unit as well as during commercial production so as to ensure that the operations don't cause any harm to human, animal life or environment. The second issue relate to extending adequate relief and rehabilitation to the injured and survivors of the dead within a time schedule in the event of any mishap.

While enactment of the National Green Tribunal Act, 2010 and rulings of the Apex and High courts have provided a sound legal system, it is necessary for the corporate to comply with the provisions in *letter and spirit* and take adequate precautionary measures, which form the core of corporate remaining responsible towards the society in the true sense.

Reference: http://www.downtoearth.org.in/coverage/30-years-of-bhopal-gas-tragedy-a-continuing disaster society. As a matter of fact, CSR regained importance in the West following the detection of unethical business practices by corporate like Enron and WorldCom. In the Indian context, fudging off accounts made Satyam Computers liable for penal action. Notwithstanding welfare activities undertaken[1], Satyam Computers disintegrated due to unethical practices, which offers lesson to others. [**Box 5.2: Lesson from *Satyam***].

Success of any commercial organization is commonly assessed from the profit, balance sheet, order books and its performance in the stock market. But the real success comes from the trust, respect and admiration, its commands in the society and in the marketplace. Trust of the consumers form the backbone of any commercial organisation. This is owned by complying with the legal requirements as well as maintaining ethical standards. In commercial dealings, at times there are conflicts between the goal of making profit and the means followed for it. There are instances, where companies compromise with the means for making profit. Corporate, which take recourse to such short term measures, and violate the rules fail to carry on business on a long term basis and fall sooner or later. On the other hand, there are corporate, which do not compromise with the means (values) even at the risk of making lesser profit. Experience world over indicate that only the latter category of corporate, which follow rules and are guided by ethical conduct, retain their position in the market and grow on a long term sustainable basis.

One such example of commitment to values, relates to Hewlett and Packard.[2] The owner-promoters retained hands-on control of their company, stamping it with their unique mix of philanthropy and financial pragmatism. The company adhered to ethical principles; continuously funding innovations, and fostering a friendly work environment. Realizing that a happy, creative workforce would ensure profitability in the long run, they adopted a holistic approach based on ethical principles, which paid off in the long run. What makes this company different is reflected in the conduct of its promoters, Bill and Dave, who *did not shun profit, rather they just did not make profit the central mission of their company.*

In the Indian context, Tata Group have maintained a record of adhering to values, which is ingrained in its group philosophy and is reflected in the observations of its founder, Jamshetji Tata, "*We do not claim to be more unselfish, more generous or more philanthropic than other people. But we think we started on sound and straightforward business principles. We consider the interests of our shareholders and the health and welfare of the employees as the foundation for our success.*" These have been reflected in a number of cases reported like the concern

Box 5.2: Lesson from *Satyam*

Satyam Computer Services Ltd., popularly known as Satyam, was incorporated on 24th June, 1987 by two brothers, B. Rama Raju and B. Ramalinga Raju, as a private limited company with just 20 employees for providing software development and consultancy services to large corporations. The company became a public company in 1991. The company promoted subsidiaries including Satyam Renaissance Consulting Ltd., Satyam Enterprise Solutions Pvt. Ltd., and Satyam Infoway Pvt. Ltd. in 1996. It was selected as one of India's most remarkable and rapidly growing entrepreneurial companies by the Switzerland-based World Economic Forum and World Link Magazine in 1997. Satyam Infoway (Sify), a wholly owned subsidiary of Satyam Computer Services Ltd. was the first Indian Internet Company listed on NASDAQ. Mr. B. Ramalinga Raju, Chairman of Satyam, was awarded the *IT Man of the Year 2000* Award by Dataquest. In 2001, Satyam became world's first ISO 9001:2000 certified company.

However, things changed suddenly in December 2008 with the World Bank's announcement that Satyam has been barred from business with the Bank for eight years for providing Bank staff with "improper benefits" and charged with data theft and bribing the staff. On January 7, 2009, B. Ramalinga Raju confessed over Rs. 7,800 crore financial frauds and resigned as chairman of Satyam. He revealed in his letter that his attempt to buy Maytas companies was his last attempt to "fill fictitious assets with real ones".

Notwithstanding the accolades owned by the company for its CSR projects like *Emergency health care 108 Ambulance Services,* which were appreciated as best practices, the company collapsed like a pack of cards in no time for its unethical conduct, forging of accounts and failure to comply with the statutory norms.

Satyam episodes left valuable lessons on the importance of Ethics in Business, which was stressed by Mahatma Gandhi. This subject came to limelight in the West following the questionable corporate policies or unethical practices like Junk Bond fiasco of USA and failure of Maxwell, BCCI and Polypeck in UK and later with the debacle of Enron in 2001 and scandals involving large US companies such as the Tyco, Quest, Global Crossings, the World.Com and the exposure of auditing lacunae, which led to the collapse of the Andersen. These had triggered passing of the Public Accounting Reform and Investor Protection Act of 2002 known as Sarbanes Oxley (SOX) Act, 2002 in USA. Similar practices for corporate governance were introduced in India by SEBI. However failure and misconduct of Satyam in 2009 provided a lesson in corporate governance and reiterated the fact that ethics and principles form the core and basic prerequisite of any business organisation and of CSR in remaining responsible to the stakeholders and the society at large.

Reference: http://www.iodonline.com/ProfWhatWentWrongWithSatyam.pdf

for an employee, who developed physical challenges while in service and in the company's response post *Taj Mumbai attack* [**Box 5.3: Looking beyond short term gains**]. Reflecting on these, Subash Menon had observed, "*Commitment of the Tata group is reflected in its motto "Leadership with Trust". The Tata group was caught in several controversies and many corporate watchers had predicted doom for the group. However, Tata group has come out with flying colours and emerged victorious. There is no other organization in India that better embodies the spirit of fair, committed and innovative entrepreneurship than the Tata Group*".

Complying with the statutory regulations relating to safety, public health and environmental protection etc., is another important aspect, which merits specific attention. There are instances of corporate compromising with environmental protection norms just to save money and show a better bottom line. There are unfortunate cases of corporate getting into unholy nexus with corrupt and rent-seeking officials of regulatory bodies, who turned blind eye to the irregularity for a consideration. There are instances of even public sectors, which run business with public money, compromising with environmental safety norms. Such negligence affects the environment costing dearly to the society with increased incidence of pollution and related diseases. While the regulatory agency is required to be geared up for discharging its duty properly; each and every corporate need to comply with regulations of its own, as an integral part of its business and ethical conduct.

Taking care of the environment by checking pollution of air and water is an important aspect of legal compliance by responsible corporate. Often the corporate shy away from modern and environment friendly technology, as it requires additional financial investment. However, there are exceptions, where the corporate invested sizeable amount and adopted state of art technology. One such case relates to Tata Steel introducing the "*Top gas Recovery Turbine (TRT)*" method of generating additional power from the blast furnace.[3] This technology involved recovery of gases from the top of blast furnaces and using the kinetic energy of gases to generate additional power, over the traditional blast furnace and contributing significantly to conservation of the environment in general and checking global warming in particular.

Another such case relates to Tata Chemicals Limited dealing with production of inorganic chemicals, fertilizers and food additives. In its integrated inorganic chemical complex at Mithapur in Gujarat, *Larox filters* with advanced technology were installed to remove solid effluents

Box 5.3: Looking Beyond Short Term Gains

Welfare of the employees and workers constitutes one of the major responsibilities of the corporate. Employees, who met with accidents and became disabled in course of working, are often considered as liabilities and are bade farewell with a monetary package. The challenge for a sensitive employer lies in empowering the person facing challenge for living a normal life as far as possible.

The support extended by the Tata Steel to one Amit Chatterjee, Chief Technology Officer provides an example of the concern for the employee. Chatterjee, a metallurgical engineer, had contributed significantly to cost reduction in steel making. As luck would have it, he was diagnosed with multiple sclerosis at the age of 40. In the initial days, he was able to move around using a stick and later in wheelchair. In a rare show of solidarity, the company provided ramps in virtually all places, where he had to go for duty. Suitable working environment enabled him to perform his professional activities with equal vigour. Reflecting on the gesture Chatterjee has observed "Having seen my life from both sides as a normal person as well as a person with disability, I can safely say that without the understanding of the employer, and the family, it is impossible to contend with disability".[1]

Terror attacks and mindless killing and injury on the night of November 26, 2008 in the Taj, Mumbai devastated the luxury hotel property significantly damaged, leaving many devastated families and incurable losses.[2] At this hour of crisis, the management led by the group chairman, Mr. Ratan Tata, made no delay on expressing whole hearted concerns toward the employees and their families.

Post tragedy, the salaries of all the employees were given to each affected employee, including those who completed, even one day as casual, until the property re-opened. A psychiatric cell was set up and in collaboration with TATA Institute of Social Science, psychological help was provided to when and where needed. Around 1600 affected persons were provided food, water, sanitation, first aid, and counselling. The dependents of employee were flown to Mumbai from where ever they lived, and taken care of in terms of mental assurance and peace. Above all as a great gesture of empathy Mr. Ratan Tata personally visited the families of all the 80 employees who were affected in any manner, whether through death or injury.

Relief and assistance was even extended to the public, who died at CST railway station, including the *bhajiawala*, *vadapav* and *pan* shop vendors. A new trust was created by the Tata's in a record time of 20 days for the relief and compensation of not only to its own employees, but others like railways and police employees and pedestrians, who had nothing to do with the Tata's. Settlement, ranging from Rs. 36 lakhs to Rs. 85 lakhs in addition of full last salary for the life time, was released to the family/ dependants of the each deceased person.

All major responsibility including education, medical, financial were also taken care for rest of their life. Such sympathetic and long term approach to the genuine needs of the employee/workers, rising above short term financial gains are reflected in the words of the group head, Mr. Ratan Tata "*The organisation would spend several hundred crores of rupees on rebuilding the property—why not spend equally on the employees who gave their lives and suffered!*" This strong organization realized its responsibility towards its employees and society, contributing a great trust and sense of belief in itself, which makes the Tata group different while leaving lessons for others in inclusive development.

References:

1. S.K. Panda, 2008, *CSR in India—Past, Present and Future*, p. 142.
2. www.tata.co.in

from waste water. Based on the principles of "*avoid, reduce and recycle*", it set up cement plant solely for consuming the solid waste. Action taken by the plant has been *recognized, as a global benchmark* in environmental compliance by the synthetic soda industry.

While compliance with laws by the corporate is important for all society, it is more important in case of a developing country like India, as the general level of awareness, education is relatively low. This in turn casts a bigger responsibility on the corporate operating here in complying with the environmental standards as well as social issues like prevention of child labour, prevention of sexual harassment at workplace, payment of compensation to workers as per law. Public awareness on the statutory liabilities of the corporate and rights and entitlements of the labour has been on increase, which is creating pressure on the corporate for compliance and checking any manipulations. Civil society and academic institutions are also facilitating compliance with statutory measures. One such example relates to the Indian Institutes of Technology's decision to shun promotional measures of the Dow Chemicals, by returning the sponsorship for a three days international conference on chemical technology and cancelling the pre-placement talks, as a mark of solidarity with the cause of the Bhopal gas victims. Notwithstanding such initiatives taken by the civil society, the corporate should itself self-regulate in complying with the legal provisions.

Social Responsibility of the Advertising Corporate

In the context of ethical and social compliance, conduct of corporate in media and advertising business has special significance. This falls under two broad categories namely, (i) corporate using media for marketing their products and pushing up sales; and (ii) corporate in media and publicity business itself.

Media represents the fourth pillar of a democracy. Its power in shaping public opinion got a shot in the arm with the advent and rapid growth of digitization and Information Technology. The corporate use information technology based advertisement to promote their products by stimulating behaviour of the consumers. Several innovative ways of advertisement are being resorted to, for generating demand—*by motivating the consumer to want something, want more of it and/or more people wanting it*. It has been noticed that in its drive to expand the consumer base, the producer company *often leaves the negative consequence of the product to be the free choice of the consumers*. In the developed countries, the educated and enlightened consumers are in a position to take a judicious view while going for a particular brand of consumer goods. However, in a developing country, the position is different due to relatively lower level of awareness, literacy and education. Further, as the regulatory mechanism in a developing country is on an evolving stage, it puts greater onus on the corporate while advertising their product in remaining responsible towards the society. As a responsible stakeholder of the society, the corporate need to look beyond their immediate and smaller interest of making gain/profit, to the larger interest of the consumer, while advertising their products.

Corporate often resort to *generating fear, jealousy and greed* within the customers for generating demand for their products. Simple gullible customers like the less educated adults and children fall prey to such advertisement and get tempted to go for the product. Often the customer is not fully aware about the products and its adverse effect on human health. Advertisements often target vulnerable groups like children, teens and influence them to buy a particular product, with the main objective of increasing the number of consumers and volume of sale for their products. *Impact of going for the product on the vulnerable section of consumer is either overlooked or ignored*. Remaining responsible towards the society requires the corporate to take care of the health and social consequences, while promoting their products.

There are examples of corporate adopting innovative measures, which had conveyed a social message to the target group of consumer and increased sale simultaneously. Hindustan Unilever Limited's advertisement relating to Surf Excel scholarship is one such case, in which two boys fight over a scratch in the pack, find a scholarship award and hand it over to an underprivileged boy, which enables him to join them at their school. In another recent advertisement, a child has shown his concern for an elderly at the cost of his dress getting dirty. Such innovative advertisements seek to instill concerns for the underprivileged/aged in the young minds and help in making the development socially inclusive, while marketing the products. Advertisement with innovation and concern for the society can make a difference in the society, while achieving the objective of increasing turnover and profit of the company. For example, advertisement on consuming noodles with vegetables increases the sale of the noodles (product) and promotes good health as well. Similarly, persuading children to watch television serials, after completing their homework, along with rearranging screening of the popular slots; would lead to increase in viewership, without affecting the study of the young children. Advertisement on promotion of electrical goods along with the habit of switching the electrical appliances off, while not in use; will help in conservation of power, a scarce commodity, while promoting sale. Undertaking *advertisements with imagination, innovation and sensitivity* can increase the demand without compromising with the interest and welfare of the consumer. Such an approach to advertisement forms another aspect of remaining responsible towards the society.

So far as the corporate in media business are concerned, in a democracy with free press, the media wields enormous power. Such power is required to be used with care in a constructive manner for forming public opinion on various contemporary issues. While this is important for all, it is more important for those in media business to remain extra-sensitive in a developing country like India.

Responsibility of the media towards the society has two aspects, *viz.* (i) as disseminator of high quality news with objectivity and credibility and (ii) adhering to open and transparent business practices with due concern and respect for the stakeholders. It has been righty said that though the media does not leave direct footprints, it leaves '*brain-prints*' on the public psyche. Media has the capacity to contribute towards stable growth improving standards of living and reducing poverty. It has the potential to support education, awareness generation on preventive health care, affecting policies and culture, as well as supporting institutional change. This requires the corporate in media business to self-regulate with internal codes of conduct for safeguarding the interest of the consumers and the society. This forms an important component of CSR for winning the credibility and trust in the society, which will in turn lead to a "*win-win*" situation for media business as well as the society.

India has been changing and the mindset of the new generation has undergone a sea change. Print and the electronic media led by Information Technology, have been the driver of changing the public mindset. Reflecting on the changing mindset of the Young India, Dr. Sanjeev Jain, head of psychiatry, NIMHANS has observed "Indians today carry a photocopy of the American Dream in their heads. It has come a long way from 1947, when Nehru had delivered his famous '*Tryst with destiny*' speech, referring at length to peace, democracy and freedom and not about getting rich". This concept has undergone a complete turnaround in the new millennium with passage of time with India seeking global economic supremacy and releasing the 'animal spirit'. Thus, while India did well in supporting economic growth; factors like illiteracy, poverty and weak; the structure lead to corruption growing to new heights. While dealing with the strategy to fulfil this new Indian Dream, it is necessary to keep in mind the eternal advice of Mahatma Gandhi s to pursue business with ethics; which has been aptly summed up by Shri Dipankar Gupta "*Getting rich is good but doing it by the rules, is even better*".[4]

Strategic Interventions for a "Win-Win" Situation

The second aspect of CSR in a developing country like India relates to corporate undertaking strategic interventions for creating a "win-win" situation for the society as well as for itself. This covers a range of activities like promoting ancillaries, supporting micro-enterprises and startups, providing microfinance to self-help groups etc. which create wealth and employment in the society and at the same time generates business, enhances turnover and profit for the corporate.

Promotion of Ancillaries

As a part of strategic intervention, corporate have been supporting setting up of ancillaries near their manufacturing units. This helped the corporate in getting supply of quality raw-material as per requirement, in time and at a reasonable price. At the same time, it led to number of new enterprises coming up in the periphery, generating employment and wealth for the youth. Many such units have come up in the backward region of the country.

Development of ancillary requires the state government actively supporting the new entrepreneur with provision of developed infrastructure like land, industrial shed, water and power connections, development of entrepreneurship and skill, loan at concessional rate of interest, subsidy. Simultaneously, the mother unit is required to support by handholding, mentoring, provision of technical guidance along with marketing facility by procuring either a part or total of its requirements from the ancillaries. Study of promotion of ancillaries by SAIL indicated[5] that with support of the Industries Department of the concerned State Government, it played an important role in industrialization in the initial phase.

Promotion of small and medium scale industries through 'shared thinking' and 'partnership' by the Public sector enterprises played an important role in development of ancillaries all-over the country in the sixties and seventies. After the economic liberalization in 1990, the private sector also pursued this for getting supply of inputs and as a social welfare measure to some extent. This aspect continue to be an important part of industrial policy for promotion of Medium, Small and Micro Enterprises.

Exploring and Exploiting Business at the Bottom of the Pyramid

The large population of rural India offers a vast opportunity in form of a big and vibrant market. Initially, the corporate sector was not serious about this segment, based on a misperception that its purchasing capacity is low and does not appear to be glamorous. This led to taking a rather a casual view based on the perceived limitation of the rural population, with low average income and limited purchasing power. This mindset got changed by considering the fact that a big market is waiting to be exploited; by aggregation of these small demands, like droplets making a sea. Prof. C.K. Prahlad had advocated converting the challenges in low income group of customers into opportunities in his famous work "*Fortune at the Bottom of the Pyramid*". Improvements in awareness and education, supported by information and digital technology have made it possible to pool such demands and serve this segment with a low transaction cost. There are several examples of the corporate adopting innovative and imaginative strategy for exploiting this potential [**Box 5.4: Aggregating the Buying Capacity of the Poor**].

As competition gets stiffer, it becomes necessary for the corporate to look beyond the traditional customer base for expansion of business. In such a case, reaching out to the poor at the bottom of the pyramid offers an untapped and unique business opportunity. Corporate, who realize and act on this early, gets a mileage over others in expanding their

Box 5.4: Aggregating Buying Capacity of the Poor

Evolving new models for expansion of the consumer base is essential for success of a corporate. As the traditional market gets saturated, business looks for new pastures, which is a must for survival. In this context, the model[1] advocated by Prahlad, the lower economic strata of the society holds a big market potential for the corporate, to be exploited for spurring economic growth. There are several examples of going out for exploiting this potential for expansion of business.

The developing countries provide several interesting examples on this. In Bangladesh, entrepreneurs managing rural phones are able to get about (100 US$ per month), i.e. 1200 US$ per annum, which is six times of their average income (about 200 US$ per annum for rural area). The earning is even higher in the bigger villages with a bigger customer base. It has been estimated that the villagers are spending about 7 per cent of their income on phone services, which is comparable with the percentage of income spent by the well-to-do persons. Similarly, in *Dharavi*, the biggest slum in Mumbai, about 80 per cent of the households were found to have television sets, over 70 per cent pressure cookers and electric mixers, 50 per cent gas stoves and over 20 per cent telephones. These facts indicate the potential available for business in the rura area and urban slums in India.

As per a survey[2] of the consumption pattern of rural India, about 300 million rural consumers accounted for about 36 per cent of the Fast Moving Consumer Goods (FMCG) like soap, detergent, shampoo, hair oil, etc. country's market with a size of Rs. 3,20,000 crore. FMCG have an average market size of Rs. 504 per household per month, which accounts for about 18 per cent of the total monthly expenditure of the household (Rs. 2,800) in rural area. Out of the FMCG segment, food products constituted 55 per cent (Rs. 280) and personal care items like cosmetics, skincare remaining 45 per cent (Rs. 224). About 17 per cent households were found to be using branded skincare products, whereas 21 per cent households do not use any beauty care products. Another assessment made by L'Oreal India indicated the rural households spend about Rs. 36 per month on skincare and cosmetics. Further, notwithstanding impact of low rainfall and bad monsoon on income from agriculture, the FMCG market in rural India has been growing faster than the urban market continuously. However, expenditure on healthcare has been too low amounting to only Rs. 56 per household, which is a matter of concern, more so because it has been about one-third of the expenditure on alcohol (Rs. 140) and about half of the expenditure on tobacco (Rs. 96).[3]

These facts indicate the huge potential for doing business with the so-called poor as consumers, which has been growing as a result of publicity in the media and television. Later has also been fuelling new hopes and aspirations for a better life among the poor. The challenge therefore lies in striking a balance between exploiting the new business opportunities on the one hand and fulfilling the expectations of the masses on the other hand. While looking for higher turnover and bigger profit from the FMCG segment for expansion of business, the corporate need to come forward to empower the poor rural households with education, healthcare and skill for making the growth and development process inclusive and sustainable.

References:

1. C.K. Prahlad, *Economist*. "*Bottom of the Pyramid*".
2. Conducted by Chrome Data Analytics & Media, a primary research and data analytics company), covering 50,000 villages across nineteen states in India.
3. "*Rural India spends more on booze than health*", *The Times of India*, November 1, 2016, p. 9.

consumer base and surviving in the market. Such a group of large number of customer offers a new market and opportunity for doing business, rather than being considered as a limitation, looking for charity. This led to creation of new business opportunity on the one hand and empowerment of the poor and disadvantaged on the other.

Exploiting business at the bottom of the pyramid provides an opportunity to reach the real *poor beyond the not so poor,* as under normal conditions it is more difficult to make the former category customers. The consumer base can be expanded by targeting the low income group, who find it difficult to purchase household utility items like television, mixer-grinder, which they need or wish to have, but don't have adequate means to fund it. Families with limited income are not able to get consumer goods, electronic appliances, as they cannot afford to pay the entire cost at a time. Acquisition of such assets provides them market access with market information and also enables them to produce goods and services for sale as per market demand. It helps in solving the problems of unemployment and poverty to a considerable extent. For this segment of the society, cost is more critical than time. Devising suitable business models for financing the total cost with a small initial deposit (down payment) and balance in installments help in overcoming this problem. Segregation of individual requirement leads to generation of huge demand. Scaling up demand with assured market eliminates uncertainty in marketing, which in turn reduces cost and ensures supply at a relatively lower price by operating on a *low margin—high turnover* approach. Simultaneously, it supports industrialization for mass production of the commodities, generates wealth and employment by making best use of the labour. Acquisition of income generating assets enables the poor household to produce, enter the market and earn their livelihood. Use of

Mobile telephone based applications further facilitates expansion of such endeavours.

Packing of branded consumer goods like soap, shampoo etc. in pouches and smaller packs for reducing unit cost and bringing it within the reach of the household with limited income offers yet another opportunity to exploit the business at the bottom of the pyramid. With a large customer base, this model help in reducing cost, creating new business opportunity for the corporate and employment opportunity for the poor.

The *e-choupal* initiative of ITC Limited offers one such example of empowering the primary producers in rural area with technology, started at the beginning of the new millennium. Over 6,400 Internet-enabled information kiosks set up under this intervention have been serving over 3.5 millions farmers in Madhya Pradesh, Karnataka, Andhra Pradesh, Uttar Pradesh, Maharashtra and Rajasthan. These centres are managed by local youth, who have been trained in Information Technology (IT) as *Sanchalaks,* providing valuable information relating to market prices, scientific farm practices, weather and risk management to the rural villagers in vernacular language at virtually no cost. This platform is being shared by other companies like Agrico division of Tata Steel for marketing agri-implements. ITC had ambitious plan to extend this to cover 15 million villagers living in 1,00,000 villages. ITC had taken up training with provision of pedal based rolling machine to the poor artisans involved in *Agarbati* Stick making in the North Eastern State Tripura. This new technology helped the artisans with higher productivity, better quality and higher income. Based on this experience, The Ministry of Panchayati Raj had initiated setting up Rural Business Hub (RBH) on Public-Private-Panchayat Partnership (PPPP) model in liaison with the Confederation of Indian Industries (CII) for providing similar IT services in the rural area.

Such models have helped in expansion of business by exploiting the existing potential and led to empowerment of the poor and disadvantaged as well. Solar Electric Light Company (SELCO), India based in Bangalore had initiated an innovative model to provide solar energy devices and services to rural people at an affordable price.[6] Over 80,000 people living in rural areas in Karnataka, Kerala and Andhra Pradesh were benefited by this initiative in getting electricity from solar energy for the first time. The company was providing a two-light solar home system for Rs.12,500 and four-light system for Rs. 20,000 including installation and one-year service contract. It had tie-up with rural banks, leasing companies and microfinance organizations for financing the purchase. In addition to social and commercial aspects, this operation supported conservation of energy and protection of environment.

Another such case related to empowering the poor fishermen with technology for reducing the risk due to uncertain weather. Qualcomm in collaboration with *MSSRF*, Tata Teleservices Ltd., and Astute Systems Technology launched *Wireless Reach* initiative "*Fisher Friend*", which enabled the fishing communities to work safely and earn more by accessing relevant information anytime, anywhere at the press of a button. Based on the success, there was plan for scaling up CDMA2000 wireless connectivity solutions to 65 Village Resource Centres in the coastal States.

Project Shakti initiative[7] of Hindustan Unilever Limited is yet another example of expanding business along with a social purpose in reaching out to the un-served. Started in 2001, about 80,000 villages in 15 states have been covered under this programme. Over 37,000 underprivileged women have been empowered as entrepreneurs with provision of training and other support under this project. An individual Shakti entrepreneur was able to earn as much, as the average household income from this endeavour, which has provided the women dignity and improved the overall standards of living of the family. Based on this experience, the company has planned to cover 1 lakh entrepreneurs and reach 600 million consumers in 5 lakh villages.

Microfinance

Micro-finance involves provision of small credit to large number of burrowers with limited means for setting up micro-enterprises. It offers yet another area of exploring business at the bottom of the pyramid. On the potential of micro-finance, Nobel laureate, Mohammad Yunus had observed, "Poor people are like bonsai tree, having all the capabilities to rise up like big trees but the problem is that they are planted in flower pots. If 2 per cent gets 98 per cent credit and 98 per cent gets 2 per cent credit that means, there is a lot to be done to reach out to those poor, who have no access to credit. The credit should be available at low cost." The Reserve Bank of India (RBI) and the National Bank for Agriculture and Rural Development (NABARD) have advised the bankers for taking up provision of micro-finance, based on which several public and private sector banks and financial institutions have taken up provision of micro-credit through NGOs. The Citibank Micro-finance Group took up supporting Hyderabad-based "*Basix*" and Mumbai-based "*Swadhaar*", since 1999, offering financial services and products to people, outside the formal banking structure. Institutional finance up to Rs. 25,000 is being provided to economically active and low income individuals. Such interventions have enabled the disadvantaged in setting up micro-enterprises and accessing the market for earning their livelihood and repaying the loan at the same time. Strength of micro-finance in empowering the poor and needy is based on the fact that in addition to doing business and improvement of economic condition, it develops saving habit as well. Provision of other financial services, like micro-insurance have been dovetailed with micro-finance, which has increased risk-taking ability of the poor and enabled him/her for undertaking new occupations.

Production and Marketing of Agricultural Produces

In the rural areas, production and processing of agriculture and dairy products (milk) on a commercial scale offer huge opportunity for business along with empowering the primary producers with assured marketing facility and higher return. India's cooperative based *Amul model* has set an example in dairy development all-over the world. However, attempts for replicating this model has not succeeded in other parts of the country, due to some reason or other and the potential has remained untapped. However, several corporate have taken up supporting the primary producers with quality inputs for production along with assured price, aggregating the produce, processing and marketing the value added product. This has led to provision of a remunerative price to the farmers, decent return on investment and general prosperity in the region as in the case with Nestle India in Moga, Punjab; Lipton in Etah, Uttar Pradesh. [**Box 5.5: Milk and fodder production for growth and employment**]

Strategic Intervention for Re-skilling and Redeploying Manpower

Remaining sensitive to the changing business scenario and taking appropriate measures for safeguarding interest of the organization as well as of the stakeholders particularly the employees and workers is yet another aspect of remaining responsible towards the society. Arrival of new technology and products often makes the earlier version obsolete, like the digital photography replacing analog version. Such developments pose new challenge to the commercial organization from time to time. The corporate need to take up diversification of the business for meeting such challenges. Normally, corporate carry on business in good times, when

Box 5.5: Milk and Fodder production for growth and employment

Spurred by rising incomes, a growing population and changing food preferences, the demand for milk and milk products has been projected to grow to at least 210 million tons by 2021-22, a rise of 36 per cent over five years. To meet this demand, production shall have to grow by 5.5 per cent per annum.[1] In 2014-15 and 2015-16, milk production grew at 6.2 per cent and 6.3 per cent, respectively. Such increase in milk production is feasible, but depends upon producing 1,764 million tonnes of fodder by 2020.[2] However, existing sources can only manage about 900 million tonnes of fodder, which will lead to a shortage of 49 per cent.[3]

Demand for private consumption has risen from five per cent per annum in the period 1998-2005 to 8.5 per cent per annum between 2005 and 2012.[4] This demand and supply gap has pushed up milk prices by an average of 16 per cent per annum in the decade 2000 – 2015. Milk production went up by 59 per cent from 92 million tonnes in 2000 to 146 million tonnes in 2015. But fodder shortages may knock India off its position as the world's top milk producer (it contributes nearly 17 per cent of global production). The milk productivity of India's livestock is less than half (48 per cent) of the global average: 987 kg per lactation compared to the global average of 2,038 kg per lactation. Availability and quality of fodder has a direct bearing on the productivity quantity and quality of milk. All the three states that topped milk productivity in terms of gram per day—Rajasthan (704), Haryana (877) and Punjab (1,032)—had earmarked more than 10 per cent of their cultivable land for pastures, according to the 2015 SOIL report.

The three types of fodder are in short supply—green (63%), dry (24%) and concentrates (76%). Only four per cent of total cultivable land in India is used for fodder production, a proportion that has remained stagnant for the last four decades. Considering the demand for milk, land under fodder production needs to be doubled, according to a December 2016 report of the Parliamentary Committee on Agriculture. Shortages are forcing states to source fodder from elsewhere. "The quality of fodder is a concern. We are now looking to source fodder from Varanasi, Uttar Pradesh", said Sudhir Mishra, who runs a dairy farm in Ranchi, Jharkhand. But major portions of grazing lands have either been degraded or encroached upon, according to the Parliamentary Committee report. However, the availability of crop residues, the largest single source of fodder, has been impacted by increasing pressure on land and the replacement of traditional cereal crops, especially coarse ones. Crop residue includes coarse and fine straws, leguminous and pulses straws. Given the importance of food and cash crops, it is very unlikely that the area under fodder cultivation will increase substantially, as has been observed by the parliamentary committee.

Milk production has a social angle as well, as bulk of the milk (about 70%) is produced by small and marginal farmers. Relatively less educated, unemployed youth, belonging to disadvantaged segments like Scheduled Caste/Scheduled Tribe, have taken bank loan and gone for dairy units with one or two cattle heads. Feed cost constitutes about 60-70 per cent of operating expenses on dairy farms. To cut costs, easy access to fodder is important for small farmers. As such non-availability of fodder will affect their productivity and income very adversely. India may have to import milk in four years, if it cannot increase fodder supply for its 299 million cattle, as rising pressure on land reduces pastures nationwide.

References:

1. State of India's Livelihood (SOIL) Report, 2015.
2. India Spend analysis of government data.
3. Gangadhar S. Patil, With pastures shrinking India may be importing milk by 2021, *Tripura Observer*, 27 February, 2017, p. 2.
4. Report of the Indian Institute of Management, Bangalore.

the going is smooth and there is profit. Once the going becomes tough and the revenue dries up; the operation is closed down. This led to dislocation and considerable hardship to the workers, as they find it difficult to get employment elsewhere with their existing skill sets. This leads to unemployment and economic hardship for the workers. There are several such instances in the labour intensive textiles, jute, tea industries; where production units with old technology closed down causing untold misery to the workers.

A socially responsible corporate on the other hand anticipates the impact of new technology on contemporary business and takes up diversification of business well in time along with re-skilling the worker for making them employable with new skill sets, as per the market requirements with new technology/product. Such strategic move ensures safeguarding the interest of the business as well as of the workers. Tata Tea's action for diversifying tea business and skilling and redeploying the existing workers offers one such example of corporate taking care of the workers and remaining responsible to the society [**Box 5.6: Diversification of Tea Plantation**].

Development of science and technology, discovery of new products with new uses generate new business opportunities for the corporate to initiate economic activities, as per the emerging requirement. Production of environment friendly green cotton, without use of chemicals, for example, meets the need of a new niche market, which in turn set new and higher standards for the business for satisfying the consumers. Once

Box 5.6: Diversification of Tea Plantation

With a view to meet the challenges emerging due to the downturn in tea prices, Tata Tea planned to diversify its tea business into horticulture, animal husbandry and pisciculture in the north-eastern region. This has been initiated in partnership with Globally Managed Services (GMS). Two pilot projects were started in the tea estates at *Borjan and Hathikuli* in Assam for production of oranges, tomatoes, a wide variety of fish, dairy products and even pork and duck meat. Based on its success, it would be taken up on a commercial scale.

According to Dipankar Borah, Tata Tea's vice-president for North India Plantation Operations (NIPO), diversifying into non-tea areas has been taken up in the existing tea estates in Assam and West Bengal, by creating a separate Agricultural Services Organization (ASO) division. Production of fruits and vegetables like chilli, tomatoes, oranges, papaya and bananas, spices like ginger and turmeric, duck meat and pork have been identified. The operation is planned to be undertaken on a "hub-and-spoke" model in a co-operative format. The company has planned to promote this venture and manage the supply chain with supply of inputs like soft loans, seeds and fertilizers and buying back the produce. The product would be marketed through organized food retailing chains across the country and would undertake export as well, in due course.

This diversification represents strategic intervention by a responsible corporate for exploring new potential, remaining competitive in the market along with welfare of the workers with limited assets as well.

Reference

"Tatas to grow fruits, vegetables and fish in north-east tea estates", Sumit Mitra, *The Financial Express*, April 05, 2007, p. 12.

the new product becomes popular, other companies are forced to adopt such practices. In such a case, the initiator derives the benefits of starting early.

Management of water and taking up micro irrigation system on a commercial scale provide one such opportunity for the corporate growth on the one hand and helping the small and marginal farmers on the other [**Box 5.7: Micro irrigation for Inclusive Development**].

Exploiting such existing/emerging opportunities requires manpower with skill and education. Providing technical manpower as per requirement of the industry offers another opportunity to the corporate sector to expand and help the society as well, in solving the problem of unemployment. Corporate have taken up intervention for upgrading the skill of the youth by forging partnership with the universities/institutes for producing knowledgeable and competent graduates as per their requirement. While

Box 5.7: Micro Irrigation for Inclusive Development

Water is essential for survival of plants and human being and plays a significant role in the agriculture based rural economy. Agriculture accounts for approximately 70 per cent of the global fresh water withdrawal and 90 per cent of its consumptive use. However, India has only 4 per cent of the world's usable water resources for meeting requirement of 16 per cent of world's population. India's economy is dependent on the monsoon and pattern of annual rainfall. Global warming and its impact on climate change have been affecting monsoon and making the rainfall pattern erratic. Accordingly, judicious use of available water has assumed an important role in economic development in general and promotion of agricultural activities in particular.

Appropriate technology like sprinkler and drip irrigation provides one of the best ways of using available water effectively. These techniques increase efficiency of water use by 50 to 90 per cent, save consumption of energy by 30 per cent, consumption of fertiliser by 28.5 per cent; at the same time increase productivity of fruits and crops by 42.4 per cent, vegetable by 52.7 per cent, reduce cost of irrigation by 31.9 per cent, facilitate crop diversification and introduction of new crop by 30.4 per cent and increase income of farmers by 42 per cent.[1] These techniques are extensively used in Israel and other countries and have contributed to development of agriculture and individual farmers significantly.

Keeping in view these advantages, initiative for adoption of this technology was introduced in India in 1992, which was given specific thrust in 2006 with launching of a Centrally sponsored Scheme for Micro Irrigation. This was upgraded to National Mission on Micro Irrigation in 2013-14 and merged with the *National Mission for Sustainable Agriculture* in 2014-15. *Pradhan Mantri Krishi Sinchayee Youjana (PMKSY)* was launched in 2015, for integrating micro irrigation as an integral component. Advantages of micro irrigation lie in its implementation and putting the system in place only within a few months, whereas traditional irrigation project takes years together.

However, experience of micro irrigation at the individual farmer level has remained mixed. Out of the total potential of about 69 million hectares, only 7.7 million hectares (about 10%) could be covered during 2015 with a target for adding 0.5 million hectare per annum which will take a long time to exploit the available potential. 82 per cent of the total coverage is limited to six states, *viz*. Andhra Pradesh, Gujarat, Rajasthan, Maharashtra, Karnataka and Haryana.[2] Its spread in the remaining states and extension of its benefits to small and marginal farmers, who really need this help, continues to be a matter of concern.

In view of its specific advantage based on use of appropriate technology, potential for production of fruits, vegetables, flowers and other agricultural commodities, which have got good demand both within and outside the country; micro irrigation provides excellent business opportunity. Apart from profit and gain at the corporate level, it has considerable social significance. Promotion of micro irrigation along with supply of agricultural inputs, marketing and processing of the agricultural produce will spur economic growth and in improving economic condition of the small and marginal farmers. In addition to consolidating business of existing corporate like Jain Drip Irrigation, others can take up this for producing quality goods and also execution of the project on a turnkey basis. Further generation of awareness about its advantage and promotion of skill for managing and maintaining the assets would be required for its expansion at the field level, which will play an important role in inclusive development.

References:

1. FICCI Report in February 2016 made by Grant Thornton.
2. livemint.Microirrigation-lags-far-behind-potential-shows-study.

enabling the youth and making them employable, such intervention helps the industry in meeting its future manpower need as well.

Looking Beyond Immediate Gains for Meeting Social Needs

The third and common component of CSR in Indian conditions relates to the corporate supporting social issues as a responsible stakeholder in the society, looking beyond immediate gains. Social activities of corporate has evolved in India through three broad phases, namely, (i) charity, (ii) philanthropy, and (iii) institutionalized philanthropy.

Charity is derived from the Latin word *'Caritas'* (meaning to care), which essentially means short term measure for meeting immediate requirement. For an individual, it relates to the emotional responsibility for assisting somebody, who is in need, as a part of religious and moral duty.

Philanthropy is derived from the Greek words *'Philos'* (meaning friend) and '*Ánthropos*' (meaning human). This relates to interventions, which are of long term nature. It requires strategy and institutional arrangements like building a school or a hospital for assisting fellow human beings with limited means, who are not in a position to avail such services from open market on payment basis. It is seen as a means for empowering individuals and communities over a long term by conferring benefits of permanent nature, looking beyond immediate problems as is the case with charity.

The institutional philanthropy represents the latest and more developed stage, where arrangements are institutionalized for meeting long term needs. It involves providing assistance on a holistic manner over a longer period of time, like providing long term training along with counselling, handholding, and provision of assets for earning livelihood. It covers management of ecosystem as well for operating on a sustainable basis.

In order to remain relevant to the society in the twenty-first century, the corporate need to look beyond compliance of law and undertake innovative practices for taking care of those, who are outside the market and need specific support. This group includes the aged, orphans, widows, destitute, persons facing challenges; whose empowerment is important for making the growth inclusive. The corporate have to take care of them without looking for immediate gains [**Box 5.8: Corporate taking care of the widows**]. Keeping in view the social needs, corporate have taken up initiatives for bridging the existing gaps in social infrastructure for furthering the cause of national development in general and welfare of the weaker section in particular. CSR, becoming mandatory under the Companies Act, with effect from 1st April, 2014, provide a rare opportunity for scaling up the welfare activities in general and for the disadvantaged segments of the society in particular.

CSR in the New Millennium

On future of CSR in India, it will be worthwhile to analyze some of the major challenges faced, the efforts being made by the Government for tackling those as well as initiative taken by the corporate under their CSR initiatives for supplementing it, with a view to ascertaining the innovative and best practices, which can be replicated for making a meaningful difference in the society.

India in the 21st Century—Challenges and Achievements

Notwithstanding various constraints, India has made significant success in various social parameters, as is evident from the achievements in respect of the Millennium Development Goals (MDGs) 2015[8], which were adopted at the beginning of the new Millennium and acted upon in the first one and half a decade (2000-15), as indicated below:

Poverty

Incidence of poverty declined from 47.8 per cent (in 1990) to 21.9 per cent (in 2015), which was better than the MDG target [of reducing it by

Box 5.8: Corporate Support for the Widows

Because of prevailing social customs and stigma, widows in general and young widows in particular face enormous social and economic difficulties. Further, those with limited income, face difficulties in bringing up their children and giving them proper education.

The Loomba Trust[1] was set up in United Kingdom in March 1998 at the initiative of Shri Raj Loomba, Chairman of the Rinky Clothing Group Company, in memory of his mother Smt. Pushpa Wati Loomba. It seeks to assist the widows with limited financial means for bringing up and educating their children. The trust provides scholarships to needy children of widows for a period of five years and has sought financial support from individuals and organisations with the appeal "contribution of 100 UK Pounds will educate a widow's child in India for one year".

The Indian Chapter of the trust was started in March 1999 with the aim to support at least 100 children in each state for pursuing education without regard to gender, religion or class. Several corporate, including Birla, ONGC, Godfrey Philips India, HSBC, ICICI Bank, British Telecom supported this cause.

On the activities of the trust, Cherie Booth[2] QC had commented "The hardship faced by millions of widows around the globe is rarely talked about, but the Loomba Trust has made great progress in bringing this issue to light and in implementing practical programmes to support these unfortunate widows and their children".

Following a sustained campaign, on 21 December, 2010 the United Nations General Assembly formally recognised, *23 June as International Widows Day.* The first *World Widows Report* prepared by the Loomba foundation[3] was launched on March 17, 2016 at the United Nations in New York, coinciding with the UN's adoption of the Sustainable Development Goals (SDG, 2030).

In India, numbers of widows are forced to leave their homes and migrate to religious places like Banaras, Vrindaban, and Mathura, where they are subjected to humiliation and exploitation. The Ministry of Women and Child Development and State Governments have taken steps for welfare of the widows including provision of monthly pension. However, this is not adequate. Solution to this problem requires an empowerment based approach for imparting quality skill to the relatively young widows for earning their livelihood and providing adequate financial assistance to the elderly ones for meeting their day to day needs for food, clothing and shelter.

In this context, non-governmental organisations like Loomba Trust as well as corporate under its CSR intervention, along with the ongoing government schemes can make a difference in the lives of widows, one of the disadvantaged groups of the society.

References:

1. The Loomba Trust, Annual Report 2004-05, www.theloombatrust. org
2. Cherie Booth QC, wife of Tony Blair, the British Prime Minister, while launching the programme in UK on the 30th March, 1998.
3. http://theloombafoundation.org/home/

half to 23.9%], as assessed by the all India Poverty Head Count Ratio (PHCR). This was attributed to higher economic growth in all sectors including agriculture and higher spending in social sector on interventions like MGNREGA, National Rural Health Mission (NRHM). Notwithstanding this reduction, over 270 million Indians continue to live in extreme poverty (in 2012), which makes elimination of poverty a challenging task.

Hunger

Malnourishment among children declined from 53.5 per cent (in 1990) to 40 per cent (in 2015), which was below the target of reducing it to 26 per cent. Malnourishment and food insecurity are interlinked. Eradicating hunger continue to be a key challenge for India. About one-quarter of the world's undernourished population, over a third of the world's underweight children, and nearly a third of the world's food-insecure people are living in India.

Health

Infant Mortality Rate (IMR), indicating the number of children dying before attaining five years age per 1,000 live births, declined from 125 (in 1990) to 49 (in 2013), against the MDG target of 42 indicating that achievements are moderate. This is attributed to implementation of child centric policy and programmes, like the National Policy on Children (2013), National Policy on Early Childhood Care and Education, Integrated Child Development Services (ICDS). However, it is necessary to speed up these giving more attention to neonatal, i.e. infant deaths, which occurs within a year of birth and childhood illnesses for improving child survival, particularly to the more vulnerable, disadvantaged communities. There have been large interstate variations with better performing Kerala (12) at one end and Madhya Pradesh (54) on the other end. This calls for giving more attention to the latter region/states.

Maternal Mortality Rate (MMR), indicating the number of death of mothers per lakh of live births, fell from 437 (in 1990-91) to 167 (in 2009), as against the target of 109 (by 2015), making the achievement somewhat slow. Institutional delivery rose from 26 per cent (in 1992-93) to 72 per cent (in 2009) and deliveries by skilled personnel increased from 33 per cent to 76.2 per cent in the same period. These are attributed to implementation of *Janani Suraksha Yojana* including cash transfer, which had impact on reducing the MMR. Ongoing interventions are required to be supplemented and speeded up in the coming decade for achieving the SDGs.

Achievements in tackling **AIDS and HIV** have been good, as not only the growing trend of incidence of HIV was checked, but in fact got reversed among the high risk categories. Prevalence rate got reduced from 0.45 per cent (in 2002) to 0.36 (in 2009), on account of greater awareness and increase in use of condom; as about 86 per cent of HIV and AIDS transmissions in India are reportedly caused by sexual activity.

Further, **incidence of Malaria** reduced significantly from 2.12 per thousand (in 2001) to 0.72 per thousand (in 2013). Incidence of **tuberculosis** (TB) was checked with incidence per lakh population reducing from 216 (in 1990) to 171 (in 2013). Access of households to **safe drinking water** increased from 68.2 per cent (in 1992-93) to 90.6 per cent (in 2011-12). However, improvement in provision of sanitation facilities remained slow.

Primary Education

Achievements in literacy and education with overall literacy rate of the 15-24 years age group at 86.17 per cent (in 2011), female literacy (rate 92.47%) coming at par with male (rate 94.81%), enrolment in primary level touching 88.04 per cent (in 2013-14), and continuation up to grade V at 86.05 per cent (in 2011-12) have remained significant. These are attributed to the enactment of the Right of Children to Free and Compulsory Education Act (RTE) in 2009 along with provision of substantial resource. However, there are gaps and regional variations, for which the interventions are required to be consolidated and improved further giving greater attention to gender (girls), geographical area (rural and tribal) and communities (minority).

Environment

In respect of environmental sustainability, forest cover increased by 5871 sq. km. to 21.23 per cent of the total land area. The energy intensity of GDP growth however remained high. This is required to be reduced through promotion of energy efficient means.

The Road Ahead

Achievements of India in various parameters in the past decade, as discussed above, are attributed to policy initiatives, action taken along with deployment of resource by the Central and State Governments as well as Civil Society (non-governmental organizations) associated with development. Taking these achievements forward for ***achieving the next phase of Sustainable Development Goals (SDG 2030) would require mobilization of substantial financial and managerial resources along with deployment of appropriate technology.***

Relevance of CSR in the Indian context is required to be appreciated in this background for bridging the gaps in the expectations and available opportunities for the masses and the youth in particular. While this issue is multidimensional in nature and require multiple stakeholders working in unison; the corporate need to appreciate that they can make a meaningful contribution for this cause through their CSR interventions by designing and implementing CSR projects in synergy with ongoing programmes of government, non-governmental organizations, the bank and other financial institutions. ***Sensitizing all the stakeholders, particularly the corporate to these realities for extending their support for making the development inclusive and sustainable is, in fact the main purpose, of this humble publication.***

CSR of Future

In this context, it is deemed relevant to briefly discuss some of the CSR initiatives for ascertaining the impact and also the scope for future course of action for making the growth socially and environmentally inclusive. These would be analyzed with reference to the three components of human resource development; relating to quality healthcare, education, skill for livelihood along with the environment related issues.

Quality Healthcare

Out of the multifarious challenges faced by India, provision of quality healthcare, which is *effective, safe* (without any side effect) and *affordable* (from cost perspective) to all citizens, is of special significance. Importance of health for an individual is best reflected in the Sanskrit *sloka* "*Shariramâdyam, khalu dharmasadhanam*"; meaning Human body or good health is the most important and comes first of all things in life. Provision of healthcare is a multidimensional and complex issue. It requires not only financial and physical resources but also favourable social parameters like faith, belief, mindset, free from prejudice; which determine habit and attitude of the target group. It *requires provision of quality services from the provider side and the right attitude to avail the services from the consumer side, for having the desired impact.* Further, the requirements are dynamic and keep on changing; as is evident from the fact that economic development brings more resources, nutritious food and reduces the incidence of diseases relating to hunger and malnutrition, but in turn leads to incidence of lifestyle related diseases like obesity, diabetic, high blood pressure, cancer etc.

In pursuance of the directive principles of State policy of the Constitution, the government has been taking up measures for providing primary, secondary and tertiary healthcare to all for decades since independence. Notwithstanding commitment for multifarious purposes, public resource to the extent of about 5 per cent of the GDP is being spent on public healthcare in India. However, status of healthcare, both in coverage and quality, continues to be a matter of concern. In the composite Sustainable Development Goal indicators, including health, India ranked 143 among 188 countries; at a position lower than Indonesia (91), Thailand (112) and Ghana (141). Provision of more financial resources along with suitable changes in the government policy has been advocated[9] for improving the healthcare services in the public sector. In this context, soft components relating to management, participation of the community and individuals, suitable change in the lifestyle and mindset are of critical importance for ensuring utilization of available financial resources optimally and achieving the desired objectives.

In a developing country, even though government is primarily responsible for provision of healthcare, mobilization of corporate support under CSR can be of considerable help in improving the healthcare services. CSR interventions for healthcare fall under three broad categories, namely, (i) creation of new physical infrastructure like buildings; (ii) filling gaps in existing health infrastructure; and (iii) improving the management by deployment of new and appropriate technology, capacity building of officers and staff etc.

CSR intervention is normally measured in terms of the amount of money provided or spent. But soft components like support for counselling, management of resources are equally important in delivering quality healthcare services. Health of an individual depends on a set of interlinked factors like availability of nutritious food in adequate quantity, access to safe drinking water, sanitation as well as awareness for using available facilities. It has been seen that mere availability of physical infrastructure like hospital does not by itself lead to better health. For example, number of toilets constructed with government fund are not being used by the target group due to some reason or other, because of which the health parameters are not improving in spite of the investment. In such cases, it is necessary to change old habits and mindset, which takes time. For this purpose, soft components like counselling for winning confidence and changing habits becomes more important than spending money and creation of physical assets. Innovative Information, Education and Communication (IEC) activities have proved to be useful in changing behaviour of the target group, leading to better use of the facilities and improvement of the health parameters. This has been established in the case of tackling HIV and AIDS, which was quite alarming at one point of time, and could be checked through media campaign for generating awareness about the disease. Similarly, adoption of small family norm got more acceptances by counselling, taking care of the mother and child, checking infant mortality; rather than forcible sterilization which failed miserably. Publicity on cigarette smoking and tobacco consumption leading to cancer similarly had a good impact on reducing the incidence of smoking.

Corporate have volunteered to support social causes like preventive healthcare measures for generating awareness about controlling blood pressure, diabetics among adults, checking obesity among children by adoption of healthy lifestyle. This provides an interesting and useful area of corporate action for welfare of the society looking beyond profit **[Box 5.9: Corporate Initiative for Preventive Healthcare, Checking Obesity].**

In provision of quality healthcare, Arvind Group have evolved a business model by mobilization of resource in providing quality eye care health services to the rich on payment and providing same service to the poor free; setting an example in inclusive development. **[Box 5.10: Business Model for Meeting Need of the Disadvantaged].**

These experiences indicate that in addition to financial resources, corporate support by mobilization in form of *corporate volunteerism for counselling* played an important role in improving the healthcare. Further use of appropriate technology like telemedicine and teleophthalmology has also been found to be effective, particularly in the interior areas. It has helped in provision of quality services at a reasonable cost and overcoming the problem arising due to acute shortage of doctor and paramedical staff in such areas.

Nutrition

The Integrated Child Development Services (ICDS) scheme was launched in selected blocks in 1975 for providing a package of six services including supplementary nutrition to children up to six years age, pregnant and

Box 5.9: Corporate Initiative for Preventive Healthcare

Preventive healthcare has assumed new dimensions with economic development and change in lifestyle. Health education for generation of awareness and adoption of healthy lifestyle are more effective means to tackle this development rather than medication.

"Swashrit", an NGO, led by a group of doctors, nutritionists, psychologists and lifestyle experts has been organizing *"Get Active"* campaign for generating awareness about healthy habits and active alternatives among school children[1]. The campaign has a mission *"To drive and instill an active lifestyle and healthy nutritional habits among school children"*. Several Medical professionals and institutions like Escorts Heart Institute and Research Centre Hospital, New Delhi, Indian Medical Association (IMA) have been associated with the initiative.

As many as 27 Habit Modification activities have been undertaken under this programme covering three categories; such as Calories In, Calories Out, Community Building including Active Tiffin, Active treasure hunt, Active inventions, Active salad, Active theatre etc. This initiative increases the intrinsic value and attraction towards active lifestyles amongst children and adolescents through fun-filled, learning activities. It has generated enthusiasm among the Principals, teachers, and parents as well.

The programme has been of considerable help to the populations, especially in low and middle income groups in checking excessive caloric intake, promoting physical activity and healthy food consumption. It has attempted to raise awareness through promotion of a holistic development approach covering emotional, physical, psychological and social aspects for healthy lifestyle amongst children and youth. Over 3 lakh children have been covered under this programme aiming at motivating them for acquiring good eating habits and remaining physically active in daily life.

PepsiCo[2] India has come forward to support this cause under its CSR initiative along with promoting healthier alternatives to Cola like juice, oatmeal etc., for meeting the changing lifestyles. This development marks synergy of action taken by the civil society and the corporate for promoting a social cause of enormous importance relating to good health.[3]

References

1. http://www.swashritsociety.com/get-active.html
2. Suman Tarafdar, *The Financial Express,* October 14, 2007, p. 4.
3. Kounteya Sinha, "1 in 5 in India is obese, overweight: Study", *The Times of India*, May 29, 2014, p. 1.

nursing mothers through a network of *Anganwadi Centre* (AWC), set up at the habitation level. This scheme was subsequently extended to the entire country and made universal as per the order of the Supreme Court,

Box 5.10: Business Models for meeting Need of the Disadvantaged

Aravind Eye Care Hospital was founded[1] in 1976 by Dr. G. Venkatswamy with a view to provide quality eye healthcare services in general and cataract surgery in particular. Its business practice is based on a model for providing free services to patients belonging to poorer section and running its commercial activities on the fees collected from the relatively affluent segment. The experiment based on *"treating vast number of non-paying patients enables the company to deliver the quality that attracts the ones that do pay"* enables the company to render social service without affecting its commercial viability on a long term basis and offers a model, which can be followed with suitable modifications by other corporate in remaining meaningful in the society, particularly in a developing country like India.

The operations model[2] is similar to McDonalds involving high volume, highly efficient operations, based on division of labour and cost efficiency. It makes the operation profitable with a gross margin of about 50 per cent and enables the setup to treat about 70 per cent of the poor patients for free. The 30 per cent that do pay are relatively affluent people who can afford the full cost of operation, but receive the same service. In fact, the company goes out of its way to actively locate non-paying customers, by looking for them systematically in the countryside and bringing them to their clinics free of cost. The clinical quality of service—the cataract operation, is second to none. The business models are built for the long-term and in the long-run, the lower costs enable them to provide better quality.

It is often said that Aravind's paying customers subsidize the 70 per cent that get the operation for free. Yet, in many ways, it is the other way around: Treating the vast numbers of non-paying patients enables the company to deliver the quality that attracts the ones that pay.

Arvind eye care provides valuable lessons for others, who make decisions based on the short-term consequences, because that is what they can see and measure. It indicates a better alternative[3] involving delivering superior quality at lower costs and at the same time even do some good for society in the process. This is of considerable significance for a developing country like India in providing affordable quality health care to the masses.

References

1. http://www.aravind.org/
2. Freek Vermeulen, "The two questions every manager must ask", *The Hindu*, April 30, 2014, p. 2.
3. Freek Vermeulen, *"Business Exposed: The Naked Truth about What Really Goes on in the World of Business".*

for having one AWC in each habitation.[10] Over last decades, coverage of ICDS expanded to 13.49 lakh AWCs under 7,073 ICDS projects, serving 820.65 lakh children below six years and 189.91 lakh pregnant and nursing mothers (as on 30.09.2016). Out of them, pre-school education is being provided to 345.44 lakh children in the age group of 3-6 years.

After two decades of starting ICDS, the Mid-Day Meal (MDM) scheme was launched in 1995 for providing nutrition support to students studying in Government schools up to Class VIII. Further, the National Rural Health Mission (NRHM) was launched for provision of health care to all with focus on institutional delivery, immunization through Health Sub-Centre (HSC) set up at Panchayat level. All capital expenditure on construction of AWC, HSC, equipment as well as recurring expenditure on salary and wage is being met by the government.

Notwithstanding deployment of substantial resources under these programmes for decades, the percentage of malnourished (stunted) children below 5 years in the country got reduced by only 9 per cent in 8 years; from 48 per cent in 2006 to 39 per cent in 2014 as per the Global Nutrition Report.[11] Another important health indicator, Maternal Mortality Rate (MMR) reduced marginally from 178 in 2010-12 to 167 in 2011-13. Such relatively slow progress is attributed to factors like illiteracy, poor socio-economic status, early age of marriage, poor knowledge of nutritional care during pregnancy, home delivery, etc. In view of its importance, it is necessary to explore alternatives including taking advantage of the mandatory CSR for supplementing resources, better managerial practices, mobilization of beneficiary etc. As a matter of fact, importance of Angan Wadi Centre in serving the children as well as empowering women has been appreciated by corporate leaders from time to time. Shri Anil Agarwal, Chairman of Vedanta Group has recently observed[12] that "achievement of the sustainable development goals would require providing gender equality and empowering women, improving maternal health. The *starting point for* meeting the goals must be the *Anganwadis*: *courtyard shelters'* started by the government in 1975, to provide food and basic healthcare in villages, where children gather along with their mothers. These are the best places to teach the women essential skills so that they become occupied, independent and empowered in the real sense, even as they continue to supervise their children. If given proper training in vocational and managerial skills, nothing will come in the way of women even from humble backgrounds becoming entrepreneurs in their own right. The more a country empowers its women, the more prosperous it becomes".

ICDS, *Sarva Shiksha Abhiyan* (SSA) and National Health Mission (NHM) are being implemented by government as flagship schemes for meeting the basic needs of a child with provision of a package of health and education services. Notwithstanding creation of physical infrastructure, deployment of staff and provision of substantial resources, *impact of these schemes vary widely from place to place*. With general economic development, requirement of the target group has also been changing. *The target group has started realizing the importance of quality of service* beyond mere coverage, as evident from the fact that even the poor in the urban slums are sending their children to English medium private schools by raising loan rather than availing free education in government schools. Limitations of the Government schemes in delivering quality services have been due to the emphasis on quantity and coverage; and quality often getting compromised. This is discussed and realized in government and the scheme is revised or replaced. One of the recent cases[13] relates to renaming the Anganwadi Centre under ICDS as *Anganwadi Pathsala* in Rajasthan for providing quality pre-school education to improve the cognitive abilities of children with focus on school readiness. ICDS scheme seeks to cover all children, irrespective of their family belonging to Below Poverty Line or otherwise. Accordingly, the new *Pathsala* seek to provide benefits of the academic and creative environment to all children.

A recent study[14] of malnutrition among children in schools run by *Brihanmumbai Municipal Corporation* (BMC), Mumbai by *Praja* Foundation indicated that even in the urban area in one of the advanced region of the country, *incidence of malnutrition increased by four times* from eight per cent in 2013-14 to thirty-four per cent in 2015-16, while sizeable portion of the Mid-Day-Meal (MDM) budget allocation remained unutilized. This has *raised doubts about efficacy of the government programmes like Mid-Day Meals (MDM) and Integrated Child Development Scheme (ICDS),* aimed at improving nutritional status of the children. Malnourishment adversely affects the growth of individual children and development of human resource of the country. As per the Global Nutrition Report 2016, hunger and malnutrition are the largest risk factor for diseases leading to a loss of about ten per cent of the GDP; greater than the loss sustained during the last global financial crisis in 2008-10. Increase in the malnutrition rate among children in a urban centre, where there is no shortage of financial resource, points towards a management failure and need for a change in the strategy for delivering the desired result.

The general experience has been that while such new interventions, announced with minor changes, make headlines, *it is failing to sustain due to lack of adequate resources, proper monitoring and community participation*. In this context, it is necessary to think "*Out of box*" for providing quality service, which will be possible by adopting decentralized model with financial support from the corporate sector under CSR, involvement of a NGO with expertise, along with active participation and supervision of the local community for ensuring quality services on a long term basis.

In the above context, *Akshaya Patra Foundation*, a non-governmental organization, has set an example in serving hot cooked meals to millions of children, by mobilizing corporate support along with government assistance at a number of places across the country. This has made a dent in tackling malnutrition among children, pregnant and nursing mothers as well as school students. The model is based on evolving synergy between CSR initiatives with ongoing Government programme and involvement of Non-Governmental Organization of repute [**Box 5.11: Serving Hot Cooked Meals to Children**].

Regular intake of micro-nutrients and vitamins, which are required in small quantity but essential for physical and mental development of the child, is another important issue. It has been established that micro-nutrient intake pay rich dividends in human resource development, which has very small financial implication. Its success depends more on managerial than financial resource. Micro-nutrient can be provided to the young children in form of fortified salt, mustard oil, and wheat at cooking stage, which offer a foolproof method in ensuring physical and mental development of the child on a holistic basis [**Box 5.12: Fortifying Supplementary Nutrition with Micro-nutrients**].

Mobilization of corporate support for social cause has got attention of the other stakeholders of the society including the judiciary. Justice Verma Committee set up after the unfortunate rape and death of a young lady in December 2012 in Delhi, had made several recommendations on checking Crime Against Women (CAW) in the Nirbhaya case. As a follow-up on the said recommendations, Ministry of Health and Family Welfare issued "*Guidelines and Examination Proforma for Medico Legal Cases of Victims of Sexual Violence*" in April 2014. These guidelines, among other things, include an appeal to all government as well as private hospitals to treat sexual assault survivors/victims free of any charge, as a part of the CSR.

Box 5.11: Serving Hot Cooked Meal to Children

The *Akshaya Patra Foundation*[1] was set up by Bhaktivedanta Prabhupada with the vision *"No child in India shall be deprived of education because of hunger"*. Its activities started in June 2000 with serving 1,500 children in 5 Government schools of Bangalore. Lack of vessels and vehicles to pack and transport the cooked food to the schools were the initial constraints, which was overcome by corporate donation *viz*. Mohandas Pai giving the first vehicle to deliver food and Abhay Jain mobilizing more donors.

The foundation set up mechanized kitchen for preparing nutritious food in hygienic conditions, which is packed in containers and transported to schools. The food is served hot to the students as mid day meal. As per the estimate, about Rs. 750 is required for providing one meal to a student daily for the entire school year. For many children coming from disadvantaged segments; this is the only complete meal, they get on a day. The food has become an incentive for the student to come, stay in the school and get both nutritious food and education. Depending upon the location, the organization followed different models *viz*., running centralized kitchens in the urban area having good connectivity, decentralized kitchens in semi-urban area and through Anganwadi Centres in rural area. The foundation functions in a transparent manner and shares its financial information as well as intellectual property with the public.

Over years, *Akshaya Patra* has expanded its coverage[2], serving 14,29,878 children in 24 locations across 10 states with freshly cooked meal on all school days. It has evolved synergy with the mid-day meal programme in 10,845 schools and has plans to cover 100 more schools Besides under a tie-up with ICDS, about 1,52,041 children[3] below 6 years age are provided supplementary nutrition in 2,594 Anganwadi centres in seven locations across five states. The foundation has taken up serving nearly 6,000 pregnant and nursing mothers across 298 Anganwadi centres from its Jaipur centre.

Serving nutritious food in adequate quantity to a mother and child plays a critical role in health and development. As per an impact study[4] by Sigma Research and Consulting Pvt. Ltd. (in 2014) there is a positive impact of this intervention in addressing the classroom hunger along with improvement in enrolment and attendance. The programme has achieved the recommended nutritional requirements of food, which was found to be healthy and hygienic. Both parents and children confirmed to taking the mid-day meal together, irrespective of caste, religion and economic status.

This intervention is implanted by a non-governmental organization with support under government scheme and of corporate under CSR, serving quality food to children in Government Schools. It has led to achieving multiple objectives of human resource development like increase in enrolment, attendance, better results in school, checking malnutrition among children and mothers along with empowerment of women.

References:

1. http://en.wikipedia.org/wiki/Akshaya_Patra_Foundation
2. http://www.akshayapatra.org/our-reach
3. http://www.akshayapatra.org/anganwadi-feeding
4. http://www.akshayapatra.org/apadmin/uploads/userfiles/images/pdf/sigma-study-2014.pdf

Box 5.12: Fortifying Food with Micro-nutrients

Micro-nutrients are minerals and vitamins, which are required in small quantity but are essential for growth of human body and mind. Failure to take micro-nutrient in required quantity, in time affects growth very adversely; some of which like absence of zinc affecting growth of brain, are irreversible in nature. These are present in balanced diet, normal food, fruits and vegetables. However poorer sections are often deprived of this which affect growth of individuals particularly children in the growing stage.

With a view to reduce micro-nutrient dietary deficiency, fortification of edible oil and wheat was first launched on a mass scale under the public health policy[1] in Gujarat. This intervention involved providing energy dense, extruded, fortified, blended, *"Ready to Cook"* food packets to all the registered beneficiaries, free of cost, through the network of Anganwadi centres (AWCs). The field functionaries Anganwadi workers and Anganwadi helpers as well as the supervising officers were given intensive trainings about the need for fortification with micro-nutrients, the new product, how to use it and how to counsel mothers and other community members about its advantages. The fortified food was easy to prepare, nutritious, safe, and tastier and was liked by the target group. As per evaluation reports[2], this intervention led to decline in severe malnutrition and increase in the number of children in the normal grade within a period of 7 to 8 months. Further it had a positive impact on the health of persons belonging to Below poverty line (BPL) families, where malnutrition was a major problem. It is likely to pay rich dividends in terms of better health and reduce incidence of diseases in the long run.

Micro-nutrient initiatives have been taken up under CSR as well. As a part of CSR initiatives of the Tata Group of Industries, Tata Trust[3] signed a Memorandum of Understanding with Government of Tripura on July 9, 2015 for promotion of health, medical facilities, education, livelihood, dairy and skill development. Supply of Iron Fortified Iodized Edible Salt {Double Fortified Salt (DFS)} at subsidized rate was started on the 9th February, 2017 as a part of this initiative, for supplementing the Mid-Day-Meal provided to the students in the schools, and supplementary nutrition provided to children below six years and pregnant and nursing mothers in the Angan Wadi Centres (AWCs) under the Integrated Child Development Services (ICDS) programme as well as the meals served to the student inmates in government hostels and patients in government hospitals. Under this joint initiative, 440 MT of DFS will be provided at a concessional rate of seven rupees a kg, lower than the maret price twelve rupees per kg for the iodized salt. Such dovetailing of CSR intervention with the ongoing government programmes will have a positive impact in Tripura[4].

Benefits of food fortification in development of human resource are substantial as compared to its financial implication. Further, there is technology for scaling it up. It provides an excellent opportunity to corporate to provide last mile connectivity under its CSR which will make a big difference in the society. This intervention will eliminate micro-nutrient and vitamin deficiency related health problems like anaemia and empower the disadvantaged.

References:

1. http://wcd.gujarat.gov.in/int1.html
2. UN MDG Report 2014: *Poverty, Malnutrition and Sanitation Remain Concerns for India*.
3. "State Government and Tata Trust launch DFS to address iodine deficiency", *Tripura Times*, February 10, 2017, p. 8.
4. As per National Family Health Survey-4 (2015-16) anaemia due to low haemoglobin level among children in 6-35 months age group (48.3%), pregnant women (54.5%) and non-pregnant women (54.4%) is a matter of concern.

Control of HIV and AIDS

In the last part of the twentieth century, there was fear of HIV and AIDS acquiring epidemic proportion in India. However, this could be dealt effectively by use of Information, Education and Communication (IEC) activities in an innovative manner for generation of awareness among the risk prone category; along with early diagnosis and treatment facilities. Number of Corporate played an important role in supplementing government efforts for prevention of HIV and AIDS under CSR interventions. Generation of awareness among the vulnerable groups was prioritized and supported, which created lasting impact on prevention of AIDS. Special programmes were organized along the highways for the high risk category like truck and lorry drivers, who represent one of the most vulnerable segment as well as the commercial sex workers. Along with National Government, civil society/Non-Governmental Organization; corporate together provided a joint forum, which helped in checking the menace and its adverse social consequences.

Welfare of the *Divyang* (Person with Disability)

Welfare of the persons facing physical and mental challenges, '*Divyang*', is another sensitive and important area. The Persons with Disabilities (Equal Opportunities, Protection of Rights and Full Participation) Act, 1995 has elaborate provisions for safeguarding the interest of the persons facing challenges. The Central and State Governments have been taking measures for their welfare by provision of aids and appliances, financial assistance, capacity building, and reservation in employment in the services in identified posts. This is a gigantic task, which requires adequate financial and managerial resources for providing services specific to each person. This cause has been taken up by a number of corporate under their CSR as number of innovative interventions. "*Operation Muskan*" programme of Tata Steel providing cleft lip and palate corrective surgeries in rural areas free of cost have brought smiles to large number of children with disability in overcoming social stigma and living a normal life. Several best practices have been developed for serving the *Divyangs* in supply of onetime aids and appliances, provision of quality skill and assets for accessing the market, web-based database with person specific information on each of the differently-abled person (done in Tripura)[15], which can be replicated and scaled up by the corporate under CSR intervention for ensuring universal coverage, which will undoubtedly fulfil a national cause in empowerment of the *Divyangs* [**Box 5.13: Empowering the *Divyangs***].

Quality Education

Along with healthcare and nutrition, provision of quality education is another important requirement for development of human resource. *Sarva Shiksha Abhiyan* (SSA) was launched in 2000-01, as a Central flagship scheme for providing universal elementary education. SSA interventions included *inter alia*, opening of new schools and alternate schooling facilities, construction of schools and additional classrooms, toilets and drinking water, provisioning for teachers, regular in service training and academic resource support, free textbooks, uniforms and support for improving learning achievement levels/outcome.[16] SSA marked continuity in provision of elementary education as a follow-up to pre-school education provided to all children below six years in the *Anganwadi Centres* under ICDS.

Subsequent developments, namely directions of the Hon'ble Supreme Court, insertion of Article 21-A in the Constitution by the Constitution (Eighty-Sixth Amendment) Act, 2002 and enactment of the Right of Children to Free and Compulsory Education (RTE) Act, 2009 seek to ensure free education to each and every child as a legal right. The Mid-Day-Meal (MDM) scheme was launched to provide nutritional support to children studying in all Government schools up to class VIII. Substantial amount of public resources have been deployed for these interventions.

Box 5.13: Empowering the *Divyangs* (Differently abled)

Persons facing physical and mental challenge represent one of the most vulnerable segments of the society. Along with provision of aids and appliances, capacity building is of critical importance for empowering them in the true sense and enabling them for leading a life at par with others. Hemophilia Federation (India) (HFI) and CSR intervention[1] of Oil and Natural Gas Corporation (ONGC) have come together with a vision to transform lives of Children with Hemophilia. The ONGC-funded and HFI-implemented Hemophiliacs Education and Transformation (HEAT) project for covering 1000 children identified with these disease.

Further, ONGC supported Muzaffarnagar based, *Asha Deep Charitable Organization,* which caters to the welfare of the needy including training the mentally impaired children. The organization was facing problem of safe transportation of differently-abled children from their residences to the institute, which could be solved by ONGC providing a van. This gives a good example of CSR providing last mile connectivity.

The Blind Relief Association (BRA), set up in 1944, has been serving the visually impaired, disabled children. The NGO is running a Government-aided, all-boys residential school providing education and comprehensive range of services free to around 200 students. The School is affiliated to the Central Board of Secondary Education. The School also has a Nursery section, which prepares children for future educational tasks through the play way method. It is organizing *Abilities Mela*[2] (show-*cum*-sale exhibition) at New Delhi with the help of several corporate for display and sale of handicraft garments and other products made by the differently-abled persons. The event was sponsored by Business and Community Foundation (BCF) of India, FICCI-SEDF, Kanoria Chemicals and Industries Ltd. (KCIL) and National Thermal Power Corporation (NTPC). As a moral boosting measure, the winning Indian team in the World Blind Games 2015 held at Seoul was felicitated in the Blind Relief Association, Delhi on 20th May, 2015.

Empowerment of the mentally challenged and disabled is an important and delicate matter. Synergy of action involving the government, the civil society and the corporate under CSR initiative with new and appropriate technology, can make a meaningful difference in their lives.

References:

1. http://ongcindia.ongc.co.in/wps/wcm/connect/ongcindia/home/csr
2. Jyoti Verma, "A fair of equal opportunities", *The Financial Express*, April 09, 2006.

However, the quality of education in the government schools varies widely. While school building have come up, teaching in general and of mathematics, science and English subjects in particular; have remained far from satisfactory. Absenteeism and accountability of teachers particularly in rural and tribal areas continue to be a matter of concern.

Provision of quality education to all has got renewed importance with adoption of SDG 2030; Goal No. 4 of which aim to "ensure that all girls and boys complete free, equitable and quality primary and secondary education leading to relevant and effective learning outcomes" and to "eliminate gender disparities in education and ensure equal access to all levels of education and vocational training for the vulnerable, including persons with disabilities, indigenous peoples and children in vulnerable situations" by 2030. Reduction of the out-of-school children would require interventions to ensure that all children start school on time, that repetition is minimized, and that every child completes primary, lower secondary and upper secondary education. The effort to get all adolescents and youth into secondary education by 2030 *poses another extraordinary challenge.* It is estimated that this will have a financial implication of US$39 billion every year to fill the funding gap and achieve this target in low and lower-middle-income countries. These include measures to increase supply, notably construction of classroom along with improvements in school infrastructure related to water, sanitation and accessibility, as well as measures to increase demand, such as removal of fees, unconditional and conditional cash transfers, scholarships or ease of restrictions to progression. It has been estimated[17] that in the school year ending 2014, about 263 million children and youth were out of school, which included 61 million at primary school age (about 6 to 11 years), 60 million at young adolescents of lower secondary school age (about 12 to 14 years), and 142 million at upper secondary school age (about 15 to 17 years). The numbers as well as complexity involved in provision of school education make this task gigantic. While there are positive aspects like high level awareness on the benefits of education and parent as well as child eager to avail it, there are challenges, both *in quantity* in covering all and in providing *quality* education to all; giving specific attention to the disadvantaged segments and less accessible geographical area.

Achieving the SDG 2030 in respect of education goals in India would require mobilization of resources as well as managerial ability. Participation of the corporate under the CSR intervention can play a meaningful role in this regard.

As discussed in the previous chapter, several corporate have taken up promotion of education under their CSR interventions. *CPSEs like SAIL* had set up schools in the peripheral area of their plants for providing quality school education to the public, in addition to extending facility from the schools run by the company for the wards of its executives/ workers. This had a positive impact in provision of quality education in the peripheral area of the plant, many of which were located in the tribal dominated interior areas. In addition to physical infrastructure, use of Information Technology (IT) based, computer aided education played an important role in improving the quality by overcoming the constraints due to shortage of trained subject teachers. This has proved to be of considerable help to the students. *In the private sector*, IT companies like Infosys and Wipro have invested sizable fund and adopted innovative measures like setting up library, science laboratory and use of IT for improving quality of education by supplementing existing arrangement in Government schools under their CSR, before it was made mandatory. There are best practices like IKEA, dealing with home furnishings including carpets, providing quality education to out-of-school children in joyful learning centres. This has induced parents for sending their children to school and in removal of the child labour related stigma, associated with the carpet industry. Such instances indicated that *a sensitive corporate can always make difference in dealing with an important social cause like provision of quality education for the children in general and avoiding child labour in particular*. This represents an innovative way of remaining responsible towards the society.

Advancement in the digital technology has also been of considerable help in overcoming the gaps in infrastructure, bridging the distance and improving quality of education, particularly in the schools located in rural and tribal areas. Computer aided education has contributed significantly in improving the quality of education in general and the shortage of subject-teachers in particular. Provision of computer along with required facilities in the schools is a basic requirement for this purpose, which has been taken up under various schemes, both by the Central and State Governments in the last decade.

However, a recent analysis[18] made during 2015-16, availability of computer facility in schools across the country appeared to be distorted. Majority of schools in Bihar (92.41%), Assam (91.3%), and Meghalaya (90.33%) do not have any computer facility. However, the position is better in Gujarat (26.7%), Delhi (16.1%) and Kerala (5.7%) schools without computer.

In view of multifarious advantages of computer based education, ongoing government programmes for computer education in the schools is required to be relooked into for addressing this issue. In this context, it would be worthwhile to mobilise the CSR intervention of the corporate, not only for the financial aspects in making the hardware available but also in providing the software and other last-mile connectivity components, like making the existing computers functional for delivering the desired services to the students. This can play a very important role in development of human resource of the country and make the CSR interventions relevant to the society in the true sense.

After CSR became mandatory, several innovative interventions taken up by the corporate have been reported. One such case relates to *Thermax* imitative for improving quality of education in the municipal schools. [Details given as Appendix, p. 353]. Strength of this intervention lies in evolving synergy with ongoing Government programmes and supplementing it with additional financial resource as well as volunteerism from the corporate for providing person specific support to each student. It has led to significant improvement in quality of education in term of increase in the percentage of students passing in first division and with distinction. Undertaking CSR Projects with imagination and commitment in synergy with Government programmes on similar lines can improve the quality of school education significantly.

Skill for Livelihood[19]

Along with health and education, provision of market oriented, quality skill for making the youth employable is another important component in development of human resource on a sustainable basis. Demographic dividend refers to the increase in the rate of economic growth due to a higher share of working population. India's demographic dividend lies in its working-age (15-59 years) population, which as of now, largely consists of youth (15-34 years). As a result, India's economy has the potential to grow more quickly than that of many other countries. With the declining working age population, particularly in the developed countries, more jobs emanating from the developed countries are bound to be outsourced and India can gain from it due to its demographic dividend.[20] According to International Monetary Fund (IMF), India's *continuing demographic dividend has the potential to add about 2 per cent to the annual rate of economic growth, if harnessed properly*. Over the next decade, 11 to 13 million more youth are expected to look for employment opportunities each year in the country.

However, the employment levels in India have remained virtually stagnant or declined in the last two decades.[21] In this regard, *lack of necessary skills among the youth and the resultant lack of employability has been the main area of concern* in India as is the case in other Organization for Economic Cooperation and Development (OECD) countries. Origin of this problem lies in the old traditional education system, which was designed to produce clerks for the colonial rulers. It is necessary to integrate skilling with the school and college education curriculum for providing required skills at an early age.

At present only 10 per cent of the Indian workforce is in the organized sector and only 2.5 per cent of the working population has vocational training, as compared to about 60 to 70 per cent in developed countries. Of the 11 million students graduating from colleges, including 4 lakhs engineering graduates each year; *only 20 per cent get jobs relevant to their skill sets*. There are about 6,900 State Government run Industrial Training Institutions (ITIs) and privately run Industrial Training Centres (ITCs) with a capacity of about 9,50,000 students. It has been found[22] that only 41, 35 and 16.2 per cent of ITI trained students in the states of Andhra Pradesh, Maharashtra and Odisha respectively; were able to get wage employment/self-employment or joined family business. The corresponding percentages for those graduating from ITCs were 22.8, 35.6 and 21.3 per cent, respectively. Another study by World Bank indicates that *more than 60 per cent of all graduates remained unemployed even three years after completion of a course*. Poor quality of training, curricula of training not aligned with the industry needs and lack of general academic skills such as problem solving, presentation skills, entrepreneurship etc. restrict employability of students after completing the regular courses. Further, *over 40 million persons were registered in employment exchanges, out of whom, only 0.2 million got jobs*. A large section of the existing labour force has outdated skills. With current and expected economic growth, this challenge is going to only increase further, since more than 75 per cent of new job opportunities are expected to be "skill-based." Industrialization will raise the demand for medium skill workers with secondary education and vocational training, but due to low rates of high school enrolment and completion, there could be a shortfall of 13 million such workers in India by 2030.[23]

The National Skill Development Corporation (NSDC) was set up in the Public Private Partnership (PPP) mode to facilitate setting up of large, high quality, for-profit vocational institutions. The National Skill Development Policy was framed with an ambitious plan to skill about 15 million youth each year and imparting skills to 350 million people by 2022. However, the actual progress in the past has been slow and only 1.4 million persons could be trained during 2012-13, against a target of skilling 8.5 million persons.

The *Skill India* initiative was launched by the new Government in 2014 for giving specific thrust and focused attention on skill development.

National Skill Development Mission was geared up with a mandate to scale up setting up 1,500 new ITIs and 5,000 skill development centres. This is an uphill task, which requires active participation of the private sector to provide quality skill as per the requirement of the industry. Further, skill development has been identified as a priority area under CSR, at serial number (ii) in the list of activities given in the Schedule VII of the Companies Act, 2013 under "employment enhancing vocational skills ...... livelihood enhancement projects." The corporate can take this up under their CSR interventions by either (i) setting up and managing skill development institute of its own; or (ii) working with Government institutes for filling the gaps; or (iii) supporting non-governmental organizations imparting skill development. Making unused facility in the plant and units available for skill development and mobilizing corporate voluntarism would add specific value and improve the quality of skill development in particular.

Skill Development and Livelihood in the Primary Sector

Agriculture continues to be an important component of the economy and is of particular relevance for development and generation of employment in rural areas. Notwithstanding the increased share of service sector in the Gross Domestic Product, agriculture continues to retain its importance. In the market based economy, production as per market demand with quality holds the key to success. For the purpose, the primary producer (farmer) is required to change the cropping pattern to suit the changing requirement of market. The farmer is required to be empowered with skill, knowledge, technology and resources to exploit existing and emerging opportunities in the market. The practice of growing traditional crops in a routine manner and running after middleman for selling the agricultural produce has to change and be replaced by cash crops like fruits, flowers, vegetables, which would give a reasonable and decent return to the producers.

Promotion of agriculture and allied activities, which provides livelihood to millions of people in the rural areas, is extremely important for the socio-economic development of India. The Central and State Governments have been implementing number of programmes and schemes for assisting the primary producers to produce and market goods as per the changing market demand from time to time. Agriculture related business provides a huge opportunity to the corporate for expansion of business on the one hand and supporting the small and marginal farmers on the other, which would make the development inclusive.

Training the unemployed youth in agriculture and allied activities is essential for production of high value crops, flowers, fruits, which has got huge market. Provision of required linkages for processing and value addition will improve commercial viability and attract the bankers to come forward to finance the venture. In respect of poverty alleviation and employment of the unemployed youth, there is no "*One size which fits all*". The approach and modalities shall have to remain flexible for meeting local conditions, the requirement of the youth as well as of the market. Corporate can play an important role in this context, by bridging the existing gap with finance as well as handholding and counselling with corporate volunteerism. This will enhance success rate and make the whole development process sustainable.

There are success stories of corporate setting up facilities for processing and marketing along with a buyback arrangement with the primary producers. This has helped in exploiting the market both within and outside the country. *E-Chaupal* initiative of ITC Ltd. offers an example in empowering the primary producers with market information along with supply of inputs and marketing facility for pursuing agriculture on a commercial scale and exploiting the market.

This model can be extended to other areas for production of food-grain, vegetable, fruits, fish, dairy products, meat etc. The farmers may be provided information, training for capacity building, required inputs along with technical guidance and a proper buyback arrangement. This would safeguard interest of the farmers, provide a decent return and at the same time render a profitable business opportunity to the corporate.

Another important aspect of Indian agriculture relates to management of soil health and checking unscientific use of chemical fertilizer and pesticides. Use of chemical fertilizer and pesticides is making the soil acidic, killing micro-organism and affecting productivity of soil for production of crops on a sustainable basis. Use of vermin compost, green manure and composting in place of chemical ones can improve soil fertility, quality and yield of agricultural products and economic return on a long term basis. Some of the best practices involving corporate support for promotion of agriculture and allied activities cover following:

(i) PepsiCo promoting potato farming commercial on scale [**Box 5.14: Aggregating Potato Farming with Technology**].

Box 5.14: Empowering the Potato Farmers with Technology

Enabling the primary producers to produce as per prevailing market demand is of critical importance for making the growth inclusive in a predominantly agriculture based rural economy like India. Government has been implementing large number of plans and programmes for development of agriculture and assisting the farmers with technology, agricultural inputs, financial assistance, loan, marketing links etc. However, the outcome and impact vary widely from state to state based on the status of the primary producers, prevailing ecosystem, and market linkage.

In this context, corporate dealing with agricultural produces can play an important role by assisting the farmers to produce quality agricultural produce and processing it for meeting the consumers' demand which will not only create more employment and business in the processing sector but will also improve the lot of the farmers on a win-win basis. One such recent case relates to Pepsico working with potato farmers in Anandapur, Arambag, Hooghly district in West Bengal.[1] Under the arrangement, PepsiCo provided seeds, pesticides, fertilisers and power tiller on rent to the small farmers, who cannot afford to buy it; along with a buyback arrangement for the produce. A specially designed power tiller fitted with an attachment was made available for potato cultivating. This mechanical intervention, almost turned farm to factory and saved at least Rs. 2,500 per bigha. It is reported that growing the special process grade potato as per company's need has enabled at least 10,000 farmers this year in getting a bumper crop and saved them from a price crash. A purchase price was agreed upon before the sowing season in October, which provided a rare business opportunity in agriculture that is usually subject to vagaries of nature. The potato farmer is hoping to make a profit around Rs. 18,000 per bigha.

Another such intervention relates to farmers in Tamil Nadu[2] technology and extension support, covering the entire value chain from input provision to facilitating financial support, product requirement. This has created an ecosystem which helps the farmers improving yield, get higher price and earn predictable income. About 20,000 potato growers were provided *Frito Lay variety* of imported seeds along with a buyback arrangement, which has resulted in increase in the income of the famers by 35 per cent in the last two to three years. It has plan to extend similar support to farmers cultivating mango and for doubling farmers' income by 2020.

Pepsi had given back 12.75 billion litres of water in 2015 alone through assorted conservation and replenishment initiatives and remained water positive. Its three manufacturing facilities in Tamil Nadu provided direct jobs to 3,500 people. *Pepsico Foundation* claimed to have invested about Rs. 114 crore between 2008 and 2016 for *Swachh Bharat* programme related to WASH, covering access to clean drinking water, benefiting more than four million people across the country.

Pepsi has been advocating Three Ps approach covering "People, Product and Planet" and sought to join Make in India campaign with a view to change its image† from manufacture of soft drinks to a socially responsible corporate dealing with more health products.

References:

1. Sambit Saha, "Aloo factor that keeps fields going", *The Telegraph*, March 05, 2017, p. 7.
2. K.T. Jagannathan and S. Vijaykumar, "PepsiCo India to focus on health products", *The Hindu*, March 04, 2017, p. 14.

† This needs to be viewed in the context of a recent call for ban on sales of Pepsi and Coca Cola drinks in the state by local traders' associations.

(ii) IKEA providing marketing facility to the cotton farmers. **[Box 5.15: Empowering the Cotton Farmers]**.

(iii) Corporate support for development of rural Maharashtra [**Box 5.16: Development of Agriculture and Allied Activities**].

A socially responsible corporate dealing with agriculture can guide, handhold and support the farmers for green production without use of any chemicals and fertilizers; which would fetch a premium price in the market, as done in Sikkim. CSR interventions, for green, organic products would get a premium price in the market and empower the primary producers in the true sense.

Skill Development and Livelihood in the Secondary Sector

The secondary sector, including construction and manufacturing, provides another important avenue to the youth for employment and earning livelihood. Manufacturing of apparel, leather goods, footwear, sports goods etc., which require relatively low skill, played an important role in generating employment in several developing countries namely Sri Lanka, Vietnam, and Bangladesh. The *Skill India* and *Make in India* initiatives have been launched by the Government for exploiting similar potential in the manufacturing sector for generating employment.

Corporate have been supporting *promotion of ancillary* with technical, financial and marketing assistance from the mother unit. These have provided employment and livelihood to the unemployed youth. Number of corporate have adopted government Industrial Training Institutes and Polytechnic for improving quality of training along with provision of the job training for making the youth employable. Such action has also helped the corporate in getting skilled manpower as per their

Box 5.15: Empowering the Cotton Farmers

Cotton, one of the important cash crops of India, provides livelihood to over 40 lakh farmers, many of whom have small and marginal landholdings. It provides the raw material for the cotton spinning and weaving industry. Cotton yarn, fabrics, apparel and garments form a major component of the textile basket for domestic consumption and exports. Cotton farming also has a social aspect. In case of monsoon failure or pest attack, or unfavourable market small and marginal cotton farmers find it difficult to recover the cost of production and repay the bank loan. Failure to repay loan at times, drive the distressed cotton farmers to commit suicide, which becomes a matter of serious concern.

Return from cotton cultivation to farmers is subject to vagaries of nature (monsoon) as well as domestic and export market conditions. During 2014-15, domestic cotton market faced a tough situation due to change in the policy of China for dismantling its buffer stock, which affected scope for export of Indian cotton to China adversely. The Cotton Corporation of India, a Central Public Sector Enterprise, took up purchase of cotton from the farmers under Minimum Support Price (MSP) operation as per Government policy. This operation has financial implication of around Rs. 2,000 crores, towards the difference between expenditure on purchase, storing, marketing and the sale realizations.

Long term solution to this problem lies in consolidating the domestic textile industry covering cotton spinning, weaving, apparel and garment making industry for ensuring that the entire quantity of cotton produced by the farmers is procured, processed and disposed of in a cost-effective manner. However, this would have sizable financial implications and would depend on competition from other countries as well as alternatives like manmade fabrics.

In this background, *IKEA*, a multi-national textile company, entering into contract farming has come as a welcome development. About 50,000 cotton growers in Punjab, Gujarat, Maharashtra and Telengana are covered under this arrangement; with *IKEA* providing technical and financial support to the cotton farmers for raising cotton with less pesticide, fertilizers and water along with assured marketing facility at a remunerative price. Farmers working with IKEA are reported to have grown cotton; with 49 per cent less pesticide, 27 per cent less chemical fertilizers, 9 per cent less water, but getting about 26 per cent higher value for their produce than the conventional farmers. IKEA is purchasing 35 per cent of its cotton requirement directly from these cotton growers and has plans to consolidate it further. These measures have helped the primary producers, improved quality, and productivity making the textile industry stronger and more sustainable. *Trident*, another textile corporate, has sponsored the *Better Cotton Initiative (BCI)*, a not-for-profit organization, and Delhi based *Action for Food Production* collaborating with IKEA for taking this endeavour forward.

> The above initiative taken by corporate has multiple benefits in improving quality, productivity, reducing outgo of public resource and empowering the primary agricultural producers. It provides an innovative example of corporate remaining responsible toward the society while doing business.

requirement. Replicating this in a coordinated manner with financial and corporate voluntarism under the CSR intervention has the potential to solve one of the main problems of the society in meeting the expectations of the youth and making the development sustainable.

Imparting market oriented skill along with mentoring, handholding, provision of financial assistance and loan; forward linkage for marketing, on similar lines would enable the youth to start their own business enterprise. There are government schemes for extending such support; but somehow there are slippages and the ultimate aim of setting up and running enterprises, by persons new to business, could not materialize as expected. There are instances of corporate taking up such initiatives, which have led to success stories in starting and running new enterprises for production and marketing of goods and services. One such case relates to *training in apparel and garment making* along *with buyback arrangement* for empowering the jail inmates in Alipore, West Bengal with help of a fashion designer. Such instances of the business remaining sensitive towards the social needs is required to be encouraged and replicated for benefit of the society and business as well [**Box 5.17: Corporate Action Making Commercial and Social Impacts**].

Corporate in the construction business, like L&T and GMR groups, have set up construction academies for skilling the youth in construction related trades, as per the requirement of the industry. Provision of quality skill development, covering both theory in the classroom and practical in workshop followed by on-the-job training has empowered the youth with quality skill. This has multiple advantages namely; youth getting employment with decent wage, corporate getting skilled labour, improvement in quality of the work, reduction in wastage, and timely completion of the project. There is considerable scope for replicating such projects under CSR, which would scale up quality skilling in construction sector along with improving quality of construction with the skilled labour and providing employment to the youth [**Box 5.18: Skill Development in Construction Sector**]. In this context, it is of interest that some corporate have taken up research for evolving low cost model for housing, which will facilitate fulfilling one of the basic needs (dwelling house) of the disadvantaged segment [**Box 5.19: Corporate Support for Affordable Housing**].

Box 5.16: Development of rural economy on sustainable basis

Recognising importance of rural India in the national development, corporate has come up for supplementing the government efforts for integrated development of selected villages as a part of their responsibility towards the society (CSR). An innovative experience in this regard relates to development of the Harisal village, with one of the worst HDI parameters, in the arid forested region of Amravati district of Maharashtra. The village has been adopted by Microsoft for development as India's first ideal digital village. The innovation is based on a two prong strategy of food security with access to fair-price shops, curbing malnutrition, and improved health care. The programme started as per the discussion Maharashtra Chief Minister, Devendra Fadnavis had with Microsoft CEO, Satya Nadella during his US trip in 2015 for providing digital solutions for chronic problems in villages.

Microsoft used its 'white space' technology, the unused spectrum between two TV channels, to provide free internet connectivity to Harisal and neighbouring villages. The corporate deputed its officials to find different technological solutions for a range of activities, such as make the villagers self-reliant, increase employment, boost their incomes, and provide medical services. Laying of optical fibre network and installing Wi-Fi in the villages along with training on use of Internet empowered the villagers to sell their produce online and get a much better price for their products; bamboo mats, vases, bowls and baskets. The change is obvious with villagers who did not know how to use a cell phone two years back, being able to communicate through Skype. Further village women were trained in weaving, in the nearby Dayalbaugh Educational Institute for working in the textile hub, being developed in the district.

A state of the art e-Classroom was built by Hewlett Packard for literacy campaign using to tackle the dismal literacy rates, supported by short films and movies in the local language and lessons on television screens. The interactive mode of teaching helped the school drop-outs before reaching the 10th or 12th standard to come back to education.

Tele-medicine centre has been set up in the village by suitable tie-ups with the Amravati Super-speciality Hospital and JJ Hospital, which enabled the villagers to get quality health care service and saved time and cost involved in travelling to the district headquarter 120 kilometres away earlier for getting similar service. Further, an eye care unit was set up in the village by tie-up with Dr. B. Venkateshwara Rao eye care centre to tackle the issue of cataracts and other eye ailments.

Solar power panels have been installed to provide power, and to train students further, ICT (Information and Communication Technology) classes are being held for them. To boost crop productivity, soil testing services have been made available to the villagers who are now advised on the crop to be sown. Facility for consultation with the specialist doctors in the city to tackle mortality related to childbirth based on satellite communications is being developed in partnership with 'C-DAC'.

Development of Meghlipara village, West Tripura District, Tripura in the North Eastern Region has been planned for sustainable development, based on the available Human and Land Resources. ONGC has supported it under CSR with help of the district administration, and Tata Trust, at the initiative of the Chairman, Executive Committee, Tripura Skill Development Mission.

These interventions based on appropriate technology and corporate support promoted by the enthusiastic officers; seek to make a difference in the lives of the villagers leading to sustainable development in the true sense.

Reference:

Krishna Thevar, "With a Little Bit of (Digital) Help, a Tiny Village Makes it to National Award's Shortlist", *The Economic Times*, April 15, 2017, p. 10.

Skill Development and Livelihood in the Tertiary (Services) Sector

Globalization and rapid urbanization have led to increase in per capita income and changes in the lifestyle. As a result, share of the services based tertiary sector in the GSDP has been increasing steadily; at a rate higher than that of the agriculture based primary and manufacturing based secondary sectors. However, unlike the other two sectors, services sector needs workers with a relatively higher level of education and skill-sets for providing quality services to the customers.

Standardization of the skill sets is essential for providing quality service as per satisfaction of the customers. For the purpose, Qualification Packs (QPs) with details as per the National Occupational Standard (NOSs) have been prepared for different trades in consultation with the industry and the Sector Skill Councils under the National Skill Qualification Framework (NSQF) by the Ministry of Skill Development and Entrepreneurship. The Private Training Providers are required to set up training centres with infrastructure as specified, apply online, get the centre physically inspected and accredited before undertaking training. On completion of the training, the trainees are required to appear in the examination and are awarded certificates by the sector skill council after clearing the examination. Cost of training is sanctioned to the private training providers based on the number of persons trained and placed under the flagship scheme *Prime Minister's Kaushal Vikash Yojana* (PMKVY-II), launched in 2016 with a target of providing skill

Box 5.17: Corporate Action Making Social Impact

Number of initiatives has been taken under Government programmes for Skill development along with support for production from time to time. However in several cases, such attempts could not sustain on a long term, due to difficulties in marketing the products.

One of the recent innovative example relates to training in sewing machine operation and garment making organised in the Presidency Correctional Facility (erstwhile Jail), Alipore, West Bengal. Unique feature of the programme lies in it being supported by Abhishek Dutta, a Fashion Designer, who has been dealing with apparel and garment stitching for government units of *Tantuja* and *Biswa Bangla*. The training was organised by converting one of the existing manufacturing premise into a tailoring unit with thirty stitching machines. Forty inmates undergoing sentence, seventeen of whom have previous experience in tailoring, were given training in apparel and garment making.

The training programme has started with stitching of kurtas, palazzos, dhoti, pants and Nehru coats, which are simpler to make and have good market demand. The fashion designer has assured to provide marketing facility for the stitched products under his brand after the training is over, which will bridge one of the most important gaps in sustaining the programme. This innovative experience has brought cheers to the inmates, who have observed that many such training programmes have been organised earlier but the present arrangement would be sustainable as it will provide marketing facility for continuing the production on a sustainable basis and making the training programme meaningful. The correctional home has plan to undertake similar programme in bakery training with help of Taj Bengal Group of Hotels, who have agreed to extend necessary support for training and forward linkage.

The above intervention, though small, would make a meaningful difference in the life of the socially disadvantaged segments in earning their livelihood. It would justify renaming *"Jail" as "Correctional Home"*, as provision of skill, financial support and forward linkage for marketing the product will empower the inmates economically, give them dignity in the society and enable them to overcome their socio-economic handicap; which is one of the main reasons behind a normal person turning criminal. The intervention seek to reverse the trend on a sustainable basis.

Reference:

"Lessons tailored for jail inmates", *The Telegraph*, April 04, 2017.

development training to 10 million youth during 2016-20. While Government has earmarked fund for skill development; active participation of the industry and business is required for achieving this gigantic task with quality.

The *Tata Trust*, the social welfare arm of the Tata group, has launched *Tata Strive* initiative for skill development in an innovative manner. Skill development training is being imparted in synergy with Non-Governmental Organizations and funding support under government schemes. Facilities in the Tata group hotels are being made available for on the job training in the hospitality trades, which have made this skill development qualitatively superior, more effective and useful for the youth **[Box 5.20: Tata STRIVE's Innovative Way of Skill Development]**. This indicate the advantages of corporate working with Government for a social purpose like skilling the youth for livelihood.

With higher level of education and change in mindset, preference of the unemployed youth has shifted to white collar jobs. In this context, IT and ITES sector provide excellent opportunity for employment of the youth as well as providing quality services within, outside the country and earning valuable foreign exchange. Skilling of the youth requires filling the gaps in school and college education along with provision of market needed special skill. IT giants like Infosys and Wipro have taken up this cause in universities and training institutions, setup for education and sharpening skill of the youth. **[Box 5.21: Improving Employability of the Fresh Engineers with Skill by the IT Industry]**.

Digital Technology based online education have led to new teaching norms, getting rid of the classroom and giving learners the flexibility to study from anywhere. This is being used by universities to provide *Massive Open Online Courses* (MOOC) to upskill, which has emerged as an excellent opportunity for the youth. Online courses in subjects like data sciences, data analytics, coding, machine learning, big data, artificial intelligence, digital transformation, digital productivity, IT security have provided today's youth, both employed and unemployed, the opportunity to up-skill and add to their résumés for meeting the requirements of the fast changing world. The companies are partnering with online platforms such as *Coursera*, *edX* and *Udacity* to foster learning among their employees with reduce costs and risks. Recruiters are increasingly looking for well-rounded candidates; those having necessary technical skills complimented with important soft skills. This has opened avenue for imparting new and quality skill sets to the youth as per the market need by using the online platform at very low cost **[Box 5.22: Open Online Courses as a Tool for Acquisition of Skill]**.

Imparting quality training to the youth for acquiring new skills also help the corporate directly in getting skilled manpower as per requirement.

Box 5.18: Skill Development in the Construction Sector

Construction and real estate related activities form an important component of the national economy. It covers a wide range of activities at individual, State and National levels from individual housing to physical infrastructure like building, road, and bridges. These activities contribute significantly to the secondary sector of the economy and generation of employment on a large scale, being particularly relevant for the less educated youth.

Like other Corporate, those in the real estate business, have also been undertaking social activities as a welfare measure for the construction workers and other disadvantaged segments of the society. *Omaxe Ltd.,* in the real estate business since 1987, set up its welfare wing *Oxame Foundation* in 2006, for pursuing the vision *"Naye Bharat Ka Nirman Bhi Aur Chaheron Par Muskan Bhi."*[1] It undertook several measures for improving the quality of life of the construction workers at the construction sites.[2] Similarly GMR Group[3] took up its social activities through *GMR Varalakshmi Foundation*[4] with thrust on education of girl children, health, hygiene and sanitation and livelihood opportunity. L&T, one of the leading corporate in the construction sector, took up a range of activities including running construction academies at Chennai, Kolkata and other places for imparting quality skill in construction related trades to the unemployed youth. This was done with a view to provide quality skill to the unemployed youth for making them employable as well as getting skilled worker for the constructions.

Corporate Social Responsibility (CSR) becoming mandatory, under the Companies Act, 2013 with effect from 1st April, 2014, has opened a new window of opportunities for the corporate dealing with construction for scaling up their existing arrangement for skilling. However, it appears that the fund earmarked under CSR is being spent for a host of activities and expenditure on skill development, which is their core competence area, is forming only a small part.[5]

At the national level, provision of skill to the unemployed youth has been assigned high priority for reaping the benefits of the demographic dividends. Under the Skill India initiative, the newly created Ministry of Skill Development and Entrepreneurship (MSDE) has launched the *Pradhan Mantri Kaushal Vikas Yojana* (PMKVY) with a target to train one crore youth during 2016 – 2020. Success of this initiative would require identifying the potential sectors for skilling, putting in place arrangements for imparting quality skill and most importantly ensuring that the trained workers are employed by the industry. This would require active involvement of the stakeholders along with mobilisation of fund, infrastructure, trainers, managers and monitoring agencies.

Active involvement of the corporate in the construction business along with fund earmarked for CSR intervention and corporate voluntarism of the executives can *play a significant role* in this context. Ex-servicemen, retiring/retired officers dealing with construction as well as from Police and Para Military Forces may be trained for being trainer in the skill development institutes, to be set up and run by these corporate under CSR intervention. Corporate voluntarism of the executive may be mobilised for running the training centres particularly for supervision and motivating the trainees.

Under the *Tata Strive* initiative for skilling in hospitability, stewardship trades; *on-the-job internship training* is provided to the trainees in the Tata

Group of Hotels. This arrangement enhances the quality with higher confidence and employability of the trainees. It enabled the trainees to provide quality service to the satisfaction of the customers and better pay package. This practice may be integrated in the construction academies with specific emphasis on the job training in the project site; to be managed by the Corporate in the real estate sector under their CSR intervention. This will create a win-win situation for the corporate and the society.

References

1. Rohtas Goel, Chairman Omaxe Ltd., "We are working for primary education of girls", *The Financial Express*, October 15, 2006.
2. S.K. Panda, *CSR in India—Past, Present and Future*, p. 227.
3. Meena Raghunathan, "Dialling in corporate social responsibility", *The Hindu*, November 18, 2007.
4. GMR Varalakshmi foundation, http://www.gmrgroup.in/empower-overview.aspx
5. http://investors.larsentoubro.com/upload/AnnualRep/FY2016AnnualRepL&T%20Annual%20Report%202015-16.pdf, pp. 16-17.

Box 5.19: Corporate support for affordable housing

With an estimated shortage of about 20 million homes in the low income and economically weaker sections in the country, provision of dwelling house, one of the basic human needs, is required to be dealt on priority. Apart from number, providing affordable housing, particularly in the sub-10 lakh category, has been a challenge for attracting private sector investment because of the perceived risks and low margins. Ongoing government interventions for assisting these segments to have a dwelling house have been small and are required to be supplemented for filling the gap.

As a part of its commitment for funding socially relevant businesses, the Tata Trust has come forward to support the *Brick Eagle Foundation* for designing an affordable housing project at Karjat near Mumbai. Urban Poverty Alleviation and Livelihoods Portfolio Wing of the Tata Trusts is dealing with this. The foundation has been provided a financial grant for extensive research on customer needs, industry best practices; and working out sustainable construction technologies in affordable housing, which can be scaled up, in two years. The project would provide a blueprint for designing affordable homes, which are aesthetic, locally relevant, scalable, and commercially viable. This project will provide a critical perspective to understand the housing needs of the economically weaker sections (EWSs) and Lower Income Group (LIG) population.

The project will help in forging partnership between the private sector, the government, academia, NGOs, and social impact funds to expedite bridging the massive housing gap for the socially and economically challenged. This move of the Tata Trust seeks to make a meaningful contribution to alleviate housing poverty in India.

Reference

Kailash Babar, "Tata Trust Gives Grant for Affordable Housing", *The Economic Times*, April 14, 2017, p. 6.

Box 5.20: Tata STRIVE's Innovative Way for Skill Development

Recognizing unemployment as one of the major problems faced by the country, the Tata Group launched the *Tata STRIVE* initiative in 2014 for provision of quality skill to the youth for making them employable. The programme is executed by the Tata Sustainability Group through the Tata Community Initiative Trust, a not for profit trust.

Tata STRIVE develops module for training and skill development, creating training capacity in identified sectors and trade as per skill gaps assessment made by the National Skill Development Corporation (NSDC), conducts training along with certification and measurement of outcome. Specific attention is given to quality of skilling by setting standards, which is aligned with the National Occupational Standards, specified by concerned Sector Skill Councils, and even exceed those in some cases. The skill development training is imparted in centres having required facilities/equipment, trained manpower; followed by On the Job Training (OJT) using the spare capacities in the Tata group companies, as well as other not for profit companies, non-Tata companies, government agencies, foundations, trusts, banks, industrial training institutes and credible NGOs.

A two-pronged strategy is adopted involving (i) setting up of own large skill development centres called Tata STRIVE Skill Development Centre (TSSDC) and smaller Tata STRIVE Extension Centres (TSEC) by utilizing the infrastructure available with other group companies/other credible organizations and (ii) working in partnership with government, NGOs, other corporate for scaling up their existing training capacity and capability.

Tata STRIVE has five TSSDCs located at Aligarh, Hyderabad, Mohali, Mumbai and Pune and 40 Extension centres. Besides, over 65 centres have been set up on partnership model, which are owned and operated by private partners along with knowledge and domain expertise support from *Tata STRIVE*. Skill development is provided in a wide range of trades namely air conditioning/ refrigeration operator, auto service operator, food and beverage services, solar PV installer, General Duty Assistant, Assistant Electrician, BPO call centre executive, housekeeping operation, Assistant Beauty Therapist, automobile sale consultant, business development executive in BFSI, Retail Sale associate and Android Application Development. Hands on training, soft skills training for 360 degree development of youth, industrial application, and project based learning through field visits and OJT mark some of the strengths of this skilling, which provide quality skill to the youths. Certification is issued after clearing the examination on completion of the course including OJT. They are also given supports for placement. Taking the Auto Service Technician trade as an example, the course is designed in collaboration with Tata Motors, keeping in view the industry standards laid down in the qualification pack by NSDC for auto technician (ASC/Q1401). The course duration is nine weeks, followed by four weeks of OJT. Blended learning approach provides students the opportunity to fine tune their skills, as they go through e-learning modules and also get themselves assessed on them.

Imparting quality skill along with practical hands on training are the major features of this initiative, which is widely respected in the industry. It is sought after by the unemployed youth due to better offers with higher wages.

Reference

http://www.tataSTRIVE.com/aboutSTRIVE.html

Box 5.21: Improving Employability of the Fresh Engineers

Phenomenal growth of the Information Technology (IT) sector in the last two decades, gave a big boost to the Indian economy. It not only generated employment and foreign exchange but also spurred growth in other sectors of the economy as well, in real estate for office space and residence, car makers, lifestyle products, holiday resorts, tour operators, gourmet, restaurants, etc. Taking advantage of the relatively low-cost employees and earning in foreign currency, Indian IT industry had invested heavily in skilling and training the fresher-employees in the vast internal training centres, developed by Infosys, Wipro, TCS even bigger than formal universities.[1]

The knowledge industry is fast changing definition of knowledge. While the customer industries are transforming very fast, Indian IT industry is relatively slow to change. In the last decade, the IT industry focussed more on satisfying the investors' insatiable appetite for returns and the investment in skilling/training manpower as a percentage of total revenue went down. The government also did not pursue this under the impression that private sector will fill the gap.

In the private education sector, while quantity was delivered, quality did not get due attention. Freshly passing out students from the engineering college often lack the basic education, technical knowledge and skill. Srinivasa Kandula of *CapGemini*, employing over a lakh of IT engineers, had expressed concern[2] over the standards of fresh engineers passing out from university to be so poor that the candidate even cannot say the subjects taught in the final semester. Providing employment to such persons requires investment of sizeable financial and managerial resource.

Following the new USA political regime's insistence on revision of the immigration policy in favour of the locals, it is feared that the Indian IT sector is going to face a tough weather in the coming years. As business will shrink, scope for hiring youth and training them with the internal resources by the IT industry will become increasingly difficult. This is likely to affect the IT industry, employment potential and the entire economy very adversely, unless a coherent policy is adopted for coordinating the effort and financial resource of the government, industry and the education sector on top priority for checking a cataclysmic de-growth, which will be more spectacular than the IT boom, the country has witnessed in the past two decades. It will be worth while to respond to this jointly by the Government and Corporate, while implementing mandatory CSR.

References

1. K. Srinivasan, "IT's new improved skill problem", *The Hindu*, March 12, 2017, p. 13.
2. NASSCOM event, February 2017.

Box 5.22: Open Online Courses as a Tool for Acquisition of Skill

In the knowledge driven world, acquisition of new and multiple skills on continuous basis is becoming increasingly important and essential for survival. Information Technology based Massive Open Online Courses (MOCC), started since 2011, has come up as a timely opportunity in this context. This covers a wide range of skill sets provided online in finance, digital marketing, data sciences, data analytics, coding, machine learning, big data, artificial intelligence, digital transformation, digital productivity, IT security, mobile apps development, analytics, handling multiple stakeholders. Technical subjects in ethical hacking, app development (Android/iOS), video marketing and YouTube marketing, and SMAC (Social, Mobile, Analytics and Cloud) have been trending. Persons with design thinking and digital marketing skills are getting package of Rs. 15 to 30 lakh at the managerial levels, depending on their experience.

Strength of MOCC over traditional courses lies in its extremely low cost and flexibility; as one can undertake these courses anytime, anywhere. One is not required to go to a classroom or purchase books and attend classes on fixed hours. Anybody can avail the course content online with a computer or a smart phone anytime, which provides the user unique advantages in respect of low cost, convenience of time and place. It has become common to see the young professionals going through this course content in metro, bus, taxi, while commuting to their workplace.

A number of organizations like ProLearn, Jigsaw Academy are providing courses, which are instructor-led and hands-on learning. This facility is being used by individuals as well as organizations. Companies are partnering with online platforms such as Coursera, edX and Udacity to foster learning among their employees, and reduce costs and risks.

In a fast changing world, the hiring policy has been changing fast with the recruiters needing smart person with latest skill and experience rather than going through the traditional way of looking at the certificate. In this context, the MOCC has been providing a win-win situation[1], on the one hand to the employees in having the freedom to take any course of interest them from top universities, mostly free if a certificate is not required and to the employers on the other, for skilling existing employees, as and when required with lesser cost and time.

MOCCs are proving to be particularly useful to the Start-up and small enterprises in the talent and business growth of their employees, who have little time and resource for training people. It has overcome the dilemma as to if the employees should be put in production work or put in training to improve productivity, as the employee can take the required course in their free time in office or at home. Some of the employers have resorted to the simple way of asking the newly selected, to be hired person to complete a predetermined set of MOCC courses before joining, which save them from the training cost. For the bigger organizations, encouraging employees to acquire new skill online in their spare time has very small additional cost implication. However, it give them the flexibility of getting better skilled employees without bearing the cost of training by sending to formal training centres, and loss of productive work. Further, it is particularly useful in case of any requirement to retrench as employees with new skill find it easier to get employment elsewhere'.

LinkedIn, job-oriented social networking service, offered more than 5,000 online courses free for a week during 2016. Ericsson in India has been actively encouraging its employees to do online courses, which is not part of their key responsibilities, to brush up their tech skills and stay employable. As a matter of fact, India has emerged as the second-biggest market after USA for the Coursera and edX online course provider with 11 per cent of all its users as against 30 per cent from the US. For Coursera, India accounts for more than 1.8 million of its users out of a total of 25 million, and is one of its fastest-growing markets.

As the world becomes flatter, the organisations have to look for employees not only with multiple skills but also acquiring new skill on a regular basis for meeting the need of in a fast changing scenario. The world-class content from Quality MOCC has come handy and can be leveraged by all organisations to build a strong employee base[2] in general and retain their competitive advantages in particular.

References

1. Varuni Khosla, Prachi Berma Dadhwal and Brinda Dasgupta, "Companies turn to online platforms to up skill staff", *The Economic Times*, April 11, 2017, p. 8.
2. Gopal Devanahalli, "Can MOOCs enable the startup ecosystem?", Manipal Global Education Services, *The Hindu*, May 3, 2017, p. 4.

It helps in upgrading skill of the existing employees/workers for meeting any emerging needs as well as for redeployment of those rendered surplus due to various reasons. As skill development for livelihood is covered in the list CSR activities notified in Schedule-VII of the Companies Act, undertaking skill development provide an avenue to the corporate in fulfilling its statutory liability. It will be worthwhile for the corporate to undertake skill development by supplementing and filling the gaps in the government's programme for skill development, particularly with corporate voluntarism and making available facilities in their plant/units for on the job training. Corporate may also support awareness generation about standardization of skillsets, and Startups by setting up incubation centre, handholding, providing financial support and buyback arrangement in the initial years. Civil society organizations, like PAN IIT, have come forward to promote skilling by mobilizing the CSR intervention of corporate along with ongoing government schemes in an innovative manner, which can be replicated and extended to other regions [**Box 5.23: *PanIIT* Alumni Skilling Disadvantaged Youth**].

Box 5.23: *PanIIT* Alumni Skilling Disadvantaged Youth

PanIIT Alumni Reach For India (PARFI) foundation was set up by a group of successful alumni of the Indian Institute Technology (IIT) with a mission to empower school drop-outs from underprivileged families with market based skill for earning livelihood. The foundation has set up 22 *Gurukuls* in ten states, out of which 13 are located in the Left Wing Extremist (LWE)/ *Naxal* affected districts. The *Gurukuls* are operating on strategic partnership model; involving (i) the state government providing support for infrastructure and mobilising trainees; (ii) the corporate providing placement support and viability gap funding under Corporate Social Responsibility; (iii) the training provider dealing with sourcing, training, placement; and (iv) individual trainee funding the cost of training through bank loan.

The training is conducted in demand driven courses for providing quality services to the satisfaction of the customer. One such *Gurukul* located at Kalyan about 40 km from Ranchi is providing training in electric fitting, plumbing, Air conditioning ductman, pipe fitting trades. NABARD assisted the interested youths in getting a bank loan of about Rs. 18,000 for payment of the training cost to the *Gurukul*. The loan amount is later recovered from the monthly salary of the trainee, after he gets employment. In addition to technical subjects; financial and credit literacy as well as soft skills in *yoga*, meditation, prayers, patriotic *values* are covered in the daily programme, with ex-serviceman appointed as Centre in charge. Acquisition of quality skill is the major strength of this intervention, which is ensured by making the trainees to bear the cost of training through bank loan (which is recovered), commitment of the trainers and close supervision. The institute began operations in October 2013 with a batch of 19 tribal youths, who had dropped out of the school. Around 276 youths, trained under this intervention, have been placed in Dubai, Qatar, Saudi Arabia and Sri Lanka.

The organisation offers partnership to corporate for implementation of CSR projects for skill development and certification of the underprivileged youth. The State Government of Jharkhand has been planning to expand these *Gurukul* centres to other districts along with scaling up the capacity to 10,000 in number and including trades in labour-intensive sectors like food processing, leather and textiles.

Training, placement with regular income and remittance to parents and dependents have given dignity and new hope to the youth; refraining them from joining militant organisation. This initiative, taken by a civil society organisation of the alumni of IITs for skilling and providing livelihood to underprivileged youth from the LWE affected districts, *provides a unique example of inclusive and sustainable development.* Replicating this model provides an opportunity for making CSR *interventions meaningful to the society* in solving problem of unemployment and making development inclusive.

Reference

Ashish Mishra, "Jharkhand tribal school dropouts train for foreign jobs", *Tripura Times*, May 29, 2017, p. 2, www.parfi.org

Environment Conservation

Environment conservation, checking pollution and carbon emission related measures are crucial for sustainable development. Study indicate that while carbon emission and global warming related issues affect all, the poor and the disadvantaged segments are affected more adversely due to their limited asset base and lower risk taking ability, in the event of any calamity leading to loss of livelihood.

Awareness about the adverse effect of environmental degradation has increased significantly in the recent years. Corporate have been taking up environment mitigation and adaptation measures by integrating it into their business plan. This include corporate like ITC Limited taking up large scale tree plantation, which has been serving both environmental and financial objectives. ONGC has undertaken construction of electric crematorium, which has been reducing cutting of trees for wood used for cremation of the dead. Inclusion of environment conservation measures "ensuring environmental sustainability, ecological balance, protection of flora and fauna, animal welfare, agro-forestry, conservation of natural resources and maintaining quality of soil, air and water"; in the list of activities to be undertaken under CSR [at serial number (iv) in Schedule VII] has provided a new opportunity to the corporate for taking this forward. Mobilization of corporate support will be of considerable help in fulfilling the Nationally Determined Contribution committed in the historic climate accord made in Paris in 2015, covering plantation in denuded hills, degraded forests for having green cover as well as promoting solar and non-conventional energy as alternative to fossil fuel [**Box 5.24: Mobilizing Corporate Support for Meeting NDC under Paris Accord in 2015**].

In this context, new technology can be promoted which provides scope for business, cost cutting as well as cleaner environment, by corporate on similar lines as done in the West [**Box 5.25: Checking Climate Change—Ford Motors**].

Further use of solar energy in transport and other sectors can be promoted as a part of environment conservation and checking carbon emission interventions under CSR [**Box 5.26: Promotion of Solar Powered Water Transport**].

Awareness about adverse impact of global warming on the climate and livelihood has sensitised the common man/woman taking interest and extending his support for the cause. One such recently reported case relate to Meenangadi village panchayat in Wayanad district of Kerala,

Box 5.24: Mobilizing Corporate Support for checking climate change

Threats from global warming have focused the global attention on the need for undertaking appropriate mitigation and adaptation measures for checking carbon emission and climate change on priority. This would require by mobilizing the support of all stakeholders of the society including the corporate. India had signed the Paris Agreement in 2015, under which it is required implement the Climate Action Plan to achieve the Nationally Determined Contribution (NDC) target of creating additional carbon sink of 2.5 to 3 billion tonnes of carbon dioxide equivalent by increasing forest and tree cover by 2030. Afforestation related projects have been included in the list of activities to be taken up under Corporate Social Responsibility (CSR) in the Schedule under the amended provisions of the Companies Act, 2013, with effect from the 1st April, 2014.

The National Forest Policy, 1988 also envisages increasing India's forest and tree cover from existing 24 per cent to 33 per cent of the total geographical area. This is an arduous task, which requires not only fund but managerial ability, identifying land, preparation of plantation material, mobilizing manpower for undertaking and maintaining plantation. While substantial fund is being earmarked under Plan and under the Compensatory Afforestation Fund, collected for diversion of forestland for non-forestry use; the challenge lies in mobilizing the resources and taking the chain of activities to its logical end in a well coordinated manner.

Ministry of Environment, Forest and Climate Change has mooted the innovative idea for mobilization of fund and managerial support of the Public Sector Banks for increasing forest cover; on similar lines as done for construction of separate toilets for boys and girls in all the Government Schools under the *Swachh Bharat Mission* during 2014-15.

The National Afforestation and Eco-Development Board deliberated on the 21st-22nd October, 2016 in Delhi for increasing green cover and explored various ways to increase the carbon sink such as creating 'city forest' ranging from 20 to 100 hectares (based on land availability), utilization of CAMPA (Compensatory Afforestation Fund Management and Planning Authority) fund, carrying out national green highway mission, giving financial incentive to states for increasing/protecting forest cover and involving multiple stakeholders—including private sector companies.

This would require looking beyond the resource available under normal budgetary provision and manpower within the Government to the Corporate, Non-Governmental Organisations and the Society at large for mobilization of fund, technology, managerial ability and people's power to accomplish the task. As an innovative idea for achieving the afforestation target, the banks have been moved to earmark at least 25 per cent of their CSR fund for afforestation and raising the plantation either by itself or by pooling resources of number of banks together along with involvement of NGOs.

It is hoped that this innovative approach based on mobilization of CSR fund along with government fund and manpower would increase forest and tree cover, enable the country to achieve the mandate of Paris Agreement and make the country greener and environmentally sustainable.

Reference

"Green Target: Government may ask banks to chip in to increase forest cover", *The Times of India*, October 31, 2016, p. 6.

Box 5.25: Checking Climate Change—Corporate Initiative for

Appreciating the importance and urgency in checking carbon emission and climate change, the responsible corporate has started realigning their production process accordingly. One such instance relate to the initiative taken by auto manufacturers Ford's integrated approach for reducing emissions by evolving partnership with other stakeholders, including the automotive industry, the fuel industry, government and consumers. This would *help continuously reducing greenhouse gas (GHG) emissions* over a period of decades in all sectors of the economy. The transportation sector for example, requires improving vehicle economy, developing lower carbon fuels, and working with the government on measures to encourage consumers to buy more fuel efficient vehicles and lower carbon fuels.

Accordingly, Ford has evolved a long-term climate strategy consisting of continuously reducing GHG emissions and energy use of its operations, developing the flexibility and capability to market lower GHG emission products, and working with industry partners, energy companies, consumer groups and policy-makers to establish an effective and predictable market, policy and technological framework for reducing GHG emissions. It seeks to promote economy-wide programme that allows market mechanisms to determine where GHG reductions can be achieved at the lowest cost. Further, it has evolved climate strategy through specific environmental goals, including reducing carbon dioxide emissions by 30 per cent per vehicle by 2025 compared to a 2010 baseline. The company achieved a 31 per cent reduction from 2000 to 2010, in recognition of which, it was awarded Goal-Setting Certificate at the Environmental Protection Agency's Climate Leadership Awards Ceremony in 2012.

The Company has reported to have reduced waste, improved fuel economy, and developed EcoBoost engines. Its reduced waste sent to landfill by 14 per cent per vehicle during 2012-13 and implemented a plan to reduce waste to sent to landfill by 40 per cent per vehicle by 2016. The company improved the fleet-average fuel economy of its U.S. car fleet by two per cent and U.S. truck fleet by three per cent from 2012 to 2013. By 2013, Ford surpassed its goal of producing 1.5 million *EcoBoost* engines globally by producing over two million. These measures taken by Ford car company indicated its being responsible to the environment.

Reference

http://www.triplepundit.com/2014/06/new-csr-report-proves-ford-motor-co-takes-climate-change-seriously/ New CSR Report Shows Ford Takes Climate Change Seriously by Gina-Marie Cheeseman on June 25, 2014.

Box 5.26: Promotion of Solar Powered Water Transport

Following signing of the Paris agreement in November 2015, India has taken several specific steps for promotion of solar and other energy of non-fossil origin. The National Solar Mission was launched along with several Policy initiatives for adding six Giga Watt (GW) solar power productions during 2016-17. This has aimed to take total solar power generation to 15 GW by March 2017. The capacity for manufacturing of module and cells is sought to be doubled to 10,000 Mega Watt (MW) and 2,000 MW respectively in another couple of years. Rs. 5,000 crore has been earmarked for installation of 4,200 MW solar rooftop systems over the next five years and developing 50 cities as solar cities. The resource, to be mobilized from the mining lease auctions, will be channelized through the District Mineral Fund for supporting wind and solar power generation firms, for stepping up the capacity of power generation from the non-conventional sources.[1]

One of the innovative way of promotion of solar energy in India relate to the launching of Aditya, the first solar-powered ferry started service between Vaikom and Thavanakkadavu, connecting Kottayam and Alappuzha districts in Kerala on the 12th January, 2017. This was recreated on the Vaikom boat jetty, which was used by the father of Nation Mahatma Gandhi to reach Vaikom for the *Satyagraha* on 9th March, 1925. The largest solar-powered boat, with 75 seats capacity, was designed with help of a French firm at Thavanakkadavu unit of Navgathi Marine Design and Constructions, Kochi.[2] The ferry, 20 meter long and 3.7 meter height with a 7 meter beam, was manufactured out of the fiber glass instead of wood or steel with 78 solar panels mounted on the roof to supply power with 700 kg of lithium-ion batteries in the two hulls which can store a total capacity of 50 KWh and speeds up to 7.5 knots/hr. It takes about 15 minutes travel time between Vaikom and Thavanakkdavu, a distance of 2.5 km on water.

Compared with conventional diesel powered boat with similar specification costing about Rs. 1.58 crore, the solar ferry costs Rs. 2.53 crore. However the operating costs of diesel powered boat is about Rs. 30.37 lakh per year, which is much higher than the solar ferry about Rs. 1.5 lakh per year. Besides the Solar powered ferries make no noise or cause any pollution, unlike the diesel powered ones. Conventional ferries release huge amount of CO_2 into the atmosphere which has always posed a threat to ecosystem. Also, the oil spill is harmful to aquatic ecosystem and to the water body, whereas solar ferry boats neither create pollution in atmosphere nor in river.

Inland water transportation is the most efficient, economic and environment friendly means of transportation of men and materials in states like Kerala with an inland water navigation system, several back waters, and canals. It serves the human and environmental needs in the best possible manner. Promoting this as per technical feasibility on a commercial scale will best serve the interest of the society and environment and check global warming. This is an area worth giving attention by the corporate working in the transport sector, as part of responsibility towards the society.

References

1. *The Economic Times*, October 19, 2016, p. 11.
2. Gopakumar Pookkottur, "Aditya ferry: Vaikom's new *Satyagraha* for clean energy", *Tripura Times*, February 09, 2017, p. 2.

led by Ms. Beena Vijayan, president of the panchayat, launching an innovative carbon-neutral project[24] on 5th June, 2017. This project envisages offsetting carbon dioxide and other greenhouse gases emitted by human activities, through a series of greening initiatives. It seeks to make the panchayat carbon-neutral with zero carbon footprints, by bringing down pollution, carbon emissions, and plastic waste. Carbon audit has been taken up for assessing emissions from power consumption, fuel use in the 9,000 houses of the panchayat and from vehicles, which will be offset by tree plantation. One lakh seedlings are being distributed to farmers for plantation during this year. Taking tree plantation as the top priority, the panchayat is trying to attract the environmentally-conscious consumer, evolve a brand and market locally grown crops such as coffee and pepper as premium, sustainable products. The panchayat has undertaken an ambitious project with an outlay of Rs. 11 crore for setting up a biodiversity park, soil and water conservation programmes and a waste treatment plant under MGNREGA. The project is supported by the environmental advocacy group like M.S. Swaminathan Research Foundation's Community Agro-biodiversity Centre and other NGOs. Supporting such measures at the grass root level under CSR will add a new meaning and value to CSR.

Operationalization of CSR

Based on the issues and developments, which are of significance to the society, as discussed in the preceding paras, each corporate need to devise its own strategy and action plan for taking up CSR projects. In this context, certain issues, which will be helpful in operationalization of CSR, are indicated below.

Institutional Mechanism for taking up CSR

Proper institutional arrangement for planning and implementation of projects is critical for success of CSR. This can be done by any one or many of the three mechanisms; namely:

Setting up a Foundation or Trust under the direct control of the corporate appears to be the common and most preferred option for implementation of CSR. Induction of persons with experience, commitment and technical expertise in such foundation help in formulation, implementation of the projects and optimization of benefits accruing from the projects.

The second option involves implementation of CSR projects through NGOs of expertise and repute. This makes the job relatively easier for the corporate. NGOs, with transparency in its operation and professional competence, are usually preferred. Entering into a Memorandum of Understanding (MoU) with NGOs of repute and expertise like Ramakrishna Mission, Population Foundation of India, Bharatiya Agro Industries Foundation, Children in Need in India would create a "win-win" situation; by enabling the NGOs to get fund for their social activities and the corporate in discharging its obligations. The MoU may be prepared specifying the role and responsibilities of the parties clearly for implementation of the project in a smooth manner.

The third option involves placing CSR fund with government sponsored mechanisms. Contribution to the Prime Minister's National Relief Fund or any other fund set up by the Central Government for socio-economic development and relief and welfare of the Scheduled Castes, the Scheduled Tribes, other backward classes, minorities and women; as indicated at serial number (viii) of schedule VII of the Act. Contribution to the National Culture Fund, National Sports Development Fund can also be made in conformity with the activities specified in the Schedule.

Out of the above three, the first one gives the maximum flexibility and recognition to the corporate, whereas the third one gives the least. The corporate go for either one or a combination of these as per their requirements.

Capacity Building, Training, and Orientation on CSR

After CSR became mandatory, the need for getting personnel trained in CSR has increased by manifold for ensuring compliance with the statutory provision and also for getting the maximum mileage out of CSR projects. Statutory provisions as well as social and sustainability aspects of CSR need to be covered with examples and best practices. For the purpose, in addition to formulating specific courses, modules on CSR; relevant provisions may be suitably included in the general course curriculums of Management and Business Administration (MBA) courses to sensitize and impart required skill to the young business executives. Specific stress may be given on the innovative models, best practices, exploring business at the Bottom of the Pyramid as strategic intervention and related subjects. XLRI-Xavier School of Management has a module on social initiative for sensitizing the management student to rural and social issues. Participants of the course are required to stay and work with the villagers in the rural area for a term. This programme is implemented in collaboration with the Tata Steel Rural Development Society for giving an exposure to the students on the other part of India, which represent the poor, the weak and the disadvantaged. Such programme may be included in all management courses along with required changes. Further it should be included in all training and orientation programmes for the corporate executives and civil servants.

Challenges of social work and the thrill of making a difference in the lives of many have attracted several people from the corporate world, who have changed their career and taken up social causes. Dilip Ranjekar of Wipro working in the *Azim Premji Foundation*, Nachiket More of ICICI Bank in the *ICICI Foundation* represent this trend of successful corporate executives of high capacity and high potential, who have opted for social welfare as a career. Such initiatives should be encouraged and supported for mobilizing managerial resources, which is of considerable importance in making CSR effective in furthering social development.

Facilitating CSR Interventions

In his work "*Market for Virtue*", Prof. David Vogel has observed, "CSR is sustainable only if virtue pays off. The supply of corporate virtue is made possible as well as is constrained by the market… While there is a place in the business system for responsible firms, the 'market for virtue' is not sufficiently important to make it in the interest of all firms to behave more responsibly." As corporate operate in market, taking up CSR by all corporate will depend on the market recognizing CSR as a factor in creation of value for the shareholders. However this process takes time. In the interim period, the corporate needs to be encouraged through social recognition, which would stimulate the value system and conscience of the corporate intaking up CSR.

In India, the corporate have enormous strength and have been contributing to national progress significantly. Recognition and encouragement will encourage the corporate, who are passive to take up CSR with interest. Further, those who are already doing CSR would scale up their activities for addressing the national task of empowering the disadvantaged with physical and financial resources at their command.

In a developing country like India, where the financial markets are evolving, the government and the civil society have important roles in promoting CSR. While financial measures like deferment, exemption of taxes are relevant, non-financial measures like recognition, awards etc.

would be more effective and useful. A beginning in this regard has been made by making CSR mandatory under the Companies Act, 2013 requiring the corporate to spend part of their profit for CSR activities with effect from April 2014. However, *the best in any individual person or firm or institution always comes up by motivation and encouragement and not by threat or pressure; as regulations in any form often stifle the initiative and creativity.* As such, promotion of CSR needs to be based on motivation, which will generate social capital, and enhance the prestige and brand name of the corporate at the marketplace, which will in turn encourage the corporate to take up CSR on a larger scale.

In this context, development of a *"CSR Sustainability Trust Mark"* for encouraging market to support responsible corporation, as advocated by Y.C. Deveshwar, Chairman ITC deserves consideration. Trust marks may be evolved like ISI marking, which may be displayed on products and services to convey to the consumer that the enterprise has a strong commitment to CSR in general and building natural and social capital in particular. These trust marks may be developed on scientific and market principles and supplemented with *ratings*, based on the extent of involvement of any particular company in creating social capital. Promotion of such a mark on voluntary basis will play an important role in the interim period, till the market gets tuned to appreciate CSR activities.

Recognition and Incentives

Numbers of corporate have created *islands of excellence* in selected areas under their CSR interventions. Some of the best practices, which came up during the study, are given in boxes in this publication. Such information will be useful to other corporate, while formulating their CSR projects. Recognition of good work done under CSR, irrespective of the quantum of money spent, will act like a catalyst and encourage other corporate to step up their CSR activities **[Box 5.27: Recognizing and rewarding innovative CSR for its intention rather than volume, similar to effort of the squirrel getting stripes].** This will also motivate the passive players to take greater interest in CSR activities. Since CSR activities touch almost all aspects of public life, performance in CSR may be included as one of the parameters for evaluating performance of corporate in selection for award and recognition. For example, the Ministry of Steel awards the Prime Minister's Steel Trophy to the best steel plant every year. CSR initiatives of the company in physical and financial terms may be considered, while deciding the award among other

Box 5.27: Recognizing and Rewarding Innovative CSR Interventions

A lesser-known, yet meaningful event of the epic, *The Ramayana,* relates to the common squirrel's contribution to making of the '*sethu*' (bridge) across the sea for reaching Lanka. Being inspired by the noble purpose, the squirrel got wet in the seawater, rolled over the sand and then shook the sand off its back on the *sethu.* Impressed by this sincere, committed though small, effort of the squirrel, *Lord Rama* patted on its back and touched it fondly with his fingers, which, according to the epic, gave squirrel its stripes.

On similar lines, in case of the CSR interventions, the spirit of involvement and sharing the prevailing concerns of the society are of greater importance than the amount, a corporate spend on CSR. It calls for mass participation by each and every corporate operating in the society. Agenda for future of CSR in India to a great extent will lie in recognizing, understanding and appreciating the CSR efforts of the corporate by the media, civil society and the Government, which will in turn promote it further in solving the national issues relating to unemployment and poverty and make the growth socially inclusive and sustainable.

parameters. Apart from recognition, CSR activities of the corporate may also be given due weightage while sanctioning new projects and considering expansion, diversification etc., along with other techno-economic parameters.

Role of Government

With justice and equality as the cornerstones of our democracy, development of the disadvantaged segment is a major task before the Government for making the growth inclusive. It requires commitment, skill and technology in addition to deployment of financial and managerial resources. Under market-oriented economy, individuals, who do not have adequate resources and skill to enter and exploit available opportunities, are required to be empowered. This is a complex process, in which CSR can be mobilised for supplementing the efforts of the government for furthering the cause of social inclusion.

Role of the government in promoting CSR has two broad aspects. The first aspect is general relating to encouraging all corporate for making the best of their CSR interventions. The second aspect is more specific relating to the CSR activities of the PSEs, which function under the direct control and supervision of the government. Action taken by the PSEs for solving social issues can set examples for others. Exemplary work of PSEs will go a long way in encouraging the private ones to take up CSR in a better manner.

Traditionally, the government system looks at the private sector with suspicion and distrust. As mutual trust and cooperation is the basic requisite for success of CSR activities, prevailing mindset within the government in dealing with the corporate need to change for making CSR meaningful. As a proactive measure for promoting CSR, Department of Public Enterprises (DPEs) had advised the CPSEs for undertaking CSR and earmarking a part of profit of the previous year for CSR activities, much before CSR became mandatory under the Companies Act, 2013. Further, formulation of CSR policy and CSR activities were incorporated in the MoU executed by the Ministry with the head of the CPSE and the compliance was being monitored periodically.

However, after CSR became mandatory, it has become equally important for corporate, both public and private, to comply with setting up board level committee, making CSR policy, earmarking a part of the profit, monitoring and reporting on CSR activities. The challenge ahead for the government lies in making the PSEs to develop best practices in promoting CSR, which will make a difference and set example for the private sector to follow.

So far as *government promoting CSR is concerned, the challenge lies in acting as a facilitator and smoothen interaction of Corporate having CSR fund to spend with the Government agencies at village, block, subdivision, district and state levels by ironing out implementation related issues*. This would help the corporate as well as the NGOs implementing CSR projects to implement the CSR projects without any difficulties.

From available information, it appears that the Government run mechanisms for mobilizing corporate support like National Sports

Development Fund, National Cultural Fund, National Population Stabilization Fund, have served a limited purpose. Guidelines on operation of these funds may be reviewed in consultation with the corporate and modified for making it more flexible and providing greater discretion to the donor-corporate. Further, due publicity may be given to the achievements for making these mechanisms more attractive and effective in mobilizing corporate support.

As per the constitutional mandate, number of plans and programmes are being launched for social welfare giving attention to the disadvantaged. The public exchequer is being looked into as the major rather the only source for funding such activities. As the corporate sector has both financial resource and management expertise, involvement of the corporate sector in the social welfare programmes may be encouraged, which will not only ease the pressure on public resources but also ensure better quality in implementation. The Ministry/Departments of Central and the State Governments dealing with education, health, sanitation, drinking water, rural development as well as welfare of the disadvantaged sections like the Scheduled Castes, Scheduled Tribes and persons facing physical/mental challenges may *evolve suitable strategy for availing the corporate support under CSR to the maximum extent possible*, which will help them not only in overcoming the constraint of resources but also in achieving the objective of providing quality service and empowering the disadvantaged.

As this would require coordination among government departments, corporate and NGOs, it will be useful to evolve suitable mechanism for facilitating implementation of CSR under the Cabinet Secretary at the Central level and the Chief Secretary at the State level.

Role of NGOs/Civil Society

As CSR primarily relates to the welfare of the society, effectiveness and sustainability of CSR interventions will require active participation of the civil society, NGOs and media. These will be of special significance in a developing country like India, where CSR is in an evolving stage.

Large numbers of NGOs are associated with the welfare of the disadvantaged sections of the society. NGOs like *Akshaya Patra Foundation, M.S. Swaminathan Research Foundation* (MSSRF), Child Relief and You (CRY), *Bharatiya Agro Industries Foundation* (BAIF), and *Population Foundation of India* (PFI) have been pursuing social causes and empowerment of the disadvantaged. NGOs, with expertise and professional competence, can play an important role in helping the corporate houses in implementation of CSR projects. NGOs may be rated based on expertise in different sectors like education, health, skill development as well as credibility in a transparent manner. Such rating will help the corporate in choosing NGO for implementation of their CSR projects.

The role of civil society in improving delivery of public service hardly needs any elaboration. However, excessive dependence on the State or foreign donor organizations for funding has been one of the major limitations of the NGOs. At times this has led NGOs into making compromises with the objectives. In order to be effective and impartial, the civil society and community-based organizations are required to develop a culture of self-reliance in due course. In this context, CSR can provide required flexibility to the NGOs. Synergy of action between the corporate and the civil society in undertaking CSR activity would help the target group and enable the NGOs to function in an effective manner.

The civil society wields power to mobilize public opinion and enforce accountability. There are instances of NGOs seeking judicial interventions through public interest litigations, for safeguarding the interest of common man. Initiatives taken by the civil society on environment conservation related matters have created pressures and enforced accountability in several cases. Active participation of the civil society will help in promoting CSR.

Encouraging NGOs to Avail CSR

Governments, at the Centre and State, have lunched number of welfare plans and programmes for provision of social services and welfare of the disadvantaged segments. Besides, organizations like Dr. Ambedkar Foundation, Maulana Azad Educational Foundation, set up with financial support from government; are also pursuing similar activities. Under these schemes, numbers of NGOs are provided financial assistance for taking up welfare activities for the disadvantaged. CAPART, operating under the administrative control of the Ministry for Rural Development, has been coordinating activities of the NGOs dealing with rural development. Suitable steps may be taken for dovetailing corporate support under CSR with the government interventions to the extent possible. Further, NGOs may be encouraged to avail corporate support, both financial and managerial, for last mile connectivity, in addition to the help from the government. This will avoid duplication, optimize use of public fund and ensure better and faster development.

Importance of Civil Society Organizations (CSOs) in effective implementation of government policies/schemes was recently highlighted by the Vice Chairman, NITI Aayog that *'an effective partnership between the government and the CSOs will go a long way in efficient utilization of government resources, especially in the social sector"*.[25] Effective coordination and collaborative approach between CSOs and the government would help in creating a lasting impact on the lives of citizens in general and in providing innovative solutions to eliminate poverty, hunger and other forms of deprivation in particular. The CSOs may be encouraged to avail CSR funding for taking up projects as per the decision of the donor-corporate.

Role of Media

The electronic and print media wields enormous power in a democracy in forming public opinion. Media may take up publicizing the CSR initiatives in general and success stories in particular for generating public awareness. In the recent years, social media like *Whatsapp, Facebook, Twitter* have been playing a critical role in reaching the masses very fast and with very little cost. The social media may be used for promoting CSR in an innovative, effective, and cost-effective manner. It will generate social capital in favour of the concerned corporate, which in turn will lead to promoting the brand name of the corporate and encourage them to promote CSR further. It will also inspire the fence-seaters to join and take up CSR activities.

Response of the industry to environment related issues in general and global warming in particular is another extremely important aspect, which is required to be pursued.

Role of Political Parties and People's Representatives

Political parties are active partners in a democracy. Role of CSR in sustainable development and advantages of synergy of action between the corporate, NGOs and government may be discussed for generating awareness among political leaders and people's representatives, which will facilitate formulation and implementation of CSR interventions in an effective manner.

The Common Man and CSR

The last but not the least important factor for making CSR effective is the involvement of the common man. It is necessary to make the common man aware about the role and objectives of the corporate, with particular reference to the fact that corporate can undertake CSR, only if it is in profit, which is essential for its survival. It is necessary to demystify the concept of sustainable development and encourage the common man to acquire skill and enter the market. Based on the famous Chinese proverb "*learning how to catch fish will ensure fish on sustainable basis, whereas looking for it free from others will be only temporary and not sustainable*"; the disadvantaged segments need to be encouraged to avail help of the corporate under CSR to acquire skill and access the market and earn their livelihood rather than looking for paid employment. Responsibility of individual towards the society, particularly the disadvantaged segments, may be suitably included in the school and college syllabus. Further, volunteers of the National Service Scheme and National Cadet Corps may be exposed to the concept of CSR, which will help in spreading awareness and promotion of CSR, and creating a "win-win" situation for the business and the society.

CSR in National Development

Several approaches have been advocated on the course, India should adopt for transforming its economy for *emerging as a global super power* in general and solving the problems of poverty and unemployment, and making the growth inclusive in particular. While there is unanimity that the agrarian base of the economy is required to be diversified from its low production, low wage and low employment base, there are differences as to whether India should take the normal course of developing the secondary sector with the industrial and manufacturing base first and then go to the tertiary sector covering services; or otherwise. China adopted the course of strengthening its manufacturing base in the last decade (2000-10), when the global situation was different with relatively less competition. China mobilized its resources and strengthened its physical infrastructure; covering the rail, road network, sea port and airport facilities, power generation, which are essential for taking up manufacturing on a large scale. In the meantime, the Information Technology (IT) and Telecom revolution has brought about sweeping changes, which have changed the level of competition in the global economy. Further, new age aggregators like *Amazon* and *Flipkart* for small merchandise; *Uber* and *Ola* cabs for taxies have evolved IT based models; which have redefined the way of doing business in the service sector by optimizing use of available resources. Strength of such platform aggregators is attributed to their ability to reduce cost for the consumer and create jobs on a large scale with relatively low capital investment; not as monolithic large organization but as large number of small entrepreneurs interconnected on an IT platform.[26]

India's young English knowing population are looking for opportunity to innovate and chalk out similar success stories in health, education and skill for livelihood sectors; covering tourism, information technology, banking, Financial services, insurance, telecommunication, capital markets. India's Unique Sales Proposition (USP) lies in its single huge market and strong financial institutions, which provides it an edge over its competitors. There is tremendous scope for creation of business and employment by exploiting the potential in different sectors. Taking the tourism and hospitality sector as a case; around eight million international tourists visit India in a year, which is about one-third of the figure for smaller countries like Thailand, Indonesia, and Malaysia. Creation of required infrastructure and conducive environment will enable exploiting the huge potential India has. Similarly, linking Aadhaar number with Jan Dhan account and Mobile phone (JAM) has opened a new window of opportunity for serving the people in making financial transactions—paperless, cashless and personless—smoother and faster. This will not only enhance productivity but also create employment with higher wage for meeting the expectations of the youth. Stable Central Government under the *visionary leadership of Shri Narendra Modi*, Hon'ble Prime Minister has generated new hopes and aspiration among the youth for carving out a new chapter of economic growth, which is socially inclusive and sustainable.

Best Practice in CSR

Mobilizing CSR for providing separate toilet for boys and girls in each government school offers one example of using CSR for tackling national issues. The importance of hygiene and sanitation in preventive healthcare for ensuring health for all at an affordable cost hardly needs any elaboration. It has been established that availability of sanitation facilities along with safe drinking water plays a significant role in bringing down the incidence of communicable diseases in general and waterborne diseases in particular.

Importance of sanitation was brought to the centre stage with the launching of the *Swachh Bharat Campaign,* by Hon'ble Prime Minister,

Shri Narendra Modi on the 2nd October, 2014. Setting up of separate toilets for girls and boys in each and every government school of the country was taken up under this national campaign. The Ministry of Human Resources Development, Development of Primary Education pursued this on a mission mode by mobilizing support of the corporate in general and the Central Public Sector Enterprises (CPSEs) in particular.

Existing gaps were assessed by a quick survey and specific target was assigned to each CPSE, which was monitored at regular intervals. 64 Central Public Sector Enterprises (CPSEs) and 11 private Corporate funded[27] construction of 1,41,636 toilets (Rs. 341.52 crores) and 3,466 toilets (Rs. 8.35 crores) respectively, whereas remaining 2,72,694 toilets (Rs. 657.54 crores) were funded under ongoing Government programmes namely *Sarva Shiksha Abhiyan* (SSA), *Rashtriya Madhyamik Shiksha Abhiyan* (RMSA) and *Swachh Bharat Kosh* (SBK). Participation of the CPSEs varied, with Coal India Limited topping the list with construction of 51,115 toilets with an expenditure of Rs. 12.77 crores and Jute Corporation of India with construction of one toilet at an expenditure of Rs. 2.5 lakh. Tata Consultancy Services and Mahindra Group were the major private corporate, which took up construction of 1,509 toilets (Rs. 3.77 crore) and 1,171 toilets (Rs. 2.92 crore) respectively.

While there are issues like water supply, maintenance, and regular use of the toilets by the target group; it is a fact that mobilization of CSR fund fulfilled a critical infra structural gap in sanitation in schools in general and for the girl students in particular. *Analysis of factors behind success of this effort* indicates that the *direction and commitment from the top* at the level of Prime Minister, which flowed down to the Central Ministries and State Governments with political representatives and senior officers including the Prime Minister's Office monitoring the progress and taking corrective action from time to time was the key for this success. Further, the intervention was *taken up in the existing schools* in consultation with the school managements. Initially, the construction was done directly by the PSUs, which was revised later. The construction was decentralized and done through the agencies of the State Government. The press and media also supported this cause. Completion of such a gigantic task, across the length and breadth of the country, by mobilizing CSR fund for bridging the gaps and completing it within a record time made *this an island of success* in CSR solving national problems. Based on this, Ministry has initiated steps for taking the total sanitation movement forward.

For sanitation and public health related requirements, it is a fact that while corporate have CSR fund and the Urban Local Bodies (ULBs) needs it, there is a gap and the two are not connected seamlessly. Corporate select projects and get it executed either directly or through a third party as per their own choice, rather than giving it to the ULBs, due to a prevailing impression that ULBs delay decision-making and implementation; misutilize resources, which make fate of the CSR project uncertain. Communication gap between the companies and the ULBs constraints aligning the available resource with the demands.

It is heartening that based on the experience of mobilizing the CSR fund for building toilet in schools, Ministry of Urban Development has initiated[28] steps for availing CSR with help of associations of industry like Confederation of Indian Industry, FICCI and ASSOCHAM to connect the companies to spend their CSR budget through Urban Local Bodies (ULBs), which need fund for urban development. Ministry of Urban Development is reportedly developing an *interactive market place* for facilitating this, which will carry list of projects in need of investments. This will help companies in choosing projects for funding under their CSR to be implemented through the ULBs concerned. A range of projects, covering construction of individual, household, community and public toilets, waste management infrastructure, Information, Education and Communication (IEC) initiatives will be listed in the marketplace seeking resource support of corporate under CSR. This will facilitate proper utilization of the CSR fund and provide better sanitation and cleaner environment in cities and towns.

Area of Concern of the Corporate in Development

While development for enlarging choice of individual is necessary for all nations, ensuring that the benefits of development reach all segments of the society is equally important. Analysis of past experience of development indicates that normally those who are educated, skilled and have assets take advantage of development in general and development in science and technology in particular for going up on the economic ladder, whereas those who lack education, skill and assets continue to lag behind. As a result, the gap between the rich and the poor gets widened. This in turn gives rise to frustration, anger and leads to violence.

In the context of corporate exploiting available business opportunity and making profit, two specific issues have surfaced as major concern. The first one relates to providing employment for livelihood. In recognition of the prevailing socio-economic conditions and for making the development socially inclusive, reservation in government services for the Scheduled Castes, Scheduled Tribes was considered and specifically provided by the framers of our Constitution. This provision continued and was later extended to Other Backward Classes excluding the financially well off creamy layer. There has been demand for similar reservation in the private sector as well, which has not been agreed to, as for this, the private sector does not come within the purview of the Constitution. Further, the private sector require the freedom in hiring and managing its own people [**Box 5.28: Affirmative action for empowerment of the disadvantaged**].

Making CSR mandatory seeks to address the social inclusion related issue, which requires using CSR interventions for provision of quality education, health and skill to the disadvantaged segments for entering and exploiting the market. There are examples of provision of quality education and skill enabling persons belonging to the disadvantaged segments to perform at par and even better than the socially and economically better off segments. This is required to be pursued under CSR for overcoming the feeling of deprivation.

The other issue relates to acquisition of private land for setting up plants and units by the corporate. This issue has been a sensitive one in the agricultural economy, as land is considered as the main asset, which determines the status of a person in the community. With economic development, even though importance of agriculture has got reduced; land continues its importance in the rural economy. As a scarce and limited commodity, land continues to be important for development particularly for setting up new plants/units. Opposition to land acquisition for the small car plant at Singur, special economic zone at Nandigram in West Bengal, setting up steel plant at Kalinganagar in Odisha bear testimony to the adverse consequence of acquisition of private land for corporate use [**Box 5.29: Acquisition of private land for corporate use**].

Corporate efforts for exploiting available opportunity for setting up new units were defeated in the first case. These developments have reiterated the need for taking care of the population living in the periphery for remaining at peace with the local community, which is of critical importance for doing business in the society.

CSR, having been made mandatory, provides an opportunity for addressing these issues in providing livelihood with a decent income to the youth for fulfilling their expectations, which is critical to development.

The **future of CSR in India** is required to be looked into in this perspective keeping in view the relevant socio-economic scenario. In

Box 5.28: Affirmative Action for Empowerment of the Disadvantaged

As a part of inclusive development, affirmative action in favour of Scheduled Tribe (ST) and Scheduled Caste (SC) by reservation of seats in the Parliament and State Legislatures and employment, in Central and State Governments in proportion to their percentage in the total population, were introduced in the Constitution as an accepted national policy. Similar provisions were made for admission into the Government educational institutions. Later, reservation in employment under government was extended to outside the creamy layer of the Other Backward Classes (OBCs).

Demands for reservation in employment in the private sector on similar lines have been raised from time to time. While supporters of this demand[1] stress on its need for ensuring social justice, overcoming deprivation and social inclusion, those against it argue that it will compromise merit and affect efficiency and productivity of the organisations. There are views that reservation primarily benefits the better off section and not the really deprived. On the contrary, provision of quality education and skill is more broad-based, empower and enable all in getting their share of development. It has been opined that it may not improve the socio-economic conditions of the disadvantaged communities significantly.[2] The corporate leaders have also argued in favour of empowering the poor with quality education and health services so that they can exploit the market in a better way instead of reservation.[3]

This issue was incorporated in the National Common Minimum Programme and, a group of corporate leaders representing major corporate had issued a statement supporting affirmative action to empower the disadvantaged segments through educational, vocational and occupational training in June 2005.[4] Even though, no specific orders have been issued on reservation in the private sector as such, Uttar Pradesh government had issued a directive to the effect that all industrial units, infrastructure projects, educational institutes, *set up with government assistance* to provide 30 per cent (10% for SC, 10% for OBCs and backward religious minorities and 10% for economically weaker sections from the upper castes) *job reservation on a voluntary basis* for augmenting the job opportunities to the disadvantaged sections.[5]

Agitation for inclusion in the reservation list by the *Gujjars* in Rajasthan, *Patidars* in Gujarat and *Jaats* in Haryana have come up in the recent past, even in the advanced states; leading to violent protest, loss of property as well as business opportunity. As a matter of fact, expansion of the opportunity for the youth is one of the major factors considered while making CSR mandatory by amendment of the Companies Act, 2013. Welfare of SC, ST and disadvantaged segments have been specifically incorporated in the list of activities in the Schedule-VII to be taken up under CSR. The corporate has to survive in a competitive environment by production of quality goods and services at a competitive rate. Technological development, competition from other producers/countries, etc. affect their competitiveness adversely. It is felt that while reservation in private sector may take its own course based on relevant factors, Corporate undertaking CSR interventions with sincerity and commitment in a planned manner will be of relevance to the disadvantaged and facilitate making the growth socially inclusive.[6]

References

1. Thorat, Sukhdeo, "On Reservation Policy for Private Sector", *Economic & Political Weekly*, June 19, 2004, pp. 25-60.
2. Mehta, Pratap Bhanu, "Affirmative Action without Reservation", *Economic & Political Weekly*, June 3, 2004, pp. 29-51.
3. Rahul Bajaj, "Devoid of Merit – Reservation will Kill Indian Private Sector", *The Times of India*, September 21, 2004, p.16.
4. "Captains courageous make a reserve sweep in private jobs", *The Economic Times*, June 01, 2005.
5. "For Maya's sake, keep 30 per cent quota", *The Economic Times*, August 11, 2007, p. 22.
6. S.K. Panda (2008), *CSR in India–Past, Present and Future*, p. 213.

course of study, number of best practices under CSR was noticed, which have made meaningful difference in the life of the target group. One of the main factor behind such success in the CSR intervention is attributed to the corporate leader's Personal commitment to CSR, owning the project and mobilizing human and financial resources for making a difference in the society. Foundations, set up and managed by the corporate have taken innovative measures and achieved significant success, as a result of committed and coordinated action. Involvement of NGOs with expertise has helped in ensuring quality of the output in general and making it sustainable in particular. Further, implementing CSR projects in synergy with the ongoing government plans and programmes has led to better use of the public resources, reduced wastage and provided better quality services. Mobilizing corporate volunteerism along with financial resources and appropriate technologies has added further value; particularly in areas needing change in habits, mindset and attitude. Instances like corporate executives counselling the rural folks to use toilets instead of defecating in the open; and teaching science, mathematics and English subjects to students of municipal schools for improving the quality of school education have set a new trend in sustainable development. CSR projects implemented with expertise, appropriate technology has brought out the best of each stakeholders; *viz.* the corporate in terms of better management gap filling, the government in achieving the coverage (number) and the NGOs motivating and guiding the beneficiaries in terms of quality. This has created examples in making the development sustainable.

Box 5.29: Acquisition of Private Land for Corporate Use

Availability of land is one of the basic prerequisites for setting up industrial units by corporate. Initially, government land was provided for this purpose. However as availability of government land got reduced, private land has to be acquired for setting up industrial units. Under normal cases, promoter of the industrial unit needs to purchase the private land required from the landowner, as a transaction between two private parties *viz.*; the landowner and the corporate. But in some cases, Government resort to acquire the private land using the statutory power under the Land Acquisition Act in the name of public interest, on the ground that setting up the industry will serve a public purpose by way of bringing in benefits of economic development in general and generation of employment in particular. This matter has been under discussion and debate in the last decade. Analysis of a few cases will bring out the major issues in acquisition of private land for corporate use.

One of the most talked about cases related to acquisition of private land for the setting up the low-budget "*Nano*" car project by Tata Motors in Singur, West Bengal. Acquisition of about 1000 acre of land for the project faced local opposition, which later turned violent and acquired political dimension. The agitation, led by Ms. Mamata Banerjee, continued and ended with the general election to the West Bengal Assembly and emergence of *Trinmool Congress*, a state political party, forming government in the State. There was a series of litigations over this land acquisition, which ended with verdict of the Hon'ble Supreme Court on the 31st August, 2016 holding the land acquisition process to be anti-farmer, done hurriedly in violation of law. It held that the enquiry process that preceded land acquisition was basically fraud and was mechanically accepted by the government. While one of judges observed that the land acquisition was for public purpose, as the project would have generated large scale employment, the bench struck down the acquisition process and ordered to return the land to the farmers within twelve weeks. The court had observed that the compensation, which has already been paid to the landowners/cultivators, shall not be recovered as the landowners have been deprived of the occupation and enjoyment of their lands for last ten years and those, who have not withdrawn the compensation, are permitted to withdraw the same.

The second case related to land acquisition for a Tata steel plant at Kalinganagar in Odisha, which met with protest from the local tribals. Police used force and resorted to firing on the agitating public on the 2nd January, 2006, in which as many as thirteen tribals lost their lives. There were uncertainties about the project for a long time. However, finally the unit was commissioned after about a decade long persuasion and efforts by the corporate and the State Government.

It is rather a coincidence that both of these projects were promoted by the Tata Group, which has a long history of adherence to ethical principles and remaining responsible towards the society. A closure look at the developments behind the turmoil indicates that these incidents happened primarily due to the general change in mindset and high expectations of the youth belonging to the tribal and other disadvantaged segments; rather than due to any particular project or corporate.

After independence, large chunks of forest and land belonging to the tribal were provided for setting up iron and steel plants, other industrial units, infrastructure and hydel projects. The older generations, born before or immediately after independence, were simple and peace loving. They were satisfied with whatever compensations they got and did not question the State authority to acquire their private land and providing it to private corporate.

However, the mindset has changed with passage of time and spread of awareness and education. Tribal youth of the twenty-first century, born in the post-1990 economic liberalization period, has cherished a dream for himself, which is different from that of his father and forefather. This is only natural in the age of media publicity, information technology and digital literacy. Lack of resources and failure to fulfil individual dream has been leading to frustration, giving rise to anger and violence. This issue is required to be addressed for having peace and development in the society including setting up projects by the corporate.

Availability of land is essential for setting up physical infrastructure like road, railway line, port and airport as well as commercial plants and projects. This is critical for expansion of the Secondary sector of the economy including manufacturing, in which India is weak. Rapid urbanization as well as infrastructure has created pressure on land. On the other hand, protecting the forest and green cover has come up as major concern for checking carbon emission and global warming. Making land available to corporate for new projects has thus become an extremely important and sensitive issue.

Analysis of the failed projects provides rich lessons. The discontentment among the landowner appeared to be partly due to a feeling that the amount of land acquired for the project is often over-assessed in excess of the actual requirement. In certain cases, after the project is completed, part of the acquired land is used for development of real estates and similar purposes, *which fetches a huge profit for the promoter—the new landowner. This led to the original landowner getting a feeling of being cheated with the paltry compensation received prior to the development of the project*.

In this background, acquisition of land for the same *Nano* project, relocated at Sanand, Gujarat, offers a different picture.[1] Setting up of the car project in the new site created *a micro climate* for industrialization, which spurred growth and attracted investment to the region. It acted as an incubator for auto ancillaries and skills, with as many as 41 auto ancillaries coming up in the area, which has been projected to rise further to 350 in the Sanand-Mandal-Becharaji region. Further, this region attracted investment and setting up of new units by Honda, Maruti-Suzuki with a capacity of 2.5 lakh cars per year, to increase further to a capacity of 15 lakh per year with an investment of Rs. 18,000 crore. AMW Motors for heavy trucks, Atul Auto for three-wheelers, Honda Motorcycle and Scooter India and Hero MotoCorp showed interest for setting up their plants and units in the area. Notwithstanding future of the *Nano* plant, the micro climate created by it in the area; attracted sizeable investment, created flow of jobs and converted the area into a hub of industrial activity. This experience made the landowners to appreciate the position and getting a better deal as a partner in exploiting benefits of economic growth and employment generation in the backward area.

It appears that the process of getting private land for corporate use can be better addressed *through voluntary negotiation* with the landowner and exploring *other alternative* like leasing of the land in place of acquiring. Further, provision of a part of the developed land to the original landowner would make him a partner in the development process, which makes the process acceptable and smooth. Acquisition of land for setting up the new capital project for the new State of Andhra Pradesh at Amaravati on these lines has got support from the landowners and come up as a model.

These cases indicate that acquisition of private land for corporate needs a holistic approach covering the following:

- Keeping the amount of land to be acquired to the barest minimum.
- Giving back part of the developed land to the original landowner, which he can use for setting up shopping complex, restaurant, automobile repairing unit, etc. for earning livelihood.
- The compensation amount may be decided in a fair and transparent manner.
- Providing employment to the affected persons in the project to the extent possible; along with provision of quality education and skill for earning livelihood in the open market.
- Due consultations with the landowners for convincing them about advantages of the project on completion.

In brief, in order to succeed the government and corporate should act in a manner, which is not only fair but appears to be fair. As a part of their responsibility towards the society, while setting up plants and units in new areas and acquiring private land for the same, the corporate need to remain sensitive to the changing expectations of landowners and support them for taking the project to its logical end. In this context, along with provision of monetary compensation, the landowner need to be convinced that not only the minimum amount of land has been acquired but also attempts have been made to give part of the developed land to them as far as possible. Corporate action for supplementing government efforts in provision of quality healthcare, education and skill for livelihood to the local population under the Corporate Social Responsibility (CSR) would further smoothen this process.

Reference

1. *The Times of India*, September 11, 2016, p. 14.

CSR becoming mandatory has made sizable financial resources earmarked with the corporate for social/environmental purpose. The challenge, ahead lies in evolving, strategy for addressing social issues. As per the Directive Principles of State Policy, government is to look after the social issues and empowerment of the disadvantaged segments. Accordingly, government has been implementing schemes and deploying resources. However, dealing with social issues requires commitment and involvement, which is difficult to assure under government managed system. Civil society organizations/NGOs show commitment and involvement. However, they face limitation of resources. There are also issues relating to transparency and disclosure with such organization.

As an important stakeholder of the society, corporate have a responsibility towards the society. However, it would be *unfair to expect that corporate will take care of all the social problems*. This is due to the fact that the main job of the corporate is to take up production and marketing of goods and services with quality and at a competitive price, for winning consumers' satisfaction to remain in business. Further, it is neither feasible nor possible for the corporate to take care of the social problems keeping in view its magnitude and diversity. In this context, Non-Governmental Organizations (NGOs), i.e. the civil society, also have a role in areas and activities, in which they have expertise and interest. However, NGO sector is handicapped due to limitation of resources. There are several instances of NGOs starting welfare activities on a smaller scale by mobilizing the resources at their command and achieving excellence, however often same fails to sustain and scale up. Provision of adequate resource with accountability can overcome this with use of technology for having better management, monitoring and transparency, which was rather difficult a decade back. CSR becoming mandatory with effect from the 1st April, 2014 has opened a new window of opportunity in this context, for mobilization of financial, managerial resources and technology for bridging the gaps in implementation of government plans and programmes. Number of best practices has been noticed in utilization of the CSR fund, some of which have been indicated in the preceding paragraphs as well as in boxes. The major challenge ahead lies in scaling up and replicating success stories for addressing the major national issues.

Innovative Model for Implementing CSR Projects

In the context of using CSR fund, construction of separate toilets for boys and girls in each government school of the entire country has been a major achievement. This happened primarily due to the leadership and close monitoring support of Hon'ble Prime Minister. Learning from the said experience, converting the noble intention for using CSR for solving national issues would require an institutionalised arrangement; clearly indicating the role and responsibility of the government, corporate, technical institution and civil society involved and monitoring the implementation and removing the differences if any in time. Further, involvement of the corporate leaders owning the project and mobilising corporate voluntarism will go a long way in delivering the desired results.

It has been found that inadequacy of financial resource, improper technology, lack of managerial skill, commitment, and inability to involve the local community and beneficiary are some of the issues which affect achieving the desired objectives in social sector plans and programmes. It is necessary to learn from the past experiences and revise the strategy and implementation suitably for achieving the desired results. Experiences of corporate implementing CSR projects, which has been discussed in the previous chapters and case study indicate that *CSR projects can be taken up on an innovative model, where the one-time cost on setting up required physical infrastructure supported by appropriate technology, along with a corpus is funded by the corporate. Financial provision under ongoing government schemes may be dovetailed for meeting the recurring expenditure towards salary and wages and cost of the consumables required for providing the services.* The project may be managed by a NGO of credibility and expertise in the area of intervention, to be selected based on past performance. The local community and the beneficiaries may be actively associated with the implementation. The interest accrued on the corpus may be used for bridging the gaps in funding, if any. A token service charge may be collected from the users for ensuring their involvement and their having a say in the management, which will go a long way in ensuring accoutability, quality and sustainability. Some CSR interventions for tackling major issues under this model, have been outlined below:

Tackling Problem of Malnutrition and Hunger

Centralised kitchen as run by the *Akshaya Patra Foundation* may be *set up in the subdivision headquarters* to start with under the CSR intervention of the CPSEs **[Box 5.11: Serving hot cooked meals to children]**. Hot cooked food may be prepared at one place centrally; transported and served to all children, expecting and nursing mothers, the target group under ongoing ICDS and Mid-Day-Meal schemes in all the *Angan Wadi Centres (AWCs)* and schools of the subdivision respectively. Essential features of this model would involve:

(i) **One time capital cost** for the construction, machineries, and vehicles for transportation along with a corpus fund to met **under CSR**; and

(ii) Fund **under ongoing government programmes** for provision of supplementary nutrition under the ICDS and Mid-day Meal along with interest from the corpus to be used **for meeting the recurring expenditure** on preparing, transporting, serving the food along with the establishment cost. The food may be supplimented with micro-nutrient and vitamins during preparation in this centralized kitchen.

This model will have a **number of advantages**, like (i) supply of nutritious food and micro-nutrient prepared in hygienic condition to the target group; (ii) Anganwadi worker/helper, school teacher, who are engaged in cooking and serving food, will be free for teaching the students; and (iii) use of CSR fund optimally. This facility may be extended to provide food to patients in the hospital, inmates of Old Age Home, street children, destitute, adolescent girls etc. in due course, by dovetailing required resources under the ongoing schemes. Addition of micro-nutrients, locally available seasonal vegetables will add value to the food served and keep the expenditure manageable. It is beyond doubt that such a coordinated approach will make a meaningful difference in CSR interventions solving the problem of malnutrition and hunger.

Trauma Care

Increase in number of vehicles has led to increase in road accidents and minor, major and fatal injury, causing lots of financial and social hardships to people. It has been established that death in road accidents can be reduced substantially, by providing required help for completing the legal formalities and medical help in time; as has been done by motivated NGO with corporate support [**Box 5.30: Highway Trauma Care Centre**]. This model can be replicated by supplementing the additional requirement along with a corpus fund in one of the District

Box 5.30: Highway Trauma Care Centre

Motor vehicle road accidents[1] has been claiming over one lakh human lives, causing misery to lakhs of families in India every year. Many of these deaths are preventable, in case the injured is shifted to a hospital within the first hour and provided emergency healthcare. Further, on account of legal formalities and apathy of lower level police functionaries; general public and hospital often don't come forward to help the injured in time in such condition.

Based on personal experience following injury sustained in an accident, when their car crashed into a tree on the Ahmedabad-Vadodara highway in 1999, when no help came their way for seven long hours, till a milkman on a bullock cart stopped and took them to the hospital; Dr. Subroto Das and his wife, Sushmita, set up the Ahmedabad-based *Lifeline Foundation*.[2] It is a non-profit organization committed to providing Emergency Medical Services (EMS) covering life saving pre-hospital trauma care to accident victims on Highways.

Persons affected by motor accidents on national highways are provided rescue, evacuation to the nearest medical center and services covering medical care like blood and medicines, legal and police related assistance. For the purpose, the foundation mobilizes ambulances, cranes and metal cutters, blood donors, hospitalization etc. at its own cost.

Lifeline has setup central control rooms to respond to distress calls on 24x7 basis. All along the highways, the helpline numbers, have been displayed on billboards. All major landmarks on the highways have been mapped and referred to, which enables the ambulance to reach the victims at the shortest possible time. Along with the nearest ambulance, the nearest hospital is informed to be in preparedness, concerned Police Station is informed and other utilities are mobilized to rescue the victims. The foundation manages to *send its teams to reach accident spots in less than 40 minutes*. The teams are trained to give basic care and ensure that critically injured people are not moved unnecessarily or in a manner that could cause further injury. The foundation uses a network of ambulances to get accident victims to hospitals in time and manages all the paperwork required at hospitals and police stations, while the accident victim undergoes treatment.

Further, it has effectively spread the directions of the Hon'ble Supreme Court of India that in road accident cases, hospitals cannot refuse to treat an accident victim in the name of waiting for police formalities, *nor can the police stall medical procedures* in the name of carrying out legal formalities. As most of the injured people end up paying sooner than later, the hospitals have realized that this is good business and usually don't turn victims away. However, Lifeline Foundation guarantees hospitals payment in case any of the accident victims cannot pay; which provide a big strength in such difficult situation.

The foundation has taken up *training the paramedics and drivers and also to upgrade the ambulances and spread the message to the people,* which support provision of emergency medical service. The foundation has taken up capacity building of the local population, like the highway toll tax plaza attendants, villagers, petrol pump attendants, doctors, paramedics and police for extending support in such emergency operations. Indian Oil Corporation Limited has a tie up with the foundation to train the attendants manning its petrol stations on highways to handle the accident victims.

Gauri Wagner, chief representative of the Netherlands Business Support Office at Ahmedabad helped Lifeline connect[3] with a Dutch non-governmental organization in 2001. Activities of the foundation are supported by corporate donors such as Asian Paints including Sushmita, spouse of Dr. Das, who runs a travel agency, as the first corporate donor.

Activities of this initiative increased[4] by manifolds from evacuating 86 injured victims in Gujarat in 2002 to over 2,187 cases in five states (Gujarat, Maharashtra, Rajasthan, West Bengal and Kerala) in 2012, covering more than 5000 kilometers of Indian Highways, supporting over 1000 Road Traffic Accidents cases in a year with a network of more than 600 ambulances and 300 care centres, making a big differences in saving lives of persons in such difficult condition and serving a great humanitarian and social purpose.

In recognition of the outstanding service to the society, Dr. Subroto Das, founder of the Lifeline Foundation was awarded[5] the prestigious national *Padmashri award* for 2017 in medicine.

References

1. As per National Highways Authority of India (NHAI) statistics (1,46,133 road accident deaths in 2015).
2. http://emsindia.in/subsectioncontent.php?secid=70&subsecid=58
3. http://www.livemint.com/Companies/ichBzVdGijModIRgwpNRHO/Subroto-Das—This-doctor-extends-a-Lifeline-to-highway-acci.html
4. http://emsindia.in/subsectioncontent.php?secid=70&subsecid=87
5. http://connectgujarat.com/dr-subroto-das-conferred-padmashri-award

Hospitals under CSR and managing the *recurring expenditure* under Government Programmes.

Provision of Preventive Healthcare, and Pre-School Education

As per the order of the Hon'ble Supreme Court, provision of *Anganwadi Centre* at habitation level has become a legal right of children. Under the National Health Mission, *Health Sub-centres* are being set up at the Gram Panchayat level. Besides, *Rajiv Gandhi Seva Kendras* are set up at the Panchayat level for supporting Rural Development programmes. Evolving synergy in functioning of these three grass-root level organizations at the Gram Panchayat level along appropriate Information

Technology (IT) based intervention can ensure provision of preventive healthcare, education and skill to the rural population as well as urban slums in a cost-effective manner. Quality physical infrastructure may be developed by consolidating available buildings and supplementing it with required equipment under CSR *as a one-time expenditure* and the recurring expenditure may be met *under the ongoing schemes*. Experiences[29] of Tripura in holistic development may be replicated with area specific modifications as required. Such an approach will go a long way in ensuring provision of basic services on preventive healthcare, IT literacy and related services to millions in the rural areas and urban slums.

Development of Agriculture and Allied Activities

Agriculture and allied activities provide livelihood to millions and form the backbone of rural economy. *E-Choupal* experiment of ITC Ltd. has set an example in empowering the villagers with information, technology and linkages. This experiment can be taken forward with focus on introduction of appropriate technology and management practices in soil testing, improving soil nutrition with vermin-compost, use of technical textiles for conservation of water, diversification for production of high value green cash crops, pulses, vegetables, flowers, fruits, and without use of chemicals. High tech agriculture on a project mode can be promoted under CSR, which will not only empower the farmers with higher and sustainable income but also attract the rural youth towards agriculture and check urbanization.

Welfare of the *Divyangs* (those Facing Physical and Mental Challenge)

Empowering the *Divyangs* (those facing physical and mental challenge) with provision of aid and appliances, special education and skill for livelihood is another issue, which need to be dealt with care and sensitivity. Welfare of persons with mental disability or multiple disabilities is somewhat more challenging. Keeping this in view, physical infrastructure has been set up and staff has been posted in the District Disability Rehabilitation Centres (DDRCs) under government scheme at district level. However barring a few exceptions, management and quality of services provided to the target group have been far from satisfactory. In certain cases, corporate have taken up this cause under CSR **[Box 5.13: Empowering the *Divyangs* Differently Abled]**.

It has been noticed that some NGOs formed by parents of the *Divyangs* are doing meaningful work, but are not able to continue and scale up due to financial constraints. Involvement of such dedicated NGOs with one-time support under the CSR, on the lines indicated above, will serve a very meaningful purpose. Available government infrastructure/ facilities may be consolidated and supplemented with required building, equipment and a corpus as *one-time grant under CSR, recurring expenditure under the ongoing government programmes, to be managed by a NGO*, dedicated to the cause; which can make a big difference in the life of the *Divyangs*.

Skill Development

Provision of quality skill as per market demand is yet another important area of concern. In this context, provision of on-the-job training has a special strength. Some of the Corporate in the construction and real estate business have taken up skill development under their CSR. Consolidating the available infrastructure, as an one-time grant under CSR, along with facility for on-the-job training in the projects under execution by the corporate, corporate voluntarism and meeting recurring expenditure under ongoing PMKVY can make a big difference in provision of short term quality skill in the construction sector. This will make lakhs of youth employable.

The *list of such possibilities, which can make a meaningful difference in the life of the poor and disadvantaged, is long*. While there is no doubt that Government will continue to be primarily responsible, the issue for consideration of the corporate is that these provide them a unique opportunity for making the best use of their CSR fund in making a difference in the life of the common man and the growth inclusive. These will be useful for both the corporate and the society as well.

Conclusion

India has been a society in transition. After over four centuries long subjugation under the Mughals and British, Indians won their political freedom in August 1947 and later economic freedom in July 1991. The transition has reached a critical phase, with the landslide victory and formation of the new government at centre in May 2014 bringing them new hopes.[30] The dreams of an aspiring new middle class have been affirmed for the first time in India's history. Charismatic leader, Prime

Minister, Narendra Modi, made millions believe that they have a future which is open, and not predetermined—that it can be altered by their own actions. It is being discussed as similar[31] to the great transformation of the West in the 19th and early 20th century, when the industrial revolution created a middle class that changed the western societies. It needs to be appreciated that the typical voter, who elected the new Government, was not a Hindu nationalist, but a young, middle-of-the-road person, who had recently migrated from a village to a small town. He had got his first job, his first cell phone and aspires to have a life better than his father's. The message of development and governance has made him forget his caste, religion, and village. The young man is somehow convinced that his battle was not against other Indians but against a state of governance that would not give him his basic necessities like a birth certificate without paying a bribe.

Present status of Indian society has been nicely summed up by G.K. Gandhi[32], that in India, the media has emerged as the security guard of the monarch (the voter) for performing that task with amazing diligence. Indian judiciary today, is known for its independence and fearlessness on issues relating to quality of life, probity in public life. So far as common man is concerned, more people today own or rent '*pucca*' homes than before. More people travel by road, train and air than before. More people travel for leisure than before. More people spend on entertainment than before. More people eat, dress and buy goods and services better than before. Hardly anyone goes without footwear or a watch now. And of course almost every home, even if it does not have other essential furniture, has a television. The middle class believes in using its money for raising comfort levels. Refrigerators, small air-conditioners or coolers are considered as essential goods and not as luxury any longer. Most Indian youth have a mobile phone and some have even two. Indian scientists have been making news in advanced field like space technology, with putting multiple satellites in one go have become a matter of discussion all-over. There is no craze for getting imported goods from abroad, as from the nano and the micro to the mega, India today produce and use almost everything that Indians need. Be it the classical arts or the folk arts, be it cinema or literature, Indians are in an era of high achievement. The world—not just NRIs but other nationalities—looks to performing Indian artists with awe, invites them and celebrates their genius.

Technology led globalization has enabled India to get integrated with the global economy and emerge as one of the major players among the developing countries. The Indian ICT industry, dealing with the IT software and IT Enabled Services, has set a record in the world. However, benefits of this development have not been evenly shared by all segments. Notwithstanding these achievements, India represents uneven levels of development, which does not validate a democracy. India continues to be a paradox with few rich on the one end and many poor on the other. In the Global Hunger Index (GHI) 2015, India ranked 80 among 104 emerging economies studied, which make hunger, undernourishment and mortality among children as the major challenges faced by the country. Similarly, in the Global Human Development 2015 report, released by the United Nations Development Programme (UNDP), India with a score of 0.609 ranked 130 out of 188 countries. Another area of concern relating to inadequate skilling for livelihood is reflected in the Labour Bureau Report 2014, which has indicated the size of India's formally skilled workforce a meager two per cent, a poor comparison with Japan (85%), Germany (75%), South Korea (96%) and United Kingdom (68%).

Human deprivation is often leading to violence claiming loss of life and property and retarding the development process. As many as fifty incidents of attack by Left Wing Extremists (LWEs) violence were reported in the run-up to the elections (during 10-16th April, 2014) leading to the death of 17 persons including eight security force (SF) personnel (Bihar-2, Chhattisgarh-5 and Maharashtra-1) and nine civilians in Bijapur and Bastar districts of Chhattisgarh. They had targeted the vehicle carrying civilians, believing that the passengers were SF personnel. In one of the bizarre incident on 12th April, 2014, they triggered a landmine blast at Bijapur District of Chhattishgarh targeting an ambulance used by CRPF personnel for returning to their base camp, killing five CRPF personnel and two civilians, besides injuries to five others. The extremist outfits blamed the Police for forcibly commandeering the ambulance and putting the life of the civilian driver and technician at risk. The LWE claimed that the teaching community was not its enemy, rather the teachers, petty shopkeepers and small traders were part of 'petty bourgeois', and its allies and that lower-level police functionaries, though not 'class enemies', were targeted by Maoists and they worked for the 'exploiter' ruling class. Unfortunately, such incidents by the Left Wing Extremists (LWEs) is yet to end with tragic and unfortunate repetition; the latest one being on the 24th April, 2017 at Sukma in Chhattisgarh, claiming lives of 25 CRPF security personnel on a single day. Apart from loss of lives, it has affected socio-economic development of the tribal dominated areas, which need maximum attention for bridging the gaps in development. It goes without saying that while weapon and armed forces can only check insurgency, the long term solution for eliminating insurgency lies in expediting development and making them socially inclusive. As rightly observed by Shri N.R. Narayana Murthy[33] of Infosys, "managing expectations of the youths and creation of job for the youth, which will give them adequate disposable income, have come up as the *most important challenge*, requiring creation of 150 to 200 million jobs in the coming decade".

Corporate represent a major stakeholder in the society and play an important role not only in making major contribution to the National Gross Domestic Product (GDP), export/and earning of foreign exchange but also in generation of employment and livelihood for the youth, a matter of critical importance for making the development inclusive. So far as the social responsibility of the Corporate is concerned, as per the provisions under the Directive Principles of the State Policy mandated in the Constitution, the executive, i.e. Governments at State and Centre are primarily responsible for socio-economic development giving particular attention to the disadvantaged segment of the society. With over 1.3 billion people spreading from Kashmir to Kanyakumari and Kutch to Cocchar, India represents unity in diversity, a rich mosaic of diverse language, culture, food, clothing, faith and religion. In a multi-party democracy, managing public affairs and delivery of basic services to the common man has been a Herculean task for the Government. Apart from availability of financial resources, management and service delivery related issues are extremely challenging for delivering services within time on a long term basis.

In this context, empowering the youth with skill, knowledge, technology, health and education for exploiting the market and earning his livelihood has emerged as the critical need for India in the twenty-first century. Further, welfare of the disadvantaged segments needs specific attention for becoming stakeholders in national development. Unless this is done, mere investment in physical infrastructure will continue to make the rich richer and widen the gap between the rich and the poor further; thereby making sustainable development a distant dream. Social welfare related initiatives taken by the corporate in the past have been of help to the society to some extent. Making CSR mandatory has opened a new window of opportunity with financial resources of about 15,000 crore Rupees, as a part of the profit of the corporate available, every year for social purpose. *Channelizing this resource with managerial skill and corporate volunteerism will be of great help for solving the major national issues like providing quality education, health, skill for livelihood and conservation of the environment.* Implementing CSR in synergy with ongoing government plans and programmes with innovation *can bring about transformative results* in growth and development in general and empowering the poor and disadvantaged getting livelihood in particular, which will make the development socially inclusive.

References

1. S.K. Panda (2008), *CSR in India—Past, Present and Future*, pp. 335-338.
2. Michael S. Malone, "How Hewlett and Packard built the world's greatest company", Penguin Portfolio.
3. "Tata steel set to use TRT method to produce power", *The Financial Times*, February 07, 2007.
4. Dipankar Gupta, "Corruption of the American Dream", *The Times of India*, 25th May, 2013.
5. S.K. Panda (2008), *CSR in India—Past, Present and Future*, p. 148.
6. *Ibid.*
7. http://www.slideshare.net/......../project-shakti-15663985
8. http://www.in.undp.org/content/india/en/home/post-2015/mdgoverview.html [*source* 2015 Millennium Development Goals: India Country Report, Ministry of Statistics and Implementation, Government of India and 2015 India and MDGs: Towards a Sustainable Future for All, United Nations.]
9. Saachi Bhalla and Nachiket Mor, "Framing the right prescription", *The Hindu*, March 21, 2017, p. 8.
10. http://pib.nic.in/newsite/PrintRelease.aspx?relid=155963
11. http://globalnutritionreport.org/, released on the 10th December, 2015.
12. Anil Agarwal, "Women's Entrepreneurship – Holding up half the sky-holders", *The Economic Times*, 10 March, 2017, p. 18.
13. "Linking nutrition with education at *Anganwadis*", *The Hindu*, April 2, 2017, p. 6.
14. "1 in 3 Mumbai Municipal school children malnourished", *Tripura Times*, June 02, 2017, p. 2.
15. S.K. Panda, 2008, "Making One plus One Eleven", ISBN: 978-81-7650-626-7.
16. http://mhrd.gov.in/sarva-shiksha-abhiyan
17. "Leaving no one behind: How far on the way to universal primary and secondary education", The UNESCO Institute for Statistics (UIS) and the Global Education Monitoring (GEM) Report, policy paper 27, July 2016.
18. National University of Educational Planning and Administration (2015-16 Survey), *The Hindu*, 8th June, 2017, p. 9.
19. N.C. Saxena, Creating Jobs through Skill Development, *INCLUSION*, January-March 2014 issue, pp. 55 to 57.

20. http://www.mbarendezvous.com/general-awareness/demographic-dividend-advantage-india/
21. 68th round of the NSSO survey.
22. International Labour Organization (ILO) study of the ITIs and ITCs.
23. Report by McKinsey & Company (2012).
24. E.M. Manoj, "Meenangadi has a green dream: carbon neutrality", *The Hindu*, March 26, 2017, p. 1.
25. Dr. Arvind Panagariya, Vice Chairman, NITI Aayog, on the 1st March, 2017.
26. Nandan Nilkeni, "How Digital will save India", *The Times of India*, July 28, 2016, p. 10.
27. Answer to Rajya Sabha Unstarred Question No. 245 by Shri Avinash Rai Khann, Hon'ble M.P. answered on 25th February, 2016.
28. Nidhi Sharma, "Private companies can choose *Swechh Bharat projects* online now". *The Economic Times*, 20 March, 2017, p. 2.
29. S.K. Panda, "Making one Plus One Eleven—Some experience of Tripura".
30. Guru Charan Das, "*Modi's moment is about middle class dignity*", *The Times of India*, 1st June, 2014, p. 12.
31. *Bourgeois Dignity*, Deirdre McCloskey.
32. Shri Gopal Krishna Gandhi, Former Governor, West Bengal, "Eclipse at Noon", 15th DP Kohli Memorial Lecture, April 15, 2014, in New Delhi, published in the *Governance Now*, May 1-15, 2014, pp. 8-9.
33. N.R. Narayan Murthy, "The New India we want", *The Economic Times*, 29th April, 2014.

6

Conclusion

Corporate or organized modern business originated with the discovery of steam engine and industrial revolution in the West. It has undergone radical changes in the last centuries. Corporate has emerged as an integral part of the society; serving the important role in its development, through productive activities and creation of wealth and employment. Corporate owes its existence to the society in general and for making profit in particular. Keeping this in view, responsibility of the business towards the society has been a matter of discussion and evolving with the change in the society.

Based on his experience and analysis of social values and lifestyle typical to India; Mahatma Gandhi had advocated the concept of trusteeship for business. Trusteeship envisaged that business should generate wealth, and use part of it to the minimum extent required. The balance amount of profit belongs to the society, which is to be retained by the business not as the owner but as trustee on behalf of the owner (society). Further, he had stressed on the need for business with ethics, which requires business to adhere to value based transactions and complying with the statutory provisions relating to human beings and environment in letter and spirit, as central to business. Approach of Mahatma Gandhi towards business is guided by the Hindu philosophy of "*live and let live*" and that "*the world has enough for everyone's need but not for the greed*". Notwithstanding the criticism about being too idealistic and not applicable to modern society, Gandhiji's philosophy of business continue to be an important milestone in the study of responsibility of business towards the society.

The Western society, guided by the capitalism and supremacy of market in the economy, offers a contrast with business guided by one and only objective of making profit. Economist Milton Friedman had reiterated this and argued that it would be wrong on the part of business to get into social activities, which is the main work of government.

The market driven, corporate-led economic development has its share of successes as well as failures. Its experience in the developing economies, struggling with limited resources and poor physical infrastructure, in fulfilling the expectations of the youth has been a matter of concern.

Socialism was advocated as an alternative to capitalism for socio-economic development and checking the exploitive tendency of the business. Under this economic model, State owned Public Sector Enterprises (PSEs) were set up and promoted for production and marketing of goods and services. However, in due course, it was realized that this model has also its limitations as the government managed PSEs failed to deliver the desired outcome.

In the subsequent period, the concept of Triple Bottom Line emerged for tackling market failures on the one hand and making the development sustainable on the other. It advocated that it would be improper to judge the success of a business enterprise based on profit alone. That it is necessary to consider impact of business on the environment, i.e. "Planet" Earth and the social aspect relating to the gap between the rich and the poor divide, i.e. "People". Accordingly, the success of business got widened from one P, i.e. Profit to "three Ps" with the inclusion of Planet for the environment and the People for social aspects. This guided Corporate Social Responsibility covering major aspects of the responsibility of corporate towards the society.

Adoption of the Sustainable Development Goals 2030 with seventeen goals in the later part of 2015 has marked completion of a full circle in experimenting with the responsibility of the business towards the society. Achieving these goals requires mobilization of the corporate acting in close cooperation with the government. This is based on the realization that even though the Government is primarily responsible for tackling social issues like provision of quality education, healthcare, and skill for livelihood as well as conservation of environment; active participation of the corporate is essential for achieving the desired outcomes on a time bound manner. This is of special significance in the developing countries like India, which has been struggling to meet expectations of a huge youth population with limited physical resources. This has come out clearly in the United Nation's latest report "Better Business, Better World".

In the Indian context, notwithstanding the success in various fields, certain incidents relating to the society have been raising questions over sustainability of the development process. For any business, sustaining the growth on a long-term basis is as important as making profit. While making profit relates to immediate gains and is short-term in nature, sustainable growth requires a more composite approach covering economic, social and environmental aspects for sustaining operations on a long-term basis. Corporate are required to comply with the laws of the land for doing business in the society. But there are situations, when mere compliance of law is not enough. Developing countries like India have vast untapped potential for expansion of business. There are instances of corporate attempt to set up business for exploiting existing potential, which failed to take up due to opposition from local people affected by such commercial activities, commonly known as the Project Affected Families (PAFs). These are primarily attributed to the frustration of the local PAFs, who got displaced and suffered due to loss of occupation; but are not satisfied with the gain from the corporate activities. There is a feeling that they have lost more and gained less, which led to disillusionment and distrust against the corporate action. This resulted in frustration, anger and violence. Often, such oppositions to corporate action particularly acquisition of homestead and agricultural land by the local inhabitants are viewed as any other law and order problem. Police action with use of force is resorted to for suppressing such protests. However, such police action becomes counterproductive and the problem gets more serious. In many cases, the proposed project failed to take up notwithstanding its technical feasibility and commercial viability, loss of opportunity for development of the area and creation of job for the local people. Taking Orissa as a case, it represents an economic paradox with vast natural resources coexisting with sizable population living in poverty with high percentage of poor people. Exploitation of the natural mineral resource offers an ideal path for economic development and lifting the poor out of poverty. However, it does not happen due to the local population and society not extending its support to corporate action. In the recent past opposition to land acquisition for setting up the steel plant by the Tata Group at Kalingnagar led to loss of lives in police firing in January 2006. Another incident related to similar opposition to land acquisition for setting up another mega steel plant at Jagatsinghpur involving one of the largest Foreign Direct Investment (FDI) by the Korean steel maker POSCO in 2007. The Tata steel project could be started after considerable time and effort by the promoter. But the second project could not succeed and has to be winded up. These cases represent poverty and human deprivation in a vicious circle, in which corporate effort got frustrated with loss of the business opportunity; best illustrating the observations of Bjorn Stigson, President, World Business Council for Sustainable

Development (WBCSD) "*Business cannot succeed in a society that is failing.*" In the process, both the corporate and the society (the poor) have been losers. It is clear that these problems need holistic approach rather than being dealt as law and order incidents with use of force.

Another area of concern in development of the country relates to the disruptive activities of the Left Wing Extremists (LWEs). Over 100 districts in ten states have been witnessing violence and loss of life and properties at periodic intervals due to unlawful activities of the LWEs. The last such reported incidents were on the 11th March, 2017 claiming lives of 12 *jawans* of CRPF personnel followed by another on the 24th April, 2017 at Sukma in Chhattisgarh, where about 300 heavily armed Maoists killed 25 CRPF *jawans*. While such untoward incidents are attributed to a number of factors, lack of basic amenities, poor education and healthcare facilities have been the prime reasons. It is rather unfortunate that such incidents have been affecting implementation of various developmental plans and programmes adversely, depriving the local populations further from getting the fruits of development. Like land acquisition, solution to this problem requires holistic approach and augmenting the ongoing developmental efforts substantially for empowering and enabling the local population to become active partner in development and live a life with dignity.

Careful analyses of recent events in the urban areas indicate yet another disturbing trend of frustration of the youth; periodically spilling over and affecting peace and tranquility in the developed areas as well. Series of agitations for inclusion in the list of backward classes for reservation in Government and Public Sector employment by the *Gujjars* in Rajasthan, *Patidars* in Gujarat and *Jats* in Haryana; indicate the limitation of opportunity available to the youth for earning their livelihood in the open market for fulfilling their dreams. Unlike the LWEs activities in the tribal areas arising due to absolute poverty and deprivation; these incidents in urban areas arose due to relative deprivation and limitation in meeting the insatiable desires of the youth in general. Such agitations in the relatively progressive and developed areas of the country have been leading to loss of property, damage of infrastructure; bringing the urban life to a virtual halt for some time. These incidents reflect the limitation of job opportunity in the private sector, which has led to the demand for increasing the share of reservation in government services. These agitations are somewhat symbolic like tip of the iceberg, with huge mass frustration of the youth in earning a decent livelihood hidden below. Such agitations have led to loss of life, property for the society as well as opportunities for the business.

Solving the socio-economic problems in a developing country like India is a complex process. It is a fact that the government is primarily responsible for dealing with the economic and social issues arising out of industrialization and economic development. These relate to the interest of the corporate as well. The process will become easier, if the corporate come forward and supplement government efforts as far as possible as observed[1] by former President Kalam, "In a large democracy, bridging the gap cannot be done only by the government. All... need to help collectively so that impact is better and commitment to a common cause is more transparent." While support of corporate is relevant for all societies, it is of particular significance in a developing country like India in addressing the basic problems of unemployment and poverty. As a major stakeholder of the society, the corporate cannot afford to remain as a silent spectator to the social issue. For running business on a sustainable basis, it is necessary for the corporate to participate and do their bit in solving the social problems in general and empowering the disadvantaged for accessing the market in particular, which, in fact, forms the core of CSR in India.

Indian corporate has a tradition of remaining sensitive to social issues. Some of them have contributed significantly in providing healthcare and education facilities to the common man without expecting any return in the commercial sense. Recent years have brought an emerging trend in integrating CSR as a part of the business strategy. This covers a range of activities like exploring business at the *bottom of the pyramid,* which has expanded the market for the goods and services produced by the corporate; development of skilled manpower for meeting the future-need of the industry, which has created a 'win-win' situation for the industry as well as the society. Mobilization of voluntary service of employees has added a new dimension to CSR based interventions in dealing with issues like change of habit and mindset. In course of the study, it appeared that while involvement of some of the corporate houses like the Tata group in social issues spread over a century, many newcomers like Infosys, Wipro have taken up the cause with equal commitment, zeal and deployment of substantial financial resources for making a difference in the society. Similarly, CSR activities of Government run PSEs like ONGC, NALCO and SAIL have increased substantially in the last 4-5 years. CSR of Indian corporate covers a wide spectrum with some highly responsible corporate on one end to private corporate and smaller PSEs on the other end, which are yet to come up with commitment. For many corporate, CSR has remained limited to participation in a few events for publicity. In this context apprehensions of former President Kalam appears to be relevant that "During the last few years, I have seen many initiatives being taken by individual companies to bridge the gap between the urban and rural India. However, I do not find a large-scale impact of these measures. All companies have been growing at 20 to 25 per cent every year and reporting substantial profits leading to an overall growth of the Gross Domestic Product (GDP). The impact of this growth has *definitely not reached* the rural population at the speed one would expect."[2]

The challenge for future of CSR in India lies in sensitizing and encouraging each and every corporate to extend its support for replicating best practices for benefit of the society. CSR activities relate to the society, which is unlike starting of an industrial or commercial venture and would take time to sink in. Good work under CSR will be appreciated by the consumer and get reflected in the brand in due course, somewhat similar to the *quality consciousness* among consumers.[3] About a decade back, only a few consumers bothered about quality and the producer were able to sell whatever they produce irrespective of the quality. However, things changed in the last decade, with consumer becoming aware, vigilant and more demanding. This has led to the producers corporate appreciating the importance of quality and giving special attention to quality in order to survive in the marketplace. Consumers' preference in favour of good corporate guided by ethics, transparency and CSR will evolve gradually on similar lines and an ordinary consumer will start preferring a socially responsible corporate. Similarly, investors' preference will also be guided by the performance of the corporate on the "*Triple Bottom Line*" parameters covering the environmental and the social aspects in addition to profit. Information Technology based greater transparency and free flow of information will enable the investors to prefer companies with better values and robust CSR initiatives, while making investment decisions. The enlightened consumers and investors looking for corporate with values and responsibility towards the society will make CSR a part of branding, which will open new chapter for CSR in India.

CSR, being made mandatory under the Companies Act with effect from the 1st April, 2014, has opened another interesting chapter in the corporate discharging its responsibility towards the society. Analysis of the CSR activities under the mandatory provisions in the first two years, 2014-15 and 2015-16, indicate the following:

- Almost all companies coming under purview of the statutory provision have set up board level CSR committees with Independent Directors and adopted CSR policy.

- Earmarking of resources for CSR varied from company to company. About two-third corporate have earmarked two per cent of the net profit of the three preceding years for expenditure on CSR activities listed in the schedule.
- Under the statutory provisions, Companies have been given full discretion in identifying, formulating and implementing CSR projects covering area and activities as per their choice. There is considerable scope for improving this in the coming days.
- The statutory provision requires each liable company to disclose its CSR activities including reasons for failure; in case expenditure falls short of the prescribed amount. CSR is to be regulated in an indirect manner based on the disclosure made by each company on the amount one is supposed to spend on CSR, the amount actually spent along with details of the projects and in case of shortfall the reasons for not spending the targeted amount. As a matter of fact under the regulations, the company as well as individual officers responsible for CSR are liable for punishment only for failure to disclose. Failure to spend the targeted amount (2% of the net profit) on CSR is not an offence under the Act and no company can be forced to spend 2 per cent of their profit. The guiding spirit of this legislation has been to guide the corporate for discharging its statutory responsibility and encourage the corporate rather than through fear of law and imposition of penalty.

While compliance in term of expenditure on CSR activities by the private corporate and state owned PSEs have improved and expanded in terms of money spent; the quality of outcome varied widely; somewhat similar to the experiences of enforcing social legislations in India. *Generation of awareness, facilitating, and recognizing good work is necessary to motivate the corporate for undertaking and expanding CSR activities in a more meaningful manner.* These are essential in the interim phase till the market, the investors and the consumers distinguish good behaviour of a socially responsible corporate over others. Other stakeholders like the government and the civil society have also an important role in promoting and recognizing the CSR, as it will supplement socio-economic development and reduce the burden of the government on the one hand and make financial resource available for social work to the civil society on the other hand. Success and future of CSR in India will therefore depend on the synergy of action of the corporate, the government and the civil society a great extent.

This second phase of CSR in India under statutory provision can be viewed as "Transformative CSR" aiming at making a difference in the society and on the life of the common men. The case studies covering selected corporate have indicated that while the public sector companies have been earmarking and spending fund, the best examples of use of CSR fund and making difference in the life of the common men have, in fact, come from the private sector. There has been a difference in improving the quality of education, health services and in imparting skill for livelihood. In many cases, the corporate have worked with the government agencies for filling the gaps on a *last mile connectivity* basis. There is an instance of scaling up by mobilizing corporate support for sanitation for providing separate toilets for boys and girls in each government school. Supply of hot cooked meal in the centralized kitchen through *Akshaya Patra Foundation* offers another example of scaling up the CSR intervention dealing with nutrition and education. A beginning has been made in mobilizing corporate volunteerism, under which the interested corporate managers are being motivated to spend their time in the community. This is an aspect, which will make a major difference for the society, particularly in the life of the disadvantaged segments in giving them confidence and achieving their hopes and aspirations. Such interventions have helped in making development participative and inclusive.

The 21st century has brought new hopes for India, the largest democracy in the world, with the biggest youth population. Channelizing this demographic dividend—energy of the youth—for constructive purpose with positive mindset, confidence, quality education and skill would decide the future of India as a major global player. As a result of expansion of the mobile based digital applications and social media, the expectations of the youth have been expanding at a geometrical progression. Simultaneously, various plans and programmes and policies implemented by the governments has been creating opportunity, however it is at a lesser rate in the arithmetical progression. As a result, the gap between the expectation of the youth and available opportunity has been increasing at a fast rate. The unfulfilled expectation is causing frustration, which in turn is leading to anger and anger leading to violence from time to time. This phenomenon is common to all parts of the world and has been surfacing more frequently in the developing and underdeveloped economies. Instances like the recent Maratha mobilization in Maharashtra indicate that youth are looking for opportunity and getting frustrated, which is leading to anger and violence. The educated youth want employment, not just work but quality work as per their ability with better remuneration and proper working condition. A number of new initiatives like "*Skill India*", "*Digital India*" and "*Make in India*" have been launched for mobilization of the human resource and taking up production. New entrepreneurship from within the disadvantaged segments is being promoted under the "*Startup India*" and "*Standup India*". The corporate, as one of the major stakeholders of the society, needs to extend their support for taking these initiatives forward, which would be beneficial to them as well in increasing production, profit and at the same time taking the society alongwith by making the development process inclusive and sustainable. The future of CSR in India is going to be decided based on these developments.

Limitations of the existing model for development and need for a paradigm shift have been referred to by Economist, Shri Montek Singh Ahluwalia[4], Deputy Chairman of the erstwhile Planning Commission "Globally the *elite is being increasingly discredited*... are increasingly getting the feeling that *elitism doesn't do enough for those who don't have the same advantages*. It is important to keep in mind that *a successful society doesn't really become a whole society, unless everybody feels that there is something in it for them.*" Expressing optimism on the future of India, Shri Ahluwalia had indicated that "the youth will have a better future. Due to slow growth rate of population, complemented by the increased rate of GDP growth in the past decade, the *per capita income is expected to grow five times faster than it used to grow in post-Independence days*. As a result, the younger will see in nine years, what the older generation saw as a structural change in 45 years. *Such developments will have a tremendous impact in lives of the younger generation*".

From the study, it appears that CSR in India started with charity based approach and evolved to philanthropic stage. CSR being made mandatory has provided an opportunity for getting it institutionalized as *Systematic CSR,* representing its latest version for dealing with issues of national importance with scale and quality. Interestingly, this coincides with the launching of the SDG 2030 for achieving the goals over the next 15 years (2016-2030). Aligning CSR interventions in meeting the financial and managerial resources would facilitate achievement of the SDG 2030 to a considerable extent.

It is necessary to identify and tackle the root causes on a principle based and purpose driven approach. With technology playing an increasing important role for reducing the man to man distance across the globe, the competition in business is going to get tougher, making it more challenging for the corporate to face the competition in the market. In order to compete and survive, the corporate would be required to innovate for satisfying the consumer which would extend beyond complying with the law. Empowered by the Information Technology led media, the consumer will have access to all relevant information on a real time basis, who would be in a better position to choose between the products and the producers' companies and taking an informed decision. In this scenario, companies having better track record in CSR will have an edge over their competitors. This will in turn necessitate getting CSR institutionalized with quality and long-lasting services to the society instead of a mere Public Relation exercise. Accordingly, CSR in the 21st century would involve looking into the following:

Firstly, *innovation and creativity will be the major plank of CSR* in the coming days. Innovations like mobile phone doing financial transactions and mobile apps providing multiple solutions to the customers offer one such instance of creativity, which will become increasingly important.

The second aspect will relate to *networking among like minded corporate for scaling up the operation* for addressing issues concerning the common citizen and of national importance. *Akshaya Patra Foundation's* intervention in serving hot-cooked, nutritious food to school students under CSR intervention of IT companies, which has addressed the problem of hunger and malnutrition in a meaningful manner, provides one such example. Its success is based on synergy in CSR intervention of Corporate, an NGO with commitment and expertise, government support under ongoing schemes, along with use of appropriate technology; which has made a dent on solving the problems of hunger and malnutrition. It has been observed that India represents a graveyard of micro level success stories by NGOs, which have failed to scale up and died of its own. Such cases are likely to be redesigned and scaled up under CSR in the coming years.

The third aspect will relate to the *corporate mobilizing their core competence and unused infrastructure for social purposes*, which will widen the ambit of CSR from being considered as a mere source of fund. The Tata Group of Hotels' support for skilling the unemployed youth in the hospitality trades by using the facilities available in the hotels offers one such example, which has given a new meaning to provision of market needed quality skill to the youth, leading to inclusive development.

Further, *Environment conservation related issues would become increasingly important in the coming years*. This is evident from the recent judgement of Uttarakhand High Court, giving legal status to the River Ganga and River Yamuna, by drawing parallel with the recent legislation by the New Zealand Parliament, declaring the Whanghui River as a living entity with full legal rights. Social media based rapid dissemination of information will bring in higher accountability on the corporate on environment related issues for adoption of global best practices. The environment laws relating to green house gas reduction, disposal of waste are likely to become more stringent. Complying with these will become a major challenge for the corporate and an integral part of CSR. In this context, following life cycle approach will gain importance as it will optimize the use of scarce resources. Initiatives for plantation as well as evolving zero waste, carbon neutral and water neutral production system taken by some companies like ITC will get standardized and taken as an integral part of CSR in the coming years.

Use of digital media, particularly social media, as a cost-effective fast means of communication with the mass consumers, particularly the youth will acquire new dimension. This important tool is required to be exploited effectively for changing the attitude and mindset on various social issues and facilitating sustainable development. IT based social media online on virtual basis in no time and zero expense will emerge as the spokesperson for promoting CSR.

Capacity building for provision of required managerial skill, positive mindset, teamwork and use of appropriate technology will gain importance in implementation of CSR projects. Further, CSR will get integrated into all core activities namely production, marketing, finance and human resource rather than dealing it in an isolated manner by a separate cadre.

CSR will become integral to Sustainable Development cutting across sectors and covering social, environmental and financial aspects. In view of its several advantages, India will provide interesting examples of CSR practices to other developing and developed countries for making the development process sustainable. For the purpose, the major stakeholders, i.e. the corporate, the civil society and the government working in synergy with a positive mindset and use of appropriate technology is essential which will bring out the best for the corporate, the country and the society at large.

It is becoming increasingly clear all-over the world that achieving and sustaining growth by the corporate will be possible if and only if there is peace in the society. There are several cases to prove that by adopting innovative measures, it is possible for a corporate to make profit and at the same time do good to the society. Socially sensitive corporate have looked beyond compliance with law and making profit; by mobilizing men, machinery and managerial ability for helping the society. These have established the strength of the CSR interventions of corporate, taken up in a planned way with innovation, commitment and interest making a difference. These cases support the fact that the apparent contradictions between the economic and social interests of a corporate can be bridged by appreciating the finer linkages between the business, the government and the society; which would usher in a new era of sustainable development in the real sense.

The twentieth century brought India to global limelight for the uniqueness in achieving political freedom by mobilization of the masses based on the principles of truth and non-violence under the leadership of Mahatma Gandhi. The twenty-first century has brought a similar opportunity for economic freedom from poverty and unemployment, and ensuring welfare for all. This would require empowerment of the masses, by bringing about synergy of action involving the corporate, the government, the civil society and the media, which will make India free from poverty, hunger, malnutrition and unemployment; leading to the establishment of a society of equals in social, economic and political spheres, as envisaged in the Constitution. In this struggle for growth with distributive justice, CSR will play an important role.

References

1. A.P.J. Abdul Kalam, *The Hindu*, 9th November, 2006.
2. *Ibid.*
3. J. Irani, interview *The Economic Times*, Kolkata, 9th August, 2005.
4. Montek Singh Ahluwalia, while addressing the Graduation Day of Bishop Cotton Boys' School, Bengaluru on the 21st January, 2017, "Elite being discredited globally", *Deccan Herald*, 22 January, 2017, p. 3A.

Statutory Provisions on CSR

Appendix 1.1

Provisions of the Section 135 of the Company Act, 2013 (Act No. 18 of 2013)

"Section 135. Corporate Social Responsibility

(1) Every company having net worth of rupees five hundred crore or more, or turnover of rupees one thousand crore or more or a net profit of rupees five crore or more during any financial year shall constitute a Corporate Social Responsibility Committee of the Board consisting of three or more directors, out of which at least one director shall be an independent director.

(2) The Board's report under sub-section (3) of section 134 shall disclose the composition of the Corporate Social Responsibility Committee.

(3) The Corporate Social Responsibility Committee shall,—

   (a) formulate and recommend to the Board, a Corporate Social Responsibility Policy which shall indicate the activities to be undertaken by the company as specified in Schedule VII;

   (b) recommend the amount of expenditure to be incurred on the activities referred to in clause (a); and

   (c) monitor the Corporate Social Responsibility Policy of the company from time to time.

(4) The Board of every company referred to in sub-section (1) shall,—

   (a) after taking into account the recommendations made by the Corporate Social Responsibility Committee, approve the Corporate Social Responsibility Policy for the company and disclose contents of such Policy in its report and also place it on the company's website, if any, in such manner as may be prescribed; and

   (b) ensure that the activities as are included in Corporate Social Responsibility Policy of the company are undertaken by the company.

(5) The Board of every company referred to in sub-section (1), shall ensure that the company spends, in every financial year, at least

two per cent of the average net profits of the company made during the three immediately preceding financial years, in pursuance of its Corporate Social Responsibility Policy:

Provided that the company shall give preference to the local area and areas around it where it operates, for spending the amount earmarked for Corporate Social Responsibility activities:

Provided further that if the company fails to spend such amount, the Board shall, in its report made under clause (*o*) of sub-section (*3*) of section 134, specify the reasons for not spending the amount."

Above provisions of Section 135 of Companies Act, 2013 on Corporate Social Responsibility (CSR) *was partially amended* vide THE COMPANIES (AMENDMENT) ACT, 2017 (NO. 1 OF 2018) notified dated 3rd January, 2018 as indicated below:

In section 135 of the principle Act,—

(i) in sub-section (1),—

(a) for the words "any financial year", the words "the immediately preceding financial year" shall be substituted;

(b) the following proviso shall be inserted, namely:—

"Provided that where a company is not required to appoint an independent director under sub-section (4) of section 149, it shall have in its Corporate Social Responsibility Committee two or more directors";

(ii) in sub-section (3), in clause (a), for the words and figures "as specified in Schedule VII", the words and figures "in areas or subject, specified in Schedule VII" shall be substituted;

(iii) in sub-section (5), for the *Explanation,* the following *Explanation* shall be substituted, namely:

Explanation.—For the purposes of this section "net profit" shall not include such sums as may be prescribed, and shall be calculated in accordance with the provisions of section 198.

Appendix 1.2

List of Activities to be taken up under CSR

SCHEDULE VII OF THE COMPANIES ACT, 2013

[With reference to the provision clause (a) of sub-section (3) under section 135 of The Companies Act, 2013. Notified *vide* no. G.S.R., 130(E) dated the 27th February, 2014]

"In exercise of the powers conferred by sub-section (1) of section 467 of the Companies Act, 2013 (Act no. 18 of 2013), the Central Government hereby makes the following amendments to Schedule VII of the said Act, namely:—

(1) In Schedule VII, for items (i) to (x) and the entries relating thereto, the following items and entries shall be substituted, namely:—

(i) Eradicating hunger, poverty and malnutrition; ***promoting health care including preventive health care*** and sanitation ***including contribution to the 'Swachh Bharat Kosh' set-up by the Central Government for the promotion of sanitation*** and making available safe drinking water;

(ii) Promoting education, including special education and employment enhancing vocational skills especially among children, women, elderly, and the differently abled and livelihood enhancement projects;

(iii) promoting gender equality and empowering women, setting up homes and hostels for women and orphans; setting up old age homes, day care centres and such other facilities for senior citizens and measures for reducing inequalities faced by socially and economically backward groups;

(iv) ensuring environmental sustainability, ecological balance, protection of flora and fauna, animal welfare, agro-forestry, conservation of natural resources and maintaining quality of soil, air and water ***including contribution to the 'Clean Ganga Fund' set-up by the Central Government for rejuvenation of river Ganga;***

(v) Protection of national heritage, art and culture including restoration of building and sites of historical importance and works of art; setting up public libraries; promotion and development of traditional arts and handicrafts;

(vi) measures for the benefit of armed forces veterans, war widows and their dependents;

(vii) training to promote rural sports, nationally recognized sports, Paralympic sports and Olympic sports;

(viii) contribution to the Prime Minister's National Relief Fund or any other fund set up by the Central Government for socio-economic development and relief and welfare of the Scheduled Castes, the Scheduled Tribes, other backward classes, minorities and women;

(ix) Contributions or funds provided to technology incubators located within academic institutions which are approved by the Central Government;

(x) Rural development projects.

(xi) Slum area development.

Explanation—For the purpose of this item, the term 'slum area' shall mean any area declared as such by the Central Government or any State Government or any other competent authority under any law for the time being in force.

Notes:

- First amendment notified on *31st March, 2014* which included **health care including preventive health care** in item (i) of the Schedule.
- Second amendment notified on *6th August, 2014*, which inserted "**slum area development**" as item (xi) in the Schedule.
- Third amendment notified on *24th October, 2014*, which included (a) "**contribution to Swachh Bharat Kosh** set up by the Central Government for the promotion of sanitation" under "sanitation" in item no. (i) of the Schedule; and (b) "**contribution to Clean Ganga Fund** set up by the Central Government for the rejuvenation of river Ganga" in item (iv) of the Schedule.

Appendix 1.3

The Companies (Corporate Social Responsibility) Policy Rules 2014

[Notified vide no. G.S.R. 129(E), dated the 27th February, 2014]

In exercise of the powers conferred under section 135 and sub-sections (1) and (2) of section 469 of the Companies Act, 2013 (18 of 2013), the Central Government hereby makes the **following rules**, namely:—

1. **Short Title and Commencement.**

    (1) These rules may be called the Companies (Corporate Social Responsibility Policy Rules, 2014.

    (2) They shall come into force on the 1st day of April, 2014.

2. **Definitions.**

    (l) In these rules, unless the context otherwise requires:—

    (a) "Act" means the Companies Act, 2013;

    (b) "Annexure" means the Annexure appended to these rules;

    (c) "Corporate Social Responsibility (CSR)" means and includes but is not limited to:

    (i) Projects or programmes relating to activities specified in Schedule VII to the Act; or

    (ii) Projects or programmes relating to activities undertaken by the board of directors of a company (Board) in pursuance of recommendations of the CSR Committee of the Board as per declared CSR policy of the company subject to the condition that such policy will cover subjects enumerated in Schedule VII of the Act.

    (d) "CSR Committee" means the Corporate Social Responsibility Committee of the Board referred to in section 135 of the Act;

    (e) "CSR Policy" relates to the activities to be undertaken by the company as specified in Schedule VII to the Act and the expenditure thereon, excluding activities undertaken in pursuance of normal course of business of a company;

(f) "Net profit" means the net profit of a company as per its financial statement prepared in accordance with the applicable provisions of the Act, but shall not include the following, namely:
   (i) any profit arising from any overseas branch or branches of the company, whether operated as a separate company or otherwise; and
   (ii) any dividend received from other companies in India, which are covered under and complying with the provisions of section 135 of the Act:

Provided that net profit in respect of a financial year for which the relevant financial statements were prepared in accordance with the provisions of the Companies Act, 1956 (1 of 1956) shall not be required to be re-calculated in accordance with the provisions of the Act:

Provided further that in case of a foreign company covered under these rules, net profit means the net profit of such company as per profit and loss account prepared in terms of clause (a) of sub-section (I) of Section 381 read with Section 198 of the Act.

(2) Words and expressions used and not defined in these rules but defined in the Act shall have the same meanings respectively assigned to them in the Act.

3. **Corporate Social Responsibility.**

(1) Every company including its holding or subsidiary, and a foreign company defined under clause (42) of section 27 of the Act having its branch office or project office in India which fulfils the criteria specified in sub-section (l) of section 135 of the Act shall comply with the provisions of section 135 of the Act and these rules:
Provided that net worth, turnover or net profit of a foreign company of the Act shall be computed in accordance with balance sheet and profit and loss account of such company prepared in accordance with the provisions of clause (a) of sub-section (1) of section 381 and section 198 of the Act.

(2) Every company which ceases to be a company covered under sub-section (1) of section 135 of the Act for three consecutive financial years shall not be required to—

(a) constitute a CSR Committee; and
(b) comply with the provisions contained in sub-section (2) to (5) of the said section till such time it meets the criteria specified in sub-section (1) of section 135.

4. **CSR Activities.**

(1) The CSR activities shall be undertaken by the company, as per its stated CSR Policy, as projects or programmes or activities (either new or ongoing), excluding activities undertaken in pursuance of its normal course of business.
(2) The Board of a company may decide to undertake its CSR activities approved by the CSR committee, through a registered post or a registered society or a company established by the company or its holding or subsidiary or associate company under section 8 of the Act or otherwise:

Provided that—
(i) if such trust, society or company is not established by the company or its holding or subsidiary or associate company, it shall have an established track record of three years in undertaking similar programmes or projects;
(ii) the company has specified the project or programmes to be undertaken through these entities, the modalities of utilization of funds on such projects and programmes and the monitoring and reporting mechanism.

(3) A company may also collaborate with other companies for undertaking projects or programmes or CSR activities in such a manner that the CSR committees of respective companies are in a position to report separately on such projects or programmes in accordance with these rules.
(4) Subject to provisions of sub-section (5) of section 135 of the Act the CSR projects or programmes or activities undertaken in India only shall amount to CSR Expenditure.
(5) The CSR projects or programmes or activities that benefit only the employees of the company and their families shall not be considered as CSR activities in accordance with section 135 of the Act.
(6) Companies may build CSR capacities of their own personnel as well as those of their Implementing agencies through Institutions with established track records of at least three financial years

but such expenditure shall not exceed five per cent of total CSR expenditure of the company in one financial year.

Permissible Limit on Overheads

- Taking into consideration general circular no. 21/2014 dated 18th June 2014, notification of Ministry of Corporate Affairs (MCA) dated 12th September, 2014 and general circular no. 36/2014 dated 17th September, 2014, the position is as follows:
- 5 per cent permissible limit[1] on CSR spend will include the following:
  - ➢ All costs associated with capacity building of a company's personnel;
  - ➢ All costs associated with capacity building of Implementing Agencies;
  - ➢ Salaries paid by companies to regular CSR staff as well as volunteers. For volunteers, calculation would need to be made on the basis of company time/hours spent specifically on a CSR Project/Programme;
  - ➢ Other administrative overheads incurred by the company in handling CSR Projects/Programmes.

(7) Contribution of any amount directly or indirectly to any political party under section 182 of the Act, shall not be considered as CSR activity.

5. **CSR Committees.**

(1) The companies mentioned in the rule 3 shall constitute CSR Committee as under.—

(i) an unlisted public company or a private company covered under sub-section (1) of section 135 which is not required to appoint an independent director pursuant to sub-section (4) of section 149 of the Act, shall have its CSR Committee without such director;

(ii) a private company having only two directors on its Board shall constitute its CSR Committee with two such directors;

(iii) with respect to a foreign company covered under these rules, the CSR Committee shall comprise of at least two persons of which one person shall be as specified under clause (d) of sub-section (1) of section 380 of the Act and another person shall be nominated by the foreign company.

(2) The CSR Committee shall institute a transparent monitoring

mechanism for implementation of the CSR projects or programmes or activities undertaken by the company.

6. **CSR Policy**.

(1) The CSR Policy of the company shall, *inter alia*, include the following, namely—

(a) a list of CSR projects or programmes which a company plans to undertake falling within the purview of the Schedule VII of the Act, specifying modalities of execution of such project or programmes and implementation schedules for the same; and

(b) monitoring process of such projects or Programmes:

Provided that the CSR activities do not include the activities undertaken in pursuance of normal course of business of a company:

Provided further that the Board of Directors shall ensure that activities included by a company in its Corporate Social Responsibility Policy are related to the activities included in Schedule VII of the Act.

(2) The CSR Policy of the company shall specify that the surplus arising out of the CSR projects or programmes or activities shall not form part of the business profit of a company.

7. **CSR Expenditure.**

CSR expenditure shall include all expenditure including contribution to corpus, the projects or programmes relating to CSR activities approved by the Board on the recommendation of its CSR Committee, but does not include any expenditure on an item not in conformity or not in line with activities which fall within the purview of Schedule VII of the Act.

8. **CSR Reporting.**

(1) The Board's Report of a company covered under these rules pertaining to a financial year commencing on or after the 1st day of April, 2014 shall include an annual report on CSR containing particulars specified in Annexure.

(2) In case of a foreign company, the balance sheet filed under

sub-clause (b) of sub-section (l) of section 38 shall contain an Annexure regarding report on CSR.

9. **Display of CSR Activities on its Website.**

The Board of Directors of the company shall, after taking into account the recommendations of CSR Committee, approve the CSR Policy for the company and disclose contents of such policy in its report and the same shall be displayed on the company's website, if any, as per the particulars specified in the Annexure.

Appendix 1.4

Clarifications on Provisions of Corporate Social Responsibility Under Section 135 of the Companies Act, 2013

"This Ministry has received several references and representation from stakeholders seeking clarifications on the provisions under Section 135 of the Companies Act, 2013 (hereinafter referred as 'the Act') and the Companies (Corporate Social Responsibility Policy) Rules, 2014, as well as activities to be undertaken as per Schedule VII of the Companies Act, 2013. Clarifications with respect to representations received in the Ministry on Corporate Social Responsibility (hereinafter referred as ('CSR') are as under:—

(i) The statutory provision and provisions of CSR Rules, 2014, is to ensure that while activities undertaken in pursuance of the CSR policy must be relatable to Schedule VII of the Companies Act, 2013, the entries in the said Schedule VII must be interpreted liberally so as to capture the essence of the subjects enumerated in the said Schedule. The items enlisted in the amended Schedule VII of the Act, are broad-based and are intended to cover a wide range of activities as illustratively mentioned in the Annexure.

(ii) It is further clarified that CSR activities should be undertaken by the companies in project/programme mode [as referred in Rule 4 (1) of Companies CSR Rules, 2014]. One-off events such as marathons/awards/charitable contribution/advertisement/ sponsorships of TV programmes etc. would not be qualified as part of CSR expenditure.

(iii) Expenses incurred by companies for the fulfilment of any Act/ Statute of regulations (such as Labour Laws, Land Acquisition Act etc.) would not count as CSR expenditure under the Companies Act.

(iv) Salaries paid by the companies to regular CSR staff as well as to volunteers of the companies (in proportion to company's time/ hours spent specifically on CSR) can be factored into CSR project cost as part of the CSR expenditure.

(v) "Any financial year" referred under Sub-Section (1) of Section

135 of the Act read with Rule 3(2) of Companies CSR Rule, 2014, implies 'any of the three preceding financial years'.

(vi) Expenditure incurred by Foreign Holding Company for CSR activities in India will qualify as CSR spend of the Indian subsidiary if, the CSR expenditures are routed through Indian subsidiaries and if the Indian subsidiary is required to do so as per section 135 of the Act.

(vii) 'Registered Trust' [as referred in Rule 4(2) of the Companies CSR Rules, 2014] would include Trusts registered under Income Tax Act, 1956, for those States where registration of Trust is not mandatory.

(viii) Contribution to Corpus of a Trust/society/section 8 companies etc. will qualify as CSR expenditure as long as (a) the Trust/society/section 8 companies etc. is created exclusively for undertaking CSR activities or (b) where the corpus is created exclusively for a purpose directly relatable to a subject covered in Schedule VII of the Act.

2. This issues with the approval of Competent Authority."

References

Ministry of Corporate Affairs General Circular No. 21/2014 *vide* letter No. 05/01/2014-CSR dated: 18th June, 2014.

A High Level Committee (HLC) was constituted to suggest measures for improved monitoring of the implementation of corporate social responsibility policies by the companies under Companies Act, 2013, *vide* OM dated 03.02.2015. HLC has submitted its report and one of the recommendations related to increasing the administrative overhead costs from present 5 per cent to not more than 10 per cent of the CSR expenditure. This should not include expenditure incurred on capacity development of implementation agencies. The Companies Act and/or CSR Rules are required to be amended to implement the recommendations.

GUIDELINES FOR CENTRAL PUBLIC SECTOR ENTERPRISES (CPSEs) ON CSR AND SUSTAINABILITY (WITH EFFECT FROM 01.04.2014)

"The guidelines are aimed at providing an over arching framework of sustainability within which CSR is firmly embedded. Therefore, CPSEs are advised to read the CSR Rules together with Guidelines to clearly understand what is expected of them by the stakeholders:

(i) It is mandatory for all profit making CPSEs to undertake CSR activities as per the provisions of the Act and the CSR Rules.

(ii) All CPSEs must adopt a CSR and Sustainability Policy specific to their company with the approval of the Board of Directors.

(iii) Board's approval of new/additional CSR activities/projects CSR activities would be treated as amendment to the policy.

(iv) It would be mandatory for all CPSEs which meet the criteria as laid down in Section 135(1) of the Act, to spend at least 2 per cent of the average net profits of the three immediately preceding financial years in pursuance of their CSR activities as stipulated in the Act and the CSR Rules.

(v) While selecting CSR activities/projects from the activities listed in Schedule VII of the Act, CPSEs should give priority to the issues which are of foremost concern in the national development agenda.

(vi) For CPSEs to fully exploit their core competence and mobiles their resource capabilities in the implementation of CSR activities/projects, align their CSR and Sustainable policy with their business policies and strategies to the extent possible.

(vii) All CPSEs are expected to act in a socially, economically and environmentally sustainable manner at all times.

(viii) As a part of their sustainability initiatives CPSEs are expected to give importance to environmental sustainability even in their normal mainstream activities.

(ix) Sustainability initiatives would also include steps taken by CPSEs to promote welfare of employees.

(x) The philosophy and spirit of CSR and Sustainability should be understood and imbibed by the employees at all levels and get embedded in the core values of the company.

(xi) CPSEs should extend their reach and oversight to the entire supply chain network.

(xii) As mentioned in the Act, CPSEs should give preference to the 'local area' in selecting the location of their CSR activities.

(xiii) CPSEs, which by the very nature of their business have no specific geographical area of commercial operations, may take up CSR activities/projects at any location of their choice within the country.

(xiv) As far as possible, CPSEs should take up the CSR activities in project.

(xv) CPSEs should devise a communication strategy for regular dialogue and consultation with key stakeholders.

(xvi) As per the CSR Rules, all companies are required to include an annual report on CSR in their Board's Report.

(xvii) It is desirable that CPSEs get baseline/need assessment survey done prior to the selection of any CSR activity.

(xviii) CPSEs are encouraged to take up CSR activities/projects in collaboration with other CPSEs."

Reference

"Transforming Lives through CSR", Confederation of Indian Industry, Central Public Sector Enterprises, 15th September, 2015.

Clarification/Frequently Asked Questions (FAQs) on the Corporate Social Responsibility (CSR) provisions laid down under section 135 of The Companies Act, 2013

Sl. No. *Frequently Asked Questions (FAQs)*

1. **Whether CSR provisions of the Companies Act, 2013 is applicable to all companies?**
   CSR provisions of the Companies Act, 2013 is *applicable to every company registered under the Companies Act, 2013* and any other previous companies law *having*
   - **net worth** of rupees five hundred core or more, *or*
   - **turnover** of rupees one thousand crore or more, *or*
   - **a net profit** of rupees five crore or more *during any financial year.*
2. **What is meaning of "any financial year" mentioned above?**
   "Any financial year" referred under Sub-Section (1) of Section 135 of the Act read with Rules 3(2) of Companies CSR Rule, 2014 **implies any of the three preceding financial years** (refer General Circular No. 21/2014, dated 18.06.2014).
3. **Whether CSR expenditure of a company can be claimed as business expenditure?**
   The amount spent by a company towards CSR cannot be claimed as business expenditure. The Finance Act, 2014 provides that any *expenditure incurred* by an assessee *on the activities relating to Corporate Social Responsibility* referred to in section 136 of the Companies Act, 2013 **shall not** be deemed to be *an expenditure incurred by the assessee for the purposes of the business or profession.*
4. **Whether the "average net profit" criterion for section 135(5) is Net profit before tax or Net profit after tax?**
   Computation of **net profit** for section 135 is as per section 198 of the Companies Act, 2013 which is **primarily PROFIT BEFORE TAX (PBT).**
5. **Can the CSR expenditure be spent on the activities beyond Schedule VII?**

General Circular No. 21/2014 dated June 18, 2014 of MCA has clarified that the statutory provision and provisions of CSR Rules, 2014 is to ensure that **activities undertaken in pursuance of the CSR policy must be relatable to Schedule VII** of the Companies Act, 2013. The entries in the said Schedule VII **must be interpreted liberally so as to capture the essence of the subjects** enumerated in the said Schedule. The items enlisted in the Schedule VII of the Act, are **broad-based and are intended to cover a wide range of activities**. The General Circular also provides an illustrative list of activities that can be covered under CSR. In a similar way, many more can be covered. **It is for the Board of the company to take a call on this.**

6. **What tax benefits can be availed under CSR?**
   No specific tax exemptions have been extended to CSR expenditure *per se*. The Finance Act, 2014 also clarifies that expenditure of CSR does not form part of business expenditure. While no specific tax exemption has been extended to expenditure incurred on CSR, **spending on several activities like contributions to Prime Minister's Relief Fund**, scientific research, rural development projects, skill development projects, agricultural extension projects, etc., which find place in Schedule VII, *already enjoy exemptions under different sections of the Income Tax Act, 1961.*
7. **Which *activities would not qualify* as CSR?**
   - The CSR projects or programmes or activities *that benefit only the employees of the company and their families.*
   - *One-off events such as marathons*/awards/charitable contribution/advertisement/sponsorships of TV programmes, etc.
   - *Expenses incurred by companies for the fulfilment of any other Act/Statute of regulations* (such as Labour Laws, Land Acquisition Act, 2013, Apprentice Act, 1961 etc.)
   - *Contribution of any amount directly or indirectly to any political party.*
   - *Activities undertaken by the company in pursuance of its normal course of business.*
   - The project or programmes or *activities undertaken outside India.*
8. **Whether a holding or subsidiary of a company which fulfils the criteria under section 135(1) has to comply with section 135, even if the holding and subsidiary itself does not fulfil the criteria?**
   Holding or subsidiary of a company does not have to comply with

section 135(1) unless the holding or subsidiary itself fulfils the criteria.

9. **Whether provisions of CSR are applicable on Section 8 Company, if it fulfils the criteria of section 135(1) of the Act?**
   Section 135 of the Act reads "Every company", i.e. *no specific exemption is given* to section 8 companies with regard to applicability of section 135, hence section 8 companies are required to follow CSR provisions.
10. **Can contribution of money to a Trust/Society/Section 8 Companies by a company be treated as CSR expenditure of the company?**
    General Circular No. 21/2014 of MCA dated June 18, 2014 clarifies that *Contribution of Corpus of a Trust/Society/Section 8 companies*, etc. will *qualify as CSR expenditure* as long as:
    (a) the trust/society/section 8 company, etc. is *created exclusively for undertaking CSR activities*, or
    (b) *where the corpus is created exclusively for a purpose directly relatable* to a subject covered in Schedule VII of the Act.
11. **Whether display of CSR policy of a company on website of the company is mandatory or not?**
    As per section 135(4) the Board of Directors of the company shall, after taking into account the recommendations of CSR Committee, approve the **CSR Policy for the company and disclose contents of such policy in its report and the same shall be displayed on the company's website**, if any (refer Rule 8 and 9 of CSR Policy, Rules 2014).
12. **Whether reporting of CSR is mandatory in Board's Report?**
    The Board's Report of a company qualifying under section 135(1) pertaining to a financial year commencing on or after the 1st day of April, 2014 **shall include an annual report on CSR containing particulars specified in Annexure**. (refer Rule 9 of CSR Policy, Rules 2014).
13. **Whether it is mandatory for Foreign Company to give report on CSR activity?**
    In case of a foreign company, the **balance sheet filed under sub-clause (b) of sub-section (1) of section 381 shall contain an Annexure** regarding report on CSR.
14. **Whether contribution towards disaster relief qualifies as CSR or not?**
    (May please refer point no. 7 to the annexure to General Circular

dated 18.06.2014 issued by Ministry of Corporate Affairs).

15. **Whether contribution in kind can be monetized to be shown as CSR expenditure?**
Section 135 prescribes "*shall ensure that company spends*". The company **has to spend the amount**.

16. **If a company spends in excess of 2 per cent of its average net profit of three preceding years on CSR in a particular year, can the excess amount spent be carried forward to the next year and be offset against the required 2 per cent CSR expenditure of the next year?**
Any excess amount spent (i.e. more than 2 per cent as specified in Section 135) **cannot be carried forward to the subsequent years** and adjusted against that year's CSR expenditure.

17. **Can the unspent amount from out of the minimum required CSR expenditure be carried forward to the next year?**
The Board is free to decide whether any unspent amount from out of the minimum required CSR expenditure is to be carried forward to the next year. However, the **carried forward amount *should be over and above* the next year's CSR allocation equivalent to at least 2 per cent** of the average net profit of the company of the immediately preceding three years.

18. **What is the role of Government in monitoring implementation of CSR by companies under the provision of the Companies Act, 2013?**
The main thrust and spirit of the law is not to monitor but to generate conducive environment for **enabling the corporate to conduct themselves in a socially responsible manner**, while contributing towards human development goals of the country.
The existing legal provisions like mandatory disclosures, *accountability of the CSR Committee and the Board, provisions for audit of the accounts of the company, etc.* ***provide sufficient safeguards*** in this regard. Government has no role to play in monitoring implementation of CSR by companies.

19. **Whether government is proposing to establish any mechanism for third parties to monitor the quality and efficacy of CSR expenditure as well as to have an impact assessment of CSR by companies?**
Government has no role to play in engaging external experts for monitoring the quality and efficacy of CSR expenditure of companies. **Boards/CSR Committee are fully competent** to engage third parties

to have an impact assessment of its CSR programme to validate compliance of the CSR provisions of the law.

20. **Can CSR funds be utilized to fund Government Schemes?**
The objective of this provision is indeed to involve the corporate in discharging their social responsibility with their innovative ideas and management skills and with greater efficiency and better outcomes.
Therefore, *CSR should not be interpreted as a source of financing the resource gaps in Government Scheme. Use of corporate innovations and management skills in the delivery of "public goods" is at the core of CSR implementation by the companies.* In-principle, CSR fund of companies should not be used as a source of funding Government Schemes. CSR projects should have a larger multiplier effect than that under the Government schemes.

21. **Who is the appropriate authority for approving and implementation of the CSR programmes/projects or a company?**
What is Government's role in this regard? Government has no role to play in this regard. Section 135 of the Act, Schedule VII and Companies CSR Policy Rules, 2014 read with General Circular dated 18.06.2014 issued by the Ministry of Corporate Affairs, provide the broad contour within which eligible companies are required to formulate their CSR policies including activities to be undertaken and implement the same in the right earnest. Therefore, **all CSR programmes/projects should be approved by the Boards on the recommendations of their CSR Committees**. Changes, if any, in the programme/project should also be undertaken only with the *approval of the Committee/Board.*

22. **How can companies with small CSR funds take up CSR activities in a project/programme mode?**
A well designed CSR project or programme can be managed with even small fund. Further, there is a provision in the CSR Policy Rules, 2014 that **such companies can combine their CSR programmes with other similar companies by way of pooling their CSR resources**. [refer rule 4 in Companies (CSR Policy) Rules, 2014].

23. **Whether involvement of employees of the company in CSR project/programmes of a company can be monetized and accounted for under the head of "CSR expenditure?"**
***Contribution and involvement of employees* in CSR activities of the company will no doubt generate interest/pride in CSR work and promote transformation from Corporate Social**

Responsibility (CSR) as an obligation to Socially Responsible Corporate (SRC) in all aspects of their functioning, companies therefore ***should be encouraged*** to involve their employees in CSR activities. However, *monetization of pro bono services of employees would not be counted* towards CSR expenditure.

Reference

Circulated *vide* Ministry of Corporate Affairs' General Circular no. 01/2016 dated 12th January, 2016.

Case Studies

CSR Initiatives of Selected Corporates

STEEL AUTHORITY OF INDIA LIMITED (SAIL)

Steel Authority of India Limited (SAIL)[1] was set up as a holding company of Steel Plants and associated input units on the 24th January, 1973, by conversion of the erstwhile public sector Hindustan Steel Limited (HSL), which was formed in 1954. Subsequently, the company was restructured in 1978, under "The Public Sector Iron and Steel Companies (Restructuring) and Miscellaneous Provisions Act, 1978". The company has four integrated Steel Plants at Bhilai in Chattisgarh, Bokaro in Jharkhand, Rourkela in Orissa and Durgapur in West Bengal and three special Steel Plants, namely, Alloy Steel Plant at Durgapur, Special Steel Plant at Salem in Tamil Nadu and Visvesvaraya Iron and Steel Plant Limited (VISL) at Bhadrawati in Karnataka. It has two subsidiaries namely, Indian Iron and Steel Company (IISCO) at Burnpur in West Bengal and Maharashtra Elektrosmelt Limited (MEL) at Chandrapur in Maharashtra. In 1998, SAIL acquired the status of a "Maha Ratna" company, being the largest steel maker of India.

Box 7.1: Vision and Credo of SAIL

Vision

To be a respected world-class corporation and the leader in Indian steel business in quality, productivity, profitability and customer satisfaction.

Credo

- We build lasting relationships with customers based on trust and mutual benefits.
- We uphold highest ethical standards in conduct of our business.
- We create and nurture a culture that supports flexibility, learning and is proactive to change.
- We chart a challenging career for employees with opportunities for advancement and rewards.
- We value the opportunity and responsibility to make a meaningful difference in people's lives.

Commitment of the company to the welfare of the society is reflected in its credo.[2] [**Box 7.1: Vision and Credo of SAIL**] "We value the opportunity and responsibility to make a meaningful difference in people's lives" with an objective of the company to conduct business in ways that produce social, environmental and economic benefits to the communities in which it operates.

The company's business philosophy encompasses a Triple Bottom Line approach covering the economic, environmental and social dimensions reflecting SAIL's commitment to build natural, human and societal capital. History of CSR in the SAIL dated back to 1972, when Mr. R.P. Billimoria, Director Personnel, Hindustan Steel Limited (HSL) had suggested adoption of a few villages near the steel towns, as part of responsibility towards the local community on 15th August, 1972 at Ranchi. Development of *Chetwa* village, located at a distance of about 20 kilometres from the Bhilai Steel Plant, was taken up as a follow-up to this idea in 1978-79. Provision of drinking water, construction of school building and an approach road for the village was taken up by the Plant in this selected village for meeting the basic needs of the local villagers. Subsequently, such Peripheral Development Programme (PDP) was extended to all villages located within a radius of 8 kilometres and later on to 106 villages located within a radius of 16 kilometres from the Bhilai Steel city. In 1978-79, the Bhilai Steel Plant spent Rs. 9.1 lakhs on these activities. Rs. 24 lakhs was allocated for such activities during the period 1980-81 to 1982-83 for undertaking a range of activities like dairy, poultry farming, vegetable growing etc.

PDP of SAIL covered three broad areas, namely:

(i) Providing health and education facilities created for the employees to the general public on a limited scale,
(ii) Employment and income generating facility through promotion of ancillaries, and
(iii) Welfare activities of general nature.

For the PDP activities, which are sort of CSR activities before liberalization, a centralized budget was being approved by the SAIL Board, which was sub-allocated to individual Plants. Peripheral Development Coordination Committees were set up at the Plant level with local officials of the State Government Authorities, social organizations active in the area, local MLA, and the Plant officials. An annual work plan was prepared as per discussion with the villagers and the village panchayats, which was debated and sent to the Board for approval. Available fund was sub-allocated after the proposals were approved. The PDP activities were taken up through the *Mahila Samiti,* set up in each Plant as an NGO, as well as other NGOs and government agencies.

The objective behind these interventions was to bring the local rural people together with the newly created industrial atmosphere and create mutual trust and understanding through intermingling of the two cultures. The Parliamentary Committee on Public Undertakings (COPUs)[3] had studied the status of social activities of the central public sector undertakings including SAIL and made several recommendations.

SAIL considered its expenditure incurred on employees, community and general public as the net social income to the various sectors of the economy. From the figures for 1987-88 to 1991-92 **(Details are given in the Table 7.1)**, it appeared that expenditure on general public went up substantially as compared to expenditure on employees during the period.

Table 7.1: Expenditure on Employee and Social Activities of SAIL during 1987-88 to 1991-92

(Amount in Rs. Crore)

Item/Year	*1987-88*	*1988-89*	*1989-90*	*1990-91*	*1991-92*	*Increase* (in %)*
Employees	384.65	407.84	498.73	560.96	629.01	63.52
Community	1028.69	1415.19	1925.45	2202.20	2781.15	170.35
General Public	1236.22	1474.25	2185.98	2592.10	4446.40	259.67
Total	**2649.56**	**3297.28**	**4610.16**	**5355.26**	**7856.56**	**196.52**

* Increase in 1991-92 over that of 1987-88.
Source: 24th COPU Report, 1993-94.

In absence of any specific guidelines on activities, development of Ancillary unit construed part of its social responsibility. This also helped in providing employment in the peripheral areas. Training for capacity building along with other facilities was taken up for assisting the youth. An ancillary development officer was posted in each Plant, who took up identification of items and assisting the local youth in production and marketing. The officer interacted with the State Director of Industries, the SSI units as well as Plant shop floor managers for locating items, which can be off loaded on the SSI/Ancillary Units. From the number of ancillary units set up by the integrated Steel Plants of SAIL during 1986 to 1992 (**Details are given in Table 7.2**), it appeared that the Plants at Bhilai and Durgapur had followed it up more actively than the Plant at Bokaro and no specific information was available for other plants.

An impact assessment study of the Peripheral Development Programme (PDP) of pre-liberalization period on the living conditions

Table 7.2: Promotion of Ancillary by SAIL during 1986 to 1992

(Number of Units Promoted)

* Increase during 1992 over that of 1986.
Source: 24th COPU Report, 1993-94.

of the people residing in the periphery was done[4] by the Rourkela Steel Plant (RSP) in 1996, which indicated the following aspects:

- Although PDP budget has been increasing; there has not been a concomitant increase in the scope of work.
- PDP takes a proactive role in addressing the local problems rather than a long-term strategy for integrated development.
- Provision of drinking water and health facilities are the priority areas. Even though these facilities are being provided by both the government and the Plant, the quality of health service provided by the Plant is superior.
- PDP is focusing on the hardware i.e., construction rather than the software i.e., personnel.

Table 7.3: Impact of PDP Activities of SAIL

Item	*Covered under PDP*	*Not Covered*
Percentage belonging to ST	74.07	72.84
Sex-ratio (number of females per 1000 males)	884	910
Per capita income (in Rs. per month)	390.01	393.49
Agriculture income of total income (in percentage)	24.11	28.24

Source: Annual Report SAIL 2003-2004, p. 18 and reply to questionnaire.

Financial Analysis

Since SAIL was involved in CSR activities even before issue of CSR guidelines by Department of Public Enterprises, an attempt was made to analyze CSR spending of CSR in two separate time spans, one before issue of guidelines and another after issue of guidelines and the findings is as given in Tables 7.4 and 7.5 respectively.

Table 7.4: CSR Expenditure with Reference to Turnover/Profit in SAIL during 2001-02 to 2003-04

Item/Year	*Unit*	*2003-04*	*2002-03*	*2001-02*
Gross Revenue (GR)	Cr. Rs.	24,178	19,207	15,502
Profit After Tax (PAT)	Cr. Rs.	2,512	(–)304	(–)1,707
Earning per share	Rs.	6.08	(–)0.74	(–)4.13
Employees	No	23,849	24,674	26,052
CSR Expenditure	Cr. Rs.	1.77	0.89	

Source: Annual Report SAIL 2003-2004, p. 18 and reply to questionnaire.

It is seen that in the earlier years, expenditure on CSR is very minimal compared to Profit after Tax to the tune of only 0.07 per cent, which is much less than 2% as mandated by recent Companies Act.

Table 7.5: CSR Expenditure with Reference to Turnover/Profit in SAIL during 2007-08 to 2011-12

(*All Figures are in Rs. Crores*)

Sl. No.	*Subject*	*2007-08*	*2008-09*	*2009-10*	*2010-11*	*2011-12*
1.	Turnover	45555	48733	43935	47041	50348
2.	Profit after tax	7537	6175	6754	4905	3543
3.	Amount earmarked for CSR	95	114	80	94	64
4.	Amount earmarked as Percentage of PAT	1.26%	1.84%	1.18%	1.91%	1.80%
5.	Expenditure incurred on CSR	119.61	83.03	78.79	68.95	61.25
6.	Exp. as percentage of earmarked	126%	72.8%	98.5%	73.35%	95.7%

Source: Annual Report SAIL 2003-2004, p. 18 and reply to questionnaire.

From Table 7.5, it appears that after issue of guidelines, CSR spending increses substantially and varies in the range of 1.2 to 1.91 per cent of Profit after Tax of same year. In absolute terms, it is almost 50 times of what SAIL used to spend before issue of DPE guidelines.

Some of the major CSR initiatives of SAIL during this period were as follows:

- *Model Steel Villages:* SAIL identified 79 villages in eight states for development as Model Steel Villages. The development activities included Medical and Health Services, Education, Sanitation, Roads, Access to water facilities, Employment generation, use of steel for storage/construction/bullock carts etc.

- *Health Camps:* SAIL organised regular health camps in various villages on fixed days for the people living in the periphery of plants/units, mines and far flung area. The purpose of the Health-Camps was to create health awareness and sensitize people on health related issues by immunization, blood-donation, water purification tablets, distributing handbills etc. and providing them medicines in the medical/health camps.
- *Health Infrastructure:* SAIL established hospitals in all its plant to create better and healthy living conditions for both its employees as well as people living in the periphery. SAIL plants hospitals had provision of specialists in the area of Gynaecology, Cardiology, Pediatrics, Ultrasound, Orthopedics etc. SAIL has also established 53 Primary Health Centres, 7 Reproductive and Child Health Centres, 18 Hospitals and 7 Super-Speciality Hospitals to provide specialized healthcare to more than 31.00 million people.
- *Education:* SAIL had opened over 139 schools in the steel townships to provide modern education to about 63,000 children. Besides adopting and providing free education and facilities to tribal children, SAIL provided assistance to over 254 schools. In addition SAIL had taken the initiative to set up seven special schools for underprivileged children at all integrated steel plant locations (2 each at Bhilai and Bokaro) providing, free education, mid-day meals, transport, textbooks and stationery items, school bag and water bottles etc. Other benefits like scholarships to deserving SC/ST undergraduate engineering students were provided.
- *Water:* SAIL created about 6000 water infrastructure facilities like bore well, hand pump, overhead tanks, ponds, etc. which benefited about 4 million people across the country.
- *Road:* SAIL took up construction and repair of all-weather roads. With this endeavour more than 73 lakhs people across 435 villages were provided connectivity to nearby towns.
- *Sports:* Promotion of sports formed an integral part of the corporate philosophy of SAIL right from its inception. The company set up 6 sports academies, i.e. Athletics Academy for boys at Bhilai, Hockey Academy at Rourkela, Football academy at Bokaro, Athletics Academy for girls at Durgapur, Archery Academy at Kiriburu and Football Academy at Burnpur.
- *Preservation of Art, Culture:* SAIL supported for preserving

ancient form of art by promoting various disappearing art-forms. Chhattisgarh Lok Kala Mahotsava and Gramin Lokotsava are being organised every year by Bhilai Steel plant. Durgapur also organized Poush Mela every year to promote the art form and providing a platform to showcase local talent.

- *Skill Development:* SAIL took steps to identify various areas where training and help to the communities can be imparted so as to make them self-sustaining units that can generate income for them. People living in the peripheral area of SAIL's plants/ units are trained to acquire skills like weaving, handicrafts, animal husbandry, *chulha* making, fishery and poultry farming etc., which will help them to earn a decent living for themselves and for their family members.

CSR Policy and CSR Committee[5]

In compliance of the provisions of the Companies Act, 2013 and Rules framed thereunder, a **Board level CSR Committee** was constituted under the Chairmanship of an Independent Director with Director (Finance), Director (Technical) and Director (Personnel) as members.

A CSR Policy for the Company was formulated with the approval of the Board, with following features:

- Create value for the stakeholders and society that are fundamentally linked to SAIL's core business strategies and operations through its services, conduct and initiatives for their sustainable development.
- Enhance value creation for the community in which it operates by identifying with the hamlet and foster goodwill from those living along the periphery towards the Company by enhancing the quality of life of people in the direct impact zone.
- Support the community by assisting the underprivileged.
- Carry out developmental initiatives in order to meet the calls of the present without compromising the ability of future to meet its needs.
- Support local populace by building the image of SAIL as patron of diverse pastoral sports, art and cultures.
- To operate in a socially, environmentally and economically responsible manner, so as to succeed by seeking social license.

The company supported construction of new roads/pathways as well as repair of damaged roads/pathways in rural areas; thereby providing connectivity for facilitating reach of education and healthcare amenities to over 77.04 lakh people across 435 villages. It took steps for development of 79 villages as "Model Steel Villages" in eight states and popularized use of solar energy through installation of Solar street lights, Solar Lanterns and Smokeless *chulhas* in the poor households.

SAIL managed number of schools and hospitals in the area of its plants and units for providing education and health facilities to its workers and staff and their families. These services were extended to families living in the peripheral areas as well. From available documents it appeared that the company took following steps exclusively for welfare of the society:

- It set up 7 health centres (Kalyan Chikitsalaya) exclusively for BPL families and provided free OPD facilities and medicines.
- The Company created infrastructure for enhancing availability of safe drinking water for people living in rural areas, by installing over 7625 water sources that lead to improvement in availability of potable water resources in rural area facing drinking water deficit.
- The Rourkela steel plant took up the 'Comprehensive Water and Sanitation Facilities' project in five peripheral villages namely, Chutiatola, Dumerjore, Ushra Colony, Baniguni and Jagdishpur in 2013-14.
- It managed Seven Special Schools (Kalyan Vidyalaya) located near the plants exclusively for BPL families, which provided free education, mid-day meal, uniform including shoes, text-books, stationery items, school bags, water bottles, transportation etc. It provided Scholarships to deserving undergraduate and postgraduate, engineering students and adopted tribal children from area affected by insurgency and primitive tribal groups. It provided skill development training in Industrial and Nursing courses for uplifting the poorer segment of the society.
- "Saranda Suvan Chhatravasa", a fully residential complex was set up at Kiriburu Mines for providing education and residential facilities to students belonging to areas affected by Maoist insurgency.
- In association with Akshya Patra Foundation, it is providing Mid-Day Meal to students of Govt. schools in and around Bhilai and

Rourkela. Under this scheme, healthy and nutritious meal is being provided daily to more than 63,000 students in 570 Govt. schools.

- Vocational Training centre namely "Bhilai Ispat Kaushal Kutir", 'Swayamsiddha' at Bhilai, Skill Development and Self-Employment Training Institute (SDSETI) at Durgapur, Garment Technician Training at Salem, JHARCRAFT centre at Bokaro and Self-employment centre "KIRAN" at Kiriburu Ore Mines are providing training along with support for income generation to 3000 village youths and 7000 women living in the peripheral villages in 2014-15.[6]
- Steps for promoting the local art and culture, by supporting organization of Chhattisgarh Lok Kala Mahotsava and Gramin Lokotsava.
- It contributed Rs. 1 Crore and Rs. 20 Crore for rehabilitation of families affected by Flash Floods in Uttarakhand and by Phyline cyclone in Odisha respectively.

In recognition of various CSR initiatives taken for welfare of the society, SAIL was awarded "ICC PSE Excellence Awards 2013" under Corporate Social Responsibility and Sustainability in Maharatna and Navratna Award Category.

2014-15[7]

For the year 2014-15, average net profit in the preceding three years was Rs. 3,872 crore. Two per cent of this amount, to be spent on CSR, came to Rs. 78 crore. Against this, the company reported to have spent Rs. 35.04 crore on projects on healthcare, drinking water and sanitation (Rs. 11.03 crore); education and livelihood generation (Rs. 10.83 crore); environment sustainability (Rs. 4.73 crore); women empowerment, care of senior citizens, people with disability (Rs. 2.96 crore); promotion of sports, art and culture (Rs. 2.34 crore); rural development (Rs. 2.05 crore) and capacity building (Rs. 1.04 crore).

On the reasons, for not being able to spend the balance earmarked amount (Rs. 42.96 crores), it was disclosed that 2014-15 being the first year of new CSR policy after implementation of the Companies Act, 2013 and the Companies (CSR Policy) Rules, 2014, considerable time was spent in deliberations and formulation of CSR Policy and projects/ activities, which affected implementation of schemes. Projects like

Swachh Bharat Abhiyan and other mission/projects were conceptualised in latter part of year and have gestation period beyond the year, however expenditure is being incurred in terms of the respective milestones. It is further reported that budget provisions for disaster relief and additional requirement remained unutilised as there was no such requirement.

2015-16[8]

The board level CSR committee was reconstituted with five members comprising Independent and Functional Directors on the 6th August, 2016.

For the year 2015-16, the average net profit in the preceding three years was Rs. 2859.9 crore, two per cent of which came to Rs. 57.2 crore. Against this, the company is reported to have spent Rs. 76.2 crore on CSR activities, which was higher than the prescribed amount.

During the year, the company spent the largest amount (Rs. 25.23 crore) on eradication of hunger, poverty and malnutrition and healthcare, followed by on promotion of education, imparting vocational skill (Rs. 17.65 crore) and on ensuring environmental sustainability (Rs. 11.39 crore). The projects were implemented in the peripheral areas through agencies like *Akshaya Patra Foundation*, Ramakrishna Mission, *Zilla Saksharata Samiti* as well as NGOs promoted by the company like *Mahila Samitis* in different plants.

Financial Parameters

It appears that SAIL had taken up CSR activities much before issue of CSR guidelines by Department of Public Enterprises. An account of financial parameter of SAIL including CSR activities in the two spells during 2000-01 to 2003-04 and 2012-13 to 2015-16 are given in **Tables 7.6 and Table 7.7** respectively.

It continued CSR activities even at a time when it was incurring loss during 2000-01 to 2003-04. In the subsequent period, during the years 2012-13 to 2014-15, CSR expenditure of the Company increased in absolute term from Rs. 53.29 crores in 2012-13 to Rs. 62.06 in 2013-14.

Analysis of available information on the CSR intervention of SAIL, a *Maha Ratna* Central public sector undertaking dealing with production of steel, indicates that as a public sector undertaking it was doing social welfare activities in the peripheral areas of its plants and units. For setting

Table 7.6: CSR Expenditure with Reference to Turnover/Profit in RSP during 2000-01 to 2003-04

Item/Year	*2000-01*	*2001-02*	*2002-03*	*2003-04*
Turnover (in Rs. Crores)	2564.91	2309.84	3144.88	3813.88
Profit/loss (in Rs. Crores)	(–)444.61	(–)1035.86	(–)593.16	(–)108.83
Cumulative Profit/loss (in Rs. Crores)	(–)2,320.39	(–)3,356.25	(–)3,949.41	(–)4,058.24
CSR Expenditure (in Rs. Crores)	0.64	0.34	0.38	1.08

Source: Reply to Lok Sabha question no. 920 for 13.07.2004.

Table 7.7: CSR Expenditure with Reference to Turnover/Profit of RSP during 2012-13 to 2015-16

S. No.	*Item/Year*	*2012-13*	*2013-14*	*2014-15*	*2015-16*
1.	Turnover (Rs. Crores)	49,350	51,866	50,627	43,337
2.	Profit After Tax (PAT) (Rs. Crores)	2,170	2,616	2,093 [3,872*]	(–)4,137 loss [2,859.9*]
3.	Expenditure on CSR/Social Investment programmes (Rs. Crores)	53.29	62.06	35.04 (against 78 crores)	76.2 (against 57.2 crores)
4.	Expenditure on CSR as a %age of PAT (in % age)	2.4	2.3	1.1	2.6

Source: Figures 2012-13, 2013-14, *vide* mail dated 14-05-2015, Annual Report 2014-15, 2015-16, *average Net Profit of the last three financial years.

up the plant large chunk of land was acquired and large numbers of people particularly scheduled tribes were displaced. The peripheral development activities were taken up for provision of education, health and livelihood support to the displaced families to some extent from the facilities developed for the workers/employees of the company. The company had taken up the CSR interventions through *Mahila Samitis* formed with women in each plant/unit. Non-governmental Organisations were also involved for implementation of projects.

Analysis of CSR activities of the company during 2000-04 indicated that it was taken up with limited resource, which was partly due to the fact that the global steel market was on a downturn and the company was incurring loss.

Endnotes

CSR activities of the company went up substantially due to improved financial parameters and instructions of the Department of Public Enterprises during 2012-13 and 2013-14.

However, after CSR was mandatory in the first year 2014-15, CSR activities got reduced substantially with an expenditure of Rs. 35.04 crores, which was less than half of the amount supposed to be spent as per the statutory requirement (78 crores). The position improved during 2015-16 with an expenditure of Rs. 76.2 crore against the mandatory requirement of Rs. 57.2 crore.

The company is a leader in the steel industry with huge physical, financial and manpower resources. There is considerable scope for improvement of CSR activities. The support for health, education and livelihood extended by the company to the people living in peripheral area of its plants and units has a special significance as the plants are located in the backward region of the country in Jharkhand, Odisha and West Bengal. Incidentally, this region is also facing disruptive activities of the Left Wing Extremists. Being a public sector company, it has advantages, which can be exploited for implementing CSR in synergy with ongoing government plans and programmes by filling the gaps on last mile connectivity basis, along with managerial support inform of corporate volunteerism of the executives. Such a strategy would not only give the best value to the company for the money spent on CSR, but also help the poor and disadvantaged living in the peripheral areas of the plants, and thereby improve the brand name of the company in the market.

References

1. Information received *vide* mail dated May 14, 2015.
2. Annual Reports of SAIL for the years 2013-14, 2014-15.
3. Twenty fourth Report of the Parliamentary Committee on Public Undertakings (COPUs) on Social Responsibilities and Public Accounting of Public Undertakings, 1993-94.
4. "*A study on Peripheral Development of Rourkela Steel Plant*", Society for Rural Industrialization (SRI), Ranchi, 2004.
5. CSR policy.
6. Chairman's address in the 43rd Annual General Meeting held on September 24, 2015.
7. AnualReport_14-15. pp. 154 -155.
8. Annual-Report_2015-16, pp. 148-149.

TATA STEEL LIMITED (TISCO)

Tata Steel Limited, earlier known as Tata Iron and Steel Company Limited (TISCO), started its commercial activities with setting up of the first modern steel plant of India, with a capacity of 1.6 lakh tonnes in 1907 at Jamshedpur, Jharkhand erstwhile Bihar. In the post-liberalization era, activities of the company spread all-over the world with the acquisition of NatSteel of Singapore (in 2004), Millennium Steel of Thailand (in 2005) and the Anglo-Dutch Steel Maker Corus Group (in 2006). Its production capacity increased from a mere 1.6 lakh tonnes in 1907 to 28 million tonnes as the 5th biggest producer of crude steel in the world and combined revenue of $24.4 billion (Rs. 1,09,800 crores). Tata Steel has manufacturing operations in 26 countries, including Australia, China, India, the Netherlands, Singapore, Thailand and the United Kingdom with a workforce of about 81,600 people. The company continued to top the list of steel producers in India and its global ranking improved from 39th in 2013 to 34th in 2014.[1]

Commitment of the Tata Group to social issues is reflected in the words of Jehangir Ratanji Dadabhoy Tata "*It was people who mattered—whether in business or in life......Every Company has a special continuing responsibility towards the people of the area in which it is located. The company should spare its engineers, doctors, and managers to advise the people of the villages and supervise new developments undertaken by co-operative efforts between them and the company.*" This spirit was further strengthened by Jamsetji Nusserwanji Tata, who held "*In a free enterprise, the community is not just another stakeholder in business but is, in fact, the very purpose of its existence*", which formed the cornerstone of its CSR.

Guided by this tradition and belief, the company took number of pioneering welfare initiatives[2], such as adoption of eight hours per working day (1912), free medical aid (1915), establishment of Community Development and Social Welfare (CD&SW) Department (1916-17), setting up a technical institute at Jamshedpur (1921), launching Community and Social Welfare Schemes (1958), and five year rural development programme for the upliftment of the villages around Jamshedpur (1978-79). With the expansion of the welfare activities, the sustainable development and inclusive growth is dealt by the Corporate Social Responsibility (CSR) department, through its operating arms. Its welfare activities included several Best practices[3] in the field of Education, Health and well being and Environment for enhancing the livelihood of the local communities.

Commitment to values and national interest appeared to have continued over 100 years by Tata Steel. Renaming "*Sakchi*", where the Plant was set up as Jamshedpur after Jamsetji, indicates the recognition and acceptance of the corporate by the local people and state administration.

CSR Policy

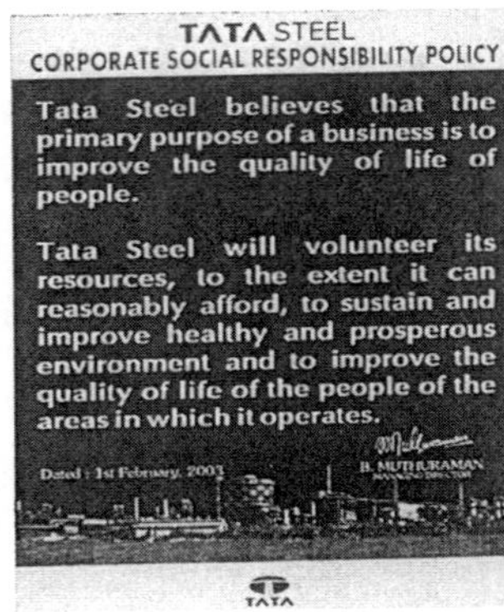

The company adopted its first CSR policy on the 1st February, 2003 *"Tata Steel believes that the primary purpose of a business is to improve the quality of life of people. Tata Steel will volunteer its resources, to the extent it can reasonably afford, to sustain and improve healthy and prosperous environment and to improve the quality of life of the people of the areas in which it operates."*

CSR Objectives

Jamsetji Tata, Founder of the group, had wished to make the community the very purpose of the Company's existence. In his words belief *"The wealth which came from the people must, wherever possible, go back to the people"* and its corporate strategy envisages placing equal emphasis on value creation and corporate citizenship making inclusive growth. As per Article 3A of the 'Articles of Association' of the company, the CSR objective of the company has been shaped through *its social and moral responsibilities to the consumers, employees, shareholders, society and the local community.* Other objective is to bring the local rural people together with the newly created industrial atmosphere and create mutual trust and understanding through intermingling of the two cultures. CSR activities of the company envisages:

- *Empower communities* by building various forms of capacity human and social capital
- Create and measure the formation of *Sustainable Livelihood*
- *Focus on Youth* through vocational Training, *Inclusion and absorption across the supply chain* as artisans, entrepreneurs and micro-enterprise.

- *Consciously* deploy technology to help people.
- *Synergize* with the local area development plans.

Modalities of Implementation of CSR Activities

The company set up a number of institutions namely Tata Steel Rural Development Society (TSRDS), the Tata Steel Family Initiative Foundation (TSFIF) and the Tribal Cultural Society (TCS) for undertaking its CSR interventions.Tata Steel Rural Development Society (TSRDS) was set up for taking up development of rural area in the periphery of the plant. It had collaboration with other NGOs working in rural areas, namely the Tribal Welfare Research Institute, Ranchi, Xavier Institute of Social Service, Ranchi, Action Aid and the Indian Institute of Public Administration.

CSR Activities

CSR interventions of Tata Steel fall under two broad categories for assisting the families,(i) living in the periphery of its Plant and Units and (ii) others living at places independent of the location of Plant/Units. A wide range of activities varying from running educational and research institutions, sponsoring sports to provision of relief and rehabilitation of families affected by calamities have been supported under the second category. Some of the best practices taken up by Tata Steel under CSR include the following:

Access to Urban Amenities

Jamshedpur Utilities and Services Company (JUSCO) was the urban civic amenities provider across the leasehold area of the company. Its services cover waste water management of municipal solid waste, public health and horticulture. Urban Services deploy Tata Steel's social initiatives in Jamshedpur. It covered the areas of education, employability, primary health care and infrastructure development to decongest the town, and the building of drains, community roads, public toilets etc.

Rural Development

Sustainable development and inclusive growth in the rural areas of India was facilitated by Tata Steel's Corporate Sustainability Services (CSS) covering sustainable livelihoods, healthcare and education.

The Tribal Culture Society launched a pilot project in 2011 in collaboration with a private residential school in Jharkhand. The society has launched project "Aakanksha", an education programme under which 118 students have been enrolled for residential school education.

Resettlement and Rehabilitation of Communities

The company paid attention to resettlement and rehabilitation of the families displaced for setting up its plant and units. Benefits extended often go beyond the entitlements stipulated in the Government policy.

Three villages Patrapur, Badarpur and Sindhigaon were completely relocated for the proposed plant site and rehabilitated in separate geographical areas within a well-planned colony with all civic amenities. The colony has been divided into ten sectors each complete with roads, drains, electrical lines and green areas. Their socio-cultural identity has been preserved.

TATA STEEL PARIVAR—Resettlement and Rehabilitation Programme

The Company's Resettlement and Rehabilitation programme sought to provide a 'better tomorrow' to the displaced families who are positioned as 'Tata Steel Parivar' covering four 'R-s' namely (i) Reassuring Communication—'Vision for a better tomorrow'; (ii) Resettling the displaced population with care; (iii) Rehabilitation—ensuring a better quality of life, income and happiness; and (iv) Recheck implementation through self and independent social audits. Through Tata Parivar cards, issued to each displaced family, improvement in quality of life is tracked.

The Company took steps to achieve the **Millennium Development Goals** in 21 villages, 14 of which are directly project impacted. For the purpose, stress is laid in (i) Bridging the health care deficit; (ii) Public-private-partnership to prevent HIV/AIDS; (iii) Social change through sports; (iv) Infrastructure development in sustainable ways; (v) Inclusive growth through sustainable livelihoods; (vi) Mid-day meal to foster the school going habit; and (vii) Mainstreaming indigenous communities.

Over the years, activities of the Tata group, including Tata Steel have expanded overseas to Iran, Bangladesh and the UK. Acquisition of Corus group has given a new dimension to Tata Steel. It appears that the group has been laying stress on **Triple Bottom Line** and Global Reporting Initiatives. Commitment of the group to CSR is reflected in the observations, "Hundred years later, critical factors to obtain a license to operate remain a CSR strategy, sound ethics and transparency in addition to core business values of Tata Steel. After all these years, ethics and transparency, along with sustainability have become part of the Tata DNA."

Philanthropic activities of the Tata group have been appreciated, on account of its commitment spread over one century since the starting of its operations, as well as undertaking suitable changes for making the interventions meaningful. Commitment and contribution of the Tata Group to education and research were appreciated by then the Prime Minister Manmohan Singh, who had called upon other business houses to follow its example and invest in the long-term development of human resource, just as they invest in making their firms globally more competitive.

However, the incidents of arising out of land acquisition for setting up a new plant *Kalinga Nagar*, Orissa and for the small car (*nano*) project at Singur, West Bengal have been matter of concern. While the Tata Group's CSR initiatives for empowerment of the disadvantaged section have been widely appreciated, there is a feeling that *"what is being done is probably not enough and something more is required to be done"*.

Tata Steel Centenary Project (TSCP), with an outlay of Rs.100 crore over five years was launched from April 2007 for efficient land and water management. This project envisaged assisting 40,000 poor tribal households living in 400 villages in Jharkhand, Chhattisgarh and Orissa. Natural resources-based interventions with focus on creation of assured irrigation facilities, setting up of water user cooperatives, development of wasteland, promotion of horticulture and agro-forestry and encouragement in improvement of agricultural output through technological upgradation are the main features of this project. Tata Steel Rural Development Society will implement the project as the nodal agency under technical support and guidance of the Central India Initiative Cell.

Tata Group, representing one of the India's biggest conglomerate dealing salt to software to steel, spent about Rs. 1,000 crore on CSR during 2013-14. Part of this fund was routed through the philanthropic trust managed by the group, excluding which the amount spent by the group companies was about Rs. 660 crore, of which biggest share came from Tata Steel. This amount was well above the two per cent of the net profit, the minimum requirement under the Companies Act. Significant amount of this was spent on skill development, health and education.

CSR activities[4] following CSR made Mandatory

As per the statutory provisions, a board level CSR committee was constituted with five members headed by Mr. Ishaat Hussain (Chairman), Mr. O.P. Bhatt, Mr. D.K. Mehrotra, Mr. Koushik Chatterjee and Mr. T.V. Narendran. Besides, a CSR Advisory Council was set up with twelve eminent personalities from academia and the development sector, having rich experience and expertise on CSR related activities.

CSR policy of the company, based on 10 core principles, was approved on the 9th September, 2014, which envisages that the company shall allocate at least 2 per cent of its average net profits before taxes of the preceding three years, towards CSR activities to sustain and improve a healthy and prosperous environment and to improve the quality of life of the communities it serves.

2014-15

For the year 2014-15[5], average annual net profit of the company in the preceding three financial years was Rs. 8,412.82 crore; two per cent of which to be spent on CSR activities came to Rs. 168.26 crore. The company disclosed expenditure of Rs. 171.46 crore on various CSR activities during the year on promotion of education including special education (Rs. 44.25 crore), promotion of Livelihood (Rs. 43.08 crore), healthcare and provision of safe drinking water (Rs. 41.19 crore etc.) and other activities.

Some of the major CSR activities related to education, skill development, and livelihood support, conservation of nature and promotion of culture. Over 15,000 adults were made functionally literate and about 13,000 middle and high school students were provided coaching on English, Math and Science. Assistance was provided to improve the quality of education in 1,000 government primary schools. Jyoti Fellowship was given to over 3,400 meritorious students from the SC/ST communities. A new scholarship programme, 'Tata Steel Scholars' was started for supporting bright SC/ST students in pursuing professional courses.

Under Project MANSI, healthcare was provided for maternal and newborn survival in 167 villages of Seraikela district, which brought down infant mortality rate by 26.5 per cent and neonatal mortality rate by 32.7 per cent for over four years. Under Project RISTA, adolescent health 47,000 adolescents were covered in 735 villages of Jharkhand and Odisha to enable to make informed decisions and choices about their sexual and reproductive health.

Skill development was taken up in partnership with other institutes, setting up Tata Steel Technical Institute at Burma mines, Jamshedpur and setting up a hospitality training centre at Kolebira, Jamshedpur, PACE Skill Training Centre at Seregada, Gopalpur, Odisha and training of 200 girls from Left-wing extremist areas in sector skill trades. Livelihood support was provided to 6,000 farmers for promotion of agriculture, popularizing System of Rice Intensification (SRI) to increase paddy productivity, construction of 366 ponds for irrigation and reducing dependency on monsoon.

Under solar street light project, over 1,400 solar street lights were installed in villages of Jharkhand and Odisha.

Promotion of tribal culture, tribal music and dance, tribal languages, literature and folklore was taken up in which nearly 15,000 youth learned tribal scripts and more than 5,000 players participated. Several sports tournaments and training camps were conducted for promotion of athletics, archery as well as football.

2015-16

For the year 2015-16[6], average annual net profit in proceeding three financial years was Rs. 7,518 crores, two per cent of which came to Rs. 150 crores to be spent on CSR activities. Against this, Rs. 204.46 crores was spent on CSR activities during the year. Major CSR activities undertaken included healthcare and provision of safe drinking water (Rs. 104.44 crores), promotion of education (Rs. 29.93 crores), promotion of Livelihood (Rs. 27.30 crores) and rural and urban infrastructure development (Rs. 18.43 crores), etc.

Analysis of the component-wise expenditure indicates that promotion of healthcare including preventive healthcare (Rs. 82 34 crore), promotion of education and special education (Rs. 29.93 crore), supply of safe drinking water (Rs. 18.31 crore), rural development projects for infrastructure and other developments (Rs. 18 crores), livelihood enhancement (Rs. 14.64 crore), and employment enhancing vocational skills (Rs. 12.28 crores) were the items of expenditure.

During the year, the company claimed to have made a positive impact in lives of 11 lakh persons, employed 1,132 youth, provided skill development facility to 1,573 youth, healthcare facilities to 5.7 lakh persons along with promotion of education, ethnicity, sports and culture.

Promotion of entrepreneurship of SC/ST families under affirmative action vendor development programme along with assured marketing facility and 18,413 employees contributing 26,290 hours under the Tata Engage initiative are some of the major initiatives.

A recent study[7] on CSR activities of 217 companies has held the Tata Group as the best performer, continuing its track record of philanthropy along with the adoption of innovative measures aligning with the Sustainable Development Goals (SDGs) 2030. The group has reengineered its strategy for implementing CSR activities in a better manner. The Tata Council for Community Initiatives has been replaced by Tata Community Initiative Trust in 2014 for pursuing Sustainability goals. *Tata Strive* initiative was launched for provision of skill for employability, entrepreneurship and community enterprises. It took up its first project in Aligarh, Uttar Pradesh for imparting skill in air-conditioning, refrigeration, electrician and solar PV installers. Subsequently, it opened three more centres at Hyderabad, Mumbai and Pune and provision of skill for meeting the requirement of auto repairs with participation of Tata Motors, Voltas as well as in BPO retail business, debt recovery and in the banking sectors.

Tata Engage initiative was started for mobilizing volunteerism in collaboration with Don Bosco Tech as a partner for developing skills ecosystem for examining challenges in ecosystem arising out of lack of life skills, attrition, quality and assessment and also developing a placement mechanism.

It gave greater focus to education, healthcare and livelihood and venturing into newer areas. In the healthcare, maternal and new born survival initiative has been taken up under public-private partnership mode in Jharkhand through the Tata Steel Rural Development Society. This intervention led to decrease in infant mortality rate from 62 to 40 and maternal mortality rate from 530 to 376 in the project areas.

Three other units dealing with CSR activities, *viz. Tata Steel Family Initiative Foundation*, *Tata Steel Tribal Culture Society* and *Tata Steel Skill Development Society* haven been revitalized for promotion of tribal culture, games and sports and language. This social initiative is reported to have touched about 16 lakh persons.

On the environment conservation front, conservation of whale-shark was supported in the Mithapur Coral Reef along the Gujarat coast making it as the only conservation effort in India which is based on generating baseline data on the endangered species, building awareness programme among the fishermen and citizens of the coastal towns and conducting scientific studies through photo identification, genetic analysis and satellite tagging. Similarly, conservation of Mahsheer fish species has been supported by the Tata Power as the second biggest conservation project after "*Save the Tiger*".

Environmental and economic impact of product, process or service was taken up on life cycle analysis by Tata Motors. Under this, the Jaguar Land Rover has made significant progress in replacing steel with recycling aluminium. Recycling of aluminium cans saved about 95 per cent of the steel in producing one unit of virgin aluminium without any environmental effect relating to mining of bauxite for aluminium matter.

Youths from socio-economic disadvantaged groups were supported by (i) identifying activities, (ii) supporting the group for quality production along with (iii) buyback arrangement which make a difference.

Empowering people by helping them develop the skills, they need to succeed in a global economy, was consolidated into a group CSR programme called **Tata STRIVE.**[8] This is one of the innovative and target oriented CSR interventions of the group for skill development. The group believes corporate social responsibility (CSR) is a critical mission that is at the heart of everything that it does, how it thinks and what it is. The Tata Group is committed to integrating environmental, social and ethical principles into the core business, thereby enhancing long-term stakeholder value and touching the lives of over a quarter of the world's population. The group's CSR programmes aim to be relevant to local, national and global contexts, keep disadvantaged communities as the focus, be based on globally-agreed sustainable development principles and be implemented in partnership with governments, NGOs and other relevant stakeholders.

Financial Parameters

Financial aspects of CSR activities of the company were studied in two spells during 2001-02, 2002-03 and later during 2014-15 and 2015-16, gist of which are given in the Tables 8.1 and 8.2 respectively. From the figures, it appears that CSR expenditure went up substantially from a meager Rs. 3.99 crores in 2002-03 to Rs. 212 crores in 2013-14. Following CSR made mandatory, 2.65 per cent of profit was reported to be spent on CSR related activities during 2014-15, which is higher than 2 per cent mandated under the Act. This position improved further to 2.71 per cent of the profit during 2015-16.

Table 8.1: Turnover, Profit and CSR Expenditure of Tata Steel India during 2001-2002 and 2002-2003

S. No.	Item/Year	2001-02	2002-03
1.	Turnover (in Rs. Crs)	7682.7	9843.66
2.	Profit After Tax (PAT) (in Rs. Crs)	204.9	1012.31
3.	Expenditure on: CSR/-Social Investment Programmes (in Rs. Crs)	3.67	3.99
4.	Expenditure on CSR as a %age of PAT (in % age)	3.67	3.95

Source: Annual Report 2001-02, 2003-04, p. 31 and reply to questionnaire.

Table 8.2: Turnover, Profit and CSR Expenditure of Tata Steel India during 2012-2013 to 2015-2016

S. No.	Item/Year	2012-13	2013-14	2014-15	2015-16
1.	Turnover (Rs. Crs)	42,317	46,309	41,785	38,210
2.	Profit After Tax (PAT) (Rs. Crs.)	5,063	6,412	6,439 [8412.82]*	4,910 [7,518]*
3.	Expenditure on CSR/-Social Investment Programmes (Rs. Crs.)	171	212	171 [168.26]#	204 [150]#
4.	Expenditure on CSR as a %age of PAT (in %)	3.37	3.30	2.65	2.71

*Average profit of preceding three years, # mandated amount for CSR.
Source: Tata Steel Ltd., *vide* letter dated 15-07-2015, Annual Report 2014-15, pp. 48-52 and Annual Report 2015-16, pp. 87-89.

Endnote

Analysis of available information on CSR interventions of the company reveals the following:

- Remaining sensitive towards the needs of the society, started by its founder, has continued and got integrated into the core values of the company. CSR has got attention and active support of the top management, which has flowed down to other levels in the organization.
- The company has strong institutional mechanism and organizations for dealing with CSR like TSRDS, TSFIF which have dedicated manpower and expertise on social issues over decades. CSR programmes of the company are being implemented through these organizations as well as other NGOs.

- The company has focused on development of the peripheral area by provision of quality education, healthcare and skill development services. Promotion of ancillaries has helped in promotion of entrepreneurship. These activities in the backward regions of the country, where its production units are located, give a special dimension to the CSR of the company.
- Evaluation and social audits have been conducted from time to time for assessing the impact of the interventions.
- Expenditure on CSR activities have remained more than two per cent of the annual profit for decades. The fact that the company continued its interventions along with provision of resource, even at a time when the global steel market was facing a downturn and plants were getting closed down, reflects on the commitment of the company towards the society in general and CSR in particular. In this context, mobilization of corporate volunteerism and filling the gaps in ongoing government programmes on last mile connectivity basis has potential for making the CSR more effective.
- CSR interventions of the company have remained consistent, focused and made an impact on the society which appears to be a *model* for other corporate.

•

References

1. Press Release, *The Economics Times*, February 18, 2014.
2. Tata Steel Annual Report 2011-2012, http://www.tatasteel.com/investors/annual-report-2011-12/html/downloads.html
3. In 2013-14, 1.5 million people in India and nearly 80,000 people in Europe and UK benefited from the Best practices of Tata Steel Group. Annual Report 2013-14.
4. Information received vide letter dated July 15, 2015.
5. http://www.tatasteel.com/investors/annual-report-2014-15/annual-report-2014-15.pdf, pp. 24, 25, 48-52.
6. http://www.tatasteel.com/investors/annual-report-2015-16/Integrated-Report-&-Annual-Accounts-2015-16-(109th Year).pdf, pp. 42, 58, 87-89.
7. *The Economic Times*, September 15, 2016, p. 14.
8. http://www.tata.com/sustainability/articlesinside/corporate-social-responsibility.

NATIONAL ALUMINIUM COMPANY LIMITED (NALCO)

National Aluminium Company Limited (NALCO) was set up as a Central Public Sector Enterprise in 1987 with headquarters at Bhubaneswar, Orissa with the vision to be a Company of global repute in the Aluminium sector. NALCO is dealing with mining, production, sale and export of aluminium. Its commitment to social responsibility is reflected in its corporate objective, *"As a responsible corporate citizen, NALCO is committed to spend around one per cent of its net annual profit on various social sector activities under its peripheral development schemes*". The main units of NALCO[1] are located at Damanjodi Koraput District (Mines and Refinery complex), Nalconagar, Angul (Smelter, mining activity and Power Plant Complex) is situated atop a set of five mountains called "Panchpatmalli".

Even though NALCO[2] was taking up philanthropic activities, it had no formal CSR policy initially. In 1998-99, it started allocating 0.5 per cent of its net profit for community development. It constructed 197 Primary Schools-*cum*-Cyclone Shelters as a rehabilitation measure after the Super Cyclone, which stuck Odisha in 1999. It set up one English-medium School in partnership with the Delhi Public School Society, and one Oriya-medium school in partnership with the Chinmaya Mission Trust, Bombay Earmarking of fund for CSR was increased to 1 per cent in 2002-03. The amount was mainly spent for developmental works in the peripheral areas through Rehabilitation and Periphery Development Advisory Committees set up by the Government of Odisha. In 2010-11, NALCO increased the allocation for CSR to 2 per cent of the net profit every year and set up a foundation for dealing with CSR activities.

Some of the social sector activities undertaken by NALCO included the following:

- Drinking water supply project was taken up in Visakhapatnam district of Andhra Pradesh covering 900 rural households. This was taken up with Community participation through voluntary labour, which met 21 per cent of the project cost for digging tranches for 15 km for laying the pipeline. Further local people were trained and supplied toolkits for repair and maintenance.
- Under the *Swachh Vidyalaya Abhiyan* programme, 354 toilets were constructed in 202 schools in Angul and Koraput districts of Odisha and Visakhapatnam district of Andhra Pradesh. Later 79 additional toilets were constructed on request of the school authorities.

- Four mobile health units were provided for covering 142 villages in Damanjodi and three units in Angul sector.
- One pair of mosquito nets treated with insecticides was provided to each family in 18 tribal villages along with water filter for checking waterborne diseases.
- It provided solar lights in two villages and solar lantern in 18 villages.

The Company got "CSR Award for Best Practices" in 2011.

Further it has constituted a Corporate Social Responsibility Committee of the Board consisting of 3 or more directors including 1 independent director as envisaged under the statute. A consolidated progress report of CSR activities is to be provided by the site-level CSR teams to the Corporate CSR on a quarterly basis, which is then be put up for consideration of the CSR Committee. On the basis of progress report, the CSR Committee recommends appropriate action with respect to any project/activity of the Policy.

Education

Considering education is the best investment in human resource development, the Company provided Rs. 13.30 crore to Delhi Public Schools and *Saraswati Vidya Mandirs* (Oriya Medium) at Angul and Damanjodi for providing quality education to the children of its own differ and staff as well as those living in peripheral areas. It took initiative to provide quality education to tribal children in the periphery villages of the Mines and Refinery. Under this programme 655 students were supported at a cost of Rs. 1.31 crore till 2014. The assistance covered expenditure on study, lodging and boarding of the students till they complete schooling in residential schools in Kalinga Institute of Social Sciences, Bhubaneswar, Koraput Development Foundation and Bikash Vidyalaya at Koraput.

It conducted education and training programme for the progressive farmers in the villages nearby its plant at Damanjodi. It also provides training in apparel stitching training to 238 persons, on which 95 per cent were girls.

Health

The Company opened Out Patient Health Care (OPD) Centre in Angul for benefit of villagers living in the areas adjacent to its plant. The villagers were given healthcare check-up and medicines free of cost.

In collaboration with Wockhardt Foundation and Lions Club it ran 8 Mobile Health Units (MHUs) in the peripheral areas of its plants at Damanjodi and Angul. These MHUs provide primary health service comprising diagnostics, free medicines and awareness building through Information, Education and Communication (IEC) activities etc., at the doorsteps. About 2,463 camps were conducted and 1,09,166 patients from periphery villages of Damanjodi and Angul were provided healthcare free of cost during 2014.

Environment and National Relief Causes

It took up plantation of 5,000 nos. of trees at an expenditure of Rs. 25.00 lakhs in the Visakhapatnam city (Andhra Pradesh) under the Green Visakha Project in liaison with the Visakhapatnam District Administration.

It adopted ISO-50001 International Standards for Energy Management System in its production units. Its Captive Power Plant at Angul got ISO-50001 Energy Management System in February 2013 and has completed the two surveillance audits successfully. The Alumina Refinery Plant, Damanjodi Unit got ISO-50001, Energy Management System Certification in March 2014. It has taken up implementation of ISO-50001 Energy Management System in Smelter Plant, Angul.

CSR Policy and CSR Committee

After CSR was made mandatory with effect from 1st April, 2104, NALCO framed its Corporate Social Responsibility Policy 2014 to regulate the CSR activities of the Company as per provisions of section 135 of the Companies Act, 2013 and rules made thereunder. Further, a Corporate Social Responsibility and Sustainability Development Committee has been constituted to look into matters related to CSR activities and sustainability development programmes.

2014-15[3]

Average annual net profit of the company in the last three financial years was Rs. 1007 crores, two per cent of which came to Rs. 20.14 crores to be spent on CSR activities during the year.

The company has disclosed an expenditure of Rs. 19.09 crores on various CSR activities during the year. Major CSR activities undertaken included sponsoring education of tribal children and operating remedial school for school drop-outs at a cost of Rs. 12.52 crores, contribution in PM national relief fund for J&K for an amount of Rs. 4 crores, providing employment enhancement skill training to persons with disabilities at a cost of Rs. 92.00 lakh etc. It contributed Rs. 10 crore to the Odisha Chief Minister's Relief Fund, for Rehabilitation and Construction works in the areas affected by the severe cyclone 'Phailin'[4] and Rs. 1.58 crore to the Uttarakhand Chief Minister's Relief Fund for relief and rehabilitation of people affected in the devastating floods.

For extending educational facilities for Peripheral village school students in the Company aided schools i.e. *Saraswati Vidya Mandirs* and Delhi Public Schools located at Damanjodi and Angul Sector and also promoting education of tribal children in residential school, Company has provided estimated fund allocation of Rs. 13.56 crores considering any possible hike of charges by educational institutions. However, the actual expenditure on this head is Rs. 12.52 crores, leaving fund of Rs. 1.04 crores on this account.

2015-16[5]

Average annual net profit of the company in last three financial years was Rs. 1312 crores, two per cent of which came to Rs. 26.24 crores to be spent on CSR activities during the year.

The company has disclosed an expenditure of Rs. 27.16 crores on various CSR activities during the year. Major CSR activities undertaken included sponsoring formal education of tribal children of Odisha in reputed schools at a cost of Rs. 20.53 crores, rural development activities in periphery villages in Madhya Pradesh at a cost of Rs. 2.03 crores, construction of toilets in schools under *Swachh Vidyalaya Abhiyan* at a cost of Rs. 1.60 crores etc.

As per latest information, NALCO spent Rs. 30.01 crore on CSR during 2016-17 (8.8% higher than the statutory amount Rs. 27.56 crore). Out of Rs. 296 crore spent on CSR (since inception till 2016-17), 45 per cent was spent on Education related activities, 26 per cent on Rural Development and 10 per cent on Social Welfare. CSR Best practices included '*Indradhanush*' project, under which 755 children, belonging to Scheduled Tribes and other economically weaker section families of the Damanjodi-Patangi area affected by Left Wing Extremists, were given residential education in a reputed school free of cost, providing financial support for education of meritorious girls from poor families under '*NALCO-ki-Ladli'* programme and taking up intensive afforestation programme in mining fills after extraction of bauxite.

Financial Parameters

Financial parameters and expenditure on CSR activities of the company were analysed based on available information. It appears that CSR activities were in a much lower profile in the first phase of the study during 2000-01 to 2003-04 (given in the **Table 9.1**) with about one per cent of the profit being spent on CSR activities. This situation has improved after a decade and the resources earmarked for CSR went up to Rs. 5 crore in 2011-12. Subsequent years 2012-13 and 2013-14 saw significant growth with about six times more resources (around Rs. 30 crores) spent annually on CSR activities. Expenditure on CSR, both in absolute term and percentage of profit, fell drastically during 2014-15, the first year of mandatory CSR, which appeared to be rather unusual. However, the position improved in the next year (2015-16) with an expenditure of Rs. 27.17 crore, which amounted to 3.72 per cent of profit against the mandatory requirement of two per cent. (given in the Table 9.2).

Table 9.1: Financial Parameters and Expenditure on CSR Activities of NALCO during 2000-01 to 2003-04

(Amount in Rs. in crore)

Item/Year	*2000-01*	*2001-02*	*2002-03*	*2003-04*
Turn Over (TO)	2,409	2,385	2,740	3,315
Profit After Tax (PAT)	656	409	521	737
CSR Expenditure	2.54	3.82	4.60	4.83
CSR Expenditure as percentage of PAT of the previous year		0.58	1.13	0.93

Source: Directors' Report 2003-04 and reply to questionnaire.

Endnotes

The company has its major mining of bauxite activity in Koraput district of Odisha, which is affected by activities of the Left Wing Extremists (LWEs), a matter of national concern. CSR activities of the company included construction of toilet under *Swachh Vidyalaya Abhiyan*, health and education. Provision of market oriented skill along with mentoring

Table 9.2: Financial Parameters and Expenditure on CSR Activities of NALCO during 2011-12 to 2015-16

Sl. No.	Subject	2011-12	2012-13	2013-14	2014-15	2015-16
1.	Turnover (in Rs. Crore)	6,927.00	7,247.00	7,024.27	7,770.62	7,156.53
2.	Profit before tax	1,197.75	905.04	917.80	2,113.42	1,102.80
3.	*Net average profit of three preceding years (in Rs. Crore)				1,006.86	1,312.09
4.	CSR obligation (2% of average profit of three preceding years)				20.14	26.24
5.	Expenditure incurred on CSR (in Rs. Crore)	5.16	30.99	29.00	19.09	27.17
6.	Expenditure as percent-tage of Profit (in %age)	0.61	5.23	4.51	1.44	3.72
7.	*CSR Expenditure as percentage of average Profit of preceding three years (in %age)				1.90	2.07

Source: As per Annual Report on CSR 2011-12, p. 74; 2012-13, p. 18; 2013-14, p. 18; 2014-15, p. 18; 2015-16, p. 22.

and guidance, through mobilisation of corporate volunteerism and working on *last mile connectivity* basis with ongoing government programmes offers considerable scope for improving quality of CSR activities. This will not only enhance the image of the company but also make a difference in the lives of people living in peripheral areas of its mining activities.

References

1. https://en.wikipedia.org/wiki/National Aluminium Company.
2. Central Public Sector Enterprises "Transforming lives through CSR", Confederation of Indian Industry, September 2015, pp. 108-110.
3. http://www.nalcoindia.com/investor/Annual-Report-2014_15.pdf, pp. 17-20.
4. Second-strongest tropical cyclone ever to make landfall in India, tropical depression on October 4, 2013.
5. http://www.nalcoindia.com/investor/35th%20Annual%20Report%20(2015-16).pdf, pp. 21-23.

OIL AND NATURAL GAS CORPORATION LIMITED (ONGC)

After Independence, development of the petroleum industry was given importance not only for promoting industrial development but also for strategic reasons. Till 1955, private oil companies did exploration for hydrocarbon resources in the country. Subsequently, Oil and Natural Gas Commission was setup as a statutory body under the Oil and Natural Gas Commission Act, 1959 with the main objectives "to Plan, promote, organize, and implement programmes for development of petroleum resources and the production and sale of petroleum and petroleum products." In 1991, under the new economic policy as part of the liberalization, petroleum sector was de-regulated and de-licensed and the Oil and Natural Gas Commission was converted into a public company, ONGC Limited under the Company's Act, 1956.

ONGC, headquartered at Dehradun has come a long way since its formation and currently is one of the largest Asia-based oil and gas exploration and production companies, and produces around 72 per cent of India's crude oil and around 65 per cent of its Natural gas. It featured as one of the eight companies from India to feature in Fortune 500s list and was ranked 357.

Commitment of ONGC to Corporate Social Responsibility is reflected in its mission statement, which reads, as "Abiding commitment to health, safety and environment to enrich quality of community life, apart from fostering a culture of trust, openness and mutual concern and imbibing high standard of business ethics."

CSR activities of the company got a major boost in 2001-02, with the adoption of Corporate Citizenship Policy, which states, "As responsible Corporate Citizens, the company shall promote education, healthcare and entrepreneurship in the community and support water management and disaster relief". In pursuance of the recommendations of the Parliamentary Committee On Public Undertakings (COPUs), ONGC had adopted comprehensive guidelines on implementation of CSR, giving more autonomy to the regions and projects for facilitating various programmes for community development. CSR at ONGC is perceived as philanthropic activity involving socio-economic developmental programmes like establishing schools and hospitals, developing agriculture and cottage industry, building infrastructure facilities, etc., around its areas of operation.

In 2003, it decided to allocate 0.75 per cent of the net profit for various Socio-Economic Development Programmes (SEDPs) undertaken by the company every year. A wide range of activities was taken up under SEDP keeping in view shared contribution by the community and well-being of the community on sustainable basis, enhancing the corporate image, Supporting national causes, and Creating enduring values, satisfaction and recognition. At the Work Centre level, the earmarked provision was redistributed for taking up projects on Education, especially info tech (35%), Healthcare, including drinking water (30%), Entrepreneurship development (25%) and General activities (10%). Further, out of the total fund earmarked for education, health and entrepreneurship development, 75 per cent of the provision is spent on new projects, and 25 per cent on maintenance and upkeep of existing projects. Payment of subsidy to local bodies, charity and religious causes are not supported under SEDP and no organization is given grant more than once in a year.

The guideline seeks contribution of beneficiaries in cash or kind for ensuring participation and avoiding a charity-based approach. Projects are implemented through Registered NGOs, recognized by the government and in existence for at least three year's voluntary participation of National Cadet Corps, Bharat Scouts and Guides, Junior Red Cross, officers' and employees' club, and *Mahila Samiti* are involved and encouraged to contribute to SEDP.

Table 10.1: Expenditure on CSR Activities of ONGC during 2000-04

(Amount in Rs. Crores)

Item/Year	*2003-04*	*2002-03*	*2001-02*	*2000-01*
Turn Over (TO)	32,927	35,387.2	23,857.4	24,270.4
Profit After Tax (PAT)	8,664.4	10,529.3	6,197.9	5,228.8
CSR Expenditure	18.46	14.40	6.24	4.59
CSR Expenditure as per cent PAT of the previous year (in %age)	0.18	0.23	0.12	

Source: S.K. Panda, 2008, *CSR in India—Past, Present and Future*, p. 316.

Analysis of CSR activities of ONGC during 2000-01 to 2003-04 (given in Table 10.1) that the amount spent on CSR during the period remained limited, less than the targeted 0.75 per cent of the profit of the previous year.

After CSR was made mandatory with effect from the 1st April, 2014, a Board level committee on CSR and Sustainable Development (SD) was set up with Shri Ajai Malhotra, Independent Director as the Chairman along with CMD ONGC, Director (HR), Director (Finance) and another Independent Director as Members. The CSR committee drafted the CSR and sustainable development policy, which was adopted by the Board. The policy envisages earmarking of two per cent of average net profit of the previous three years to be spent on CSR activities every year, in five thrust areas equally @ 20 per cent each on (i) promoting healthcare, (ii) ensuring environmental sustainability, (iii) promoting education, (iv) rural development, (v) protection of heritage monuments, setting up homes for women and orphans, promotion of rural sports and other activities listed in the Schedule-VII of Companies Act, 2013.

For sanction of CSR projects, power has been delegated under which projects of Rs. 10 lakh are cleared by Virtual Corporate Committee, up to Rs. 20 lakh by the Screening Committee, up to Rs. 25 lakh by the functional Directors, up to Rs. 50 lakh by the Director (HR), up to Rs. 1 crore by the CSR committee and the Board having full powers.

The ONGC Foundation was set up on the 20th October, 2014 for implementation of CSR projects.

2014-15[1]

In the first year of mandatory CSR, the average net profit in the three preceding years came to Rs. 33,030 crore. The CSR expenditure for FY 2014-15 as 2 per cent of the average profits came to Rs. 660.61crore. Against this Rs. 495.23 crore was spent on CSR activities during the year. The reason for lower utilisation was stated to be due to (i) major initiatives undertaken were mostly in transition phase so the allocated earmarked budget could not be spent; and (ii) some of the flagship projects undertaken were of long gestation period with budget spread over 3-5 years, thus resulting in lesser utilisation of earmarked budget for the financial year 2014-15.

Some of the major CSR initiatives under implementation during the year 2014-15 included:

Healthcare

- **Varisthajana Swasthya Sewa Abhiyan:** ONGC and Help-Age India Initiative to provide basic medical facilities to elderly in terms of medical consultancy, medicine distribution, basic diagnostic test, special health camp and palliative care at their doorstep, 20 Mobile Medicare Units (MMUs) are engaged for taking basic healthcare to the doorsteps of the elderly in 35 blocks in 17 districts in nine states, 11,86,020 beneficiaries were treated for chronic illness such as Hypertension, Diabetes, Osteoarthritis, Dyspepsia and Skin problems etc.

- **Community Hospital in Lakhimpur-Kheri, Uttar Pradesh:** Capital expenditure of Rs. 4.5 crore was spent by ONGC for 26 bedded Community Hospital for meeting Primary and Secondary health service requirements of economically backward class families.
- **Aids and Appliances to persons with disability:** In association with Artificial Limbs Manufacturing Corporation of India (ALIMCO) and Bhagwan Mahaveer Viklang Sahayata Samiti (BMVSS), Jaipur commonly known as Jaipur Foot benefiting 45,495 persons with Disabilities. Beneficiaries were provided Orthopedic, Hearing and Visually Aids and Appliances at a cost of Rs. 26.2 crore in 61 Backward Districts in 39 operational areas.
- **Government General Hospital (GGH), Kakinada:** Rs. 1.9 crore was spent to construct a separate building, blood bank, additional equipment for blood bank, general surgery and general medicine departments for people of East Godavari District in operational area of ONGC.
- **ONGC Mission Ujala:** Eye screening of students was taken up in Government Schools in the National Capital Region under National Blindness Control Programme in collaboration with reputed NGO, PRAANI. 3,000 children were detected with refractive errors and assisted with medicines and spectacles under this project.

Education and Vocational Courses

- **ONGC-GICEIT Computer Education Programme:** Employment related free computer education was imparted to economically underprivileged Youth in association with Bhartiya Vidhya Bhawan's Gandhi Institute of Computer Education and Information Technology (GICEIT) at five work centres of ONGC located at Mehsana, Dehradun, Nazira, Karaikal and Rajahmundry. More than 8295 students received computer training during 2014-15.

- **ONGC—The Akshaya Patra Foundation:** A centralized fully automated mechanized kitchen was set up to provide mid-day meals to about 1,90,840 students enrolled in all the government schools of Surat district.
- **Community School at Sitapur, Uttar Pradesh:** The school was built up at a cost of Rs. 2.7 crore which was operated by the Shanti Devi Memorial Charitable Trust.
- **ONGC Super 30:** Residential Coaching facility was provided to IIT aspirants at Sivasagar, Assam at a cost of Rs. 67 lakh for underprivileged and below poverty line students, who are unable to get proper coaching to qualify engineering exams.

Projects for Physically and Mentally Challenged

- **ONGC Centre for vocational rehabilitation for the differently abled:** Rs. 1.3 crore was provided to Tamana School of Hope, Vasant Vihar, New Delhi for setting up of Autism Centre and provide vocational training to the mentally challenged young adults and children for their economic rehabilitation with vocational skills.
- **ONGC—Cheshire Home Project for physically and mentally Challenged:** Children with disabilities living in slums area of Mumbai were assisted with help of Cheshire Homes (India) Mumbai with rehabilitation treatment and aids to help them lead a normal life.

Environment Sustainability

- **Eastern Swamp Deer Conservation Project (Phase II):** Swamp Deer were taken from Kaziranga National Park and translocated in Manas National park to conserve and increase the viable population of Eastern Swamp Deer in their natural habitat at a cost of Rs. 89 lakh.
- **Harit Moksha: Green Cremation System:** Mokshda Paryavaran Evam Van Suraksha Samiti (MPEVSS) set up Mokshda Green Cremation Systems (MGCSs) 30 units of green cremation system in 8 cities of 7 different states at a cost of Rs. 9.2 crore. The project helped in saving approximately 13,700 tonnes of wood and reduced 26,500 tonnes of GHG emissions.
- **Development of Backward Districts:** In Jaisalmer district of Rajasthan, 49 Wind Turbine Generators (WTGs), with a capacity

of 102.9 MW, was set up in association with M/s. Suzlon Energy Ltd. with a contribution of Rs. 562 crore.

Others

- **Hortoki Water Supply Scheme:** Rs. 90 lakh was spent on safe drinking water to the people of Hortoki Village, Kolasib District, Mizoram to supply more than 40 lpcd of water till 2014.
- **Rajeev Gandhi International Sports Complex, Dehradun:** ONGC in association with Government of Uttarakhand is building a Cricket stadium-*cum*-sports complex at a cost of Rs. 50 crore.
- **Dashratha Deb Stadium at Agartala:** An Indoor sports complex was set up at a cost of Rs. 24.3 crore.
- **IIIT, Agartala:** ONGC has extended support of Rs. 3 crore for setting up a new IIIT Campus in Agartala.

The company got Golden Peacock Award 2014 for CSR, ABP News Global CSR Excellence and Leadership Award for Best Overall CSR practices, 4th Annual Greentech CSR Platinum Award 2014 in petroleum exploration sector, Madan Mohan Malviya Golden Award for outstanding contribution in the field of Education, P.L. Roy CSR Award on 'International Day of Older Persons' for its CSR initiative during the year.

2015-16[2]

The average net profit in the three preceding years came to **Rs. 29,843.83 crores, two per cent of which came to Rs. 596.87 crores.** Against this Rs. 421 crores was spent on CSR Activities. Some of the major projects taken up by the ONGC under CSR included the following:

- Under the **Varisthajana Swasthya Sewa Abhiyan,** provision of basic medical facilities was provided to elderly in special health camp and palliative care at their doorstep in collaboration with the Help-Age India through a network of 20 Mobile Medicare Units (MMUs) in nine states in ONGC operational areas at a cost of Rs. 16.45 crore. Over 11 lakhs elderly patients were treated for chronic illness.
- **Empowering the differently abled under ONGC Swavalamban Abhiyan.** 95,737 appliances were distributed to

44,975 persons with disabilities through Artificial Limbs Manufacturing Corporation of India and Bhagwan Mahaveer Viklang Sahayata Samiti in 100 locations in 25 states **at a cost of Rs. 26.24 crore**.

- Under the Swachh Vidyalaya Abhiyan, 8202 toilets were made functional and 3800 schools were provided water facility at a cost of Rs. 125.7 crore. In association with Oroville Foundation, community led total sanitation were taken up in 5,599 schools at a cost of Rs. 7 crore. Besides, Rs. 1.07 crore was spent on construction of individual household latrines in Tamil Nadu, Jammu & Kashmir. In a special move, garbage and waste generated by tourists in high altitude was removed with help of Indian Mountaineering Foundation at an expense of Rs. 16 crore.
- **Nephrology and cardiac care unit was set up in the** ONGC-Sardar Vallabhbhai Patel Rotary General Hospital at Ankleshwar, Gujarat at a cost of Rs. 13 crore.
- **Bone Marrow Transplant Centre was set up in HM Patel Centre** for Medical Care and Education in Karamsad, Gujarat through Charutar Arogya Mandal at a cost of Rs. 65.58 lakh.
- **Ramakrishna Mission Hospital** was set up at Khar, Mumbai at a cost of Rs. 95.51 lakh with the help of Ramakrishna Mission.
- **Community hospital was set up at Lakhimkpur-Kheri** in Uttar Pradesh at a cost of Rs. 5 crore through Chandan Healthcare.
- **Government Hospital at Ziro of Arunachal Pradesh was provided** X-Ray machine, Ultra Sound Machine and ambulance facilities at a cost of Rs. 65.45 lakh.
- **ONGC-MRPL wing** was set up in government hospital at Mangalore at a cost of Rs. 12.78 crore
- Oncology department was set up in a multi-storied building in the **King George Hospital** at Vizag along with equipment at a cost of Rs. 15 crore.
- **Popularization of Sanskrit language** was taken up through Sanskrit Promotion Foundation at a cost of Rs. 5.57 crore and Rs. 12 crore was provided to Vivekananda Yoga Anusandhan Sanstha, Bangalore.
- **Computer education, training modules for English speaking**, personality development and advance computer training was provided to youth for employment at Mehsana, Karaikal, Rajahmundry, Dehradun and Nazira at a cost of Rs. 10 crore through the Bharatiya Vidya Bhavan.

Financial details on Gross Revenue, Profit and Expenditure on CSR

Financial parameters and CSR activities of the company was studied based on available information for the periods 2000-01 to 2003-04 and 2011-12 to 2015-16. **(Table 10.2)** From the available information, it appears that CSR expenditure of the company went up substantially from less than Rs. 5 crore during 2000-01 to about Rs. 20 crore in 2003-04 and touching Rs. 500 crore in 2014-15 which indicates a growth by 100 times. However, the trend has remained uneven till CSR became mandatory in 2014-15. CSR expenditure during 2014-15 and 2015-16 has been less than the prescribed amount.

Table 10.2: CSR Expenditure with reference to Turnover/Profit of ONGC during 2011-12 to 2015-16

Sl. No.	*Subject*	*2011-12*	*2012-13*	*2013-14*	*2014-15*	*2015-16*
1.	Turnover (in Rs. Crore)	76,887.06	83,308.96	84,202.78	83,093.47	78,565.19
2.	Profit before tax (in Rs. Crore)	36,642.57	30,544.33	32,431.93	26,555.24	23,390.32
3.	*Net average profit of three preceding years (in Rs. Crore)				33,030.00	29,843.83
4.	CSR obligation 2% of average profit of three preceding years				660.61	596.88
5.	Expenditure incurred on CSR (in Rs. Crore)	N.A.	261.57	341.30	495.23	421.00

Source: Annual Report 2012-13, p. 127; 2013-14, p. 146; 2014-15, p. 85; 2015-16, p. 80.

Endnotes

The company has been undertaking a wide range of activities under CSR, out of which provision of nutritious meal with help of Akshaya Patra Foundation, empowering the differently abled, elderly healthcare, relocating swamp deer, construction of toilet under *Swachh Vidyalaya Abhiyan*, appear to be useful and interesting. As a *Maharatna* public sector undertaking, the company has the potential to tackle the problems of unemployment and poverty by empowering the youth and the poor with assets, skill and technology. There is scope for bringing in innovation and improving the quality under CSR interventions by working with ongoing government schemes and filling gaps *on last mile connectivity* along with mobilizing the corporate volunteerism of its executives; which will give a better value for the money spent on CSR and make a difference in the life of the people.

References

1. http://www.ongcindia.com/wps/wcm/OngcHTML/Annual_Report_2014_15/anextures_to_Board's_report.html, Annexure-C.
2. http://www.ongcindia.com/wps/wcm/PDF/AnnualReport/annual_report15-16.pdf, pp. 80-85, 93-96, 229.

RASHTRIYA ISPAT NIGAM LIMITED (RINL)

Rashtriya Ispat Nigam Limited[1] was set up in year 1971 as a central public sector enterprise under Ministry of Steel for pursuing steel manufacturing and allied objective. Its Vision envisages, "To be a continuously growing world class company". It has only one integrated Steel Plant at Visakhapatnam (VSP). It has been producing a wide range of steel wire, rods, bars, rounds, angles, channels, beams, blooms and billets and has acquired *Navaratna* (nine jewels) status with expansion of business.

Commitment of the Company to Corporate Social Responsibility (CSR) is reflected in its corporate objective, "Concern for Society, Environment and Sustainability" as well as in its preamble that "The focus of CSR is to share the profits derivative from the Society to the well-being of Society." The company claimed that its policies on CSR have been designed in accordance with the provision of the Companies Act as well as guidelines issued by the Department of Public Enterprises.

Salient Features of CSR Initiatives[2]

A Committee with help of the Personnel (Welfare & CSR) Department dealt with the formulation and implementation of guidelines on CSR. The company formulated its first **CSR policy[3] in February 2006** with a mandate to allocate two per cent of the net profit of the previous year for CSR activities. Some of the major CSR activities of the company covered the following:

The company took up drinking water supply through gravity under the "**Jaladhara**" scheme. This involves construction of small check dams across natural streams/springs through which the water is tapped and taken to a filter tank, collected water is filtered by medium like, sand, gravel and bricks, which is stored in a ground level service reservoir. This water is supplied to the target groups through pipes. This has been taken up in 19 villages in 3 phases during 2007-2012 with involvement of *D. Sarada* trust, an NGO. An amount of Rs. 67 lakhs was spent and about 5400 villagers are benefited under this project. As per an impact study[3], the results are quite encouraging which has reduced incidence of diseases in the villages.

It supported plantation of saplings for environmental conservation, generation of awareness about water conservation and adoption of appropriate technology for recycling, eliminating wastage and tapping additional sources.

Mahila Mandals[4] were set up and assisted by the company in the rehabilitation and skill development programmes. Visteel Mahila Samithi took up construction of additional Class rooms at the Zilla Parishad High School (ZPHS) of Konda Koppaka Village in Anakapalle Mandal. In 2011, it took up Girl Child Education, Health, Social Empowerment etc. in the mining operation areas.

Developmental activities were undertaken in the peripheral areas of the Plant covering setting up model steel village in Visakhapatnam District. With a view to propagating the use of steel in rural areas, construction of steel intensive buildings was promoted for use as community halls, Panchayat office. The company took up construction of bus shelters and distributed steel bullock carts to individual farmers.

The Company runs schools and a 160-bed hospital for provision of education and healthcare facilities respectively to its employees. These facilities are extended to general public living in the peripheral area, other than employees on payment are extended these facilities to some extent. User fee is collected from the non-entitled patients for provision of healthcare facilities. The company supported promotion of sports.

During 2011-12[5], a budget of ₹12 crore was approved for FY 2011-₹12 for CSR activities to be taken up as per Policy and in compliance with Guidelines issued by DPE. It is mentioned that during last 5 years, the total expenditure towards CSR has been varying up to 1.5 per cent approx. with a cumulative approved budget of 1.3 per cent. During 2012-13[6], a provision of Rs. 15 crores was kept for CSR, as 2 per cent or the profit of the previous year as per the guidelines of DPE and Rs. 16 crores was spent. The company got the IPE-CSR Corporate Governance award for the year. During 2013-14[7], Rs. 20.31 crores was spent on CSR activities.

After CSR became mandatory with effect from 1st April, 2014, a **Board Sub-Committee on CSR** and Sustainability was constituted with three members namely Shri K.M. Padmanabhan as Chairman, Shri S.K. Srivastava and Shri Sunil Gupta as members, all of whom are independent Directors. As on the 31st March, 2015, Constitution of the board sub-committee on CSR and Sustainability was later revised with three Independent Directors namely Prof. S.K. Garg as Chairman, Shri A.K. Jain and Prof. Sushil as members.

The company's CSR and Sustainability Policy[8] was revised keeping in line with the requirement of Companies Act, 2013 and the CSR Rules, 2014 and the specific environment in which the company operates and was approved by the board on the 8th September, 2014.[9] It was redrafted and approved by the board on 27th March, 2015. The nature of activities as well as area of implementation has been outlined in the policy and the share of CSR expenditure between the local area and other area has been kept in an indicative ratio of 80:20.[10] CSR activities were taken up by three different ways namely: (i) collaborating with an NGO, (ii) Government organization, and (iii) doing it directly through RINL trust. NGO with a minimum of 5 years of sustained experience were associated for taking up CSR projects.

For the year 2014-15[11], the average Net profit of the company for the last three financial years comes to Rs. 711.29 Cr, accordingly prescribed CSR Expenditure (2% of profit) comes to Rs. 14.23 Cr. Against this, Rs. 14.04 crores was spent on CSR activities during the financial year

During the year 2014-15, the major CSR activities undertaken include provision of education, female literacy (Rs. 601 lakh), solar light and energy devises in old age home and plantation (Rs. 83 lakh), construction of toilet in schools (Rs. 81 lakh), contribution to CM's relief fund and for cyclone relief (Rs. 503 lakh), and construction of multipurpose halls (Rs. 32 lakh). These activities were undertaken in the peripheral area of the plant and in rural areas of Himachal Pradesh.

The company joined the *Swachh Bharat Abhiyan* and *Swachh Vidyalaya Abhiyan*[12] initiated by Hon'ble Prime Minister, Shri Narendra Modi and taken up constructing 86 toilets in 33 schools spread across 7 mandals at a cost of around Rs. 95 lakhs. The company has also assisted construction of 4 Additional Class Rooms and supplied equipment's at a cost of Rs. 4.14 lakhs.

For the year 2015-16[13], the average Net profit of the company for the last three financial years comes to Rs. 326.56 Crores accordingly prescribed CSR Expenditure (2% of profit) comes to Rs. 6.53 Crores Against this, Rs. 8.73 crores was spent on CSR activities during the financial year 2015-16.

During the year 2015-16, the major CSR activities undertaken include providing free education to BPL children (Rs. 456 lakh), construction of educational infrastructure in school (Rs. 49 lakh), free education to differently abled children (Rs. 32 lakh), plantation of trees (Rs. 1.13 lakh), and construction of road, bus centre, community centre (Rs. 38 lakh).

Financial Parameters

Financial parameters and expenditure on CSR activities of the company

Table 11.1: CSR Expenditure on Social Activities of RINL during 2000-01 to 2002-03

Component/Year	*2000-01*	*2001-02*	*2002-03*
Turnover (in Rs. crores)	3,436	4,081	5,058
Profit before Tax (in Rs. crores)	(291)	(75)	521
(i) Peripheral Development Activities	0.0215	0.0150	0.0110
(ii) Vocational Training Programmes	0.0050	0.0150	0.0165
(iii) Contributions	0.1000	0.2300	0.5000
(iv) Total Expenditure on social activities (in Rs. crores)	0.1265	0.2550	0.5275

Source: Annual Report and reply to questionnaire.

were analyzed based on available information. It appears that CSR activities were in a much lower profile in the first phase of the study during 2000-01 to 2002-03 (given[14] in the **Table 11.1**), social welfare activities was on a low key, however the expenditure increased continuously during the period. With about one per cent of the profit being spent on CSR activities.

The expenditure on CSR in the year 2002-03 was Rs. 52.75 lakh, which increased to Rs. 20.31 crores in 2013-14. However, the expenditure on CSR activities decreased to Rs. 14.04 crores in 14-15 and to Rs. 8.73 crores during 2015-16 (in the **Table 11.2**), Decline in the profit level during 2011-12 to 2014-15 and company incurring loss during 2015-16 had an adverse impact on its CSR activities.

Table 11.2: Financial Parameters and Expenditure on CSR Activities of RINL during 2011-12 to 2015-16

Sl. No.	*Subject*	*2011-12*	*2012-13*	*2013-14*	*2014-15*	*2015-16*
1.	Turnover (in Rs. Crore)	14,462	13,553	13,488	11,675	12,271
2.	Profit before tax (in Rs. Crore)	1,110	526	549	103	(1,417)
3.	Amount to be spent on CSR (as 2% of average profit of three preceding years)				14.23	6.53
4.	Expenditure incurred on CSR (in Rs. Crore)	12	15	20.31	14.04	8.73

Source: Annual Report and disclosure on CSR 2012, p. 111; 2013, p. 33; 2014, p. 26; 2015, p. 53; 2016, p. 43.

Endnotes

The company has its mining and production activities in Andhra Pradesh

State, in areas which is affected by activities of the Left Wing Extremists (LWEs), a matter of national concern The company has taken up construction of toilet under *Swachh Vidyalaya Abhiyan*, health and education, school buildings, etc. under its CSR interventions. While these are important, provision of market oriented skill along with mentoring and guidance through mobilization of corporate volunteerism and bridging gaps in the ongoing government programmes on *last mile connectivity* basis would help in improving the quality of services provided to the target group and tackling the LWE activities. This will not only enhance the image of the company but also make a difference in the lives of people living in peripheral areas of the plant and mines.

References

1. https://www.vizagsteel.com
2. Information received vide letter dated July 15, 2015.
3. Annual Report 2006-07, The Ministry of Steel, the Government of India, pp. 82-85.
4. Study by Department of Social Work, Andhra Pradesh, 2013.
5. Mahila Mandal is a village level forum for women to discuss their personal, social, political, spiritual and economic concerns.
6. Media Release dated October 30, 2014, under heading Nobel Gesture by *Visteel Mahila Samithi.*
7. https://www.vizagsteel.com/images/Annual%20Report%20 2011-12%20(English).pdf, pp. 28-33.
8. https://www.vizagsteel.com/images/Annual%20Report%20 2012-13%20(English).pdf, pp. 33-41.
9. https://www.vizagsteel.com/images/Annual%20Report%20 2013-14%20(English).pdf, pp. 26-29.
10. https://www.vizagsteel.com/images/Annual%20Report%20 2015-16.pdf, pp. 42-47.
11. https://www.vizagsteel.com/images/Annual%20Report%202014-15.pdf, pp. 52-57.
12. Ministry of HRD has launched programme to provide separate toilets for boys and girls in all Government schools till 2015 end, 1.58 lakh toilets as well as dysfunctional toilets have been taken up by Public Sector Undertakings/Corporates for construction/repairs.
13. https://www.vizagsteel.com/images/Annual%20Report%20 2015-16.pdf, pp. 42-47.
14. Reply to questionnaire vide no. PL/CO/1(82)/2004/579 dated 29.11.2004.

ITC LIMITED

ITC was incorporated on August 24, 1910 under the name Imperial Tobacco Company of India Limited, which changed to India Tobacco Company Limited in 1970 and then to I.T.C. Limited in 1974. In recognition of the Company's multi-business portfolio encompassing a wide range of businesses—Fast Moving Consumer Goods comprising Foods, Personal Care, Cigarettes and Cigars, Branded Apparel, Education and Stationery Products, Incense Sticks and Safety Matches, Hotels, Paperboards and Speciality Papers, Packaging, Agri-Business and Information Technology, the Company was rechristened as ITC Limited with effect from September 18, 2001.[1] The company with the production and managing of a wide range of activities covering Fast Moving Consumer Goods (FMCGs), tobacco, hotels, paperboards and packaging, agri-business.

Commitments of the company to social obligations are indicated[2] in its vision[3] "ITC's abiding vision to create larger societal value for the nation and its stakeholders has powered a multi-pronged strategy to address the larger challenges of widespread social inequities and environmental degradation. The key priority of this strategic objective is to leverage its enterprise strengths to contribute to the creation of large scale sustainable livelihoods and environmental resources. Towards this, ITC has crafted unique and innovative interventions within the ambit of its operations as well as in partnership with stakeholder communities."

In the year 2015, the Company has completed 10 years of being carbon positive, 13 years of water positive and solid waste recycling positive for 8 years, which reflects its sustainability performance.

ITC continuously strives to improve processes and systems at all its Units to minimize its environmental impact as far as possible, create a work environment that is safe, healthy, productive and fair for its employees and proactively engage with its suppliers and partners to maximize value for all stakeholders. In regulation of its CSR initiatives, the company has got several awards including, the Green Manufacturing Excellence Award in 2014.

Salient Features of CSR Initiatives[4]

e-Choupal

This initiative, started in 2000, aims at providing last mile connectivity to leverage Information Technology (IT) to build capability at the grassroots through empowerment of the small farmer. ITC *e-Choupal* is a continuously evolving platform, embracing new products, technologies and services in tune with the changing needs of rural India, serving agricultural communities as both producers and consumers. By providing access to technical and market information, this intervention seeks to enhance competitiveness in the global market.

ITC's *e-Choupals* have been extended to 40,000 villages and 4 million farmers in 17 states, making it the world's largest rural digital infrastructure by 2013-14. As per a latest report[5] , *e-Choupal* system is a critical component of ITC's rural development programmes, under the 'Choupal' umbrella, the quality of lives in rural India has improved, enabling a larger mainstreaming of farmers to the opportunities offered in the national economic growth process. Recipient of a number of global awards, ITC *e-Choupal* has not only brought the benefits of digital technology to farmers, but has created a larger rural ecosystem, which together have ensured that fortune was created 'FOR' the bottom of the pyramid, rather than merely seeking a fortune 'AT' the bottom of the pyramid. This fundamental approach of enlarging rural purchasing power as well as creating sustainable livelihoods continue to be the cornerstone of ITC's transformational impact in rural India.

In his Budget speech[6], the Hon'ble Minister of Finance also emphasized on the importance of digital India and further quoted that "The National Optical Fibre Network Programme (NOFNP) of 7.5 lakh kms. Networking 2.5 lakh villages is being further speeded up by allowing willing States to undertake its execution, on reimbursement of cost as determined by Department of Telecommunications". This speedy progress in the field of IT will enable many other villages to connect with the programme like *e-choupals*.

Afforestation

The Social and Farm Forestry Programme, started in 1998, over 1,63,000 hectares has been planted leading to large-scale carbon sequestration besides creating over 70 million person days of employment by 2013-14.[7] ITC's pulpwood is largely sourced from renewable plantations under this Programme, which provides livelihood opportunities to tribals and small farmers. Leveraging its experience in afforestation, ITC embarked on an innovation to address the food-fibre conflict by creating an Agro-Forestry model that synergises tree growing along with crop production.

This ensures both food and wood security and helps in the conservation of precious natural resources. ITC's Agro-Forestry model is designed to allocate 25 per cent of the land to forestry and the remaining 75 per cent land is available for agricultural crops. As a result, multi-cropping is possible throughout the tenure of the tree life-cycle. In addition, through Agro-Forestry, the leaf litter increases the carbon content, and replenishes soil nutrients restoring fertility.

Environmental Conservation

On the environmental conservation, the company claims to have achieved and sustained status as a 'water positive' issue and also become 'carbon positive' organization. The company is striving towards achieving a 'zero solid waste' discharge status, having recycled over 90 per cent of solid waste produced. As per a study[8], 99.9 per cent of the total waste generated is being successfully re-cycled by the company.

Under the integrated watershed development programmes, nearly 98,325 hectares has been covered in rural areas providing critical irrigation to water stressed areas benefiting about 1,27,394 persons by 2013-14. The watershed development programme was taken up in Yavatmal district of Maharashtra during 2007-12. Study revealed that income as a result of the watershed interventions has increased income of agriculturalists and farm labourers by about 50 per cent.

Livestock Development

Under the Livestock Development initiative, animal husbandry services was provided to over 10,00,000 animals which increased milk yields which started in 2003-04 substantially. Artificial Insemination (AI) services was provided at doorsteps to produce cross-bred progeny with significantly higher yields, and thereby converted a low-yielding asset into a profitable new livelihood opportunity. A comprehensive package of services, covering AI and other aspects of cattle health, is provided through Cattle Development Centres (CDCs), which are manned by local youth trained as technicians.

Over 261 CDCs, spread across are operating in 7 states. It is estimated that 3.98 lakh cross-bred progeny have been born and animal husbandry services were provided to over 10 lakh breedable cattle. A state-of-art milk procurement network and transparent measurement system is being implemented through which more than 35,000 farmers will be benefited through higher realizations for their milk.

Women's Empowerment

Women's Economic Empowerment programme was started in 2000 with a view to empower poor women by forming micro-credit Self Help Groups (SHGs). About 1,682 operational SHGs with 20,230 members have been covered under this with a cumulative savings of 3.52 crores.

These groups have taken up activities like *agarbatti* production, which got a fillip with the introduction of pedal machines, which increased output and income. 1,368 pedal machines were operational in the states of Bihar, Uttar Pradesh, Tamil Nadu, Andhra Pradesh, Madhya Pradesh and Maharashtra. The women owned and managed scenting units dispatched a total of 319 million sticks with a turnover of Rs. 4.17 crores during the year 2013-14.

Primary Education

ITC has supported primary education in rural areas with provision of infrastructure in Government primary schools in the vicinity of its operating units. Under the "Read India Plus Programme" aiming at improving education levels of children in and around ITC's production units over 30,000 students were assisted during 2014, taking the total number of children covered up to 3.36 lakhs. Infrastructure support was provided to 47 government primary schools during 2014 and 1,011 schools since inception. More than 2,400 youths were provided skill enhancement training including 38 per cent from the SC/ST communities, as a part of Company's affirmative action.

CSR Policy and CSR Committee

After CSR was made mandatory under the Companies Act, 2013, ITC set up the CSR and Sustainable Committee with five members headed by Mr. Y.C. Deveshwar (Chairman), Mr. A.V. Girija Kumar, Mr. R.E. Lerwill, Mr. S.B. Mainak and Ms. M. Shankar with the mandate to review, monitor and provide strategic direction to the companies CSR and sustainability.

In accordance with the statutory provision, ITC formulated the **CSR policy** which envisages directing ITC's CSR Programmes, *inter alia*, towards achieving one or more of the following: enhancing environmental and natural capital; supporting rural development; promoting education and vocational skills; providing preventive healthcare; providing sanitation and drinking water; creating livelihoods for people, especially those from disadvantaged sections of society, in rural and urban India; preserving and promoting traditional art and culture, and promoting sports.

The three most important stakeholders for ITC's CSR programmes/ projects are: Rural communities in the Company's operational areas. The communities residing in close proximity to our production units. The Central and State Governments, encourage Public Private Partnerships (PPPs).

The identified CSR Activities were implemented through a number of NGOs/Trusts namely like BAIF Development Research Foundation, Pratham Education Academy, CII-ITC centre of Excellence for sustainable Development.

2014-15[9]

As per the disclosure made by the company, it had made an average profit of Rs. 10,646.11 crores in the preceding three years. Two per cent of this to be spent on CSR comes to Rs. 212.92 crores. Against this, the company has reported to have spent Rs. 214.06 crores during the year, which is higher than the mandated requirement.

The identified CSR activities were implemented through a number of NGOs/Trusts namely like BAIF Development Research Foundation, Pratham Education Foundation, SEWA Bharat, Foundation for Ecological Security, ITC Sangeet Research Academy, CII-ITC Centre of Excellence for Sustainable Development.

Out of the activities undertaken, the largest amount Rs. 2,900 lakh was spent on ensuring environmental sustainability, followed by Rs. 2,709 lakh on education, Rs. 2,431 lakh on eradicating hunger, poverty, Rs. 2,142 lakhs on protection of national heritage, arts and culture, Rs. 2,017 lakhs as contribution to PM's Relief Fund, and. Rs. 1,497 lakhs on rural development projects. CSR activities were taken up in the states of Maharashtra, Rajasthan, Andhra Pradesh, Telangana, Karnataka, Tamil Nadu, Jammu & Kashmir, Kerala, Pucucherry and Punjab.

2015-16[10]

Average annual net profit of the company in the last three financial years was Rs. 12,338.22 crore, two per cent of which came to Rs. 246.76 crore to be spent on CSR activities during the year.

The company has disclosed an expenditure of Rs. 247.50 crore on various CSR activities during the year. Major CSR activities undertaken included health and sanitation, drinking water, eradication of poverty at a cost of Rs. 57.95 crore, environmental sustainability, soil and moisture conservation at a cost of Rs. 54.12 crore, Agricultural development at a cost of Rs. 50.85 crore, improving quality of education at a cost of Rs. 24.19 crore etc.

Some of the major highlights of CSR activities of 2015-16 covers empowering 4 million Indian farmers in 40,000 villages across 10 states under *e-Choupal*, covering 2,60,000 hectares under the Integrated Watershed Development Programme greening over 2,25,00 hectares and generated more than 100 million person days of employment under the Livestock Development Programme, animal husbandry service to over 13,00,000 milch animals. Under Women Empowerment Programme livelihood opportunities to over 50,000 women, Primary Education Programme benefiting over 4,60,000 children, the Skills and Vocational Training Programme over 31,000 youths, construction of over 15,400 individual household toilets under Health and Sanitation Programme, Creation of sustainable livelihoods for around 6 million people, many of whom represent the weakest in society.

Skilling and Vocational Training

Given the inadequate availability of skilled manpower and the Government's efforts to promote vocational education and training, Company's Vocational Training programme played an active role in building and upgrading skills of marginalized youth to better meet the emerging needs of the job market. 13,180 youths were enrolled for training under different courses during the year. Of the total students enrolled, 10,378 (79% of enrolled) completed training and 3,280 (32% of trained) students were provided placement. The students trained included a healthy mix of women and SC/ST candidates. To cater to the ever growing need for professionally trained human resources in the hospitality industry, Company continues to work with the Welcomgroup Graduate School of Hotel Administration together with Dr. TMA Pai Foundation. This institution continues to be ranked among the top educational institutions in the sector. Graduates of the institution are today part of several leading hotel chains of the world. In addition, Company also opened a Culinary Institute at Chhindwara in 2014, where cooking skills are imparted to youth from disadvantaged sections of society. Leveraging its core competencies in the FMCG sector, Company launched an employability programme to skill unemployed youth in FMCG sales and distribution across various locations of the country. Candidates who successfully completed the programme were certified by the National Skill Development Corporation and have been gainfully employed in the FMCG sector. A programme to promote entrepreneurship for self-help groups from economically weaker sections of society was launched in selected districts of Odisha. This initiative targeted to equip unemployed rural youth to become entrepreneurs and small businessmen capable of generating independent earnings by selling products on a direct-to-home sale model. This initiative has resulted in generating a sustained supplementary income for economically disadvantaged youth and will be further scaled up in the future.

Health and Sanitation

Company invested in impacting public health through multiple routes. To promote a hygienic environment through prevention of open defecation and reduce incidence of water-borne diseases, 3,578 individual household toilets were constructed during the year. With this, a total of 8,254 low-cost sanitary units have been constructed so far in Company's factory catchment areas. In areas with water quality problems, 19 plants providing safe drinking water to about 28,000 rural households have been installed in the state of Andhra Pradesh.

'Swasthya Choupal', Company's *e-Choupal* Rural Health initiative was consolidated in 7 districts of Uttar Pradesh and expanded to 3 new districts in Madhya Pradesh with a coverage of over 450 villages.

Solid Waste Management

Company's Solid Waste Management programme, christened 'WOW—Wellbeing Out of Waste' inculcates the habit of source segregation and recycling among school children, housewives and general public as well as industries and business enterprises. The WOW movement today extends to Hyderabad, Chennai, Bengaluru, Coimbatore and some towns of Telangana, enjoying the support of over 3 million citizens, 5,00,000 school children, 350 corporate, more than 1,000 commercial establishments and around 200 industrial plants. On the occasion of the 3rd anniversary of National Recycling Day, Company launched a novel pilot programme in 12 selected wards of Bengaluru with the support of the Bruhat Bengaluru Mahanagara Palike (BBMP) and a similar programme in 30 wards of Coimbatore to create sustainable livelihoods for rag pickers and waste collectors by propagating source segregation at each household and facilitating effective collection mechanisms in collaboration with Municipal corporations.

Incense Sticks (Agarbattis) and Safety Matches[11]

The *Agarbatti* category sustained its high growth trajectory anchored on a diverse range of high quality products, growing franchise for the 'Mangaldeep' brand and enhanced distribution reach. Mangaldeep continues to be the fastest growing *agarbatti* brand in the country aided by a well-crafted portfolio of offerings born out of deep consumer insight and increasing brand salience. During the year, Company also fortified its leadership position in the 'Dhoop' segment which has a relatively high salience in the northern markets. Investments were made during the year to enhance quality, availability and improving supply chain responsiveness.

Although bamboo and charcoal are available in India, the *Agarbatti* industry continues to import raw *battis* primarily from Vietnam as imports are allowed into the country at a low rate of customs duty. This is resulting in loss of livelihood creation opportunities for women and tribals in rural areas, particularly in the North-East. In this context, it is pertinent to note that Company has implemented several measures including facilitating the mechanization of *agarbatti* manufacturing at vendor locations and backward integration by vendors into raw *batti* manufacturing using indigenous inputs towards enhancing the competitiveness of the domestic industry *vis-à-vis* imports. **Suitable changes in policy need to be implemented** towards encouraging indigenous raw *batti* manufacturing thereby facilitating the creation of sustainable livelihood opportunities for the weakest sections of society.

Interest taken by the Chairman of the Company itself appears to be driving spirit behind making the CSR intervention mode productive and useful. It appears that there has been a quantum jump in the expenditure in CSR both in absolute term and as a percentage of the profit after tax during 2014-15 as compared to the previous years. Interest taken by the top management along with resources would make the company a pioneer in the field of CSR.

Financial details on Gross Revenue, Profit and Expenditure on CSR

Company's gross income for the year 2014-15 stood at Rs. 49,964.82

crores, while net profit rose 9.4 per cent to Rs. 9607 crores. And nearly 59 per cent of net segment revenue is derived from businesses other than cigarettes.[12]

From the statement on financial details of the company **(Table 12.1)** it appears that CSR expenditure of the Company increased both in absolute term from 106.63 crore (2013-14) to 214.06 crore (2014-15). CSR Expenditure went up further to Rs. 247.5 crore during 2015-16.

Table 12.1: CSR Expenditure with Reference to Turnover/Profit of ITC during 2011-12 to 2015-16

Sl. No.	*Subject*	*2011-12*	*2012-13*	*2013-14*	*2014-15*	*2015-16*
1.	Turnover (in Rs. Crore)	34,871.86	41,809.82	46,712.62	49,964.82	51,582.45
2.	Profit before tax	8,897.53	10,684.18	12,659.11	13,997.52	14,958.39
3.	Net average profit of three preceding years (in Rs. Crore)				10,646.11	12,338.22
4.	CSR obligation 2% of average profit of three preceding years				212.92	246.76
5.	Expenditure incurred on CSR (in Rs. Crore)	N.A.	82.34	106.63	214.06	247.50

Sources: Annual Report 2012-13, p. 11; 2013-14, p. 11; 2015, p. 83; 2016, p. 89.

Endnotes

ITC Limited has been a pioneer in conservation of environment and empowerment of the poor and disadvantaged segments. Leveraging information technology for empowering the primary producers with market information and access are good and innovative initiatives.

References

1. http://www.itcportal.com/about-itc/profile/history-and-evolution.aspx
2. Report and Accounts 2004 and other published literatures sent *vide* Corporate Communication Department's letter No. PRC/18 dated 24.12.2004 in reply to the questionnaire.

3. Chairman's Statement "*Sustainability Report 2014*" and "*Redefining Corporate Contribution – ITC: In pursuit of the triple bottom line*", 93rd Annual General Meeting held on July 30, 2004.
4. "*Transforming lives and landscapes, ITC's rural development philosophy at work*", Publication of ITC Limited, October 2003.
5. Report Submitted by Asia-Pacific Association of Agricultural Research Institutions ITC *e-Choupal*, A success story (September 2014).
6. 2015-16 Budget speech of Minister of Finance, para 82.
7. ITC Sustainability Report -2014.
8. Study carried out by Access Livelihoods Consulting.
9. http://www.itcportal.com/about-itc/shareholder-value/annual-reports/itc-annual-report-2015/pdf/report-accounts-2015.pdf, pp. 82-84.
10. http://www.itcportal.com/about-itc/shareholder-value/annual-reports/itc-annual-report-2016/pdf/ITC-Report-and-Accounts-2016.pdf
11. Annual Report 2015-16, p. 51.
12. Address by Chairman, ITC limited, 104th Annual General Meeting, July 31, 2015.

BHARTI AIRTEL LIMITED

Bharti Airtel Limited[1], erstwhile Bharti Tele-Ventures Limited, was incorporated on July 7, 1995. Over decades, it has emerged as a leading Multi National telecommunications services provider Company (MNC), with headquarter in New Delhi. The company is operating in 20 countries across South Asia and Africa with over 300 million subscribers.

Commitment of the Company to Corporate Social Responsibility (CSR) is reflected in the words of Shri Sunil Bharti Mittal, CMD of the Company "*'Sustainability' is as much about securing a balance between economic priorities and environmental protection as promoting inclusion and empowerment in society. At Bharti Airtel, we have always believed in making sustainability an intrinsic part of our business agenda.*" As a part of CSR intervention, the company has undertaken several community welfare programmes with Education at the forefront and including other activities like disaster relief, environment protection, blood donations etc.

Based on the view that the business success is not just about profits and shareholder returns, the Company has been pursuing wider socio-economic and cultural objectives and endeavoured to not just live up to it, but to try and exceed the expectations of the communities in which it operate. Its CSR activities cover (i) Promoting education including special education, employment enhancing vocation skills especially among children and livelihood enhancement projects; (ii) Eradicating hunger, poverty and malnutrition, promoting preventive health care and sanitation and making available safe drinking water; and (iii) Contributions or funds provided to technology incubators located within academic institutions, which are approved by the Central Government.

Education

The Company set up the "*Bharti Foundation*" in 2000 with an objective to make quality education accessible to the underprivileged children in rural area. The foundation has been implementing welfare programmes in the fields of primary, elementary, senior secondary and higher education.

Under the "*Satya Bharti School Programme*" quality education is provided to the underprivileged children, with a special focus on the girl child free. Under this initiative, 254 Satya Bharti Schools, 185 Primary Schools, 64 Elementary Schools and 5 Senior Secondary Schools are operating in 6 states. Enrolment of 49 per cent of girls out of total 40,934 students and engagement of 54 per cent of the total 1,551 teachers being female reflects the importance attached by the company to gender related issues.[2] This programme has made a sustainable impact on the communities, where the schools are located.

Subsequently, "*Satya Bharti Learning Centres Programme*" was started in 2012 for bringing the out of school children by providing bridge courses to out-of-school children back to the school and main streaming them into age-appropriate classes in the Government schools. These Centres were initially set up in the Government Schools in the rural areas of Rajasthan. One Cluster in charge and one Cluster Assistant managed each Centre with 12 to 20 children. 334 such centres were made operational with 10,548 children in Rajasthan, out of which 4,052 students could be mainstreamed. Salient features of the programme are given in Table 13.1:

Table 13.1: Achievements of *Satya Bharti Learning Centres* (As on March, 2015)

Number of Centres	334
Number of State	1
Number of Children Impacted	10,548
Number of Children enrolled	6,496
Number of Children Mainstreamed	4,052
Percentage of Girl Students	52%
Number of Education Volunteers	415

Source: Programme Factsheets—http://www.bhartifoundation.org

Quality Support Programme for education was started in 2012-13 with a view to support the government schools for improving the overall quality of education by adopting the best practices followed in the *Satya Bharti Schools*. Around 4,280 students studying in 9 Schools were covered under this programme till 2015. Strength of this intervention lies in its focus on optimal utilization of Government resources and sharing of best practices.

Health and Sanitation

Inspired by the Hon'ble Prime Minister's call to the Corporate sector to improve sanitation, the company launched '*Satya Bharti Abhiyan'* in 2014 to improve sanitation facilities in the rural areas of Ludhiana district in Punjab, Rs. 100 crore was allotted for construction of toilets and reaching out to each and every rural household, which lacked sanitation facilities, over three years. Improvement of sanitation facilities in Government Schools in rural areas was also supported under this programme. This initiative focuses as much on infrastructure development as on awareness and behavioural change of the rural communities. 252 Satya Bharti Schools were covered under this programme (till 2015).

CSR Policy and CSR Committee[3]

After CSR was made mandatory under the Companies Act, 2013, the company constituted a 3-member CSR Committee including one Independent Director was on the 29th April, 2014. The CSR Committee is responsible for formulating policy and giving its recommendations to Board of Directors. The Committee is to meet at least twice a year to review the implementation of CSR programmes/activities of the Company.

Further it framed its CSR policy[4], which envisages creating and supporting programmes that bring about sustainable changes through education and use of technology.

CSR Activities in 2014-15[5]

Average net profit before tax of the Company in the preceding three financial years was Rs. 6,998.6 crores and prescribed CSR Expenditure (2% of the amount) of the said amount came Rs. 140 crore.

Under the *Satya Bharti School Programme*, promotion of education was taken up which covered early 52,000 school students through 254 Satya Bharti Schools, 334 Learning Centres in rural areas in India. Under the *Satya Bharti Abhiyan*, with an outlay of Rs. 100 crore, sanitation activities were undertaken in rural area.

It appeared that the company took up developmental activities in Africa, under 'Adopt a School' Programme. Over 24,000 students are covered under this initiative to help curb the spread of the deadly Ebola through its subsidiaries in collaboration with Governments and NGOs.

CSR Activities in 2015-16[6]

For the year 2015-16, the company had Rs. 9,450.2 crore as the average net profit before tax in the preceding three financial years. Two per cent of this amount came to Rs. 189 crore as the amount prescribed for CSR activities. Against this, the company reported to have spent Rs. 53.47 crore.

Being in the initial years of implementation, the Company is persistently exploring new opportunities to increase its CSR expenditure to the prescribed level. As a socially responsible company, it is committed to play a larger role in India's sustainable development by embedding wider economic, social and ecological objectives.

Under the *Satya Bharti School* Programme, against an outlay of Rs. 22.47 crore (Operating Expenditure) and Rs. 9 crore (Capital Expenditure), Rs. 19.65 crore and Rs. 9 crore were spent respectively for promotion of education benefitting over 73,000 underprivileged children in rural areas. Under the *Satya Bharti Abhiyan* for sanitation Rs. 10.2 crore was spent on construction of toilets benefiting over 63,000 users in 12,700 households living in 559 villages in Ludhiana district of Punjab.

Besides Rs. 0.69 crore was spent on employment enhancing vocation skills (in footwear design and development skill to youth) at Chhindwara, Madhya Pradesh, Rs. 0.1 crore for providing education to underprivileged girl child in Dehradun, Uttarakhand, Rs. 0.2 crore on maintenance of old age homes in Jodhpur, Rajasthan and Rs. 2.69 crore on public policy and research through Carnegie India.

In recognition of its CSR initiatives, the Company was awarded Global CSR Award in the year 2011-12 and Mr. Rakesh Bharti Mittal, Vice Chairman, Bharti Enterprises was conferred with Hari Chand Award for Corporate Citizen of the year 2013.

Analysis of Financial Parameters

From available information (given in **Table 13.2**), it appears that gross revenue, profit after tax and earnings per share of the Company increased

Table 13.2: Financial Parameters and Expenditure on CSR activities of Bharti Airtel during 2012-13 to 2015-16

Sl. No.	*Subject*	*2012-13*	*2013-14*	*2014-15*	*2015-16*
1.	Turnover (in Rs. Crore)	45,350.90	49,918.50	55,496.40	60,300.20
2.	Profit before tax	6,454.80	8,377.40	15,655.30	10,039.80
3.	*Net average profit of three preceding years (in Rs. Crore)			6,998.70	9,450.20
4.	CSR obligation (2% of average profit of three preceding years)			139.97	189.00
5.	CSR Expenditure (in Rs. Crore)	29.56	40.45	41.10	53.47

Source: Bharti Airtel, Annual Report 2012-13, p. 27; 2013-14, p. 34; 2014-15, p. 58; 2015-16, p. 60; * as average profit of previous 3 years.

consistently year after year. However, trend of expenditure on CSR activities remained uneven.

Endnotes

CSR activities of the company increased substantially after CSR became mandatory. The company focused its CSR activities on education and sanitation. While the company may take measures for increasing its expenditure on CSR to the mandated percentage in the coming years, promoting corporate voluntarism with participation of its executives and employees will improve quality.

References

1. Name of the Company has been changed from Bharti Tele-Ventures Limited (BTVL) to Bharti Airtel Limited (Bharti Airtel) with effect from April 24, 2006.
2. Report of Bharti Foundation http://www/bhartifoundation.org/wps/wcm/connect/bhartifoundation/BhartiFoundation/Home/Resources/PG programme%20 factsheet
3. CSR policy – Airtel 2014.
4. http://www.airtel.in/airtel-annual-report-2014-15/pdf/Airtel%20DLX%20AR%202014-15.pdf. P58-Annexure D
5. 2014-15_CSR%20Ann%20D%20%20page%2058-59.pdf
6. http://www.airtel.in/airtel-annual-report-2015-16/pdf/annual-report-2015-16.pdf

NATIONAL THERMAL POWER CORPORATION LIMITED (NTPC)

National Thermal Power Corporation Limited (NTPC), a Central Public Sector Undertaking (CPSU) was incorporated under the Companies Act, 1956 under the Ministry of Power, Government of India with headquarters at New Delhi. Its core activities include generation and sale of generated electricity power to the distribution companies along with allied activities. The company also undertakes consultancy on turnkey basis comprising of engineering, project management, construction management and operation and management of power plants. It has also ventured into oil and gas exploration and coal mining activities.

During 2014-15, the Company generated 1048.403 BU of power, 8.4 per cent higher than the previous year. Further it added 22,566 MW capacities during the year (2014-15) against a target of 17,830 MW.[1]

Commitment of the company to social issues is reflected in the statement of its CMD[2], "CSR in NTPC is a deeply ingrained belief of doing business by adding value to the community and society on a sustainable basis through dedicated policies, institutional setup and engagement process to promote inclusive growth". Its CSR objective envisages "To contribute to sustainable power development by discharging corporate social responsibility". It has a CSR-Community Development Policy, which covers a wide range of activities starting from the grassroots unit level up to the regional and national level covering implementation of various programmes and activities. CSR activities are taken up through its CSR wing 'NTPC Foundation'.

In recognition of its CSR initiatives for welfare of society, NTPC was awarded FICCI CSR Award 2012-13 Golden Peacock CSR Award 2013, and ASSOCHAM CSR Excellent Award 2013.

CSR Policy and CSR Committee

NTPC constituted a Board level Corporate Social Responsibility and Sustainability Committee comprising at least three Directors with one Independent Director. CSR and Sustainability Policy of the company was framed in consonance with the CSR Policy framework enshrined in the section-135 of Companies Act, 2013 (Act) and in accordance with the DPE Guidelines, 2014 that are effective from 1st April, 2014. The policy aims to benefit of marginalized, disadvantaged, poor and deprived sections of the community and the environment.

A three-tier structure, i.e. Unit, Regional and Corporate Level is responsible for planning, implementation, monitoring and reporting on CSR and Sustainability projects. Some of the major CSR activates undertaken by the company included the following:

Education

Considering education as a unique present investment for future, the company spends up to 20 per cent of its CSR provision for it. It is running 48 schools with proper infrastructure in the peripheral locations of its plants which is benefiting about 20,000 students. Solar Lamps are distributed to meritorious school students in order to motivate them and also to create awareness about non-conventional energy.

It supported technical studies in the polytechnic at Kaladungi in Uttarakhand. Construction of classrooms and installation of Solar Street lights at SadhanaVidyalaya, Kannamangala village in Karnataka, provision of equipments to underprivileged children in Kathashala, at Govindpuri in New Delhi, "Awakening India" by Ramakrishna Mission, and Cluster Innovation Centre (CIC) of Delhi University were supported by the Company under its CSR initiative.

The company also took initiative of construction of toilets for girls in the primary schools for supporting education and reducing drop-outs for girls. It supported Jyoti Foundation, Dehradun by providing scholarship to meritorious students for pursuing professional courses. It partnered with Food Relief Foundation of ISKCON for providing Mid-Day meal to underprivileged school students in the National Capital Region. It supported infrastructure in Schools giving attention to female, adults, running coaching providing Scholarships, Study material and uniforms etc. to deserving students and personality development programmes.

Health

Setting up of basic infrastructure for health, sanitation and hygiene was supported under its CSR in the neighbouring areas, which benefitted to over 1 lakh persons. The Hospitals and dispensaries of the company set up in the townships provided medical care and facilities to the villagers living nearby. Further, its Mobile Health Clinics provided healthcare facility to more than 60,000 persons[3] belonging to underprivileged sections of society at their doorsteps in 80 villages.

About 1200 Medical Health check-up Camps and 365 Eye camps were organized in which about 2000 surgeries were performed. The Company also provided financial assistance to Impact India Foundation for the "Lifeline Express Project" (camp) at Dalmau Railway station in Raebareli district, U.P. for providing general treatment and surgical operations to poor people. It supported the District Hospital, Aurangabad, Bihar in getting medical equipments for modular ICU. Directly Observed Treatment-*cum*-Designated Microscopy Centre (DOTs-*cum*-DMC) with Mobile ambulance facilities was operated at 12 NTPC hospitals under Revised National Tuberculosis Control Programme (RNCTP) which supported about 5000 patients.

Under the *'Swachh Vidyalaya Abhiyaan'*, launched by Hon'ble Prime Minister, the Company constructed more than 24,000 toilets in schools.[4]

It organized 100 Animal Health Camps and provided animal health related facilities to villages located nearby its units. NTPC along with South Eastern Coalfields Limited (SECL) has decided to set up a medical college and hospital in Chhattisgarh with a financial assistance of Rs. 100 crores each.

Skill Development[5]

It has set up a multi-skill centre at NTPC Talcher, Kaniha to impart vocational skills in the areas of retail Information Technology (IT) enabled services and telecom with focus on employability. The Company has signed a MoU with Ministry of Skill Development and Entrepreneurship for skill development projects to be implemented in collaboration with National Skill Development Corporation (NSDC) and National Skill Development Fund (NSDF).

It has set up Indian Institute of Information Technology (IIIT) at Naya Raipur in Chhattisgarh for developing professionals. It has set up "Labs on wheels" on vehicle fitted with LCD TV for imparting science education based on models hands-on learning to the underprivileged children. Each Mobile Science Lab will cover a set of about 20 schools and benefit about 1.50 lakh students.

More than 2500 women were trained in various vocational courses. Tool kits and sewing machines were provided to 300 women after training.

For empowering Physically Challenged and Economically weaker section of the society, an Information and Communication Technology (ICT) centre was established at Delhi University. It supported four Government Blind Schools at Ajmer, Lucknow, Thiruvanthapuram and

Mysore, and set up ICT Centre at Guwahati University and Devi Ahilya Vishwavidyalaya, Indore during 2013-14.

2014-15[6]

Average annual net profit of the company in the last three financial years was Rs. 14,173.78 crore, two per cent of which came to Rs. 283.48 crore to be spent on CSR activities during the year.

The company has disclosed an expenditure of Rs. 205.18 crore on various CSR activities during the year. Major CSR activities undertaken included education, conservation of heritage, renewable energy, vocational training and capacity building, health and sanitation, provision of safe drinking water, promotion of sports and culture etc. at different locations across the country including corporate centre and other national level activities at a cost of Rs. 33.68 crore, Sonebhadra district at a cost of Rs. 16.51 crore, Vishakhapatnam district at a cost of Rs. 14.55 crore, Angul district at a cost of Rs. 14.12 crore, Bilaspur district at a cost of Rs. 10.39 crore, Korba district at a cost of Rs. 10.73 crore, Singrauli district at a cost of Rs. 9.68 crore, Karimnagar district at a cost of Rs. 8.66 crore etc.

Rs. 78.30 crore remain as unspent amount on CSR head as the year being the first year after the Section 135 of the Companies Act, 2013 came into force w.e.f. 01.04.2014, formulating new policy, putting new systems and procedures into place and mobilizing additional resources have taken substantial part of the year after receiving clarification in June, 2014. Also directive from the Administrative Ministry was received in October, 2014 regarding construction of 24,000 toilets in schools across 17 states. Surveying the locations, finalizing the sites in consultation with local authorities has taken considerable time.

2015-16[7]

Average annual net profit of the company in last three financial years was Rs. 13,567.43 crore, two per cent of which came to Rs. 271.35 crore to be spent on CSR activities. Inclusion of unspent amount of Rs. 78.30 crore of the previous year makes the total amount Rs. 349.65 crore to be spent on CSR activities during the year.

The company has disclosed an expenditure of Rs. 491.80 crore on various CSR activities during the year. Major CSR activities undertaken included *Swachh Vidyalaya Abhiyan* (Rs. 278.70 crore) education and skill development (Rs. 54.49 crore), rural development (Rs. 44.21 crore), healthcare and sanitation (Rs. 39.76 crore), protection of environment (Rs. 33.85 crore).

Financial Parameters

Analysis of the financial parameters including expenditure on CSR (given in **Table 14.1**) indicates that the turnover of the company went up during 2011-12 to 2014-15 but fell marginally during 2015-16. Profit before tax of the company increased during 2012-13 but fell in subsequent years. Expenditure on CSR activities increased substantially from Rs. 69.24 crore in 2012-13 to Rs. 109.77 crore during 2013-14. During 2014-15, Rs. 205.18 crore was spent against the mandated requirement of Rs. 283.48 crore which amounted to 1.44 per cent against statutory obligation of two per cent. During 2015-16, expenditure on CSR activities increased substantially to Rs. 491.18 crore, which was 3.6 per cent of the mandated requirement.

Table 14.1: CSR Expenditure with Reference to Turnover/Profit of NTPC, during 2011-12 to 2015-16

Sl. No.	*Subject*	*2011-12*	*2012-13*	*2013-14*	*2014-15*	*2015-16*
1.	Turnover (in Rs. Crore)	62,480.88	66,200.24	72,644.02	73,915.69	71,236.00
2.	Profit before tax	12,326.16	16,578.63	13,904.65	10,546.65	10,058.67
3.	Net average profit of three preceding years (in Rs. Crore)				14,173.78	13,676.64
4.	CSR obligation 2% of average profit of three preceding years				283.48	273.53
5.	Expenditure incurred on CSR (in Rs. Crore)	N.A.	69.24	109.77	205.18	491.80

Source: Annual Reports 2012-13, p. 35; 2013-14, p. 35; 2014-15, p. 39; 2015-16, CSR amount spent Rs. 491.80 crore included Rs.78.30 crore for FY 2014-15, p. 39.

Endnotes

NTPC is one of the leading central public sector undertakings dealing with generation of thermal power. It appears that CSR activities of the company increased from 2012-13 onwards initially due to instruction of the Department of Public Enterprises and subsequently following CSR being made mandatory. The company implemented its CSR activities on health, education, sanitation, skill development activities. Its CSR activities can play an important role by empowering the disadvantaged segments in the coal mining areas, which provides the feedstock for its plants. In this context, working with the ongoing plans and programmes of the government and filling the gaps on last mile connectivity basis along with mobilization of corporate voluntarism can add value to CSR. On the environment side, as the company is consuming coal for generating power, taking up plantation activities in the denuded hills in an organized manner and promoting solar energy on a large scale would make the CSR interventions meaningful.

References

1. Press Information Bureau, GoI, Ministry of Power dated 15 April, 2015.
2. http://www.ntpc.co.in/en/corporate-citizenship/corporate-social-responsibility.
3. NTPC's 38th Annual Report 2013-2014.
4. Chairman's address in the 39th Annual General meeting held on dated 18th September, 2015.
5. *Ibid.*
6. http://www.ntpc.co.in/annual-reports/4340/download-complete-annual-report-2014-15 ANNEXURE-VII to Directors' Report.
7. http://www.ntpc.co.in/annual-reports/6304/download-complete-annual-report-2015-16, ANNEXURE-VII to Directors' Report.

NATIONAL BUILDING CONSTRUCTIONS CORPORATION LIMITED (NBCC)

NBCC was incorporated in 1960 as a wholly owned Government of India undertaking under the Ministry of Urban Development[1] for undertaking Civil Engineering Construction Projects of varied nature. The Company's areas of operations broadly falls under three main segments, i.e. (i) Project Management Consultancy (PMC), (ii) Real Estate Development, and (iii) EPC Contracting. Over years, it has expanded its activities within the country and abroad and emerged as a schedule 'A' companies with 'Navratna' Status.

Commitment of the company to social obligations is reflected in its vision *"to establish itself as a responsible corporate entity conscious of its social responsibilities to all stakeholders including the Government, clientele, shareholders, employees, local community and society at large."* It has a CSR Policy which aims at socio-economic development and ensuring that benefits reach the targeted beneficiaries, with emphasis on dissemination of information and knowledge and counselling amongst rural populace. It also seems to empower them to avail benefits of Government Schemes.

NBCC was renamed as the NBCC (India) Limited and has emerged as a leading public sector undertaking dealing with construction related activities.

CSR Vision of the company seeks to establish itself and fulfil its role as a socially responsible corporate entity. To act in a socially responsible manner to contribute to the socio-economic development of the communities we operate in, by building stronger, developed, sustainable communities and raise the quality of life of the people of the country.

CSR Mission of the company seeks to undertake holistic development initiatives/projects in the community at large, to take up CSR projects in the area of quality education, skill development and livelihoods, healthcare, infrastructural development in rural areas, training and awareness, employee sensitization towards CSR, etc. to improve the quality of life and standard of living of the rural populace as first priority. NBCC will act as a good Corporate Citizen, subscribing to the ten principles of United Nations Global Compact for implementation.

Some of the CSR activities[2] undertaken by the company relates to:

- Skill and entrepreneurship training programme in domestic data entry operations for 150 young people through Sahaj e-Village Limited. One of the students, Ms. Hina Khan, trained by Sahaj e-Village in Bahraich has started her own business.

- It is running a merit-*cum*-means scholarship scheme for meritorious girls in Bihar and Mizoram with financial assistance of Rs. 500 per month for 1050 students (50 each).
- It is going to construct 100 toilets on a pan-India basis with an outlay of Rs. 5 crore.

Skill and Entrepreneurship Development Programmes

As a part of its CSR activity, NBCC is running "Skill and Entrepreneurship Development Programme" with a view to generate employment and develop entrepreneurship for benefit of the unemployed educated youth.

The training is imparted through reputed agencies such as M/s GRAS Education and Training Services Pvt. Ltd., M/s Centum Work skills, M/s Calance Software Pvt. Ltd., M/s Sahaj e-Village Limited. As it is the skill level achieved through training which determines the productivity as well as ability to adapt to the changing industrial environment.

Unemployed youth from disadvantaged segment of the society are being trained in Data Entry Operation, Retail Operation, Site Accounting (Tally), and Electrician etc. As per the data available, the company has trained to about 750 youth in their various training and skill enhancement programmes during 2012-15.

Merit-cum-Means Scholarship Scheme

It is providing Merit-*cum*-Means Scholarship to meritorious girls from the underprivileged families. Scholarship at the rate of Rs. 500 per month was given to students studying in standard VI to XII and 300 meritorious girls in Bihar, Mizoram, Uttarakhand and Delhi were assisted during 2011-12.

The company signed an MoU with M/s Shrimati Pushpawati Loomba Memorial Foundation, an NGO working for widows and provided Rs.6.00 lacs as scholarships to the poor children of widows for continuing studies.

Development of Infrastructure

The company took up a survey in the Sawai Madhopur District of Rajasthan to identify the need and requirement of the rural poor. On the basis of Baseline Survey[3] and discussions with Local Authorities, Dispensaries were set up in the Chhan, Barod, Bahrawada Kalan villages. Besides One school Building was constructed at Meikalan during 2013-14. The company constructed bus stands at a cost of Rs. 18.50 lakhs.

Partner to Total Sanitation Campaign of Government of India

The company joined the Government in support of Right to Education and Total Sanitation Campaign and set up 24 toilet blocks in Tripura, Mizoram, J&K and Gujarat. It took up introduction of new technology based Bio-digester Toilets at Balmiki Basti, Mandir Marg, New Delhi, which was inaugurated by the Hon'ble Prime Minister of India, Mr. Narendra Modi. During 2014-15, it spent Rs. 9.91 lakh for construction of toilets in schools. It has also signed a Memorandum of Understanding with *Smt. Pushpawati Loomba Memorial Foundation,* an NGO working for widows, to carry out the programme of construction of school toilets.

Rehabilitation of Earthquake Victims in Sikkim

The company joined in rehabilitation of earthquake affected families of Sikkim by providing low cost houses. Each house with a minimum area of 48.54 sq.m. was taken up at a cost of Rs. 15 lakhs per house. The structure has been designed to withstand natural calamities and provide adequate space for livelihood to the affected families.

The company got "Excellent" rating from MoUD for each of the Fiscal years from 2004 to 2010 and also with an "Excellence Award" from Ministry of Heavy Industries and Public Enterprises.

CSR Policy and CSR Committee[4]

As per provision under Section 135 of the Companies Act, 2013, a **CSR Committee** is constituted for monitoring implementation of the CSR projects and submitting its recommendations to the Board of Directors periodically.

The **CSR Policy** was prepared and approved by the Board of Directors on 13.08.2014, salient features of which envisages to:

- Covers all the project enumerated in Schedule VII of Companies Act, 2013.
- All the Proposal/Requests should come through the District Administration/District Authorities in prescribed formats.

- The proposals are recommended by the Board Level CSR Committee and approved by the Board of Directors of NBCC for implementation.
- After Implementation, Mid-term/Impact Assessment by Third Party is carried out.

2014-15[5]

The company had an average annual net profit of Rs. 214.93. crore for the last three financial years. Based on prescribed CSR guidelines, the company is to spend 2 per cent of the net profit amounting to Rs. 4.30 crore.

NBCC has disclosed an expenditure of Rs. 4.35 crore during the year for undertaking number of activities including the following:

- Construction of two number of dispensaries and school in Sawai Madhopur, Rajasthan at a cost of Rs. 2.56 crore.
- Construction of biodigester toilets in Uttar Pradesh and Rajasthan at a cost of Rs. 46.5 lakh.
- Skill development in EDC Bawana, Delhi at a cost of Rs. 11.9 lakh and in Barrage, Uttar Pradesh at a cost of Rs. 10.29 lakh.
- Rainwater harvesting in Gurgaon at a cost of Rs. 23.6 lakh.

2015-16[6]

The company had Rs. 243.97 crores as average annual profit in the last three financial years, two per cent of which amounting to Rs. 4.87 crores was to be spent on CSR activities during the year.

NBCC has disclosed that Rs. 8.70 crores was spent during the year, which included Rs. 4.31 crores on the ongoing CSR projects of previous financial years and Rs. 4.39 crores on the projects taken up/completed during financial year 2015-16. Some of the major projects undertaken included the following:

(i) Construction of community and public toilets in Delhi at a cost of Rs. 3.6 crore.
(ii) Construction of 92 bio digester toilets in schools at a cost of Rs. 4.06 crore in Uttar Pradesh, Rajasthan, West Bengal, Uttarakhand, Assam and Tripura.
(iii) Skill development at project site at a cost of Rs. 30.17 lakh,

supply of appliances to physically challenged through ALIMCO at a cost of Rs. 24.64 lakh.

In recognition of its work in the field of sanitation, NBCC was conferred with the *Swachh Bharat Ratna Award*-2015.

Financial Details[7]

From the financial parameters and expenditure on CSR of the company (given in the **Table 15.1**), it appears that turnover and profit of the company have gone up continuously during the period from 2011-12 to 2015-16. However, expenditure on CSR activities fell from Rs. 2.21 crores in 2011-12 to Rs. 1.83 crores in 2012-13, but increased substantially to Rs. 5.75 crore during 2013-14. In 2014-15, the expenditure on CSR activities got reduced to Rs. 4.35 crore. However, expenditure on CSR activities increased substantially to Rs. 8.70 crore during 2015-16, which accounted to 3.56 per cent of the net average profit of three preceding years.

Table 15.1: CSR Expenditure of NBCC with Reference to Turnover/Profit of NBCC during 2011-12 to 2015-16

Sl. No.	*Subject*	*2011-12*	*2012-13*	*2013-14*	*2014-15*	*2015-16*
1.	Turnover (in Rs. Crore)	15,016.15	16,490.73	4,008.77	4,360.97	5,749.23
2.	Profit before tax (in Rs. Crore)	289.83	301.64	333.52	391.01	436.21
3.	*Net average profit of three preceding years (in Rs. Crore)				214.93	243.98
4.	CSR obligation 2% of average profit of three preceding years				4.30	4.88
5.	Expenditure incurred on CSR (in Rs. Crore)	2.21	1.83	5.75	4.35	8.71
6.	Expenditure as percentage of Profit (in %age)	1.16%	0.88%	2.33%	1.57%	2.82%
7.	*CSR Expenditure as percent-tage of average Profit of preceding three years (in %age)				2.03%	3.57%

Sources: Annual Report 2011-12, p. 47; 2012-13, p. 72; 2013-14, p. 72; 2014-15, p. 70; 2015-16, p. 73 and Annual Report on CSR.

Substantial increase in expenditure in CSR activities during 2013-14 may be due to the instructions of the Department of Public Enterprises. Reduction, both in absolute term and as percentage of profit during 2014-15, after CSR was made mandatory, appeared to be rather unusual. However, the position changed during 2015-16 when CSR activities increased substantially. It appears that the company has taken up sanitation along with education, skill and healthcare related activities under its CSR activities.

Endnotes

NBCC (India) Limited has emerged as a leading central Public Sector Undertaking engaged with construction related activities. Construction sector, both in public and private, is an important economic activity and offers lot of scope for productive employment to the youth, which is one of the major areas of concern of the society. Imparting skill development training in the construction related trades namely carpentry, masonry, electrician, rod binding etc. will make the CSR activities more meaningful, in solving the problem of unemployment particularly among the relatively less educated to a considerable extent. Working with the *Skill India* initiative of the government, mobilizing volunteerism of the executive and staff and promoting Start-up for undertaking quality construction are areas worth looking into, as these will not only help the unemployed youth in getting employment but also in improving quality of the construction with the skilled labour and completion of the projects in time.

References

1. Previously Known as Ministry of Works, Housing & Supply (MoWHS).
2. Central Public Sector Enterprises "*Transforming lives through CSR*", Confederation of Indian Industry, September 2015, pp. 111-114.
3. The survey was undertaken by Tata Institute of Social Sciences in 30 villages of Tehsil Khandar.
4. Information received vide letter dated July 15, 2015.
5. http://www.nbccindia.com/nbccindia/nroot/pdfdata/AnnualReports/2014-2015/NBCC_ANNUAL_REPORT_2014_15.pdf, pp. 67-72.
6. http://www.nbccindia.com/nbccindia/nroot/pdfdata/AnnualReports/2015-2016/56th%20Annual%20Report%202015-16.pdf, pp. 68-75.
7. Letter no. NBCC/CSR/2015/915 dated 10.06.2015.

INFOSYS LIMITED

Infosys is one of the leading Information Technology (IT) Company of Indian origin, which has spread its wings all-over the world. Set up and guided under the able leadership of N.R. Narayan Murthy from a humble beginning it has been one of the most successful Indian companies in the field of IT services. With view to meet the challenges of technological development, Infosys[1] is committed to it is no longer adequate to simply meet expectations—we have to exceed it every time, and in every way. From delivery, to sales, consulting, operations, and each and every business enabling function—from people, to processes, infrastructure and systems—the company seek to bring about change that addresses the new reality of a pervasively digital and interconnected world based on innovation and continuous improvement. Along with its commercial activities, it has taken up Corporate Social Responsibility (CSR) initiatives in a meaningful manner under the able leadership and keen and close interest of its mentor.

Infosys set up a CSR committee with four members headed by Shri K.V. Kamath. It has adopted a CSR policy and set up Infosys Foundation for undertaking CSR initiatives with focus on supporting projects in eradication of hunger and malnutrition, promoting education, art and culture, healthcare, destitute care and rehabilitation, environmental sustainability, disaster relief and rural development projects. The CSR activities are undertaken through its own foundations and other Non-Governmental Organizations.

Infosys Foundation

The company established the Infosys Foundation in 1996 as a not-for-profit trust for social welfare activities. Over years, it has grown as a pioneer and guide in implementing programmes in the areas of healthcare, education, hunger eradication, rural development, disaster relief, arts and culture, and destitute care across India. In the year 2015-16, the Foundation's work included setting up of a *Centre for Artificial Intelligence* at the Indraprastha Institute of Information Technology, Delhi, help in rebuilding communities in calamity-hit Visakhapatnam and flood-affected Chennai, aid in building toilets in schools in Odisha, conservation of the endangered Olive Ridley turtles and partnership with *Bharatiya Vidya Bhavan* in 11 states to promote underprivileged artists. The Foundation also supported the construction of water facility and enclosures for animals at the Bannerghatta National Park in Bangalore, and efforts to conserve India's vast medical heritage.

Infosys Foundation USA

Infosys Foundation USA took on a leadership role in supporting and expanding access to Computer Science (CS) and Maker education across the U.S., especially in underrepresented and underserved communities. In fiscal 2016, as part of its mission to prepare students for an increasingly digital future, Infosys Foundation USA engaged and invested in CS and Maker-related programmes in CS professional development, CS teacher support, CS diversity and Making, Research and curriculum development.

Infosys Science Foundation

The Infosys Science Foundation (ISF) was set up by Infosys in 2009 to encourage the pursuit and practice of the sciences. The Infosys Prize, governed by the ISF, recognizes some of the finest research connected to India. The prize winners are awarded a purse of Rs. 65 lakh (tax-free in India) and a citation by a jury of global renown across six different fields in India and abroad. The winners were felicitated by the President of India, Pranab Mukherjee, in a ceremony in New Delhi on February 13, 2016. The winners of the Infosys Prize serve as role models for young researchers and scholars. Jurors and winners of the prize give public talks around the country under the Infosys Science Foundation Lectures, to talk about their work and instil a love for science and research among young students.

The ACM—Infosys Foundation Award

The Association for Computing Machinery (ACM), and the Infosys Foundation award set up in 2007 recognizes the finest recent innovations by young scientists and system developers in the computing field each year.

2014-15[2]

In the preceding three years, the company made an average net profit of Rs. 12,133 crore, 2 per cent of which Rs. 243 crores was to be spent on CSR. Against this, the company has disclosed to have spent Rs. 239.54

crores on CSR during the year and that the balance amount of Rs. 3.46 crore were meant for projects under implementation. That this amount was booked as spent in April 2015 upon receiving the pending documents.

Some of the major CSR activities taken during the year relate to contribution to *Akshaya Patra Foundation* (Rs. 36.83 crore) for eradicating malnutrition and hunger, for improving quality of education through Chennai Mathematical Institute (Rs. 33.25 crore), rural development, malnutrition and hunger eradication, healthcare and medical facilities, improving quality of education through Ramakrishna Mission (Rs. 26.03 crore), improving quality of education through Indian Institute of Science (Rs. 21.20 crore), Infosys Science Foundation (Rs. 20.99 crore) and Spark IT programme (Rs. 15.59 crore), healthcare and medical facilities through Public Health Foundation (Rs. 10.00 crore) and improving quality of education, destitute care and rehabilitation through International Institute of Information Technology, Bangaluru (Rs. 6.60 crore).

2015-16[3]

In the preceding three years, the company made an average net profit of Rs. 12,800 crore, 2 per cent of which comes to Rs. 256.01 crore. Against this Rs. 202.3 crore was spent on CSR activities during the year.

Some of the major expenditure on CSR during the year relates to eradication of malnutrition and hunger (Rs. 15.64 crore) through *Akshaya Patra Foundation*, improving quality education (Rs. 15.00 crore) through Ramakrishna Mission, improving healthcare and medical education (Rs. 12.77 crore) through *Swachh Bharat Mission*, Hud Hud Cyclone relief (Rs. 12.35 crore) and destitute care and rehabilitation/ disaster relief in Chennai (Rs. 12.10 crore). It has been disclosed that the balance amount is meant for improving quality of education through International Institute of Information Technology, Bangalore, taking care of the destitute and rehabilitation by Khushi Trust and Spark IT Programme, Raichur and workshop through destitute care and rehabilitation.

Financial Parameters are given in Table 16.1.

Impact Assessment

As per a study[4] of some of the best practices, CSR interventions of the

Table 16.1: CSR Expenditure of INFOSYS with reference to turnover, profit during 2014-15 and 2015-16

Sl. No.	*Subjects*	*2014-15*	*2015-16*
1.	Turnover (in Rs. Crore)	47,300.00	53,983.00
2.	Profit before tax (in Rs. Crore)	16,798.00	20,693.00
3.	Net average profit of three preceding years (in Rs. Crore)	12,133.00	12,800.00
4.	CSR obligation 2% of average profit of three preceding years	242.66	256.00
5.	Expenditure incurred on CSR (in Rs. Crore)	239.54	202.30

Source: Annual Report 2014-15, p. 50; 2015-16, p. 56.

Infosys group through its Infosys Foundation set up in 1996, has been noteworthy in the traditional areas like education, healthcare, art and culture, destitute care, rural development as well as new areas *viz.* creation of ecosystem for spread of science, technology, engineering and mathematics (STEM), forging alliance with International Mathematics Union, the New York Academy of Science and in the field of renewable energy.

Endnote

Infosys, one of the leading IT companies, has scaled great heights and created a name due to untiring efforts of its mentor Shri Narayana Murthy. In addition to emerging as a giant corporate in the IT sector, maintaining high standards and commitment to ethics, it has taken up series of CSR activities through Infosys Foundation. It has given preference to improving the quality of education and nursing young talents. Provision of nutritious meals in collaboration with the *Akshaya Patra Foundation* is another important intervention which has been effective in solving the problem of malnutrition and hunger. Rural development, education and healthcare interventions through the Ramakrishna Mission, popularisation of science education through Indian Institute of Science, Infosys Science Foundation and Spark IT programme provide lessons for other corporate in using CSR as an effective tool in development of the country.

References

1. https://www.infosys.com/investors/reports-filings/annual-report/annual/

Documents/infosys-AR-16.pdf, p. 41; CSR, pp. 69-73, Annual Report 2015-16.

2. https://www.infosys.com/investors/reports-filings/annual-report/annual/Documents/infosys-AR-15.pdf, CSR, pp. 64-66. Annual Report 2014-15.
3. https://www.infosys.com/investors/reports-filings/annual-report/annual/Documents/infosys-AR-16.pdf, p. 41, CSR, pp. 69-73, Annual Report 2015-16.
4. *The Economic Times*, September 15, 2016, p. 14.

RELIANCE INDUSTRIES LIMITED (RIL)[1]

Reliance Industries Limited (RIL) is one of the largest private sector companies of India and a major global player in the integrated energy value chain. It has a growing presence in the retail and digital services in India. Built on strong values, RIL is steadfastly rooted in the culture of safety, integrity and commitment. The Company's vision is to create value for the nation, enhance quality of life across the entire socio-economic spectrum and build an inclusive India. Reliance endeavours to create replicable and scalable models of development through an integrated approach and maximising societal value for all to create value for its stakeholders and society.

RIL set up a 4 member Corporate Social Responsibility and Governance Committee[2] (CSR&G Committee) including two independent directors. The Board level Committee meet at least twice a year to review the implementation of CSR programmes/activities of the Company.

The committee formulated and recommended, a Corporate Social Responsibility (CSR) Policy indicating the activities to be undertaken by the Company, which was approved by the Board.[3] The key philosophy of all CSR initiatives of the Company is guided by three core commitments of Scale, Impact and Sustainability and has identified six focus areas of engagement, namely (i) Rural Transformation: Creating sustainable livelihood solutions, addressing poverty, hunger and malnutrition; (ii) Health: Affordable solutions for healthcare through improved access, awareness and health seeking behaviour; (iii) Education: Access to quality education, training and skill enhancement; (iv) Environment: Environmental sustainability, ecological balance, conservation of natural resources; (v) Protection of National Heritage, Art and Culture: Protection and promotion of India's art, culture and heritage; and (vi) Disaster Response: Managing and responding to disaster.

Reliance's CSR policy aimed at improving lives, living and livelihood for a stronger and inclusive India, covering five areas, as indicated below:

Health

Reliance provides affordable solutions for quality healthcare through improved access to healthcare services and spreading awareness. The outcomes of healthcare related initiatives include providing access to quality primary and secondary care services to the deprived population, conducting need-based health camps and providing consultation and medicine, amongst others. Efforts have been made to ensure better maternal and child healthcare services and improve delivery through innovative research programmes. Through the *Drishti* programme, Reliance has worked with the visually impaired.

Education

Reliance seeks to provide quality education, training and skill enhancement to improve the quality of living and livelihood. The Company focusses on promoting primary and secondary education, enabling higher education through scholarships, promoting higher education through setting up and supporting universities and skill development through vocational training.

Sports for Development

Reliance focusses on using sports as a medium to encourage learning and inculcate leadership amongst the youth. The programme uses sports and activities as a tool for development to bring about positive change. Under this initiative, talented young students are groomed further to build their skills in sports.

Disaster Response

Reliance works towards organising timely relief and rehabilitation of communities affected by natural calamities. Efforts are also made to build capacities of local communities to cope with disasters and develop expertise and resources to respond to it in a timely manner.

Arts, Culture and Heritage

The initiative towards protecting Indian Arts, Culture and Heritage is aimed at supporting and promoting artists and craftsmen, preserving traditional art and handicraft and documenting India's rich heritage for the benefit of future generations.

All along, Leveraging of technology for creating a multiplier effect is stressed under CSR for the socio-economic development of the marginalised communities. Reliance's approach to social development is aligned to the broad dimensions of sustainability, namely (i) Planet: Water harvesting and conservation, provision of clean drinking water, energy conservation, environment protection and cleanliness; (ii) People: Providing access to quality education, scholarship opportunities for pursuing higher education, promoting skills in sports, ensuring access to quality healthcare including maternal and child health services, and improving food and nutrition security; (iii) Products and Processes: Process improvements through technology and innovations for optimal outcomes; (iv) Prosperity: Promoting sustainable agricultural practices, skill building for alternative livelihoods, employment and income generation; (v) Disaster relief to mitigate human suffering during natural calamity; and (vi) Peace and Partnerships: Aligning with organisations and governments for synergistic efforts for larger impact.

Reliance Foundation (RF)

Reliance Foundation (RF) was set up as the CSR arm of the company in 2010 with the objective to create and support meaningful activities through innovative institutions to address some of the pressing developmental challenges of India. The Foundation is working with focus on (i) health, (ii) education, (iii) rural transformation, (iv) development of the arts and culture along with (v) disaster relief.[4]

Education related activities accounted for 45 per cent of the total CSR budget in 2010. However, in 2014-15 healthcare became the main activity with 80 per cent of total expenditure. It supported a wide range of activities from free eye surgeries and HIV/AIDS treatment to mobile medical units providing healthcare to people at their doorstep. Sir HN Reliance Foundation Hospital and Research Centre and the Dhirubhai Ambani International School are two major institutions set up by the company.

The Foundation activities reported to have touched the lives of more than four million people living in over 5,500 villages and urban locations including some of the remotest villages. The Foundation provided water in 50 villages such as Sakpa in Gangakhed cluster, Parbhani district in Maharashtra, which have been hit by severe drought. It has built 7,368 farm ponds and renovated 2,000 ponds to solve the water woes of villages. It encouraged formation of 519 Village Farmers' Associations (VFAs) for managing the assets on a sustainable basis.

It mobilised and supported 15 number of the Village Farmers Associations (VFAs) of Jalara, a water-starved village in Madhya Pradesh, to build a lake at a cost of Rs. 54 lakhs which provided water to about 200 households of the village. It also supported villagers of Bhanpura,

Madhya Pradesh with Jatropha plantation for biodiesel making and power generation and getting water supply which helped in promoting environment and green technology.

Activities of the Foundation are summed up by Ms. Nita Ambani, founder and Chairperson of RF, "It is all about a mindset change. You can do a lot of good even if you don't have a lot of wealth. But when you have the wealth, it helps you to do better. And wherever there is a need, we would."

2014-15[5]

Average annual net profit of the company in the last three financial years was Rs. 26,648 crore, two per cent of which came to Rs. 532.96 crore to be spent on CSR activities during the year.

The company has disclosed an expenditure of Rs. 760.58 crore on various CSR activities during the year, which included Rs. 101.69 crore for eradicating hunger, malnutrition, environmental sustainability and rural development projects through Reliance Foundation "Bharat India Judo Initiative" enhancing rural livelihood project, Rs. 9.65 crore for eradicating hunger, poverty and malnutrition through enable access to need based specific content in agriculture, fisheries, public health, disaster response, Rs. 3.14 crore for static and mobile medical units and organizing camps for primary and preventive healthcare, Rs. 1.28 crore for cornea transplantation and other activities for visually impaired, Rs. 1.5 crore for autism project, Rs. 24.25 crore to develop innovative technology which will help trained medical students and clinicians for better diagnosis, Rs. 5.5 crore for health partnership with non-governmental organizations, Rs. 7.07 crore for disaster relief, Rs. 4.01 crore for scholarship, Rs. 4.06 crore for promoting sports and education, Rs. 553.89 crore for HN Reliance Foundation Hospital and Research Centre on manufacturing location, Rs. 1.88 crore for community development, Rs. 10.24 crore for promoting education etc.

2015-16[6]

Average annual net profit of the company in the last three financial years was Rs. 27,889 crore, two per cent of which came to Rs. 557.78 crore to be spent on CSR activities during the year.

The company has disclosed an expenditure of Rs. 651.57 crore on various CSR activities during the year. Major CSR activities undertaken included healthcare at a cost of Rs. Rs. 314 crore, rural transformation at a cost of Rs. 104 crore, education at a cost of Rs. 215 crore etc.

It is indicated that CSR activities of the company touched lives of over 6 million people so far including more than 19 lakh farmers and fisher folks living in over 10,500 villages across 14 States and 2 Union Territories. Some of the major works undertaken related to following:

Mission Zero Malnourishment Project

With a view to minimise malnourishment among children in 22 villages in Nagothane, Mizoram; paediatric check-ups, medication and nutritious food support was provided to malnourished children, who in a period of 6 months became normal in the Phase I of the project. There is follow-up with workers and teachers to start Phase II of the project.

Similar intervention for abating malnourishment among children in urban slums was taken up in Mumbai and rural areas in several states with a focus on community ownership. Services provided include screening, medical check-up, medication, nutritional supplements as well as functional linkages with *anganwadi* and nutritional rehabilitation centres. 12,283 children covered in Mumbai have been screened under this initiative and severely and moderately malnourished children have shown 14 per cent and 49 per cent improvement rates, respectively. In Shahdol, 87.5 per cent of the 249 malnourished children have been linked to either nutritional rehabilitation centres or *anganwadi* centres, of which 21 per cent have shown improvement.

Skill Development Among Rural Youth

In line with the Skill India Campaign, the youth were provided with necessary skills to ensure employability. In a pilot programme, 100 youth were trained as retail assistants, of which 69 were employed. More than 1,000 students were provided functional English supplementary classes to enhance capacity in spoken and written English. Eleven stitching centres were set up for training women.

Other areas of interventions relate to supporting over 17,000 people to reach nutrition self-sufficiency, bringing 6,749 ha of land under improved cultivation practices, plantation of over 5.4 lakh saplings, creation of 103 lakh cubic metre of rainwater harvesting capacity, securing 107 villages secured for drinking water through sustainable rainwater harvesting initiatives, rehabilitation of 8 villages from tiger reserve forest

Environment, providing over 5 lakh health consultations to patients through Reliance managed hospitals, mobile and static medical units and various health camps, screening 8,480 women for anaemia of which over 3,165 diagnosed and received follow-up treatment for it and 12,283 children for malnutrition of which 1,459 received follow-up for malnutrition, Project ASMAN for improving maternal and child health outcomes Health, scholarships to over 687 meritorious students to pursue higher education.

Financial Parameters

From the available information on financial parameters (given in **Table 17.1**), it appears that the expenditure on CSR activities of the company has been substantial and remained higher than the two per cent statutory limit.

Table 17.1: CSR Expenditure with Reference to Turnover/Profit of RIL during 2013-14 to 2015-16

Sl. No.	*Item/Year*	*2013-14*	*2014-15*	*2015-16*
1.	Gross Revenue (In Rs. Crore)	4,01,302	3,40,814	2,51,241
2.	Profit After Tax (PAT) during the year*/average profit of last 3 years (In Rs. Crore)	21,984*	26,648	27,889
3.	Expenditure on CSR/Social investment programmes (In Rs. Crore)	712.28	760.58	651.57
4.	Expenditure on CSR as a %age of average profit of last 3 years (in percentage)	3.24*	2.85	2.33

Source: Annual report 2013-14, 2014-15, 2015-16.

Endnotes

RIL, the largest leading corporate of India, had undertaken CSR activities on a large scale even before it became mandatory. CSR activities covered a wide range of activities *viz.* education, healthcare, livelihood support, rural development, heritage conservation, environment and safety initiatives for the community with huge financial investment. Working in synergy with Government schemes for solving major national issues and mobilization of corporate voluntarism provide avenues for making its CSR interventions more effective and meaningful.

References

1. *"Reliance foundation-want to do good"*, Mint, October 16, 2015,
2. http://www.riil.in/pdf/csr_policy.pdf
3. CSR Policy http://www.ril.com/getattachment/d5fd70ef-e019-47e5-bb83-de2077874505/Corporate-Social-Responsibility-Policy.aspx
4. http://www.reliancefoundation.org
5. http://www.ril.com/ar2014-15/RIL%20AR%202014%20-15.pdf
6. http://www.ril.com/ar2014-15/directors-report.html, sl. no. 19, Annexure II.

THERMAX LIMITED

Thermax Limited's core activities relate to deals Power and Environment covering power generation, heating, cooling, renewable energy; and air pollution control, chemicals and water and waste water treatment; areas respectively. It is guided with a Vision "*To be a globally respected, high performance organisation, offering sustainable solutions in energy and environment*".

It set up *Thermax Social Initiative Foundation* (TSIF) in 2007 as its CSR arm to design and implement CSR programmes. TSIF, in partnership with Pune Municipal Corporation (PMC), started its work with focus on improving the quality of education. The interventions started in one school in 2007 and have grown covering over 2,100 students in six schools. In 2013, '*Leadership Institute for Teachers*' (LIFT) programme was launched for training teachers of English as well as Marathi medium municipal schools in the PMC area. Over 130 teachers from 40 schools have been covered under this making an impact on nearly 5,200 children. TSIF was later renamed as *Thermax Foundation (TF)* in 2015-16.

Thermax Limited set up a CSR committee with the Chairperson, one Director and two independent Directors as per provision of Section 135 of the Companies Act.

The CSR committee had formulated the CSR Policy[1], which has been adopted by the Board. The policy is based on the belief that in a society characterised by widening inequalities of income and opportunity, education is the single most powerful instrument of change that gives a child choices in life and enabling him to go out of the vicious cycle of poverty, which in turn transform the life trajectory of the family. Accordingly, the company is focussing on education of economically underprivileged children. Besides, it aims at addressing social discrimination through affirmative action, skill development and employability initiatives. The company lays specific emphasis on the involvement of its employees in implementing CSR activities.

As a part of its CSR intervention, the company supports deserving and credible NGOs doing quality work through evaluation and assessment of the need of the projects and extending help in increasing their impact. The credibility of NGO and people involved are assessed before funding a project. The activities are supported based on values, transparent and honest communications and collaborative decision making. Besides funding, the foundation also provides mental and strategic guidance for the projects funded on a continuous basis.

CSR Activities During the Year 2014-15[2]

The average net profit of the company in the three preceding financial years was Rs. 494 crores, two per cent of which, to be spent on CSR, came to Rs. 9.88 crore. Against this, the company contributed Rs. 9.96 crores to *TSIF*, which has reported an expenditure of Rs. 8.43 crores during the year. Some of the major activities undertaken relate to:

- Adoption and running of municipal schools Education in Pune (Rs. 4.24 crores);
- *Teach for India* (TFI) programme Education in Pune (Rs. 1.60 crores);
- Support to Residential school for orphans, street children, extremely impoverished tribal children Education West Bengal (Rs. 75 lakhs); and
- Support to Model residential school for blind girls Education Alandi Devachi, Pune (Rs. 50 lakhs).

CSR Activities During the Year 2015-16[3]

The average net profit in the preceding three financial years was Rs. 448.31 crore, two per cent of which came to Rs. 8.97 crore. Against this, the company reported to have contributed Rs. 9 crore to the *TF* for undertaking CSR activities. *TF* reported having spent Rs. 13.76 crore on CSR activities during the year, which includes the following major interventions:

- Adoption and running different municipal schools in Pune through Akanksha Foundation (Rs. 8.77 crore).
- Teach for India programme implemented through *Teach to Lead* organisation (Rs. 1.6 crore).
- Support to Residential school for urban street children and extremely impoverished tribal children through *Parivar Education Society* (Rs. 1.45 crore); and
- Support to Model Residential School for blind girls through the *National Federation for the Blind,* Maharashtra (Rs. 80 lakh).

Thermax Foundation in association with '*Umeed Foundation*' implemented "*Nanhe Kadam*" for childhood development in the Matoshri English Medium Schools for children from the local community. This pilot project with 135 children up to three years, aims to identify nutritional deficiencies in children and take corrective action at the initial stage itself so that by the time the children begin school, they are equipped for appropriate learning skill give specific attention to overcome nutritional deficiency to overcome stunting of the brain.

Being a Vidya Niketan School, KCTVN used to take students in 3rd standard through a test conducted by PMC School Board. Since the Vidya Niketan concept was discontinued from the academic year 2015-16, KCTVN has added grade 1 to its existing grades 3 to 10. It plans to add junior and senior KG in the coming years. The Foundation constructed two more floors in the school building to accommodate the additional numbers of students.

Thermax Foundation supported eight schools till 2016-17, which was scaled down to five schools in PMC area during 2016-17 on account of higher expenditure due to addition of another grade each year and reduction in funding, due to company's lowered profits and lower fund for foundation under CSR. Attempts were made to identify other corporate to fund the remaining three schools.

Under the Pune City Connect (PCC) intervention, the Foundation focussed on to improving the quality of education in municipal English medium as well as Marathi and Urdu medium schools, in collaboration with PMC and some other corporate and NGOs of the city. PCC has the ambitious and noble goal of reaching out to every municipal school in Pune by training the trainers and improving the quality of education within the next three years.

Keeping in view importance of trained teachers in improving quality of education, the foundation has supported leadership institution in Pune, where year-long professional development programmes are being organised for teachers of government and low income private schools. 224 teachers, about 80 per cent of the English medium school teachers, were trained under this programme.

"*Aakar*" initiative was taken up in 2016 in collaboration of the Integrated Child Development Services (ICDSs) scheme for strengthening non-formal, pre-school education benefitting about 50,000 children in 1,413 *anganwadis*.

Under corporate volunteerism programme, the company is encouraging its employees to *teach for India* for two years in the under-resourced schools.

The foundation has adopted *Jagriti School for Blind Girls*, functioning under the National Federation of the Blind, Maharashtra for imparting career oriented education and skill development.

The foundation in partnership with *Zensar Foundation*, Pune Municipal Corporation and the *Unnati Foundation* initiated *Unnati Skill Development Centre* in Pune in 2014. 270 youths in 13 batches have been trained and 192 trained youths have been placed in various companies, others have opted for higher studies.

Financial Details on CSR

Analysis of the expenditure made on CSR during 2014-15 and 2015-16 (details given in **Table 18.1**) indicated that the company has spent more than two per cent of its profit on CSR activities as required under the statute.

Table 18.1: Financial Parameters and Expenditure on CSR Activities of Thermax during 2014-15 and 2015-16

Sl. No.	*Subject*	*2014-15*	*2015-16*
1.	Total income (in Rs. Crore)	4719	4462
2.	Profit before tax (in Rs. Crore)	497	437
3.	*Net average profit of three preceding years (in Rs. Crore)	494	448.31
4.	Expenditure incurred on CSR (in Rs. Crore)	9.96	9
5.	CSR Expenditure as percentage of Profit (in %age)	2	2

Source: Annual Report 2014-15 and 2015-16.

Impact

Educational standards in eight schools of Municipal Corporation of Pune, adopted by the foundation under its CSR intervention, has seen noteworthy success[4] with hundred per cent students in the K.C. Thackeray Vidya Niketan English Medium School (KCTVN) having passed and those having distinction (scoring more than 75% mark) increasing from 22 per cent in 2012-13 to 77 per cent in 2015-16. Number of students selected for higher education with full scholarship in the *Azim Premji University* increased from 5 per cent in 2012-13 to 28 per cent in 2015-16. Achievements in respect of secondary schools, which were started in 2014-15, improved similarly with 98 per cent students passing, 30 per cent having distinction and 3 per cent getting full scholarship for higher studies. Emboldened by this success, steps have been initiated for imparting quality education for students of the backward *Mushahar* (traditional rat eaters) community in Bihar.

Endnotes

CSR initiatives of *Thermax Limited* during 2014-15 and 2015-16, provide following lessons:

- The company *focused on education and improving its quality of education* with students from lower socio-economic background studying in municipal and government schools as the targets group.
- In addition to the fund available under CSR, it is *mobilising support from other likeminded corporate.*
- Corporate *volunteerism of its executive and employees is being mobilised* for supporting the CSR activity.
- Its strategy is based on providing additional support in the existing schools *as the last-mile connectivity.* The activities are being *monitored objectively* based on the percentage of students, who have achieved distinction in various categories. The deployment of resources is being reviewed based on the progress of the activities.
- Even though financial resource deployed is relatively small (less than Rs. 10 crore per year); it is beyond doubt that *CSR initiatives taken up with commitment and sincerity* in collaboration with Government and Non-Governmental bodies can deliver the best and *bring value for the corporate* and the society in respect of funds spent on CSR. The strategy, objectivity and approach of this corporate to CSR provide rich lessons to others in making the interventions meaningful in achieving inclusive development.

References

1. thermaxglobal.CSRpolicy-2015.
2. thermaxglobal, 34th#annualreport. 2014-15 and CSR report. pp. 26-29.
3. thermaxglobal, 35th Annual Report-2015-16; pp. 44-49.
4. Utkarsh Majumdar, *et al.*, "Blending CSR with Responsible Growth", *The Economic Times*, 15th September, 2016, p. 14.

Appendix 3

CSR Initiatives of Associations of Corporate

Federation of Indian Chambers of Commerce and Industry (FICCI)

FICCI was set up in 1927 as an apex business organization of the corporate for inspiring economic nationalism as a political tool to fight against discriminatory economic policies. FICCI claims to promote quality, competitiveness, transparency, accountability among its member corporate, business-government-civil society partnership, spread ethics-based business practices and enhance the quality of life of the common people.

FICCI's involvement with CSR activities dates back to the pre-Independence period. Addressing[1] members of FICCI, Mahatma Gandhi had observed, "I cannot forget the services rendered by the commercial clans, but I want you to make Congress your own and we would willingly surrender the reins to you. The work can be better done by you. But if you decide to assume the reins, you can do so only on the condition that you should regard yourselves as trustees and servants of the poor, your commerce must be regularized for the benefit of the toiling millions".

With a view to promote CSR among its members, FICCI set up "FICCI-Socio-Economic Development Foundation (FICCI-SEDF)", as a not-for-profit body on 5th December, 1995. SEDF acts an institutionalized arrangement and provides guidance and assistance to the member corporate for implementation of welfare projects under CSR.

CSR Initiatives

FICCI-SEDF is acting as an implementing agency of the CSR programmes run by various corporate in adherence to the Companies (CSR), Rules 2014. It assists companies and other stakeholders to get an understanding on the trends and current practices of CSR in India. It aims at generating social consciousness among the member business houses, leading to a healthier and happier social environment.

It provides assistance for the implementation of programmes on provision of health services, elimination of child labour, training of health workers, improving conditions of primary health centres, running mobile health centres, sanitation etc. This could be well understood with the study of their ongoing and previous projects.[2]

In 2014, FICCI SEDF has collaborated with *Abbott India Limited* as the implementation partner for their CSR initiative for raising awareness and enabling the community to maintain a healthy and hygienic environment.

As to their previous projects, in partnership with *Population Services International (PSI), Y.R. Gaitonde Centre for AIDS Research and Education (YRGCARE), Karnataka Health Promotion Trust (KHPT) and The International Labour Organization (ILO)*, FICCI SEDF launched Project Connect (2006-11). Project Connect aimed at mobilizing companies to implement workplace HIV/AIDS programmes and policies and to support HIV/AIDS programmes for high risk informal workers/ communities through their commitment to corporate social responsibility. Also, in the year 2006-07, FICCI-SEDF's AHEAD (Action for Harnessing Employment Avenues for Disabled) Strategy focussed on enhancing the employability of persons with disabilities. FICCI-SEDF in partnership with *AADI* initiated JEEVIKA, a project, for enhancing employment and livelihood opportunities for persons with disabilities in the National Capital Region.

Further, with assistance from *Rajiv Gandhi Foundation*, it has launched Mobile AIDS Counselling Services Project, under which over 3 lakh people have been covered.

In the quest to increase the participation and recognition of the work done in the field of CSR, the FICCI also instituted 'Corporate Social Responsibility Award' India's first CSR award in 1999. The award acknowledges efforts of the companies which engage in CSR in a strategic and systematic manner and integrate it with their overall corporate strategy. Till 2013, a number of companies including HPCL, ITC Limited, Mahindra and Mahindra, Cairn India, SAIL, Tata Tea, Infosys, Tata Chemicals, HINDALCO, TISCO, TELCO, Lupin, Gujarat Ambuja Cement, etc. have been recognized for their exemplary work in the area of CSR.

In 2015, FICCI SEDF has collaborated with *Magma Fincorp Limited* to enable them in achieving their commitment to build and maintain 50 toilets, especially in girl's schools of Andhra Pradesh, Madhya Pradesh, Haryana and West Bengal in locations adjoining their factories. The intervention involves awareness generation programmes in close association with the local and national Government for large scale and long-term sustainable impact.

The foundation also collaborated with *The Bank of Tokyo-Mitsubishi UFJ, Ltd. (BTMU)* to enable them in achieving their commitment towards ensuring sanitation and hygiene through the "Swachh Bharat Swachh Vidyalaya" Campaign. Under the project, BTMU wishes to build and maintain 200 toilets, especially in girl's schools of Andhra Pradesh and adjoining areas, conduct awareness programmes and work closely with the local and national Government for large scale and long-term sustainable impact.

In 2016[3], FICCI has signed a MoU with the Government of Haryana at the "Call to Action"—*Beti Bachaon, Beti Padhao* event. As part of B3P initiative, FICCI would encourage its members to consider projects for the promotion of gender equality and women empowerment. Ministry of Rural Development in association with FICCI-SEDF organized a seminar at Pravasi Bharatiya Kendra, New Delhi for providing CSR opportunities in the domains namely watershed management, marketing of self-help groups, solid and liquid waste management, Sansad Adarsh Gram Yojana.

Confederation of Indian Industry (CII)

Confederation of Indian Industry (CII), an association of corporate bodies, was set up with effect from 1st January 1992, by evolution of erstwhile Engineering and Iron Trades Association (EITA) formed in 1895.

With a view to undertake CSR initiatives, CII set up the Social Development Council in 1995, to (i) Ensure that the benefits and opportunities emerging out of the economic reforms and industrial growth are made available to all; (ii) Facilitate Indian industry's responses to the needs of a developing India; and (iii) Build-up strong partnerships across the sectors for better Governance, Accountability and Empowerment. CII has been pursuing its member corporate for undertaking social welfare activities relating to promotion of health, women empowerment, education and literacy, control of HIV/AIDS, community development, empowerment of disadvantaged youth, disabled people etc. For these purposes, it has been collaborating with a number of NGOs.

CSR Initiatives

CII has dedicated a CII Foundation (CIIF)[4] which undertakes a wide range of developmental and charitable activities in India through corporate sector engagement, by providing strategic guidance on CSR, and developing and managing high impact programmes. Since its inception in 2011, CIIF has undertaken a range of projects in the areas of skill development, maternal and child health, sanitation, livelihood creation, women empowerment, water conversation, and disaster relief and rehabilitation.

In an endeavour to initiate the rehabilitation after the disaster of June 2013 rains and cloudburst in Uttarakhand, the Foundation took up rebuilding 8 completely damaged primary schools in district Tehri Garhwal. The school intervention includes reconstruction of Schools, Providing all furnishings, Providing learning aids and softer Interventions aimed at enhancing the learning experience for children and teaching skills of faculty. In addition to the relief interventions, CII Foundation initiated the Uttarakhand Rehabilitation Project for the affected families. These included initiatives focussing on education, skilling, employment, community livelihood, women empowerment and environment.

Another project titled "Plantation for Environmental Awareness and Creative Education (PEACE)" supported by Godrej & Boyce has been initiated in Kunjo-Maikot village, Chamoli District. The project aims at reducing the risk of slope instability by planting the trees in and around school premises and village, rebuilding the recreational facility such as playground for organizing games for the school children, making available to school children educational material and other items such as school bags, stationery, solar lantern and establishing prefabricated toilets in the school premises.

In 2005, The CII Foundation launched Woman Exemplar Programme which recognizes exemplary women working at the grassroots and aims to promote women's empowerment at the çommunity level by discovering, recognizing and supporting those who have, against all odds, excelled and contributed significantly to the development process in India.

In the year 2014, the scope of the initiative was expanded beyond recognition, into a programme and was brought under the aegis of CII Foundation. The initiative is now named the CII Foundation Woman Exemplar Programme.

In order to encourage and promote innovative CSR initiatives, CIIF is introducing the Business Impact Awards—Transformation through CSR, presented by TVS Group. The award identifies and recognizes exemplary CSR projects that have positively impacted the community and business through CII. The Award will be given around the following thematic areas: Education, Sustainable livelihoods, Health, Environment Sustainability, Women empowerment and Gender equality.

The Foundation in partnership with Bombay Stock Exchange and Indian Institute of Corporate Affairs (IICA) has created an online platform called *Sammaan* in order to bridge the gap between Corporate and NGOs. It is a first of its kind initiative in the world which enables companies to undertake effective CSR activities by connecting them to non-profit and non-governmental agencies with legitimate records. *Sammaan* adopts a rigorous process to list NGOs and projects across India, from which the corporate can choose to fund and monitor their CSR grants.

In 2015[5], CII Foundation initiated rehabilitation projects in Uttarakhand for the families affected by floods by rebuilding schools, ITI, placement of ITI pass outs from disaster impacted areas. It also collaborated with Godrej & Boyce to enable farmers to earn supplementary income through plantation of herbs. As part of women empowerment programme, CII Foundation in collaboration with the Bajaj Group recognized three outstanding women with Woman Exemplary Awards.

CII Foundation has taken up Mission-Sanitation in Schools (SoS) for construction of toilets in the schools. Mission SoS is a multi-stakeholder driven initiative where CII Foundation in collaboration with companies like Bosch, SRF and the Government is working towards achieving the overall vision of *Swachh Vidyalaya*.

The foundation with the support of TIL has chosen to strengthen the Integrated Child Development Services/*Anganwadi centres* in West Bengal through PPP model by providing direct support in terms of infrastructure, equipment, capacity building, reducing undernutrition etc. during the year, six Anganwadi Centres have been adopted in Metiabruz area of Kolkata covering 70-100 beneficiaries in each centre. UNICEF is the technical partner to the programme.

CII Foundation in its efforts towards mainstreaming persons with disabilities (PwDs) into the workforce, organized a series of job fairs across the country. The job fairs brought together perspective employers and deserving candidates to enable on-the-spot job interviews. The retail, hospitality and IT sectors led in offering jobs. Some of the leading employers included Aegis, Wipro, Concentrix, Reliance Retail, Vishal Mega Mart, EXL, TCS, Lemon Tree and Max Fashion. National Foundation for Corporate Governance (NFCG) and the National Handicapped Finance and Development Corporation (NHFDC) partly supported this initiative.

In order to provide soft skill coaching to the undergraduate, postgraduate SC/ST students from various trades like Engineering, Law, MBA etc. and thereby improving employability of these students CII-Pune Zonal Office in association with English Language Teaching Institute of Symbiosis (ELTIS) organized the unique programme where the course curriculum is designed with inputs from both industry and institutes.

In 2016[6], CII Foundation undertook several activities across various verticals of social development. Post Uttarakhand Flood, CIIF undertook various rehabilitation projects to reach out to the affected communities. CIIF completed reconstruction of eight completely damaged schools and strengthened the learning environment of these schools.

CIIF undertook projects towards construction of 203 toilets in Government schools of Bihar, Chhattisgarh, Tamil Nadu, Maharashtra, Delhi and Rajasthan. CIIF launched second phase of Mission SoS to support Open Defecation Free (ODF) communities by constructing public community toilets across 60 cities by engaging with community, industry and urban local bodies.

CIIF mobilized corporate support to create 24 model Anganwadi Centre in Kolkata covering 1250 beneficiaries. Infrastructure support included repair and reconstruction of schools, pre-school education toys, mats, utensils, water dispenser, educational aids, medical kit etc. *Anganwadi* workers have been trained on nutritional assessment, nutritional supplements and early childhood education, child psychology, child centred approach, school readiness instrument etc.

Three women who did exemplary work in the social development were identified for the 12th edition of CII Foundation Women Exemplar Programme.

CIIF in partnership with Uttarakhand Skill Development Society and SNS Foundation is training the youth in auto technician and electrician courses.

The initiative undertaken with support from the Department of Prisons, Tamil Nadu and Bharat Heavy Electrical Ltd. (BHEL) is providing welding training to the inmates of Trichy Central Prison to build their capacities and help them find a job on their release to lead a normal life.

Community based Risk Reduction for Healthcare and Hygiene project initiated in 10 villages of Bandipore district of J&K aims to implement participatory and community action oriented risk reduction activities, ensure medical preparedness and quick response post disaster by developing capacity of healthcare providers and village response committee.

Further to relief efforts, CIIF is developing long-term rehabilitation initiatives in Chennai and Cuddalore in close consultation with the Government of Tamil Nadu. The projects undertaken in first phase is revival of agriculture and restoration of livelihood.

The Associated Chambers of Commerce and Industry of India (ASSOCHAM)

ASSOCHAM was established as an apex industry body in 1920, for safeguarding the interests of industry and trade, acting as an interface with government on policy issues, and interacting with counterpart international organizations to promote bilateral economic issues. It has 1,00,000 companies and professionals as members.

Its vision is to "Empower Indian enterprise by inculcating knowledge that will be the catalyst of growth in the barrier-less technology-driven global market and help them upscale, align and emerge as formidable players in respective business segments".

ASSOCHAM, in its mission to foster balanced economic, social and industrial development, set up the *ASSOCHAM FOUNDATION FOR CORPORATE SOCIAL REPSONSIBILITY (AFCSR)*. The foundation aims at taking ahead the objective of CSR to embrace responsibility for the company's actions and to encompass a positive impact on the environment, economical and social aspect of the community at large. With a view to pursue matters relating to the welfare of the SC and ST, it has set a separate Trust "*ASSOCHAM Foundation for Inclusive Growth of SC and ST*". It started the ASSOCHAM RESPONSIBLE ORGANIZATION EXCELLENCE AWARDS 2014-15 and organized the 7th Global CSR Summit-*cum*-Responsible Organization Excellence Awards on 20th February, 2015 at New Delhi to discuss the holistic perspective of CSR in the region with insights from various stakeholders with a human touch.

Endnotes

More details on the financial involvement of the associations of corporate houses on CSR activities were not available. Analysis of available information on CSR activities indicated the following:

- Interventions of the associations appear to be threefold namely to (i) Sensitize the members and creating awareness about CSR, (ii) Encourage members for pursuing CSR, and (iii) Implement certain schemes on pilot basis. Out of these, sensitization and creation of awareness appears to be of critical importance.

- The associations can play an important role in making CSR interventions of the member company more effective by circulating best practices and developing Standard Operating Procedures (SOPs) which can be adopted by the members with suitable modification.
- Promotion of strategic CSR will help the member companies and the disadvantaged on a 'win-win' basis.

References

1. 4th Annual session of FICCI held on 7th April, 1931.
2. *Source*-http://www.ficci-sedf.org/projects.html
3. http://ficci-sedf.org/past-events.html
4. http://www.cii.in/CII_Foundation
5. http://ciifoundation.in/NewsLetter_List.aspx?CallFor=ServiceBroucher
6. *Ibid*.

Government Initiatives for Promoting Corporate Contribution for Social Purpose

NATIONAL CULTURE FUND (NCF)

Launching of the National Culture Fund (NCF) on the 29th March 1997, marked the beginning of government efforts for institutionalizing mobilisation of corporate support for public purpose. The fund was set up as a trust under the Charitable Endowments Act, 1890 with a view to encourage participation of the corporate, both Private and Public, Government, NGOs as well as individuals and mobilize resources for preservation and conservation of the cultural heritage of India. With a view to encourage contribution, 100 per cent tax rebate is provided on all contributions made to the fund under Section 80G (2) of the Income Tax Act. Further, the corporate houses are guaranteed mileage for projecting their donations by putting plaques at the site developed with the resource support as well as in other forms of advertisement.

The fund is managed by a Council with the Union Minister, Culture, as the Chairman; and up to 24 members including 12 eminent persons from the corporate sector and private foundations.

The fund was started with an initial contribution of Rs. 2,00 lakhs made by the Ministry of Culture in 1996-97 against the commitment to contribute Rs.19,50 lakhs. Fund raised and utilised in the subsequent years[1] are given in **Table 19.1**.

Renovation of the Taj Mahal, Agra; Shaniwarwada Palace, Pune; Ramakrishna Mission Institute of Culture, Kolkata; Humayun's Tomb, New Delhi; Synagogue Clock Tower, Cochin; Ramana Maharshi Centre for Learning, Bangalore; Jnana Pravaha Trust, Varanasi; and Tomb of Yusuf Qattal, New Delhi are some of the major works taken up under this Fund. Besides, publication and training programmes are also organised with financial support from the Fund.

During the year 2014-15[2], Visual Archives of Kulwant Roy collection project was completed as per a MoU signed with India Photo Archives Foundation in 2007. Besides, one leadership training programme was conducted with help of British Museum, UK to impart museum management and leadership skills to museum professionals. One new project for upgradation of Archaeological Survey of India (ASI) site

Table 19.1: Fund raised and Utilised under NCF during 1996-97 to 2014-15

Year	*Fund raised by contribution from Govt. (in Rs. lakh)*	*Fund raised by contribution from sources other than Govt. (in Rs. lakh)*	*Utilization on projects (in Rs. lakh)*
1996-97	200	Nil	Nil
1997-98	200	10.60	Nil
1998-99	200	17.71	Nil
1999-2000	Nil	37.38	25.46
2000-01	Nil	54.58	0.79
2001-02	1	2657.10*	101.39*
2002-03	100	106.54	7.79
2003-04	200	862.36	46.71
2004-05	20	204.42	182.27
2005-06	210	201.56	232.33
2006-07	200	230.51	353.40
2007-08	300	153.54	135.59
2008-09	319	150.72	247.41
2009-10	Nil	118.24	27.63
2010-11	Nil	316.45	197.15
2011-12	Nil	153.90	308.19
2012-13	Nil	573.25	304.75
2013-14	Nil	226.50	232.48
2014-15	Nil	221.33	248.34
Total	**19,50**	**62,96.67**	**26,51.69**

Source: Information received from the Ministry of Culture.

museum of Red Fort was started as per a MoU signed with BHEL in October 2014. Besides, capacity building of ASI management staff professional and training of craftsman were funded.

Two MoUs were signed between HUDCO for restoration of the Sunderwala Mahal and with ASI and STC for conservation of Jai Prakash Yantra in Jantar Mantar, Delhi respectively.

During the year 2015-16[3], conservation of Sunderwala Mahal, New Delhi project (started as per MoU with HUDCO in 2012) was completed. Besides, a project titled "Treasuries of Indian Museums" for documentation of Salar Jung Museum, Hyderabad; National Museum, Delhi; Indian Museum, Kolkata; Allahabad Museum, Allahabad and Chhatrapati Shivaji Maharaj Vastu Sangrahalaya (CSMVS), Mumbai were completed.

National Culture Fund was awarded the SKOCH Award on the 10-11th December, 2015. Information on resource mobilisation and expenditure under the fund during 2015-16 could not be found in the annual report of the Fund nor of the Ministry.

Endnotes

From the available information, it appears that in nineteen years since its constitution, Rs. 19.5 crores from government and Rs. 62.96 crores, total Rs. 82.46 crores was mobilised to the fund, out of which Rs. 26.51 crores could be spent. This amount appears to be too small as compared to the public fund being spent and the fund required for the desired objectives. Rs. 26 crores was mobilised from sources other than government during 2001-02. In the remaining years, such contribution has remained less than Rs. 3 crores per year. After CSR was made mandatory, only Rs. 2.21 crores could be mobilised during the year 2014-15, which is too small as compared to the total fund available for CSR activities.

References

1. Information received from the Ministry of Culture.
2. Annual Report 2014-15, pp. 54-56.
3. Annual Report 2015-16, pp. 67-68.

NATIONAL SPORTS DEVELOPMENT FUND (NSDF)

The National Sports Development Fund (NSDF) was set up by the Ministry of Youth Affairs and Sports, the Government of India in 1998-99 with the primary objective of mobilizing resources from non-governmental sources, including the private/corporate sector and Non-Resident Indians (NRIs), for supplementing the efforts of the government. Donations to this fund are fully exempted under the Income Tax Act.

The fund is administered by a council with the Union Minister, Youth Affairs and Sports as the Chairman and up to 24 members. Many eminent sports persons and leaders of the corporate world and private foundations are represented in the Council.

In order to make contributions to the Fund attractive, 100 per cent exemption from income tax is available on all contribution to the Fund. To begin with, the Government of India made a contribution of Rs. 2.00 crore to the Fund as seed money during the year 1998-99. Further Government contribution is on matching basis to the contributions received from other sources.

Many sports persons were assisted from the fund, of which performance of Shri R.V.S. Rathore was noteworthy. Shri Rathore was provided Rs.78.23 lakhs financial support during 2002-04. He was the lone silver medal winner of Olympics 2004.

The Council was last reconstituted in March 2012 and the last meeting of the Council was held on 4th June, 2015. The Executive Committee was last constituted in May 2014.

The rising popularity of wrestling, boxing and archery in the country has caught the attention of the Sports Ministry which has approved a lucrative scheme—National Prize Money Circuit—for the three disciplines, with total prize money of Rs. 15 crore to come from the National Sports Development Fund (NSDF).[1] Under this scheme, four tournaments will be conducted in a year in every discipline with top eight sportspersons participating in each category. The participants will be selected on the basis of their national ranking, The four circuit tournaments carry a bumper cash award of Rs. 5 crore—Rs. 1.25 crore per tournament—in every discipline. The tournaments, to be held in all four zones, will be organized by the ministry in collaboration with SAI and the national federations.

Performance of NSDF in mobilizing resources for development of sports along with mobilization of resources for promotion of sports under Corporate Social Responsibility which has been made mandatory from

1st April, 2014, were looked into by Department Related Parliamentary Standing Committee[2] on Human Resource Development. From the report of the Committee, it appears that 121 sports person have been sponsored in 14 different sports discipline for their custom-wise training under coaches of international repute by the NSDF. It appears that India Infrastructure Finance Company Limited a PSU under Ministry of Finance has agreed to contribute at the rate of Rs. 10 crores per annum for three years to NSDF, out of which Rs. 10 crores for 2015-16 has been received. However, the Committee observed[3] "the Committee is unhappy to note that most of the PSUs are not aware of NSDF. Also no funds from CSF are allocated for promotion of sports". Based on action taken by various Public Sector Undertaking and Public Sector Banks in promotion of sports, the Committee in its report had recommended the Department of Sports and Sports Authority of India to nominate an exclusive nodal officer in each region for coordinating with PSUs/PSBs so that they can contribute to the NSDF as well as adopt a sports discipline/game or a centre.

NSDF has given financial assistance to outstanding sportspersons, Sports Federations and other organizations. Top level sports persons, who are medal winning prospects in Olympics, Commonwealth Games, Asian Games and other international competitions, are selected for financial assistance from NSDF. The assistance is given for their customized training, both in India and abroad, to prepare them for winning medals in international events. Target Olympic Podium (TOP) Scheme was formulated within the overall ambit of National Sports Development Fund (NSDF) with the objective of identifying and supporting potential medal prospects for Olympic Games. The selected athletes are provided financial assistance for their customized training at Institutes having world class facilities and other necessary support. Benchmark for selection of athletes under the scheme is in relation to international standards and consistency in performance. The athletes, who are prospective medal winners, have been identified through a process of research and consultation with the National Sports Federations and National Coaches/Experts of the relevant disciplines. The TOP Scheme continues for support of potential athletes for 2020 and future Olympic Games and other major international competitions. Performance of selected athletes supported under the scheme is reviewed on annual/semi-annual basis. The total money available[4] in the Fund, was Rs. 113.14 crore (as on 31.12.2014), which changed[5] to Rs. 118.70 crore (as on 31.01.2016). (Details given in **Table 20.1**). During 2016-17, Rs. 1145.72 lakhs was contributed to the fund[6] by sources other than Government during 2016-17 including Rs. 1000 lakhs by India Infrastructure Finance Company Limited (IIFCL).

Table 20.1: Contribution and Expenditure from NSDF during 2010-11 to 2015-16

(Amount in Rs. lakh)

Year	*Amount donated*	*Contribution from Govt.*	*Expenditure*	*Remark*
2010-11	–	20,00	6,49.7	Individuals (8) organizations (8)
2011-12	11,00	–	11,34.12	Individuals (35) organizations (9)
2012-13	10,00	5,00	12,31.2	Individuals (26) organizations (8)
2013-14	10,00	5,00	15,37.12	Individuals (11) organizations (11)
2014-15	10,00	3,75	12,56.	Individuals (19) organizations (13)
2015-16	5,82.6	5,00	22,46.34	Individuals (74) organizations (22)
Total	**97,46.34**	**66,41.68**		

Source: Annual Reports.

Endnotes

Non-availability of adequate resource has been often stated as one of the major constraints in the promotion of sports and games in the country, which are essential for the development of human resources and team spirit. Performance of National teams in the International-sporting events has also been a matter of national prestige and concern. Mobilisation of corporate support, both in financial and managerial assistance forms, can play an important role in achieving excellence in sports at the international level, which is a matter of concern and surface at regular intervals after each Olympic and major international sports events. Numbers of corporate are sponsoring sports persons and some have set up sports academies as a part of their business strategy. The National Sports Development Fund was an attempt to institutionalise the arrangement for ensuring smooth flow of resources for supporting sports persons, who have potential for achieving excellence and getting medals for the country at international level. However, the contribution by corporate to the Fund has remained limited both in number and amount. Even after the CSR was made mandatory, flow of resources from the corporate has remained meagre, restricted to Rs. 10 crore during 2014-15 and Rs. 5.8 crore during 2015-16. This indicates that there is a lot to be done for using this fund as a medium for channelizing corporate support for achieving the desired objectives of promotion of sports in general and getting excellence in particular.

References

1. http://timesofindia.indiatimes.com/sports/more-sports/others/Ministry-clears-prize-money-circuits-in-three-disciplines/articleshow/3510 .
2. 271st Report of the Committee, December 2015, p. 86.
3. *Ibid.*
4. Annual Report 2015, pp. 159-160.
5. Annual Report 2015-16, pp. 130-131, 188.
6. Written reply in the Lok Sabha on the 16th March, 2017, PIB Release ID: 159335.

POPULATION FOUNDATION OF INDIA (PFI)

Family Planning Foundation was set up by an enlightened, socially committed and philanthropically-inclined group of industrialists led by Mr. JRD Tata in 1970. The Foundation is dedicated to promote formulation and implementation of gender sensitive population and development policies, strategies and programmes. Its vision[1] relates to "Promoting, Fostering and Inspiring sustainable and balanced human development with a focus on population stabilization through an enabling environment for an ascending quality of life with equity and justice." It seeks to accomplish this by extending technical and financial support to individuals and civil society institutions, piloting innovative approaches, and building support at the national, sub-national and community levels. In recognition of the work, Founder-Chairman of the Foundation, Mr. JRD Tata was conferred the prestigious UN Population Award for the year 1992. The Foundation was renamed as *Population Foundation of India (PFI)* in 1993.

The Foundation deals with funding and promoting population-related activities in the country in planning for small families as a socially acceptable and sustainable behavior norm. It advocates holistic approach looking beyond family planning and the immediate concern with contraceptives covering a wide range of reproductive and child health programmes. It seeks to spearhead non-governmental efforts towards a rights-based, gender-sensitive approach to human development with a close cooperation and coordination from official agencies both at the Centre and in the states.

The Foundation is managed by a Governing Board with Dr. Vinay Bharat Ram as the Chairman and the Advisory Council headed by Dr. M.S. Swaminathan.

In pursuance of its objectives, the foundation provides a forum for pooling of experiences and sharing of professional expertise to strengthen and enlarge the operational base of the Family Welfare programme through a number of projects with a view to:

- Extend full support and provide guidance in formulating and influencing population policies and programmes.
- Serve as a catalytic agent to promote programmes at different levels directed towards the goal of population stabilization and development.

- Improve the quality of life of the people through programmes with special emphasis on reduction of neo-natal mortality, infant mortality, maternal morbidity and mortality, adolescents' health needs, HIV/AIDS prevention and care, unmet need for contraception, women's health and their reproductive rights and gender issues.
- Strengthen Non-Governmental Organizations, community-based organizations, self-help groups, Panchayati Raj institutions and the organized sector on population, health and social development issues with the goal of empowering the community as a whole.
- Advocate at all levels to promote quality of life and sustainable development.

Keeping in view the importance of family planning, the Foundation positions itself in the broader context of Reproductive Health and Comprehensive Primary Healthcare, for better acceptability and effectiveness. It is focusing on results-based management of the programmes by using baseline and end line surveys, setting specific targets, developing measurable indicators.

Activities of the Foundation cover the following broad areas:

Advocating for Family Planning and Reproductive Health

The foundation, in collaboration with corporate Ranbaxy Community Healthcare Society, implemented a project in the field of Reproductive Child Health (RCH), fort covering 1 lakh persons during 2001 to 2007. It was funded by PFI and partner corporate on 50:50 basis. Appraisal of the project done in 2005 indicated that use of contraceptive preventive rate increased to 65.4 per cent (from a baseline figure of 50%) and coverage of ANC also increased substantially.

Community Action for Health

Population Foundation of India hosted the Secretariat of the Advisory Group on Community Action (AGCA), constituted by the Ministry of Health and Family Welfare (MoHFW) in August 2005. The AGCA guided the implementation of a pilot project on community action for health in 36 districts in nine states during 2007 to 2009.

Entertainment Education

The Foundation has been working to harness the power of entertainment education to alter and transform deeply entrenched social behaviors' and promote women empowerment, their health and well being. It promoted audio-visual means to disseminate messages on family planning, with a focus on age at marriage and spacing child births. In March 2014, it launched a trans-media serial *Main Kuch Bhi Kar Sakti Hoon* (I, a Woman, Can Achieve Anything) which was quite effective.

Health of the Urban Poor (HUP)

HUP provides support to the Ministry of Health and Family Welfare in planning, reviewing of State Programme implementation plans and developing frameworks and policies for urban health. The foundation entered into a partnership with USAID India in October 2009 to start a comprehensive Health of the Urban Poor (HUP) programme. The programme envisaged the development of a responsive, functional and sustainable urban health system that provides need-based, affordable and accessible quality healthcare and improved sanitation and hygiene for the urban poor. HUP has been recognized for providing support in the implementation of the National Urban Health Mission (NUHM).

Strengthening NGO Capacity

PFI along with Sir Dorabji Tata Trust supported CINI Kolkata for undertaking a project to strengthen the NGO capacity in Jharkhand to implement Reproductive and Child Health Programmes through Life Cycle Approach (LCA) and to improve maternal and child health status. The project is implemented in Churchu Block of Hazaribagh district in Jharkhand with *Nav Bharat Jagruti Kendra* as the implementing agency in the field.

Adolescent Reproductive Health

This programme was implemented by PFI in collaboration with the Tata Steel Family Initiatives Foundation in 5 urban *bastis* in Jamshedpur during 2003-05. The basic objective of the project was to provide information to the adolescent boys and girls on reproduction and sexual health. This innovative project resulted in creating awareness among boys and girls about puberty, and removed the myths about sexuality. This intervention is likely to have a long-term impact in decision-making regarding marriage, children, sharing the parental responsibility, as well as prevention of HIV/AIDS.

It was learnt[2] that the Foundation is attempting re-orientation of its strategy from funding other NGOs and implementing projects to capacity building, handholding and supporting other NGOs along with field work.

Financial Details

An account of income the foundation from different sources and expenditure on broad heads is given in the Table 21.1.

Table 21.1: Income and Expenditure of PFI during 2013-14 to 2015-16

(Amount in Rs. lakh)

Income	*2013-14*	*2014-15*[3]	*2015-16*[4]
1. From Investment	273.41	515.20	373.09
2. Rent	571.01	317.50	237.43
3. Grant-in-Aid from International Agencies	2273.69	2836.62	3028.98
4. Grant-in-Aid from National Agencies	173.32	132.45	97.83
Total	**3291.43**	**3801.77**	**3737.33**
Expenditure			
1. Projects, Programmes & Implementation	258.22	238.45	229.08
2. For International Aided Projects	2273.69	2836.62	3028.98
3. For National Aided Projects	173.32	132.45	97.84
4. Project Development	–	–	–
5. Monitoring and Evaluation	–	–	–
6. IEC	–	–	–
7. Management and Administration	266.58	229.30	68.17
Total	**2971.81**	**3436.82**	**3424.07**

Source: Annual Report of PFI.

Analysis of the financial accounts of PFI indicates that interest on investments and rents constitute its main source of income, while conduct of action-oriented research forms the main expenditure.

Endnotes

The foundation, which is a civil society (Non-Governmental Organization), was originally set up by the corporate. It has mandate to deal with issues relating to population planning in particular, which is an extremely important issue in the context of national development. It has developed expertise in population and health-related issues the area and has team of technical persons.

However, after CSR was made mandatory with effect from the 1st April 2014, there has not been any visible increase in the corporate contribution to the Foundation during the years 2014-15 and 2015-16. Consequently, there has been no impact on the projects implemented with corporate funding under CSR.

Advocating for using the potential of this foundation and its playing an active role in implementation of CSR projects will give a distinct advantage to the corporate as well as better services to the people with help of this foundation.

References

1. Annual Report, 2014-15.
2. Discussion with the Executive Director on May 30, 2007.
3. Population Foundation of India, Annual Report 2014-15, p. 49.
4. http://populationfoundation.in/Publications/view/21/10, p. 57.

Bibliography

Books

"Ashes to Ashes: America's Hundred Year Cigarette War, the Public Health, and the Unabashed Triumph of Philip Morris", Klugar, R. Vintage Books, (1997).

"Applications of Game Theory", Ram Kumar Mishra, Shaheen, Jayasree Raveendran and Suresh Deman, Academic Foundation, New Delhi (2014).

"Banker to the Poor: Micro-Lending and the Battle against World Poverty", Yunus, Muhammad, Public Affairs, Perseus Books Group (2007).

"Behind the Swoosh: The Struggle of Indonesians Making Nike Shoes", Ballinger, J. and Olsson, C., Global Publications Foundation (1997).

"Beyond Good Company: Next Generation Corporate Citizenship", Googins, B.P. Mirvis and S. Rochlin, Palgrave Macmillan (2007).

"Bowling Alone: The Collapse and Renewal of American Community", Putnam, R.D., Simon & Schuster (2000).

"Business Ethics – Facing up to the Issues", *The Economist*, Viva Books Private Limited (2004).

"Business Ethics: Managing Corporate Citizenship and Sustainability in the Age of Globalisation", Crane, A. and D. Matten Collins, J., Oxford University Press (2007).

"Business is People", C. Northcote Parkinson and M.K. Rustomji; Vision Books Private Limited (1998), ISBN: 81-7094-474-0.

"Capitalism's Achilles Heel", Baker, R., John Wiley & Sons (2005).

"Civil Society, the conservative meaning of liberal politics", Cahoone Lawrence, Blackwell Publishers, 2002.

"Communitisation – The Third Way of Governance", R.S. Pandey, Concept Publishing Company Private Limited, (2010), ISBN: 81-8069-646-4.

"Confessions of an Economic Hit Man", Perkins, J. Berrett-Koehler Publishers (2004).

"Corporate Management Strategy for Economic Justice, Trusteeship – the

Gandhian Alternative", Gidwani Sushila, Gandhi Peace Foundation (1986).

"Corporate Social Responsibilities: Making Good Business Sense", Holme R. and Watts P., London, Rio Tinto and Royal Dutch/shell (2000).

"Corporate Social Responsibility – Concepts and Cases, The Indian Experience", C.V. Baxi and Ajit Prasad, Excel Books (2005), ISBN: 81-7446-449-2.

"Corporate Social Responsibility in India", Sanjay K. Agarwal, Response Books (2008), ISBN: 978-0-7619-3623-2.

"*Corporate Social Responsibility in India—Past, Present and Future*", Sanjay Kumar Panda, ICFAI University Press, (2008) ISBN 978-81-314-1965-6.

"Corporate Social Responsibility: Doing the Most Good for Your Company and Your Cause", P. Kotler and Lee, N., John Wiley & Sons (2005).

"Corporate Social Responsibility and International Development: Is Business the Solution?", Hopkins, Michael, Earthscan (2007).

"Corporate Social Responsibility in Europe: Rhetoric and Realities", Barth, R. and F. Wolff (eds.), Edward Elgar Publishing, (2009).

"Corporate Social Responsibility: Doing the Most Good for Your Company and Your Cause", Kotler, P. and N. Lee (eds.), John Wiley & Sons (2005).

"Corporation be Good! The Story of Corporate Social Responsibility", Fredrick, W., Dog Ear Publishing, (2006).

"Creating a World without Poverty: Social Business and the Future of Capitalism", Yunus, Muhammad, Public Affairs, Perseus Books Group (2007).

"Deep Economy: The Wealth of Communities and Durable Future", McKibben, B., Holt Rinehart and Winston, (2008).

"Directors" Remuneration, Report of a Study Group Chaired by Sir Richard Greenbury", Greenbury, R. Gee, (1995).

"Fair Trade for All", Stiglitz, J., Oxford University Press, (2005).

"Flat and Crowded: Why We Need a Green Revolution – and How it Can Renew America", Friedman, T.L. Hot, Farrar, Straus and Giroux, (2008).

"From Higher Aims to Hired Hands: The Social Transformation of American Business Schools and the Unfulfilled Promise of Management as a Profession", Khurana, R., Princeton University Press, (2007).

"Good to Great: Why Some Companies Make the Leap ... and Others Don't", Collins, J., Harper Business (2001).

"How Hewlett and Packard built the world's greatest company", Michael S. Malone, Penguin Portfolio.

"How Hewlett and Packard Built the World's Greatest Company", Michael S. Malone, Penguin Portfolio.

"It's Only Business! India's Corporate Social Responsiveness in a Globalised World", Meera Mitra, Oxford University Press (2007).

"Lobbying the Corporation: Citizen Challenges to Business Authority", Vogel, D., Basic Books (1978).

"Making Corporate Responsibility Work: Lessons from Real Business", Olsen, L., Ashridge, Centre for Business and Society, (2004).

"*Making One plus One Eleven*", Sanjay Kumar Panda, Star Publication, (2008), ISBN: 978-81-7650-626-7.

"Moral Imagination and Managerial Decision-making", Werhane, P.H., Ruffin Series in Business Ethics (1999).

"Mulberry Sericulture in New Ares-Empowering Tribal Women", Sanjay Kumar Panda, Concept Publishing Company Pvt. Ltd. (2014). ISBN-13:978-93-5125-029-6.

"New Strategies for Reputation Management: Gaining Control of Issues, Crises and Corporate Social Responsibility", Griffin, A. Kogan Page, (2008).

"Perspective on Corporate Social Responsibility", Crowther, D. and L. Rayman-Bacchus (eds.), Ashgate (2003).

"Pet Food Politics: The Chihuahua in the Coal Mine", Nestle, Marion., University of California Press, (2008).

" Principles of Modern Political Science", J.C. Johari, Sterling Publishers Private Limited.

"Provision of healthcare for all, India 2020, A vision for the new Millennium", Kalam, A.P.J. Abdul & Rajan, Y.S. (1998).

"Rethinking Corporate Social Responsibility", R.K. Mishra, Punam Singh, Shulagna Sarkar, MacMillan Publishers India Limited (2011).

"Revolutionising Corporate Social Responsibility, Towards a Sustainable Tomorrow", R.K. Mishra, Shulagna Sarkar, Punam Singh, Academic Foundation, New Delhi (2015).

"Setting Global Standards: Guidelines for Creating Codes of Conduct in Multinational Corporations", Sethi, S., John Wiley & Sons (2003).

"Small but Meaningful: CSR in Practice", Maheswar Sahu, Jeevan Prakash Mohanty, Northern Book Centre, New Delhi (2015).

"Socially Responsible Investment (SRI)", Sunil Sinha, Rating Scan (2007).

"Strategic Corporate Social Responsibility – Towards a Sustainable Business", RK Mishra, Shulagna Sarkar, Punam Singh, Bloomsbury Publishing India Limited (2013).

"Strategic Management: A Stakeholder Approach", Freeman, R.E., Harper Collins College Div., (1984).

"Sustainable Futures – Imperatives For Managing The Social Agenda", Dr. Bhaskar Chatterjee, Notion Press, Chennai (2012).

"The 86 Per cent Solution: How to Succeed in the Biggest Market Opportunity of the 21st Century", Mahajan, Vijay and Kamini Banga, Wharton School Publishing (2005).

"The Corporate Responsibility Code Book", Leipziger, D., Greenleaf Publishing (2003).

"The Corporate Social Responsibility Reader", Burchell, J. (ed.), Routledge (2008).

"The Difference Makers: How Social and Institutional Entrepreneurs Created the Corporate Responsibility Movement", Waddock, S., Greenleaf Publishing (2008).

"The Fortune at the Bottom of the Pyramid: Eradicating Poverty through Profits", Prahlad, C.K., Wharton School Publishing (2004).

"The Fortune at the Bottom of the Pyramid", Prahlad, C.K., Wharton School Publishing (2005).

"The ICCA Handbook on Corporate Social Responsibility", International Congress and Convention Association, John Wiley & Sons (2006).

"The Market for Virtue: The Potential and Limits of Corporate Social Responsibility", Vogel, D., Brookings Institute Press (2005).

"Tomorrow's History: Selected writings of Simon Zadek, 1993-2003", Zadek, S. and Raynard, P., Greenleaf Publishing (2004).

"When Good Companies do Bad Things", Schwartz, P., John Wiley & Sons (1999).

"The Business of Social Responsibility", Harsh Shrivastava and Shankar Venkateswaran; Books for Change, (2000), ISBN: 81-87380-11-X.

"The Ethical Organisation: Ethical Theory and the Behaviour", Kittson and Robert Campbell Alan (1996).

"The India Way", Peter Cappelli, Harbir Singh, Jitendra Singh and Michael Useem; Harvard Business Press (2010), ISBN: 978-1-4221-5555-4.

"The Place of Social Capital in Understanding Social and Economic Outcomes", Woolcock, *Canadian Journal of Policy Research*, 2(10) issue.

"The Planetary Bargain, Corporate Social Responsibility Matters", Michael Hopkins, Earthscan Publications (2003).

"Win in India, Win Everywhere – Conquering the Chaos", Ravi Venkatesan, Harvard Business Review Press, Boston, Massachusetts.

Journals/Reports

"2015 Millennium Development Goals: India Country Report", Ministry of Statistics and Implementation, Government of India.

"A framework for analysing corporate social responsibility", Moser, M.R. *Journal of Business Ethics*, Vol. 5, No. 1, February 1986.

"A need for greater ethical consciousness", Niharika Joshi, *Indian Management*, Vol. 45, Issue-1, January 2006.

"A review of the theories of corporate social responsibility: Its evolutionary path and the road ahead", Lee, M.P. *International Journal of Management Reviews*, Vol. 10, Issue 1, March 2008.

"*A study on Peripheral Development of Rourkela Steel Plant*", Society for Rural Industrialization (SRI), Ranchi, 2004.

"An analysis of linkage between economic value added and corporate social responsibility", Mittal, R.K., *et al.*, *Management Decision*, Vol. 46, Issue 9, 2008.

"Analyzing Philanthropic Aspects of Corporate Social Responsibility: A Study on Select Industrial Cases", Bibhas Chandra and Pattanayak J.K., *Journal of Managerial Finance and Research*, Vol. 6, No. 1, January-June 2010.

"Are individuals who agree that corporate social responsibility is a "Fundamentally Subversive Doctrine" inherently unethical?", Mason, S. and P.E. Mudrack, *Applied Psychology*, Vol. 46, Issue 2, April 1997.

Azim Premji, Chairman, Wipro's address in Annual Bank Conference on Developmental Economics, The World Bank, 2003.

"Board members, corporate social responsiveness and profitability: Are trade-offs necessary?", O'Neill, H.M., *et al., Journal of Business Ethics*, Vol. 8, No. 5, May 1989.

"Bowling Alone: America's Declining Social Capital", R.D. Putnam, *Journal of Democracy*, (1995).

"Business and beyond – Leadership, through Quality and Excellence", Address in the 4th annual session of FICCI on 7th April, 1931, FICCI Publication.

"Business ethics and company codes: Current best practices in UK", Simon Webley, Institute of Business Ethics (1992).

"Business Ethics in the Textile, Clothing and Footwear (TCF) Industries": Code of Conduct, Jean-Paul Sajhau (1997), working paper, ILO, Geneva.

"Business Ethics in the Textiles, Clothing and Footwear (TCF) Industries": Code of Conduct, Sajhau Jean-Paul, (1997), working paper 110, ILO, Geneva.

"Business in the Community, CSR research review", London, United Kingdom website.

"CBI at work", Confederation of British Industry 1996, CBI News.

"Cleaning up, A special report on business and climate change", Emma Duncan, *The Economist*, June 2nd, 2007.

"Consumers and corporate social responsibility: Matching the unmatchable?", Backmann, S.C. *Australasian Marketing Journal*, Vol. 15, Issue 1, 2007.

"Corporate Code of Ethics: Purpose, Process and Content Issues", G.R. Weaver (1993), *Business and Society*, Vol. 33(1).

"Corporate governance and corporate social responsibility (CSR): The moderating roles of attainment discrepancy and organisation slack", Arora, P. and R. Dharwadkar. '*CORPORATE GOVERNANCE: An International Review'*, Vol. 19, Issue 2, March 2011.

"Corporate social responsibility and development in Africa: Redefining the roles and responsibilities of public and private actors in the mining sector", Campbell, B., *Resources Policy*, Vol. 37, Issue 2, June 2012.

"Corporate social responsibility and organisational effectiveness: A multivariate approach", Zahra, S.A. and M.S. LaTour, *Journal of Business Ethics*, Vol. 6, No. 6, August 1987.

"Corporate social responsibility and social entrepreneurship", Journal Economics & Management Strateg, Vol. 16, Issue 3, Fall 2007.

"Corporate social responsibility and socially responsible investing: A global perspective", Hill, R.P., *et al., Journal of Business Ethics*, Vol. 70, No. 2, January 2007.

"Corporate social responsibility and workers skills: An examination of corporate responses to workplace illiteracy", Anderson, C.J., *Journal of Business Ethics*, Vol. 70, No. 4, (February 2007).

"Corporate social responsibility in Ghana: Lessons from the mining sector", Boon, E.K. and F. Ababio, IAIA09 Conference Proceedings, 29th Annual Conference of the International association for Impact Assessment (Ghana Accra, International Conference Centre, 2009), Available at Social Responsibilities and Public Accounting of Public Undertakings.

"Corporate social responsibility in the international insurance industry", Scholtens, B., *Sustainable Development*, Vol. 19, Issue 2, March/April 2011.

"Corporate Social Responsibility is Bunk", Henry G. Manne, Dean Emeritus of the George Mason University School of Law, November 24, 2006.

"Corporate social responsibility: A theory of the firm perspective", McWilliams, A. and D. Siegel, *The Academy of Management Review*, Vol. 26, No. 1, January 2001.

"Corporate social responsibility: The role of Fortune 100 companies in domestic and international natural disasters", Johnson, B.R., *et al., Corporate Social Responsibility and Environmental Management*, Vol. 18, Issue 6, November/December 2011.

"Corporate social responsibility: Three key approaches", Windsor, D., *Journal of Management Studies*, Vol. 43, Issue 1, January 2006.

"Corporate social responsibility", Walker, B., *Business Ethics: A European Review*, Vol. 1, Issue 1, January 1992.

"Corporate Social Responsibility Report – Making a meaningful difference in people's lives", Steel Authority of India Limited, August 2006, p. 32.

"Creating Jobs through Skill Development", N.C. Saxena, INCLUSION, January-March 2014 issue.

"CSR as reputation insurance: Primum non nocere", Minor, D. and J. Morgan, *California Management Review*, Vol. 53, No. 3, Spring 2011.

"CSR Special – How India Inc plan to spend Rs. 15,000 crore on social sector," *The Governance Now*, May 16-31, 2004, Vol. 05, Issue 8.

"Does corporate social responsibility influence profit margins? A case study of executive perceptions", *Corporate Social Responsibility and Environmental Management*, Blomgren, A., Vol. 18, Issue 5, September/October 2011.

"Does corporate social responsibility matter in the food industry? Evidence from a nature experiment in China", Kong, D., *Resources Policy*, Vol. 37, Issue 3, June 2012.

"Eclipse at Noon", Shri Gopal Krishna Gandhi, Former Governor, West Bengal, 15th D.P. Kohli Memorial Lecture, April 15 2014, in New Delhi, published in *The Governance Now*, May 1- 15, 2014.

"Global Nutrition Report", released on the 10th December, 2015.

"Investigating in Development, A Practical Plan to Achieve the Millennium Development Goals", World Bank.

"Leaving no one behind: How far on the way to universal primary and secondary education", The UNESCO Institute for Statistics (UIS) and the Global Education Monitoring (GEM) Report, policy paper 27, July 2016.

"Measuring Social Capital: Current Collections and Future Directors", Australian Bureau of Statistics (2000).

"Mid Year Review of CPSEs 2006-2007", Department of Public Enterprises Finance Minister's Budget Speech 2007-08, February 28, 2007.

"Reforms in Governance and Administration", an approach paper of the second Administrative Reforms Commission.

"Study of the ITIs and ITCs", International Labour Organization (ILO).

"The business case for corporate social responsibility: A review of concepts, research and practice", Carroll, A.B. and K.M. Shabana, *International Journal of Management Reviews*, Vol. 12, Issue 1, March 2010.

"The false development promise of corporate social responsibility: Evidence from multinational oil companies", Fredrick, W.C., *International Affairs*, Vol. 81, Issue 3, May 2005.

"The Future of the Company", *The Economist*, December 22, 2001

"The influence of a retailer's corporate social responsibility program on reconceptualising store image", Gupta, S. and J. Pirsch. *Journal of Retailing and Consumer Services*, Vol. 15, Issue 6, November 2008.

"The Millennium Development Goals Report 2007", United Nations, New York, 2007.

"The multiple bottom lines of corporate citizenship: Social investing, reputation and responsibility audits", Waddock, S., *Business and Society Review*, Vol. 105, Issue 3, Fall 2000.

"The relationship between corporate social responsibility and shareholder value: An empirical test of the risk management hypothesis", Godfrey, P.C., *et al.*, *Strategic Management Journal*, Vol. 30, Issue 4, April 2009.

"The Social Responsibility of Business is to increase its profits", Milton Friedman, *The New York Times Magazine*, September 13, 1970.

"Towards an integrated framework of corporate social responsibility, responsiveness and citizenship in sport", Walker, M. and M.M. Parent. *Sport Management Review*, Vol. 13, Issue 3, August 2010.

"Towards CSR: Why ethical analysis is indispensable and unavoidable in corporate affairs", Fredrick, W.C., *California Management Review*, Vol. 28, No. 2, Winter 1986.

"What is corporate social responsibility all about?", Hopkins, M., *Journal of Public Affairs*, Vol. 6, Issue 3/4, August-November 2006.

American Academy of Sciences, *The Economist*, June 2007.

Annual Report 2006-2007, Ministry of Steel, Government of India.

ONGC Annual Reports, Ministry of Steel, Government of India.

Chairman, ITC Limited address at the 96th AGM, July 27, 2007.

NMDC Chairman's address in the 49th Annual General Meeting held on the 31st August, 2007.

SAIL Annual Report, 2003-04.

Parliament

Twenty-fourth Report of the Parliamentary Committee on Public Undertakings (COPU) on Social Responsibilities and Public Accounting of Public Undertakings, 1993-1994.

Lok Sabha question no. 920 for July 13, 2004 reply to.

Newspaper articles

BS Bureau

"Acceptable formula on CSR is ready: Moily", *Business Standard*, 27 June, 2012.

"Dialogue, not negotiation, is the way forward", Bhattacharyya, A.K. *Business Standard*, 14 May, 2012.

"Will the government's business responsibility norms improve corporate governance?", Bhattacharyya, A.K., *Business Standard*, 13 June, 2012.

BL Bureau

"Corporate must wake up to social responsibility", *Business Line*, 17 November, 2006.

"CSR, an acceptable marketing tool: Lowe Lintas Survey", *Business Line*, 11 August, 2011.

"Make CSR mandatory for India Inc.", Raghavan, B.S. *Business Line*, 25 May, 2012.

The Economic Times (ET) Bureau

"A long list of woes!" Nitin Podar, *The Economic Times*, April 24, 2007.
"B.K. Birla Reminisces about the Austere life in the Tumultuous Days before Independence", Anuradha Himatsingka, *The Economic Times*, August 14, 1997.
"Corporate social responsibility: Should government force Cos to spend or should companies volunteer?", Sharma, S.D., *The Economic Times*, 19 May, 2012.
"CSR may become mandatory if Companies Bill is passed with house panel suggestions", *The Economic Times*, 13 June, 2012.
"Giving till it heals", Sachs Jeffrey D., *The Economic Times*, April 6, 2005.
"Inclusive Growth, How Globalisation Affects Developing Counties", Joseph Stiglitz, *The Economic Times*, March 23, 2007.
"Private companies can choose Swachh Bharat projects online now". Nidhi Sharma, *The Economic Times*, March 20, 2017.
"Rio+20: Policy mix based on 'Less Excess and More Access' credo will help achieve sustainability", Bhagwati, J., *The Economic Times*, 23 January, 2012.
"The healthier poor", J.D. Sachs, *The Economic Times*, September 03, 2007.
"The New India we want", N.R. Narayan Murthy, *The Economic Times*, 29th April, 2014.
"Three routes to sustainable CSR", Dipankar Gupta, *The Economic Times*, May 26, 2005.
"Trusteeship of Wealth", Special Report on CSR, *The Economic Times*, November 8, 2004.
"Women's Entrepreneurship – Holding up half the sky-holders", Anil Agarwal, *The Economic Times*, 10 March, 2017.
"XLRI students to get a feel of the rural mural", Father Casimir Raj, *The Economic Times*, August 19, 2005.
Economic Times Group, Arup Gupta, Mumbai, *The Economic Times*, October 18, 2007.
Interview, J. Irani, *The Economic Times*, Kolkata, August 9, 2005.

The Hindu Bureau

"BHEL donates classroom implements", *The Hindu*, 23 June, 2012.
"Workshop held on CSR", *The Hindu*, 11 July, 2010.

"Meenangadi has a green dream: carbon neutrality", E.M. Manoj, *The Hindu*, March 26, 2017.

"Carlos Slim overtakes Bill Gates", Fortune, dated 6th August, 2007, quoted in *The Hindu*, 8th August 2007.

"CSR not charity, but part of business process", *The Hindu*, 19 May, 2010.

"Framing the right prescription", Saachi Bhalla and Nachiket Mor; *The Hindu*, March 21, 2017.

"Governance key to equitable growth", M.G. Devasahayam, *The Hindu*, August 14, 2005.

"ICICI Bank move on human development", Nachiket Mor, *The Hindu*, August 16, 2005.

"India's Nutritional Crisis, National Family Health Survey (NFHS III)", *The Hindu*, March 02, 2007.

"Institution-industry partnership, NASSCOM HR summit", July 19, 2005, *The Hindu*, August 14, 2005.

"Linking nutrition with education at Anganwadis", Anil Agarwal, *The Hindu*, April 2, 2017.

"Microsoft Corp's founder Bill Gates pledges $900 million for TB eradication", on Friday, 27 January 2006 at Davos, Switzerland, *The Hindu*, January 28, 2006.

"The role of civil society in good governance", P.K. Doraiswamy, *The Hindu*, August 26, 2007.

Marcos Espinal, WHO, *The Hindu*, January 28, 2006.

National University of Educational Planning and Administration (2015-16 Survey), *The Hindu*, 8th June, 2017.

The Financial Express

"Gates Foundation gives $75 million for pneumonia vaccine research", *The Financial Express*, April 09, 2006.

"Making the difference", Abhinav Kanchan, media head, FICCI, *The Financial Express*, February 09, 2006.

"Reducing chronic poverty", Shashanka Bhide, *The Financial Express*, October 8, 2007.

"Tata Steel set to use TRT method to produce power", *The Financial Express*, February 07, 2007.

"Wall Street Profits Fuel Philanthropy", The Financial Express, April 09, 2006.

"We should encourage young minds to deliver more on CSR", Sanjeev Duggal, *The Financial Express*, February 12, 2006.

Special Supplement on Indian Chemical Industry, *The Financial Express*, September 29, 2007.

The Times of India Group (TNN)

"Corruption of the American Dream", Dipankar Gupta, *The Times of India*, May 25, 2013.

"How Digital will save India", Nandan Nilkeni, *The Times of India*, July 28, 2016.

"Microsoft launches teaching tools for schools", *The Times of India*, 9 June, 2012.

"Modi's moment is about middle class dignity", Gurucharan Das, *The Times of India*, June 01, 2014.

The Financial Times

"Social responsibility is not charity, it's a duty", Saroj K. Poddar, President, FICCI, *The Financial Express*, February 26, 2006.

"A century that forged a company of steel", *The Financial Express*, August 25, 2007.

"Five years under the thumb", *The Financial Express*, July 30, 2007.

"Small Fish, big catch", Rajiv Tikoo, *The Financial Express*, October 8, 2007.

"Tata group's integrity, understanding, excellence, unity and responsibility drive other corporate too", Indian Chemical Council Annual Awards, Subhash Menon, *The Financial Express*, September 09, 2007.

"Tata steel set to use TRT method to produce power", *The Financial Times*, February 07, 2007.

"Tatas to take global their famed corporate social responsibility", G. Nair, *The Financial Express*, June 07, 2007.

"Yunus calls for legislation on micro credit Banks", *The Financial Express*, February 02, 2007.

D.N. Sahaya, Governor of Tripura in seminar on social responsibility organised by the Seraikela-Kharsawan District Chamber of Commerce & Industry (SKDCCI) on October 28, 2007, Jamshedpur, *The Financial Express*, October 30, 2007.

Economic Survey, 2006-07.

Lord Michael Hastings, interview, *The Financial Express*, October 21, 2007.

World Institute of Sustainable Energy, G.M. Pillay, *The Financial Express*, August 11, 2007.

Index